Communications in Computer and Information Science 2773

Series Editors

Gang Li, *School of Information Technology, Deakin University, Burwood, VIC, Australia*
Joaquim Filipe, *Polytechnic Institute of Setúbal, Setúbal, Portugal*
Zhiwei Xu, *Chinese Academy of Sciences, Beijing, China*

Rationale
The CCIS series is devoted to the publication of proceedings of computer science conferences. Its aim is to efficiently disseminate original research results in informatics in printed and electronic form. While the focus is on publication of peer-reviewed full papers presenting mature work, inclusion of reviewed short papers reporting on work in progress is welcome, too. Besides globally relevant meetings with internationally representative program committees guaranteeing a strict peer-reviewing and paper selection process, conferences run by societies or of high regional or national relevance are also considered for publication.

Topics
The topical scope of CCIS spans the entire spectrum of informatics ranging from foundational topics in the theory of computing to information and communications science and technology and a broad variety of interdisciplinary application fields.

Information for Volume Editors and Authors
Publication in CCIS is free of charge. No royalties are paid, however, we offer registered conference participants temporary free access to the online version of the conference proceedings on SpringerLink (http://link.springer.com) by means of an http referrer from the conference website and/or a number of complimentary printed copies, as specified in the official acceptance email of the event.

CCIS proceedings can be published in time for distribution at conferences or as post-proceedings, and delivered in the form of printed books and/or electronically as USBs and/or e-content licenses for accessing proceedings at SpringerLink. Furthermore, CCIS proceedings are included in the CCIS electronic book series hosted in the SpringerLink digital library at http://link.springer.com/bookseries/7899. Conferences publishing in CCIS are allowed to use Online Conference Service (OCS) for managing the whole proceedings lifecycle (from submission and reviewing to preparing for publication) free of charge.

Publication process
The language of publication is exclusively English. Authors publishing in CCIS have to sign the Springer CCIS copyright transfer form, however, they are free to use their material published in CCIS for substantially changed, more elaborate subsequent publications elsewhere. For the preparation of the camera-ready papers/files, authors have to strictly adhere to the Springer CCIS Authors' Instructions and are strongly encouraged to use the CCIS LaTeX style files or templates.

Abstracting/Indexing
CCIS is abstracted/indexed in DBLP, Google Scholar, EI-Compendex, Mathematical Reviews, SCImago, Scopus. CCIS volumes are also submitted for the inclusion in ISI Proceedings.

How to start
To start the evaluation of your proposal for inclusion in the CCIS series, please send an e-mail to ccis@springer.com.

Constantine Stephanidis · Margherita Antona ·
Stavroula Ntoa · George Margetis ·
Gavriel Salvendy
Editors

HCI International 2025 – Late Breaking Posters

27th International Conference on Human-Computer Interaction, HCII 2025
Gothenburg, Sweden, June 22–27, 2025
Proceedings, Part III

Springer

Editors
Constantine Stephanidis
University of Crete and Foundation for Research and Technology - Hellas (FORTH)
Heraklion, Crete, Greece

Margherita Antona
Foundation for Research and Technology - Hellas (FORTH)
Heraklion, Crete, Greece

Stavroula Ntoa
Foundation for Research and Technology - Hellas (FORTH)
Heraklion, Crete, Greece

George Margetis
Foundation for Research and Technology - Hellas (FORTH)
Heraklion, Crete, Greece

Gavriel Salvendy
University of Central Florida
Orlando, FL, USA

ISSN 1865-0929 ISSN 1865-0937 (electronic)
Communications in Computer and Information Science
ISBN 978-3-032-12775-4 ISBN 978-3-032-12773-0 (eBook)
https://doi.org/10.1007/978-3-032-12773-0

This Springer imprint is published by the registered company Springer Nature Switzerland AG
The registered company address is: Gewerbestrasse 11, 6330 Cham, Switzerland

Foreword

The HCI International (HCII) conference was founded in 1984 by Gavriel Salvendy (Purdue University, USA, Tsinghua University, P.R. China, and University of Central Florida, USA) and the first event of the series, "1st USA-Japan Conference on Human-Computer Interaction", was held in Honolulu, Hawaii, USA, on 18–20 August. Since then, HCI International has been held jointly with several Thematic Areas and Affiliated Conferences, with each one under the auspices of a distinguished international Program Board and under one management and one registration. Twenty-seven HCI International Conferences have been organized so far (every two years until 2013, and annually thereafter).

Last year, we celebrated 40 years since the establishment of the HCII conference, which has been a hub for presenting groundbreaking research and novel ideas and collaboration for people from all over the world. Over the years, this conference has served as a platform for scholars, researchers, industry experts, and students to exchange ideas, connect, and address challenges in the ever-evolving HCI field. The conference has evolved itself, adapting to new technologies and emerging trends, while staying committed to its core mission of advancing knowledge and driving change.

The 27th International Conference on Human-Computer Interaction, HCI International 2025 (HCII 2025), was held as an 'on-site' conference at the Gothia Towers Hotel and Swedish Exhibition & Congress Centre, in Gothenburg, Sweden, on June 22–27, 2025, with the additional option for 'on-line' participation. It incorporated the 21 thematic areas and affiliated conferences listed below.

A total of 7972 individuals from academia, research institutes, industry, and government agencies from 92 countries submitted contributions. 1430 papers and 355 posters (as short research papers) were included in the volumes of the proceedings published just before the start of the conference. Additionally, 439 papers and 104 posters were included in the volumes of the proceedings published after the conference, as "Late Breaking Work". The contributions thoroughly cover the entire field of human-computer interaction, highlight the evolving role of computers in diverse contexts, and demonstrate how HCI research is shaping and improving user experiences across a wide range of domains, influencing technological progress and its effective integration into various sectors. The volumes constituting the full set of the HCII 2025 conference proceedings are listed on the following pages.

I would like to thank the Program Board Chairs and the members of the Program Boards of all thematic areas and affiliated conferences for their contribution towards the high scientific quality and overall success of the HCI International 2025 conference. Their manifold support including paper reviews (via a single-blind review process, with

---

The original version of the book has been revised. The title, Color of this book has been corrected.
A correction to this book can be found at https://doi.org/10.1007/978-3-032-12773-0_29

a minimum of two reviews per submission), session organization, and their willingness to act as goodwill ambassadors for the conference is most highly appreciated.

This conference would not have been possible without the continuous and unwavering support and advice of Gavriel Salvendy, founder, General Chair Emeritus, and Scientific Advisor. For his outstanding efforts, I would like to express my sincere appreciation to Abbas Moallem, Communications Chair and Editor of HCI International News.

September 2025 Constantine Stephanidis

HCI International 2025 Thematic Areas and Affiliated Conferences

- HCI: Human-Computer Interaction Thematic Area
- HIMI: Human Interface and the Management of Information Thematic Area
- EPCE: 22nd International Conference on Engineering Psychology and Cognitive Ergonomics
- AC: 19th International Conference on Augmented Cognition
- UAHCI: 19th International Conference on Universal Access in Human-Computer Interaction
- CCD: 17th International Conference on Cross-Cultural Design
- SCSM: 17th International Conference on Social Computing and Social Media
- VAMR: 17th International Conference on Virtual, Augmented and Mixed Reality
- DHM: 16th International Conference on Digital Human Modeling & Applications in Health, Safety, Ergonomics & Risk Management
- DUXU: 14th International Conference on Design, User Experience and Usability
- C&C: 13th International Conference on Culture and Computing
- DAPI: 13th International Conference on Distributed, Ambient and Pervasive Interactions
- HCIBGO: 12th International Conference on HCI in Business, Government and Organizations
- LCT: 12th International Conference on Learning and Collaboration Technologies
- ITAP: 11th International Conference on Human Aspects of IT for the Aged Population
- AIS: 7th International Conference on Adaptive Instructional Systems
- HCI-CPT: 7th International Conference on HCI for Cybersecurity, Privacy and Trust
- HCI-Games: 7th International Conference on HCI in Games
- MobiTAS: 7th International Conference on HCI in Mobility, Transport and Automotive Systems
- AI-HCI: 6th International Conference on Artificial Intelligence in HCI
- MOBILE: 6th International Conference on Human-Centered Design, Operation and Evaluation of Mobile Communications

Conference Proceedings – Full List of Volumes

1. LNCS 15766, Human-Computer Interaction — Part I, edited by Masaaki Kurosu and Ayako Hashizume
2. LNCS 15767, Human-Computer Interaction — Part II, edited by Masaaki Kurosu and Ayako Hashizume
3. LNCS 15768, Human-Computer Interaction — Part III, edited by Masaaki Kurosu and Ayako Hashizume
4. LNCS 15769, Human-Computer Interaction — Part IV, edited by Masaaki Kurosu and Ayako Hashizume
5. LNCS 15770, Human-Computer Interaction — Part V, edited by Masaaki Kurosu and Ayako Hashizume
6. LNCS 15771, Human-Computer Interaction — Part VI, edited by Masaaki Kurosu and Ayako Hashizume
7. LNCS 15772, Human-Computer Interaction — Part VII, edited by Masaaki Kurosu and Ayako Hashizume
8. LNCS 15773, Human Interface and the Management of Information: Part I, edited by Hirohiko Mori and Yumi Asahi
9. LNCS 15774, Human Interface and the Management of Information: Part II, edited by Hirohiko Mori and Yumi Asahi
10. LNCS 15773, Human Interface and the Management of Information: Part III, edited by Hirohiko Mori and Yumi Asahi
11. LNAI 15776, Engineering Psychology and Cognitive Ergonomics: Part I, edited by Don Harris and Wen-Chin Li
12. LNAI 15777, Engineering Psychology and Cognitive Ergonomics: Part II, edited by Don Harris and Wen-Chin Li
13. LNAI 15778, Augmented Cognition, Part I, edited by Dylan D. Schmorrow and Cali M. Fidopiastis
14. LNAI 15779, Augmented Cognition, Part II, edited by Dylan D. Schmorrow and Cali M. Fidopiastis
15. LNCS 15780, Universal Access in Human-Computer Interaction: Part I, edited by Margherita Antona and Constantine Stephanidis
16. LNCS 15781, Universal Access in Human-Computer Interaction: Part II, edited by Margherita Antona and Constantine Stephanidis
17. LNCS 15782, Cross-Cultural Design: Part I, edited by Pei-Luen Patrick Rau
18. LNCS 15783, Cross-Cultural Design: Part II, edited by Pei-Luen Patrick Rau
19. LNCS 15784, Cross-Cultural Design: Part III, edited by Pei-Luen Patrick Rau
20. LNCS 15785, Cross-Cultural Design: Part IV, edited by Pei-Luen Patrick Rau
21. LNCS 15786, Social Computing and Social Media: Part I, edited by Adela Coman and Simona Vasilache

22. LNCS 15787, Social Computing and Social Media: Part II, edited by Adela Coman and Simona Vasilache
23. LNCS 15788, Virtual, Augmented and Mixed Reality: Part I, edited by Jessie Y. C. Chen and Gino Fragomeni
24. LNCS 15789, Virtual, Augmented and Mixed Reality: Part II, edited by Jessie Y. C. Chen and Gino Fragomeni
25. LNCS 15790, Virtual, Augmented and Mixed Reality: Part III, edited by Jessie Y. C. Chen and Gino Fragomeni
26. LNCS 15791, Digital Human Modeling and Applications in Health, Safety, Ergonomics and Risk Management: Part I, edited by Vincent G. Duffy
27. LNCS 15792, Digital Human Modeling and Applications in Health, Safety, Ergonomics and Risk Management: Part II, edited by Vincent G. Duffy
28. LNCS 15793, Digital Human Modeling and Applications in Health, Safety, Ergonomics and Risk Management: Part III, edited by Vincent G. Duffy
29. LNCS 15794, Design, User Experience, and Usability: Part I, edited by Martin Schrepp
30. LNCS 15795, Design, User Experience, and Usability: Part II, edited by Martin Schrepp
31. LNCS 15796, Design, User Experience, and Usability: Part III, edited by Martin Schrepp
32. LNCS 15797, Design, User Experience, and Usability: Part IV, edited by Martin Schrepp
33. LNCS 15798, Design, User Experience, and Usability: Part V, edited by Martin Schrepp
34. LNCS 15799, Design, User Experience, and Usability: Part VI, edited by Martin Schrepp
35. LNCS 15800, Culture and Computing; Part I, edited by Matthias Rauterberg
36. LNCS 15801, Culture and Computing; Part II, edited by Matthias Rauterberg
37. LNCS 15802, Distributed, Ambient and Pervasive Interactions: Part I, edited by Norbert A. Streitz and Shin'ichi Konomi
38. LNCS 15803, Distributed, Ambient and Pervasive Interactions: Part II, edited by Norbert A. Streitz and Shin'ichi Konomi
39. LNCS 15804, HCI in Business, Government and Organizations: Part I, edited by Fiona Fui-Hoon Nah and Keng Leng Siau
40. LNCS 158045, HCI in Business, Government and Organizations: Part II, edited by Fiona Fui-Hoon Nah and Keng Leng Siau
41. LNCS 15806, Learning and Collaboration Technologies: Part I, edited by Brian K. Smith and Marcela Borge
42. LNCS 15807, Learning and Collaboration Technologies: Part II, edited by Brian K. Smith and Marcela Borge
43. LNCS 15808, Learning and Collaboration Technologies: Part III, edited by Brian K. Smith and Marcela Borge
44. LNCS 15809, Human Aspects of IT for the Aged Population: Part I, edited by Qin Gao and Jia Zhou

67. CCIS 2529, HCI International 2025 Posters — Part VIII, edited by Constantine Stephanidis, Margherita Antona, Stavroula Ntoa and Gavriel Salvendy
68. LNCS 16331, HCI International 2025 — Late Breaking Papers: Part I, edited by Masaaki Kurosu and Ayako Hashizume
69. LNCS 16332, HCI International 2025 — Late Breaking Papers: Part II, edited by Masaaki Kurosu and Ayako Hashizume
70. LNCS 16333, HCI International 2025 — Late Breaking Papers: Part III, edited by Hirohiko Mori, Yumi Asahi, Dylan D. Schmorrow and Cali M. Fidopiastis
71. LNCS 16334, HCI International 2025 — Late Breaking Papers: Part IV, edited by Don Harris, Wen-Chin Li, Norbert A. Streitz and Shin'ichi Konomi
72. LNCS 16335, HCI International 2025 — Late Breaking Papers: Part V, edited by Margherita Antona and Constantine Stephanidis
73. LNCS 16336, HCI International 2025 — Late Breaking Papers: Part VI, edited by Pei-Luen Patrick Rau and Heidi Krömker
74. LNCS 16337, HCI International 2025 — Late Breaking Papers: Part VII, edited by Adela Coman, Simona Vasilache and Abbas Moallem
75. LNCS 16338, HCI International 2025 — Late Breaking Papers: Part VIII, edited by Jessie Y. C. Chen, Gino Fragomeni and Xiaowen Fang
76. LNCS 16339, HCI International 2025 — Late Breaking Papers: Part IX, edited by Vincent G. Duffy
77. LNCS 16340, HCI International 2025 — Late Breaking Papers: Part X, edited by Vincent G. Duffy, Qin Gao and Jia Zhou
78. LNCS 16341, HCI International 2025 — Late Breaking Papers: Part XI, edited by Martin Schrepp
79. LNCS 16342, HCI International 2025 — Late Breaking Papers: Part XII, edited by Martin Schrepp and Matthias Rauterberg
80. LNCS 16343, HCI International 2025 — Late Breaking Papers: Part XIII, edited by Fiona Fui-Hoon Nah and Keng Leng Siau
81. LNCS 16344, HCI International 2025 — Late Breaking Papers: Part XIV, edited by Brian K. Smith, Marcela Borge, Robert A. Sottilare and Jessica Schwarz
82. LNCS 16345, HCI International 2025 — Late Breaking Papers: Part XV, edited by Helmut Degen and Stavroula Ntoa
83. LNCS 16346, HCI International 2025 — Late Breaking Papers: Part XVI, edited by June Wei, George Margetis, Helmut Degen and Stavroula Ntoa
84. CCIS 2771, HCI International 2025 — Late Breaking Posters: Part I, edited by Constantine Stephanidis, Margherita Antona, Stavroula Ntoa, George Margetis and Gavriel Salvendy

85. CCIS 2772, HCI International 2025 — Late Breaking Posters: Part II, edited by Constantine Stephanidis, Margherita Antona, Stavroula Ntoa, George Margetis and Gavriel Salvendy
86. CCIS 2773, HCI International 2025 — Late Breaking Posters: Part III, edited by Constantine Stephanidis, Margherita Antona, Stavroula Ntoa, George Margetis and Gavriel Salvendy

https://2025.hci.international/proceedings

27th International Conference on Human-Computer Interaction (HCII 2025)

The full list with the Program Board Chairs and the members of the Program Boards of all thematic areas and affiliated conferences of HCII 2025 is available online at:

http://www.hci.international/board-members-2025.php

HCI International 2026 Conference

The 28th International Conference on Human-Computer Interaction, HCI International 2026, will be held jointly with the affiliated conferences at the Montréal Convention Centre (Palais des congrès de Montréal), in Montreal, Canada, 26–31 July 2026. It will cover a broad spectrum of themes related to Human-Computer Interaction, including theoretical issues, methods, tools, processes, and case studies in HCI design, as well as novel interaction techniques, interfaces, and applications. The proceedings will be published by Springer (part of Springer Nature) in a multi-volume set. More information will become available on the conference website: https://2026.hci.international/.

General Chair
Constantine Stephanidis
University of Crete and ICS-FORTH
Heraklion, Crete, Greece
Email: general_chair@2026.hci.international

https://2026.hci.international/

Contents

Advances in Immersive and Multimodal Interaction

Artificial Intelligence for Creativity, Education, and Design

Pattern Flow: A Parametric Approach to Pattern Generation with Future Integration of Shape and Color Grammars

Elaheh Babaei[1](✉), Huiwon Lim[2], and Joel Priddy[1]

[1] Graphic Design, Penn State, University Park, PA 16802, USA
{eqb5545,jdp19}@psu.edu
[2] Iowa State University, Ames, US
hwlim@iastate.edu

Abstract. This research focuses on a web-based parametric design platform for generating complex patterns, bridging computational methods with the rich traditions of textile arts. By leveraging parametric modeling, the system provides an environment where shapes, proportions, and relationships can be manipulated in real time, promoting user-driven creativity. A prototype demonstrates diverse pattern outcomes while maintaining an intuitive interface. Early evaluations with pilot users suggest that the parametric engine supports flexibility in exploring design variations, distinguishing it from tools that limit user input or require advanced technical knowledge.

Although the research highlights the efficacy of a parametric model, our long-term objective is to integrate Shape Grammar and Color Grammar in future iterations. Such a hybrid approach aims to unite rule-based generation (Shape Grammar) with systematic color relationships (Color Grammar), expanding both aesthetic complexity and user control. Ultimately, this study lays the groundwork for a robust design tool that balances usability with algorithmic sophistication, offering a valuable framework for computational pattern generation.

Keywords: Generate Patterns · Usability · Algorithmic Generation · Real-Time Manipulation · User-Driven Creativity

1 Introduction

Pattern generation has garnered growing attention in computational design, particularly in fields such as textile arts, surface design, and decorative motifs. Modern digital tools provide unprecedented control over geometric and color compositions. However, many pattern-generation platforms either oversimplify user interaction or demand specialized expertise to navigate complex rule systems. To bridge the gap between expert-driven computational tools and accessible design solutions, this study proposes a web-based parametric platform called Pattern Flow.

This study examines the parametric core of Pattern Flow, developed in Rhino/Grasshopper software, illustrating how it facilitates real-time user control over shape and color parameters. The novelty of this work lies in establishing parametric design as the cornerstone for future integration of Shape Grammar and Color Grammar. By delineating the balance between immediate user flexibility (parametric rules) and advanced generative algorithms (Shape and Color Grammars), this study seeks to progressively refine the platform's capabilities.

C. Stephanidis et al. (Eds.): HCII 2025, CCIS 2773, pp. 3–6, 2026.
https://doi.org/10.1007/978-3-032-12773-0_1

2 Methods

2.1 Theoretical Background

Parametric design refers to a design processes in which geometric and visual outputs are driven by adjustable parameters [1]. Originally developed in architecture and product design, parametric tools allow designers to rapidly iterate on form through real-time manipulation of dimensions, angles, and relational constraints. In pattern generation, this translates into adjusting variables (e.g., shape size, repetition intervals, curvature) to quickly explore aesthetic outcomes. Automatic graphic pattern generation plays a pivotal role in the patter design industry [2].

Shape Grammar involves defining production rules that transform an initial shape into progressively complex patterns or designs [3]. When applied to textiles or decorative arts, Shape Grammar can systematically generate patterns that adhere to specific style constraints. Color Grammar builds upon this concept by structuring color relationships through rule-based interactions [4]. While these grammatical approaches offer algorithmic rigor, they often require expert-level knowledge to define and manage the rules effectively. Hence, this study proposes beginning with a parametric foundation that is more user-friendly and flexible, gradually introducing Shape and Color Grammars as optional or advanced features.

Most commercial and research-based pattern generators employ simple transformations, like repeating tiles or basic symmetrical compositions. Tools that allow deeper generative control either limit user interaction to pre-set options or demand proficiency in scripting languages. Our Pattern Flow system aims to bridge this gap by proving an accessible interface with parametric flexibility, laying the foundation for more advanced grammar-based features.

2.2 Parametric Platform

At the core of Pattern Flow is a parametric model developed in Rhino/Grasshopper that manages relationships between shape variables and layout variables. Users can adjust input numeric values to control parameters such as radius, number of sides, and the density of the base geometry, instantly updating the rendered pattern on the screen.

Figure 1 illustrates one of our rule-based workflows, inspired by the work of Ulu and Sener [5], for generating patterns. In this workflow, the base motif, a cypress tree with its reference point, is arrayed around the center of the base polygon (Rule 1). Then the polygon, with the arrayed motif, is transformed into three polygons, whose centers form a triangle (Rule 2). These geometries are then mirrored across the XZ plane (Rule 3) and subsequently mirrored across the YZ plane (Rule 4) to generate the base pattern.

Figure 2 shows the translation of this logic to a parametric algorithm in Rhino/Grasshopper, where more control is provided on the process by defining the input variables including number of sides of the polygon, polygon radius, move factor, and the coordinates of the reference point on the base motif (bottom, in between, top).

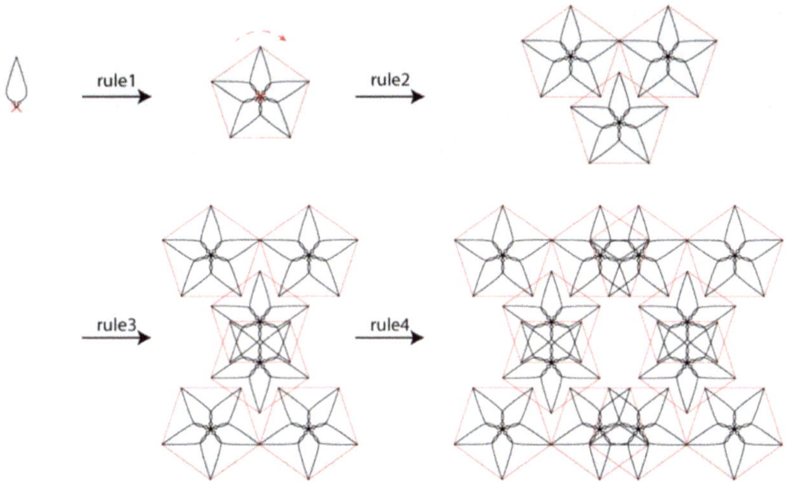

Fig. 1. An example of using a rule-based workflow to generate patterns.

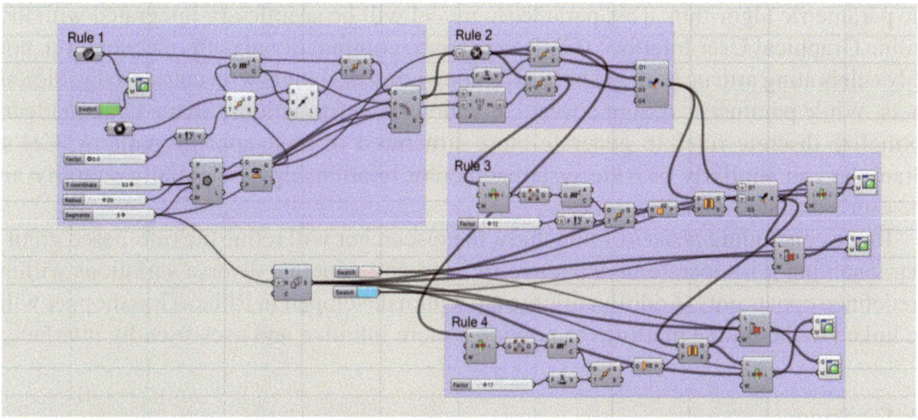

Fig. 2. Parametric algorithm developed in Rhino/Grasshopper.

2.3 Prototype

Initial prototypes generated complex, repetitive motifs by varying just a few parameters. For example, adjusting the scale and rotation parameters in real time yields patterns that evolve from simple polygons to intricate tessellations (Fig. 3). Test patterns demonstrated a high degree of variability without overwhelming the user.

Comparisons with popular pattern generators revealed that Pattern Flow offers greater flexibility in shape manipulation. While some existing systems provide advanced generative algorithms, they often limit real-time customization or require scripting knowledge, our parametric approach fills this gap by maintaining both accessibility and adaptability.

(a) (b) (c)

Fig. 3. Prototype 1. a test with a simple graphic motif to find how users can change parameters to generate a pattern with the motif: (a) reference point at the top of the motif, (b) reference point in between the top and the bottom part of the motif, (c) reference point at the bottom of the motif.

3 Conclusion

This study presented the first phase of Pattern Flow, a web-based parametric design platform for pattern generation. By facilitating real-time manipulation of shape, layout, and color, our approach achieves an optimal balance between technical depth and ease of use.

The next phase of this study will integrate Shape Grammar and Color Grammar into the parametric algorithm. This parametric model will be seamlessly integrated with the online Graphical User Interface (GUI) to enhance computational pattern generation, not only celebrating artistic heritage but also empowering designers with cutting-edge digital tools. While parametric design covers continuous transformations, Shape Grammar can formalize discrete rules to generate more structured or style-specific patterns. Color Grammar can similarly provide systematic color relationships, potentially simplifying the user's decision-making process.

In the concluding phases of this study, the researcher will refine the rule-based grammar, enabling it to operate on a parametric seed and generate diverse variations within predefined constraints. Additionally, the algorithm developed in Rhino/Grasshopper will be linked to the online platform to provide a more intuitive and user-friendly interface.

References

1. Liu, W., Kolisnyk, O.: Parametric modeling as an innovative approach in graphic design. Art Des. **1**, 34–45 (2024)
2. Abdi, A., Safabakhsh, R.: An automatic graphic pattern generation algorithm and its application to the multipurpose camouflage pattern design. IEEE Trans. Cybern. **53**(8), 4748–4762 (2022)
3. Stiny, G., Gips, J.: Shape grammar and the generative specification of painting and sculpture. In: IFIP Congress (2), vol. 2, no. 3, pp. 125–135, August 1971
4. Knight, T.W.: Color grammar: designing with lines and colors. Environ. Plann. B. Plann. Des. **16**(4), 417–449 (1989)
5. Ebru, U., Şener, S.M.: A shape grammar model to generate Islamic geometric pattern. In: 12th Generative Art International conference, Italy, pp. 290–297 (2009)

Designing Meaning Across Cultures a Framework for HCI from an Interdisciplinary Perspective

Mario Bisson, Stefania Palmieri, and Claudia Spinò(✉)

Politecnico di Milano, 20160 Milan, MI, Italy
{mario.bisson,claudia.spino}@polimi.it

Abstract. Design in Human-Computer Interaction (HCI) has evolved beyond usability toward systems that offer engaging experiences, systematically leveraging the mechanisms that regulate perception and meaning-making. Ongoing research reveals new layers of complexity regarding the role of context and subjectivity in perception (Levitt-Frank & Shoshana 2023), which risk limiting the transversality of experiences and challenging the creation of universally meaningful interactions (Plocher et al. 2021). Design practice has progressively integrated holistic theories of cognition, leading to structured methods that—borrowing from Norman (2004)—focus on the visceral and behavioral levels of emotion, while the reflective level—the domain of higher-order meaning and identity—remains elusive. This paper proposes an unedited transdisciplinary framework powered by a systemic perspective to coordinate tools and technologies in support of embedding powerful, intersubjective meanings into design. A broad literature was reviewed to: (1) integrate models describing the phenomenology of interaction; (2) analyze the state of the art in cross-cultural HCI design; (3) identify relevant findings in anthropology and psychology and explore their implications for HCI; (4) contextualize cross-cultural design in the aftermath of cultural globalization. Findings show that, just as the embodied nature of perception establishes a shared perceptual baseline (Plocher et al. 2021), cognitive structures exhibit universal patterns as well and while contents and functions may vary, their scaffolding remains stable across human experience (Lang & Kundt 2023). The interdisciplinarity of the proposed framework enables a more systemic and organic understanding of HCI: one that acknowledges complex, evolving phenomena and harnesses the embodied and cognitive foundations of human experience.

Keywords: Embodied Cognition · Scaffolding Theory · Ritual Design

1 Introduction

Globalization and mass consumption have given rise to a widespread commodification of virtually any industry sector. Many companies have reacted to this market flattening by opting for differentiation strategies whose key asset is the brand identity and the value system it communicates. In this context, an almost Platonic dualism occurs: the brand

C. Stephanidis et al. (Eds.): HCII 2025, CCIS 2773, pp. 7–20, 2026.
https://doi.org/10.1007/978-3-032-12773-0_2

is the intangible depositary of transcendental and immanent ideas, while the product plays the role of its tangible embodiment: a condensation and actualization of a variety of complex meanings that do not just need to be perceivable but enable captivating and compelling interactions (Vaidya et al. 2021). This perspective poses non-trivial issues, as embedding abstract ideas into products requires entering a strongly subjective and layered dimension, shaped by individual peculiarities and socio-cultural context, which has become almost a taboo in the scientific community: findings keep highlighting the relevance of subjective and cultural differences in perception, which make it irreducible to a standard model valid for every individual. Nonetheless, when it comes to praxis, we maintain it is useful to both recognize and keep into account such findings, which can be enlightening in developing designs destined to specific contexts, and, contextually, to focus on available studies which have instead outlined a common ground of perception. We propose that an integrated perspective on the mechanisms that regulate individual and collective meaning-making processes can empower a practical framework for meaningful and cross-cultural design praxis for HCI. In the following chapters we will in the first place (1) cover the functioning of cognitive processes and provide a definition and an integrated model of interaction; (2) analyze the state of the art in HCI approaches, tools and technologies and; (3) introduce ritual as a cultural universal and propose its contribution in HCI practice; (4) we then contextualize findings in the light of the current cultural paradigm.

2 Cognition, Interaction and Affect

The field of Human-Computer Interaction and the research that regards it are in constant and rapid evolution, at the same pace with technological advancements following the exponential curve described by Moore's Law: if the first theories and studies on Human Factor design focused on making the use of one complex and task-specific machine understandable for a highly specialized operator, today we are in front of a variety of novel approaches concerned with the interaction of one or more users with a network of multiple interconnected machines in a IoT of ambient intelligence (Wadhwa et al. 2024), where agency is shared in different proportions between humans and machines (Mueller et al. 2020), now interpretable as a coupled system cooperating towards a goal, rather than as the mere use of a passive tool by a human agent. Technological advancements, in fact, keep opening to new horizons in terms of human-computer relationships, with concepts such as tangibility, affect, enactivism, embodiment and embedment being mentioned and elaborated on with increased frequency in pertinent literature (Höök, 2018; Bennett et al., 2021). These concepts - and all the approaches and theories that stem from them - are the signal of the shift from a perspective of Interaction between humans and computers, to one of Integration (Mueller et al. 2020; Cornelio et al. 2022), where Integration is not only meant as physical (as made possible by the use of wearable devices and embedded and ambient technologies), but also as psychological, through designs that acknowledge and leverage the very processes of cognition for natural and seamless user experiences, indeed, the aforementioned relevant terms belong to the third wave of theories developed in the context cognitive-behavioral psychology, which proved to particularly resonate with the objectives of HCI and HCInt research. In fact, in the past, theories of cognition (Hanson 1984; Rumelhart 1999) proposed that the mind, akin to a computer, worked as an information processing organ that created and manipulated internal representations of the outside world. Later, this model was expanded upon by theories that have gradually considered and analyzed the interconnectedness of mind, body and external world and acknowledged that to fully grasp the complexity of cognition and interaction, it is impossible to separately analyze each element, as their mutual influences are inextricably interwoven. In this chapter we are going to investigate the function of cognition and affect and to provide a model of interaction that integrates different perspectives and theories.

2.1 Evolutionary Function of Affect

In the first place, from an evolutionary perspective, we can establish that affect and cognitive processes are functional to homeostasis: we can perceive, interpret and store for short or long-term external and internal stimuli (interoception), so that we can be aware of our needs and program our behavior accordingly (Cea 2023). Cognition is therefore predictive (Clark 1998) and embodied (Varela et al. 1991; Wilson 2002). To this end, we evolved to experience affect and emotions, as perceiving different stimuli with distinct hedonic valences (good or bad), is more convenient (Damasio 2020): for instance, affect is at the core of the phenomenon of motivated attention, where we tend to prefer and promptly focus on emotionally charged stimuli, because the intensity of the affect they elicit makes them feel more urgent and relevant to our preservation (Ali, 2023; Cea 2023). Findings identify this evolutionary transition marker as the very origin of consciousness, in fact affect, as "an additional layer of homeostatic regulation that allows sentient organisms to thrive at increasingly more complex levels of organization and interaction". Cea (2023) is the basis of Unlimited Associative Learning, which allows organisms to behave not exclusively on the basis of an inherited predefined set of automatic reflexes, but to open-endedly create and occasionally rewrite long chains of links of stimuli and actions that form an internal compass to perceive and navigate the world (Birch et al. 2020). UAL is one of the key factors in the subjectivity of perception, as the associations that shape our understanding of the world are strongly influenced by a wide range of variables, like social and cultural context and are defined by subjective experiences, making them unique for every individual. The subjectivity implied by UAL along with the agency of the environment, constituted by affordances (Gibson 1979; Mangalam et al. 2024) and sociocultural affordances (Ramstead et al. 2016), contribute to the enactivity (Thompson 2010) and situatedness (Robbins 2009) of cognition.

2.2 Towards a Model of Interaction

While foundational to understanding interaction, many cognitive theories still leave its dynamic and reciprocal nature underexplored. Hornbæk (2017) condensed findings that proposed definitions of interaction from different perspectives to unify them under an agreeable statement, from a HCI outlook. He first describes interaction as embodied and situated: "What we view as interaction emerges in a situation and cannot be reduced back to either the human or the world. This view also emphasizes how our bodies shape everything we think and do." then, to provide a broader definition, referencing

(Bunge 2009), he sustains that: "[...] interaction concerns two entities that determine each other's behavior over time. In HCI, the entities are computers (ranging from input devices to systems) and humans (ranging from end- effectors to tool users). Their mutual determination can be of many types, including statistical, mechanical, and structural. But their causal relationship is teleologically determined: Users, with their goals and pursuits, are the ultimate metric of interaction." This definition highlights interaction's reciprocity, shared agency, and goal-oriented nature, framing it broadly while clarifying key conceptual issues. It is therefore considerable an agreeable and satisfying definition that frames the matter from a broad perspective and that addresses and clarifies a number of relevant conceptual questions. In addition to it, it seems relevant to the scope of the research to also break down and schematize the different dimensions and stages interaction is articulated into. To do so, in Fig. 1, we reference the Theory of Action (Norman 1986); the Action Cycle Theory (Marks 2023); an embodied perspective on cognition and affect (Cea 2023); The emotional design theory (Norman 2004). The Theory of Action, for simplicity, proposes a sequential succession of phases, while the Action Cycle Theory, an enactivist theory that shows many points of contact with Norman's cognitive engineering concepts, emphasizes, despite being limited to the visual system, the determining role of affect in decision making and the loop of action-feedback involved in interaction; (Cea 2023) perspective, instead, is useful to sharpen the passage from the conscious part of the experience, namely the "purely felt" one, to the aware one; the Emotional Design Theory formulated by Norman, instead, is useful to discern the different types of emotion elicited in different phases, embracing a holistic perspective in which the way objects participate in reflective meaning-making processes is questioned and the issues that arise from its inherent complexity and contextuality are posed. Even if it constitutes a simplification of reality, since perception, interpretation and action take place in a continuum and their temporal dimension can be approximated to simultaneity, we can affirm that the model in Fig. 1 suits a variety of cases, satisfyingly describing, rather than the phases, the dimensions of interaction and the emotional levels mainly, but not exclusively, involved in each one. Based on the type of user, of technology and of goal, even the feedback of the System can be affectively intense and activate the visceral and reflective levels of emotion, beside the strategic planning of future behaviors. To exemplify, if a person is using their laptop computer to fill out an Excel spreadsheet, it is likely that each time they click a cell, or even the first time ever they click a cell, the behavioral level of emotion and the planning and executing processes will be mainly involved, as the feedback of the System is not emotionally charged; on the other hand, in the case of an artistic installation of ambient technology that reacts to the body movements of people without requiring them to perform any specific task, it is likely that visceral and reflective areas of emotions will be more strongly activated and that the planning and executing processes will take place in function of them. The model also emphasizes how some processes in particular belong in a blurred area, as detecting affordances is both part of the creation of the user model and the first step of programming behavior, similarly, executing action is both the result of said program and the trigger of almost instant new actions from the machine itself and therefore of their perception and interpretation by the user.

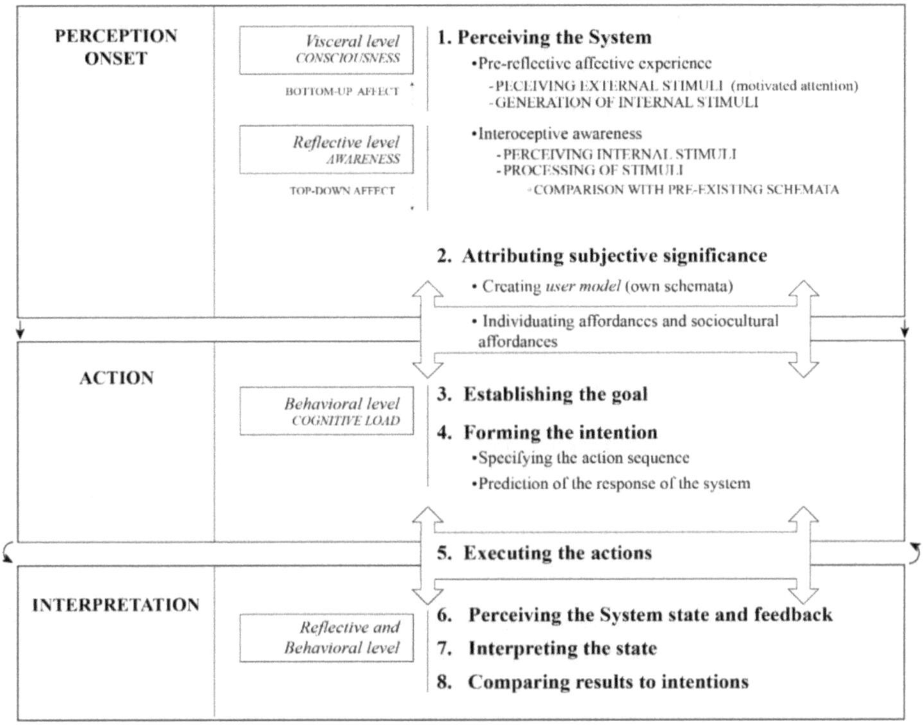

Fig. 1. An integrated model of interaction-

3 HCI Frameworks and Toolkits

As thus demonstrated, interaction is a complex phenomenon regulated by a variety of processes that act on different levels. Such processes can be leveraged in HCI design to achieve interactions that enable a spectrum of experiences that can range from simply acceptable, effective, pleasurable to even meaningful and emotional. In this chapter, our goal will be that of mapping the state of the art in said practice: what has, until now, been done to methodically leverage the very nature of human perception to create enticing HCI designs?

3.1 State of the Art

As widely renown, psychology has been informing HCI practices for as long as this field has existed. HCI researchers have in fact already investigated the findings of the third wave of cognitive-behavioral theories and bridged them to practice: a wide literature mentions and elaborates on concepts such as Tangible User Interface (TUI), Natural User Interface (NUI), Affective Interaction and Human Computer Integration. We will now provide (Fig. 2) a list of technologies, inputs and outputs used by these approaches, based on literature findings (Mueller et al.2020; Cornelio et al. 2022; Guribye et al. 2016; Zhou et al. 2024; Duarte et al. 2022; Liao et al. 2023) and shortly address the perspective, the tools and the goals of each one.

Tangible User Interface. This area of research emphasizes material engagement and embodied interaction, grounding computational processes and data in physical, sensorimotor forms (Hornecker et al. 2006), offering affordances that allow users to navigate the interaction also using their spatial intelligence, as it has been shown to help with cognitive tasks (Van Gennip et al. 2016). In addition, the perceptual qualities of the physical tokens can provide perceptual transparency (Mueller et al. 2020) over symbols lying on flat screens. They often involve different input technologies embedded in the token or in the surfaces it interacts with, like pressure sensors, temperature sensors and so on and their feedback can be output in a variety of systems.

Natural User Interface. This approach focuses on interactions that leverage users innate bodily behaviors, such as gestures, gaze, posture, and facial expressions, to control and communicate with digital systems (Wigdor & Wixon 2011) enabling cognitive offloading. These interfaces often rely on multimodal input technologies such as gesture recognition, voice input, eye tracking, and facial analysis.

Affective Interaction. The field of affective interaction seeks to enrich HCI by integrating the user's emotional states into the core of interaction, creating systems that perceive, interpret, and respond to affect as part of meaningful engagement (Picard 1997; Rosa et al. 2020). Unlike early affective computing's focus on detecting discrete emotional categories, contemporary affective interaction emphasizes context-sensitive, culturally nuanced, and embodied experiences of emotion (Ahmadpour et al. 2025). These systems leverage multimodal sensing, including AI models and algorithms for facial analysis, voice prosody, physiological signals, and haptics, to build richer, real-time models of user affect (Mueller et al. 2022).

Human Computer Integration. This field of research involves systems that augment the user's body, actions, or outcomes through tightly coupled technologies such as wearables, implants, or neural interfaces (Cornelio et al. 2022). These integrations vary in how control and agency are distributed between user and system. Design must ensure users retain a clear sense of agency, which depends on real-time feedback, adaptive autonomy, and strong sensorimotor coupling (Mueller et al. 2020).

3.2 Research Gap

Findings highlight how the aforementioned approaches are still mainly limited to small-scale experiments or art exhibitions and that, while their use and combination of the technologies in Fig. 2 is informed by embodied and enactive cognition theories, these are interpreted and put to practice based on their understanding and common sense, but there is a lack of a structured method (Duarte et al. 2022). Moreover, there are no consistent proposals that suggest cross-cultural tools to intentionally and methodically craft cross-cultural experiences involving higher-domain meaning. It appears that available literature vertically focuses on the cognitive processes of interaction, while, despite acknowledged and recognized, the highly subjective and contextual nature of meaning-making processes stays unaddressed and understandably so: it seems that the universal nature of cognition can only lead us this far, nonetheless, we maintain that other types of universal scaffoldings exist across cultures and that in order to identify them, it is useful to adopt a wider trans-disciplinary outlook on the matter.

TECHNOLOGIES

INPUT			OUTPUT
BIOSENSORS •body temperature sensors •weight sensors •body mass sensors •blood glucose sensors •ECG sensors •EDA sensors •EEG sensors •EMG sensors •breathing sensors	SENSORS •movement sensors •light sensors •sound sensors •temperature sensors •pressure sensors •accelerometers •gyroscopes	HUMAN COMPATIBLE •Epidermal technologies •Subdermal technologies •Transdermal technologies •Deep implanted technologies •Pass through technologies	•VR/AR HMDs •CAVE •screens •holographic fans •smart surfaces •tangible interfaces (buttons, controllers etc.) •bionic limbs •sound systems •LED light •vibration motors •microcontrollers •actuators

INPUT

UNAWARE	AWARE
BIOMETRIC •body temperature •weight •body mass •blood glucose •ECG •EDA •EEG •EMG •breathing	BEHAVIORAL •facial expressions •eye movement •whole body manipulation **•hand tracking** •one hand manipulation •two hand manipulation •fingers manipulation

OUTPUT

VISUAL	HAPTIC
•light •Animation •Image •3d scene	•vibration •force •heat
AUDIO	**OTHER**
•sound effect •music	•shapechanging behavior

Fig. 2. A list of tools for HCI.

4 A Cultural Universal: Rituals

In this chapter, we are going to demonstrate that beside the functioning of human cognition, that as a common and hollow structure, supports the infinitely diverse nuances of human experience, another transversal and ubiquitous phenomenon does exist as well and contributes to the presence of a common scaffolding. Ritual and ritual behavior exist across all ages and cultures and are performed for a variety of reasons and while their content or scope varies greatly, its essence remains unchanged (Kapitány et al., 2020), in fact, as (Lang et al. 2020) maintain: "Humans seem to come equipped with the psychological capacity to engage in ritual. Rituals are a culturally inherited, behavioural trademark of our species."

4.1 Definition

Anthropologists started to investigate rituals as a means of demonstrating some inherent difference between ethnicities to justify colonialist practices, instead, they unveiled and analyzed a consistent pattern of shared behavior valid across cultures (Bell et al. 2021), proposing, over time, numerous definitions for it. Before going through them, it is important to introduce another relevant theme borrowed from the anthropologic field that helps us understand the gradient of different functions and social roles rituals can have.

Egemony and the Ritual Spectrum. According to de Pina Cabral (1997), societies operate as Egemonic Systems—metaphorically like spotlights—that legitimize certain experiences by granting them symbolic power, which is expressed through institutional support, representation, and ritualization (e.g., starting a family through marriage). In contrast, experiences outside this spotlight occupy a liminal space, lacking validation or facing institutional rejection (e.g., robbery). Egemonic Systems evolve through a bottom-up dynamic, as marginalized groups push for their experiences to gain legitimacy, often transitioning from "nocturnal expressions" (individual, informal rituals) (Whitehouse, 2024) to "diurnal expressions" (socially recognized rituals). The former type of ritual has become particularly relevant in modern and post-modern societies, with New Age practices that involve a shift of spirituality towards the private sphere and the ritualization of the secular dimension (Bell et al. 2021; Frost 2022). All these factors that will be clearer when we will cover the value ritual offers individuals, explain why, according to (Davis-Floyd et al. 2022), "[…] ritual should not be thought of as something fixed, concrete, and discrete, but rather can most usefully be understood as existing on a spectrum from loosely patterned and thinly symbolic (like conversation) at one end, to highly patterned and densely symbolic (like a Catholic mass or a presidential inauguration) at the other."

Characteristics and Neuro-Cognitive Functions. Now that we have defined the context within which rituals are formed and occur, we can proceed to define their characteristics and functions. According to (Legare et al. 2020), "Rituals are socially stipulated, conventional behaviours. They are (i) predefined sequences of action characterized by rigidity, formality and repetition, which is (ii) embedded in systems of meaning and symbolism, and which (iii) contains non-instrumental elements that are causally opaque and goal demoted." This affirmation addresses some of the main points regarding rituals: their rigid and repetitive nature, their symbolic value and most importantly their causal opacity, i.e. the absence of a causal correlation between the actions performed in the ritual and the result it is supposed to achieve. All these characteristics, that can at first seem incomprehensible and irrational, are easily explained if we take a look at the evolutionary origin of rituals and ritual behavior and the function they serve on a neuro-cognitive level: borrowing from (Tonna et al., 2019; Lang et al. 2020), when we face anxiety due to unpredictable threats that go well beyond our resources, we experience a high level of neuro-cognitive entropy, meaning that we feel like we are not able to make reliable predictions to inform our behavior and we therefore feel distressed or overwhelmed. This triggers ritualized behaviors: their rigidity and repetitiveness create predictable sensory stimuli, fostering a sense of control by increasing the rate of successful predictions and therefore reducing internal entropy. While this explains causal opacity and repetitiveness, the attribution of symbolic meanings to these practices can be explained by another characteristic of our meaning-making processes, deeply rooted in our brain structure, in fact, according to (Davis-Floyd et al. 2022), "Because the wiring of the brain is mostly bottom-up (from the lower, more primitive areas to the neocortex) rather than top-down, the messages evoked from the lower emotional or behavioral levels of the brain can be very compelling." They also add "Through symbols and the systems of meaning (like myths, paradigms, and other types of belief systems) that underlie them, ritual bridges levels of the brain, entraining various neurocognitive structures through the associative linkages symbols provide. In other words, the ritual process integrates the neural networks of the conscious mind with those of the lower brain structures, which are not normally accessible to consciousness." This explains how rituals help individuals and communities make sense of otherwise abstract and intangible identities and values.

The Grammar of Rituals. It seems now appropriate to break down and analyze the constituent elements that concur to classify an action as a ritual, in fact, to paraphrase (Legare et al. 2020), rituals show a universal grammar, governed by core structural constraints, yet endowed with enough plasticity to enable wide cultural variation; humans naturally come equipped with the ability both to acquire ritual practices and to facilitate their transmission, which can take place both vertically (between generations) and horizontally (between communities). Figure 3 summarizes findings about the grammar of rituals, referencing the foundational work of (Turner 1969) and (Van Gennep 1960) and the enlightening inputs by Davis-Floyd et al. (2022), Trillò et al. (2022), Bell et al. (2021), Reynolds et al. (2017).

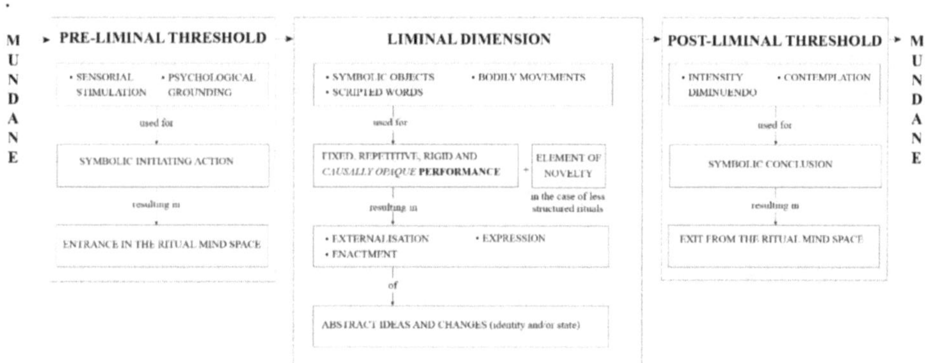

Fig. 3. Ritual structure with involved actions and requirements.

4.2 Bridging Theory to Practice

Now that we have defined the functioning and the structure of rituals, we can draw a connection between the HCI practices that we mapped in the previous chapter and ritual, by synergistically putting into system available tools following the scaffolding provided by ritual grammar to the end of implementing new types of social and cultural affordances. We propose that Systems should be designed in a way to recreate the structure of ritual processes, offering an affordance for repetitive, fixed and rigid behaviors and for the attribution of personal meaningful significance by users.

Pre-liminal Threshold. The incipit of the interaction corresponds to the pre-liminal threshold: similarly, to what happens in a ritual, this phase has the function of setting forth the beginning of the experience, signaling to the user. In this phase it is useful to use attention-capturing strategies, for example, leveraging the mechanisms of motivated attention through visual/haptic/audio feedback with attracting rhythms, or the strategies of the Natural User Interface, where voice, bodily movement or hand gesture trigger a reaction in the system: objects that activate at our signal in a natural way awaken our instinct to anthropomorphize things, a universal human tendency (Aggarwal et al. 2007; Guthrie, 2012).

Liminal Dimension. The main phase of interaction corresponds to the liminal space. Depending on the type of System, the technologies involved and the goals the user approaches it with, the content of the interaction will vary, but the function of this phase must be that of offering affordances that enable repetitive strongly patterned behavior and induce a focused and mindful state of mind. Harnessing a Tangible User Interface approach, with its embodied strategies, fosters a sense of presence, thanks to physical tokens and haptic/visual/audio feedback. This is the phase where emotional change takes place, therefore it is relevant to instill meaning into designated interaction: configurability of the tokens allows for tangible representation of abstract phenomena, fostering externalization and representational significance (Hornecker et al. 2006), while Affective Computing strategies, providing representational visual/haptic/audio feedback for emotional states and biometric data, fosters sense of presence, immersion self-reflection (Sliwinski et al., 2017). Furthermore, despite cultural differences, it has long been found (Krout 1935; Aboudan 1996) that some primordial gestures retain a biologically grounded, cross-cultural meaning due to the intrinsic link between emotion and the body. Movements like approaching or withdrawing, and spatial metaphors such as high vs. low, are commonly associated with shared emotional and conceptual interpretations across cultures (Parkinson & Walker 2016). Therefore, the design of affordances and interfaces for meaningful interactions should keep into account such findings.

Post-liminal Threshold. The conclusion of the interaction, corresponding to the post-liminal threshold, should gently dismiss the user, creating an intensity diminuendo in the sensory stimuli and a distinctive codified signal to set off the end of the interaction.

5 Implications in Post-modern Society

The New Age phenomenon reflects the ritualization of secular life and a shift from collective to individualized spirituality, marked by rituals ranging from loosely to highly codified forms. This shift is tied to structural changes in modern and post-modern societies and the effects of globalization on individuals' identity formation in their reflective project of the self (Giddens 1991): where once individuals shaped their identities in response to localized cultural frameworks (Turner, 2024), even if of course, ever evolving and constantly influencing one another, they now navigate a vast array of lifestyle and ideological choices enabled by the internet and social media, leading to the emergence of micro-identities and the erosion of cohesive social fabrics (Kossowska et al. 2023). While this fragmentation can isolate, digital platforms also facilitate the formation of meaningful communities, especially for stigmatized groups (Santaolalla-Rueda et al. 2024), but also for more trivial but deeply felt matters, like lifestyles, hobbies, passions and so on. Acknowledging the discussed phenomenon does not mean denying the subjectivity of culture but having a precious reading key to interpretate such diversity, identifying it with the mix of vertically and horizontally transmitted cultural elements. In fact, brands that recognize such dynamics have the opportunity to connect with emerging social groups by offering products that support and validate their idiosyncratic rituals and identities through culturally resonant affordances (Markum et al., 2023).

6 Future Work and Conclusions

In this work, we proposed an integrated model of interaction and bridged existent HCI and HCInt approaches and toolkits to a wider framework that, to the end of cross-culturaility, leverages the cultural universal constituted by rituals and ritualized behavior, contextualizing it, thanks to a trans-disciplinary outlook, in the phenomena of New Age and networked individualism fostered by post-modern social structure and media. We maintain that this framework represents a step further, on the course researchers have already embarked, towards holistic approaches that recognize and investigate the complexity involved in HCI. The next step is to test the proposed framework and expand on it, as to the end of transversality, the framework has a general outlook that needs concrete applications and verticalization on specific projects and contexts to verify its solidity and detect possible weaknesses. Another challenge that needs to be assessed through its use is that of ensuring it effectively supports designs that offer ritual affordance *and* fit mass production and everyday use, to avoid limiting its use to the design of speculative art installations.

Disclosure of Interests. The authors have no competing interests to declare that are relevant to the content of this article.

References

Norman, D.A.: Emotional Design: Why We Love (or Hate) Everyday Things. Basic Books (2004)
Giddens, A.: Modernity and Self-Identity: Self and Society in the Late Modern Age. Polity Press (1991)
Bell, C., Kreinath, J.: Ritual. The Wiley Blackwell Companion to the Study of Religion, pp. 382–399 (2021). https://doi.org/10.1002/9781119092797.ch27
Davis-Floyd, R., Laughlin, C.D.: Ritual: What It Is, How It Works, and Why. Berghahn Books (2022). https://doi.org/10.3167/9781800735286
Trillò, T., Hallinan, B., Shifman, L.: A typology of social media rituals. J. Comput. Med. Commun. **27**(4), Article zmac011 (2022). https://doi.org/10.1093/jcmc/zmac011
Turner, R.: Finding likeness: neural plasticity and ritual experience. In: Kapferer, B., Gold, M. (eds.) Egalitarian Dynamics: Liminality, and Victor Turner's Contribution to the Understanding of Socio-Historical Process, pp. 339–355. Berghahn Books (2024). https://doi.org/10.3167/9781805395881
Tonna, M., Marchesi, C., Parmigiani, S.: The biological origins of rituals: an interdisciplinary perspective. Neurosci. Biobehav. Rev. **98**, 95–106 (2019). https://doi.org/10.1016/j.neubiorev.2018.12.031
Kapitány, R., Kavanagh, C., Whitehouse, H.: Ritual morphospace revisited: the form, function and factor structure of ritual practice. Philos. Trans. R. Soc. B Biol. Sci. **375**(1805), Article no. 20190436 (2020). https://doi.org/10.1098/rstb.2019.0436

Whitehouse, H.: Rethinking ritual: how rituals made our world and how they could save it. J. Roy. Anthropol. Inst. **30**(1), 115–132 (2024). https://doi.org/10.1111/1467-9655.14048

Legare, C.H., Nielsen, M.: Ritual explained: interdisciplinary answers to Tinbergen's four questions. Philos. Trans. R. Soc. B Biol. Sci. **375**(1805), Article no. 20190419 (2020). https://doi.org/10.1098/rstb.2019.0419

Vaidya, G., Kalita, P.C.: Understanding emotions and their role in the design of products: an integrative review. Arch. Des. Res. **34**(3), 5–21 (2021). https://doi.org/10.15187/adr.2021.08.34.3.5

Bennett, D., et al.: Emergent interaction: complexity, dynamics, and enaction in HCI. In: Extended Abstracts of the 2021 CHI Conference on Human Factors in Computing Systems, pp. 1–7. Association for Computing Machinery (2021). https://doi.org/10.1145/3411763.3441321

Hornbæk, K., Oulasvirta, A.: What is interaction? In: Proceedings of the 2017 CHI Conference on Human Factors in Computing Systems, pp. 5040–5052. Association for Computing Machinery (2017). https://doi.org/10.1145/3025453.3025765

Markum, R.B., Wolf, S., Hoefer, M., Maas, F.: Designing tangible interactive artifacts for religious and spiritual purposes. In: Proceedings of the 2023 Designing Interactive Systems Conference (DIS 2023 Companion Publication), pp. XYZ–ABC. Association for Computing Machinery (2023). https://doi.org/10.1145/3563703.3591463

Zhou, N., Devleminck, S., Geurts, L.: Tangible affect: a literature review of tangible interactive systems addressing human core affect, emotions and moods. In: Proceedings of the 2024 Designing Interactive Systems Conference, pp. 424–440 (2024). https://doi.org/10.1145/3643834.3661608

Hornecker, E., Buur, J.: Getting a grip on tangible interaction: a framework on physical space and social interaction. In: Grinter, R., Rodden, T., Aoki, P., Cutrell, E., Jeffries, R., Olson, G. (eds.) Proceedings of the SIGCHI Conference on Human Factors in Computing Systems, pp. 437–446. Association for Computing Machinery (2006). https://doi.org/10.1145/1124772.1124838

Cornelio, P., et al.: The sense of agency in emerging technologies for human–computer integration: a review. Front. Neurosci. **16**, Article no. 949138 (2022). https://doi.org/10.3389/fnins.2022.949138

Mueller, F.F., et al.: Next steps for human-computer integration. In: Proceedings of the 2020 CHI Conference on Human Factors in Computing Systems, pp. 1–15. Association for Computing Machinery (2020). https://doi.org/10.1145/3313831.3376242

Wadhwa, M., Shrivastava, U.: Ubiquitous computing: a comprehensive review. In: Shaw, R.N., Siano, P., Makhilef, S., Ghosh, A., Shimi, S.L. (eds.) ICEEE 2023. LNEE, vol. 1115, pp. 591–600. Springer, Singapore (2024). https://doi.org/10.1007/978-981-99-8661-3_42

van Gennip, D., Orth, D., Imtiaz, M.A., van den Hoven, E., Plimmer, B.: Tangible cognition: bringing together tangible interaction and cognition in HCI. In: Proceedings of the 28th Australian Conference on Computer–Human Interaction (OzCHI 2016), pp. 662–665. Association for Computing Machinery (2016). https://doi.org/10.1145/3010915.3011863

Duarte, E.F., Méndez Mendoza, Y.L., Nobre de Queiroz, M.J., Baranauskas, M.C.C.: Embodiment in interactive installations: results from a systematic literature review. In: Proceedings of the 21st Brazilian Symposium on Human Factors in Computing Systems (IHC 2022), Article no. 14, pp. 1–13. Association for Computing Machinery (2022). https://doi.org/10.1145/3554364.3559118)

Liao, L., Liang, Y., Hong, L.E., Ye, Y., Wu, G.: A systematic review of global research on natural user interface for smart home system. Int. J. Ind. Ergon. **95**, Article no. 103445 (2023). https://doi.org/10.1016/j.ergon.2023.103445

Guribye, F., Gjøsæter, T., Bjartli, C.: Designing for tangible affective interaction. In: Proceedings of the 9th Nordic Conference on Human-Computer Interaction (NordiCHI 2016), pp. 17:1–17:10. Association for Computing Machinery (2016). https://doi.org/10.1145/2971485.2971547

Hanson, P.P.: Computation and CognitionZenon W. Pylyshyn Cambridge, MA: Bradford Books, MIT Press, 1984. Pp. xxiii, 292. Dialogue **25**(4), 811–814 (1986). https://doi.org/10.1017/S0012217300049854

Thompson, E.: Mind in Life: Biology, Phenomenology, and the Sciences of Mind. Harvard University Press (2010)

Marks, D.F.: The action cycle theory of perception and mental imagery. Vision **7**(1), 12 (2023). https://doi.org/10.3390/vision7010012

Cea, I.: The somatic roots of affect: toward a body-centered education. In: Fossa, P., Cortés-Rivera, C. (eds.) Affectivity and Learning, pp. 555–583. Springer, Cham (2023). https://doi.org/10.1007/978-3-031-31709-5_29

Damasio, A.: Feeling & knowing: making minds conscious. Cogn. Neurosci. **12**(2), 65–66 (2020). https://doi.org/10.1080/17588928.2020.1846027

Wilson, M.: Six views of embodied cognition. Psychon. Bull. Rev. **9**, 625–636 (2002). https://doi.org/10.3758/BF03196322

Birch, J., Ginsburg, S., Jablonka, E.: Unlimited associative learning and the origins of consciousness: a primer and some predictions. Biol. Philos. **35**, 56 (2020). https://doi.org/10.1007/s10539-020-09772-0

Norman, D.A.: Cognitive engineering. In: Norman, D.A., Draper, S.W. (eds.) User Centered System Design: New Perspectives on Human-Computer Interaction, pp. 31–61. Lawrence Erlbaum Associates (1986)

Ali, K.: A review of emotions, behavior and cognition. J. Biomed. Sustain. Healthc. Appl. **3**(2), 165–176 (2023). https://doi.org/10.53759/0088/JBSHA202303016

Turner, V.: The Ritual Process: Structure and Anti-Structure. Aldine Publishing Company (1969)

Krout, M.H.: The social and psychological significance of gestures: a differential analysis. Pedagog. Semin. J. Genet. Psychol. **47**(2), 385–412 (1935). https://doi.org/10.1080/08856559.1935.10533779

Aggarwal, P., McGill, A.L.: Is that car smiling at me? Schema congruity as a basis for evaluating anthropomorphized products. J. Consum. Res. **34**(4), 468–479 (2007). https://doi.org/10.1086/518544

Höök, K.: Designing with the Body: Somaesthetic Interaction Design. MIT Press, Cambridge (2018)

Parkinson, C., Walker, T.T., Memmi, S., Wheatley, T.: Emotions are understood from biological motion across remote cultures. Emotion **17**(3), 459–477 (2016). https://doi.org/10.1037/emo0000250

Guthrie, S.E.: Anthropomorphism. In: Runehov, A., Oviedo, L. (eds.) Encyclopedia of Sciences and Religions. Springer, Cham (2012). https://doi.org/10.1007/978-1-4020-8265-8. 100218

Aboudan, R., Beattie, G.: Cross-cultural similarities in gestures: the deep relationship between gestures and speech which transcends language barriers. Semiotica **111**(3/4), 269–294 (1996)

de Pina Cabral, J.: The threshold diffused: margins, hegemonies and contradictions in contemporary anthropology. Afr. Stud. **56**(2), 31–51 (1997). https://doi.org/10.1080/00020189708707867

Clark, A.: Being There: Putting Brain, Body, and World Together Again. MIT Press, Cambridge (1998)

Sliwinski, J., Katsikitis, M., Jones, C.M.: A review of interactive technologies as support tools for the cultivation of mindfulness. Mindfulness **8**(6), 1375–1390 (2017). https://doi.org/10.1007/s12671-017-0712-3

Plocher, T., Rau, P.-L.P., Choong, Y.-Y., Guo, Z.: Cross-cultural design. In: Salvendy, G. (ed.) Handbook of Human Factors and Ergonomics, 5th edn., pp. 252–279. Wiley (2021). https://doi.org/10.1002/9781119636113.ch10

Levitt-Frank, M., Shoshana, A.: Subjectivity and individual psychology. J. Individ. Psychol. **79**(3), 275–290 (2023). https://doi.org/10.1353/jip.2023.a909959

Ahmadpour, N., et al.: Affective interaction and affective computing – past, present and future. In: Extended Abstracts of CHI Conference on Human Factors in Computing Systems (CHI EA 2025). ACM (2025). https://doi.org/10.1145/3706599.3706743

Picard, R.W.: Affective Computing. MIT Press, Cambridge (1997)

Sekhavat, Y.A., Sisi, M.J., Roohi, S.: Affective interaction: using emotions as a user interface in games. Multimed. Tools Appl. **80**(4), 5225–5253 (2020). https://doi.org/10.1007/s11042-020-10006-4

Lang, M., Kundt, R.: The evolution of human ritual behavior as a cooperative signaling platform. Relig. Brain Behav. **14**(4), 377–399 (2023). https://doi.org/10.1080/2153599X.2023.2197977

Rumelhart, D.E.: Parallel Distributed Processing. 1: Foundations (12th ed.). MIT Press (1999)

Freeman, R.B.: The Senses considered as perceptual systems. James J. Gibson. Q. Rev. Bio. **44**(1), 104–105 (1969). https://doi.org/10.1086/406033

Mangalam, M., Hajnal, A., Kelty-Stephen, D.G. (eds.): The modern legacy of Gibson's affordances for the sciences of organisms. Taylor & Francis (2024)

Ramstead, M.J.D., Veissière, S.P.L., Kirmayer, L.J.: Cultural affordances: Scaffolding local worlds through shared intentionality and regimes of attention. Front. Psychol. **7**, Article 1090 (2016). https://doi.org/10.3389/fpsyg.2016.01090

Robbins, P., Aydede, M.: A short primer on situated cognition. In: Robbins, P., Aydede, M. (eds.) The Cambridge Handbook of Situated Cognition, pp. 3–10. Cambridge University Press (2001). https://doi.org/10.1017/CBO9780511816826.001

Varela, F.J., Thompson, E., Rosch, E.: The Embodied Mind: Cognitive Science and Human Experience. MIT Press (1991)

Bunge, M.A.: Causality and modern science. Dover Publications, New York (1979)

Wigdor, D., Wixon, D.: Brave NUI World: Designing Natural User Interfaces for Touch and Gesture. Elsevier (2011)

Frost, J.: Ritualizing nonreligion: Cultivating rational rituals in secular spaces. Soc. Forces **101**(4), 2013–2033 (2022). https://doi.org/10.1093/sf/soac042

Lang, M., Krátký, J., Xygalatas, D.: The role of ritual behaviour in anxiety reduction: An investigation of Marathi religious practices in Mauritius. Philos. Trans. Royal Soc. B: Bio. Sci. **375**(1805), Article 20190431 (2020). https://doi.org/10.1098/rstb.2019.0431

Van Gennep, A.: The rites of passage. Phoenix Book, University of Chicago Press (1960)

Reynolds, C., Erikson, E.: Agency, identity, and the emergence of ritual experience. Socius Soc. Res. Dyn. World **3**, 1–14 (2017). https://doi.org/10.1177/2378023117710881

Kossowska, M., Klodkowski, P., Siewierska-Chmaj, A., Guinote, A., Kessels, U., Moyano, M.: Internet-based micro-identities as a driver of societal disintegration. Humanit. Soc. Sci. Commun. **10**, Article 955 (2023). https://doi.org/10.1057/s41599-023-02441-z

Santaolalla-Rueda, P., Fernández-Muñoz, C.: Potaxies and Fifes: The formation of new subcultures on TikTok. Societies **14**(12), Article 265 (2024). https://doi.org/10.3390/soc14120265

Mnemonic Design with GenAI for Digital Security Management

Tojin T. Eapen[1], J. Scott Christianson[2(✉)], Kai Wang[3], Petra Kugler[4], and Josh Folk[1,2,3,4]

[1] Center for Creative Foresight, Vancouver, USA
tteapen@cforesight.org
[2] Trulaske College of Business, University of Missouri, Columbia, MO, USA
christiansonjs@umsystem.edu
[3] AI Ager, New York, USA
[4] OST Eastern Switzerland University of Applied Sciences, St. Gallen, Switzerland

Abstract. This paper introduces a novel and systematic approach to enhance the memorization and recall of complex numeric codes by leveraging generative AI to produce blended visual mnemonics. The technique encodes numbers as memorable composite images, blending occupations, organisms, and objects to represent numeric values. This approach helps balance code complexity and memorability, making numeric codes both easier to use and more secure. Visual mnemonics using our approach have broad applicability, benefiting children, older adults, users with memory impairments, and users under high-pressure conditions who must recall crucial numeric codes, such as passwords, PINs, or private cryptographic keys.

Keywords: Mnemonic design · Generative AI · Conceptual blending · Picture mnemonics · Numeric codes · Security · Usability

1 Introduction

The capacity to accurately recall numeric information is increasingly central to both everyday security practices and critical, high-stakes scenarios in modern digital life. Whether memorizing a smartphone passcode, recalling an emergency contact number, or executing a complex security protocol under pressure, users must navigate the tension between memorability and security. The longer and more complex the code, the more secure it is, but it is also more challenging to recall and store [1]. Moreover, certain user groups, such as children and older adults, may have difficulty memorizing emergency numbers and PINs that are typically easy for average users to recall [5]. The resulting trade-off commonly leads users to adopt simpler but less secure codes, inadvertently increasing vulnerability. Moreover, the repercussions of not recalling numeric credentials can

J. Folk—Independent Consultant.

C. Stephanidis et al. (Eds.): HCII 2025, CCIS 2773, pp. 21–32, 2026.
https://doi.org/10.1007/978-3-032-12773-0_3

be substantial, ranging from the inconvenience of resetting a device to the irrevocable loss of digital assets, as seen in the case of significant financial losses associated with lost cryptocurrency private keys [17,22,23]. Similarly, the loss of an iPhone passcode can mean that the user is locked out and needs to reset the phone, which can lead to the loss of valuable data [2].

2 Background

Prior research into mnemonic strategies has established that techniques such as phonetic encoding, chunking, and visual association can improve numeric recall [3,7,8,14]. Numerical mnemonics have been used in the past to aid in the recall of passcodes [9]. However, conventional mnemonic techniques, such as the Phonetic Method, often require extensive training and may not be suitable for all user groups, particularly individuals with cognitive impairments, children, or older adults [4,12,13]. An alternative approach is the use of visual mnemonics, which leverage imagery to enhance recall. Although visual mnemonics have demonstrated promise in previous studies [15,16], current methods have yet to fully capitalize on emerging AI technologies that could streamline and improve the generation of effective mnemonic aids.

Recent advances in artificial intelligence, particularly in generative models, enable the automated synthesis of evocative and memorable imagery using image generators such as OpenAI's DALL-E [18]. Conceptual blending, a cognitive strategy that merges disparate concepts, can be combined with generative AI tools to produce novel, highly distinctive images that represent numeric sequences [11]. By mapping numbers to composite visuals incorporating familiar cities, organisms, and objects, users gain memorable mental anchors. For example, a short numeric code such as a PIN might translate into a hybrid image of a "bee-camera," while a more complex numeric sequence could integrate a cityscape with multiple distinct image elements to create a richer mental cue.

This paper introduces a generative AI-driven system that produces picture mnemonics by transforming numeric codes into intuitively memorable visual imagery. This approach aims to preserve or enhance the security of numeric codes without placing undue cognitive burdens on users. By offering accessible, user-centric mnemonic solutions, this work addresses a critical gap in digital security research in the domain of visual mnemonics. Potential applications range from helping children memorize emergency contact numbers to facilitating users with cognitive impairments in recalling PIN codes. Visual mnemonics can also help users and professionals in securing high-value digital assets in an evolving threat landscape.

3 Encoding Scheme

Effective memorization of numeric codes is crucial for secure access systems, particularly for users with memory-related challenges. This section presents a systematic approach for encoding numeric values into visually distinctive and memorable mnemonics, utilizing the principles of bisociation and trisociation, which involve blending two or three concepts to create an integrated visual concept [11]. The methodology involves mapping numeric values to a predefined set of objects, organisms, and occupations to generate blended image mnemonics. By associating abstract numeric data with vivid and tangible visual cues, this technique enhances memorization while ensuring usability and accessibility.

In our system, numbers from 0 to 255 are mapped to specific organisms, objects, and occupations. This mapping allows numbers expressed in base-256 to be represented as images that conceptually blend elements from these various categories. The lookup table in Table 1 shows representative mappings.

The encoding process involves mapping numeric values to corresponding visual elements using a predefined lookup table. Numbers in base-256 format are associated with an occupation, an organism, and an object to create bisociated (two-element) or trisociated (three-element) images [11]. These images provide a unique and memorable representation of the numeric codes. More complex images can be generated by intersecting four, five, or six categories.

The proposed encoding methodology transforms numeric values into easily memorable visual mnemonics by mapping base-256 representations of numbers onto predetermined categories: cities, organisms, and objects, derived from a lookup table. To encode a given numeric code N as a trisociated image, it is first converted from its original format (e.g., decimal) into a base-256 sequence $[a, b, c, \dots]$, where each element corresponds to a byte. Using the lookup table T, each byte is then associated with a specific object $T_{\text{object}}[i]$, an organism $T_{\text{organism}}[i]$, and an occupation $T_{\text{occupation}}[i]$.

For shorter codes consisting of two bytes, a bisociated mnemonic is generated by combining the components of the organism and the object in a phrase such as "object-like-organism." For codes involving three bytes or more, the approach is extended to a trisociated mnemonic by including the occupation category. This can be used to produce trisociated sets such as *(occupation, organism, object)*. Finally, these selected concept components are combined to form a mnemonic, which can be presented simply as text for verbal recall or used to generate a visual mnemonic to aid memory. Picture mnemonics can be created using AI image generators by utilizing prompts such as *"draw an image of a fork that looks like a lemon."*

Thus, using the above table, a four-digit PIN such as `1427` converts to base-256 $(5, 147)$, mapping to the set *(organism:aloe, object:guitar)*. Similarly, the number `12216814` is equivalent to $(186, 105, 238)$ and maps to *(occupation:postman, organism:gazelle, object:toy)*.

Table 1. Lookup table used to generate picture mnemonics

N	Object	Organism	Occupation	N	Object	Organism	Occupation
0	Abacus	Aardvark	Accountant	128	Easel	Jellyfish	King
1	Accordion	Acorn	Actor	129	Envelope	Jujube	Knight
2	Adapter	Albatross	Actress	130	Eraser	Juniper	Knitter
3	Adhesive	Alligator	Administrator	131	Fan	Kale	Laborer
4	Airplane	Almond	Advocate	132	Faucet	Kangaroo	Landlord
5	Alarm	Aloe	Aesthetist	133	Feather	Kingfisher	Lawyer
6	Amplifier	Alpaca	Agronomist	134	Fence	Kiwi	Lecturer
7	Amulet	Anemone	Airman	135	Fireplace	Kiwifruit	Librarian
8	Anchor	Anise	Analyst	136	Flashlight	Koala	Lifeguard
9	Antenna	Ant	Animator	137	Flask	Ladybug	Linguist
10	Apron	Antelope	Announcer	138	Flute	Lavender	Locksmith
11	Aquarium	Apple	Anthropologist	139	Fork	Leek	Machinist
12	Arch	Apricot	Appraiser	140	Funnel	Lemon	Magician
13	Arrow	Armadillo	Architect	141	Gear	Lemur	Manager
14	Ashtray	Asparagus	Archivist	142	Globe	Lice	Manufacturer
15	Atlas	Avocado	Artist	143	Glove	Lion	Marketer
16	Awning	Axolotl	Astronomer	144	Goggles	Lizard	Mathematician
17	Axe	Badger	Athlete	145	Gondola	Llama	Mechanic
18	Baby	Bamboo	Attendant	146	Grill	Lobster	Mediator
19	Backpack	Banana	Auditor	147	Guitar	Longan	Merchant
20	Bag	Baobab	Author	148	Hairbrush	Lotus	Meteorologist
21	Ball	Barley	Aviator	149	Handbag	Lychee	Microbiologist
22	Balloon	Barracuda	Baker	150	Handcuffs	Macadamia	Miner
23	Banjo	Basil	Banker	151	Hanger	Macaw	Minister
24	Barbell	Bat	Barber	152	Harmonica	Mackerel	Model
25	Barcode	Beans	Barrister	153	Hat	Mahogany	Musician
26	Barometer	Bear	Biochemist	154	Helmet	Mango	Musicologist
27	Basket	Beaver	Biologist	155	Hook	Mangosteen	Naturalist
28	Bat	Bee	Botanist	156	Hose	Mantis	Navigator
29	Bathtub	Beetle	Brewer	157	House	Marigold	Negotiator
30	Battery	Beetroot	Broker	158	Hovercraft	Marlin	Networker
31	Beach	Bison	Builder	159	Igloo	Meerkat	Neurologist
32	Bed	Blackberries	Butcher	160	Iron	Mole	Notary
33	Beehive	Bluebell	Buyer	161	Jacket	Mongoose	Novelist
34	Bell	Blueberry	Captain	162	Javelin	Monkey	Nurse
35	Belt	Bluejay	Carpenter	163	Jigsaw	Mouse	Nutritionist

(*continued*)

Table 1. (*continued*)

N	Object	Organism	Occupation	N	Object	Organism	Occupation
36	Bench	Broccoli	Cartographer	164	Jug	Mulberry	Observer
37	Bicycle	Bumblebee	Caterer	165	Kaleidoscope	Mushroom	Obstetrician
38	Billboard	Butterfly	Cellist	166	Key	Nightingale	Optician
39	Binder	Butternut	Chauffeur	167	Keyboard	Nutmeg	Optometrist
40	Binoculars	Cabbage	Chemist	168	Kite	Ocelot	Organizer
41	Blackboard	Cactus	Chiropractor	169	Knife	Octopus	Orthodontist
42	Blanket	Camel	Clerk	170	Ladder	Okra	Painter
43	Blender	Capybara	Coach	171	Lamp	Olive	Paralegal
44	Blimp	Cardamom	Cobbler	172	Lantern	Onion	Paramedic
45	Blinds	Carrot	Collector	173	Leash	Orange	Pathologist
46	Blueprint	Cashew	Comedian	174	Lighter	Orchid	Pharmacist
47	Book	Cassava	Composer	175	Lock	Ostrich	Philosopher
48	Bookcase	Cat	Conductor	176	Lunchbox	Otter	Photographer
49	Boomerang	Caterpillar	Confectioner	177	Magazine	Owl	Physicist
50	Bottle	Cauliflower	Consultant	178	Mailbox	Panda	Physiotherapist
51	Bow	Celery	Contractor	179	Map	Pangolin	Pilot
52	Box	Centipede	Cook	180	Marker	Panther	Planner
53	Bracelet	Chameleon	Copywriter	181	Matchbox	Papaya	Plumber
54	Brick	Cherry	Counselor	182	Microphone	Parrot	Poet
55	Briefcase	Chestnut	Critic	183	Microscope	Parsley	Policeman
56	Brooch	Chia	Cryptographer	184	Mirror	Passionfruit	Politician
57	Broom	Chickpea	Curator	185	Monitor	Peach	Porter
58	Bubble	Cicada	Dancer	186	Monocle	Peacock	Postman
59	Bucket	Cinnamon	Decorator	187	Mug	Peanut	Potter
60	Bugle	Clam	Designer	188	Napkin	Pear	Programmer
61	Building	Clove	Detective	189	Nebula	Peas	Psychiatrist
62	Bulb	Cockatoo	Dietitian	190	Necklace	Pecan	Psychologist
63	Bulletin	Cockroach	Diplomat	191	Net	Pelican	Publicist
64	Bumper	Coconut	Director	192	Newspaper	Penguin	Publisher
65	Bunk	Coffee	Diver	193	Notepad	Pepper	Queen
66	Burglar	Coral	Doctor	194	Nutcracker	Persimmon	Quilter
67	Burner	Coriander	Driver	195	Oboe	Pig	Radiographer
68	Bus	Corn	Editor	196	Oil	Pigeon	Radiologist
69	Butter	Cotton	Educator	197	Palette	Pineapple	Rancher

(*continued*)

Table 1. (*continued*)

N	Object	Organism	Occupation	N	Object	Organism	Occupation
70	Button	Cow	Electrician	198	Pan	Piranha	Ranger
71	Buzzer	Crab	Embalmer	199	Pants	Pistachio	Realtor
72	Cake	Cranberry	Engineer	200	Paper	Pitaya	Registrar
73	Calendar	Crane	Entertainer	201	Parachute	Platypus	Researcher
74	Camera	Crocodile	Entrepreneur	202	Passport	Plum	Restaurateur
75	Can	Crow	Epidemiologist	203	Peeler	Pomegranate	Reviewer
76	Candle	Cucumber	Ergonomist	204	Pencil	Pomelo	Sailor
77	Car	Currant	Evangelist	205	Periscope	Porcupine	Salesman
78	Cardboard	Cypress	Examiner	206	Phone	Potato	Scientist
79	Cargo	Daffodil	Executive	207	Pillow	Pumpkin	Sculptor
80	Carpet	Dandelion	Fabricator	208	Pin	Quail	Seamstress
81	Carriage	Date	Farmer	209	Plank	Rabbit	Secretary
82	Cart	Deer	Fashionista	210	Plate	Raccoon	Singer
83	Castle	Dingo	Filmmaker	211	Puzzle	Radish	Socialite
84	Catapult	Dog	Financier	212	Quilt	Rambutan	Sociologist
85	Cauldron	Dolphin	Fisherman	213	Quiver	Raspberry	Soldier
86	Ceiling	Dragonfly	Florist	214	Ring	Rhino	Statistician
87	Cement	Duck	Forecaster	215	Road	Rhubarb	Stockbroker
88	Chainsaw	Durian	Foreman	216	Rope	Rooster	Strategist
89	Chair	Eagle	Founder	217	Roulette	Rose	Surgeon
90	Chalk	Earthworm	Freelancer	218	Scissors	Saffron	Surveyor
91	Chalkboard	Eel	Gardener	219	Shell	Salamander	Tailor
92	Charger	Eggplant	Gemologist	220	Shirt	Sapodilla	Taxidermist
93	Chimney	Elderberry	Geneticist	221	Shoe	Seahorse	Teacher
94	Clip	Elephant	Geographer	222	Slide	Seal	Technician
95	Clipboard	Elm	Geologist	223	Soap	Shark	Technologist
96	Clock	Fennel	Glazier	224	Socks	Sheep	Therapist
97	Cloud	Fig	Goldsmith	225	Speaker	Shoebill	Tiler
98	Coaster	Finch	Governor	226	Spoon	Skunk	Trader
99	Coat	Fir	Groundskeeper	227	Star	Sloth	Trainer
100	Coffee	Firefly	Guide	228	Stone	Snail	Translator
101	Comb	Fish	Gunman	229	Straw	Snake	Treasurer
102	Compass	Flamingo	Hairdresser	230	Sundial	Spider	Trucker
103	Computer	Fox	Historian	231	Syringe	Spinach	Tutor
104	Cork	Frog	Homemaker	232	Table	Squash	Typist

(*continued*)

Table 1. (*continued*)

N	Object	Organism	Occupation	N	Object	Organism	Occupation
105	Cradle	Gazelle	Horticulturist	233	Tablet	Squirrel	Umpire
106	Crayon	Ginger	Host	234	Telescope	Starfish	Undertaker
107	Crowbar	Giraffe	Hostess	235	Tissue	Stingray	Underwriter
108	Cup	Goldfish	Hotelier	236	Toothbrush	Strawberry	Urbanist
109	Cupcake	Goose	Hunter	237	Towel	Sunflower	Usher
110	Curtain	Gooseberry	Illustrator	238	Toy	Sweetsop	Valet
111	Dart	Gorilla	Immunologist	239	Train	Tamarind	Veterinarian
112	Deck	Gourd	Industrialist	240	Trombone	Tiger	Violinist
113	Desk	Grape	Innkeeper	241	Trumpet	Tomato	Vocalist
114	Detergent	Guava	Inspector	242	Ukulele	Toucan	Volunteer
115	Diaper	Hawk	Instructor	243	Umbrella	Tulip	Voyager
116	Digital	Hazelnut	Intern	244	Unicycle	Turtle	Waiter
117	Diploma	Heron	Interpreter	245	Vase	Vanilla	Warden
118	Dirigible	Hibiscus	Inventor	246	Violin	Vulture	Washer
119	Dish	Hippo	Investor	247	Volcano	Walnut	Weaver
120	Doll	Hornet	Janitor	248	Vortex	Walrus	Welder
121	Donut	Horse	Jeweler	249	Waffle	Watermelon	Winemaker
122	Door	Housefly	Jockey	250	Whistle	Whale	Writer
123	Doormat	Hummingbird	Journalist	251	Windmill	Wheat	Yachtsman
124	Drawer	Hyacinth	Judge	252	Window	Woodpecker	Yardman
125	Drawing	Iguana	Juggler	253	Wrench	Yam	Yeoman
126	Drill	Jackfruit	Juror	254	Yacht	Zebra	Yodeler
127	Drum	Jasmine	Keeper	255	Yoyo	Zucchini	Zoologist

4 Illustrative Cases

4.1 Device Passcodes

Research suggests that blending concepts into vivid mental images enhances memorability, often more so than recalling numeric codes alone, due to their distinctive and "bizarre" nature [10].

Consider encoding a four-digit numeric code, such as an ATM PIN or the last four digits of a Social Security Number. To illustrate, take the number `1427`. In binary coding, it is represented as `10110010011`, and in base-256 as (5, 147). To create a bisociated image, we use a lookup table to map base-256 representations onto an organism-object encoding scheme.

For the code (5, 147), 5 maps to "aloe" (organism) and 147 maps to "guitar" (object). Thus, the resulting mnemonic is encoded as *(guitar, aloe)*. The mnemonic image can be generated using an AI image generator with a prompt such as "aloe inspired guitar" to create a mnemonic similar to the one in Fig. 1.

Fig. 1. Illustration of a bisociated mnemonic *(aloe, guitar)* and a trisociated mnemonic *(postman, gazelle, toy)* generated using Google Gemini's image generator.

A single image can encode larger numbers through *trisociation*, a technique that blends three distinct concepts into one cohesive visual [11,20]. For example, consider the seven-digit code `12216814`, which converts to the base-256 sequence [186, 105, 238]. Using our predefined lookup table, these values correspond to the concepts *postman*, *gazelle*, and *toy*. These can then be integrated into a visual mnemonic using a prompt such as: *"generate an image of a postman with a gazelle-inspired toy"* A sample image generated by employing this prompt is presented in Fig. 1.

However, there is a notable trade-off between bisociated and trisociated images. While trisociation enables the encoding of more extensive information within a single image by combining three concepts, such images may be more difficult for users to recall compared to bisociated images, which blend only two concepts and are often simpler and more intuitive.

4.2 Social Security Numbers

Social Security Numbers (SSNs) are vital numeric identifiers but are often challenging to memorize due to their complexity. Using our method, one can encode SSNs as vivid, blended visual mnemonics with the help of the lookup table. For example, consider an SSN such as `123-45-6789`, which is equivalent to [(7, 91), (125, 21)] in base-256. This could be translated into a set of two bisociated mnemonics such as *[(anemone, chalkboard), (iguana, ball)]*, which can be converted into a visual mnemonic, as shown in Fig. 3. For some authentication applications, users are generally required to recall the last four digits of their SSN. In such cases, only a single bisociated image is required to support the recall of the code (Fig. 2).

Fig. 2. Illustration of a picture mnemonic that encodes the SSN `123-45-6789`.

4.3 Emergency Numbers

Various forms of identification numbers, such as national identification numbers and telephone numbers, can be critical to remember in specific circumstances. For instance, the telephone number `+1 202-501-4444` corresponds to the U.S. Department of State's Overseas Citizens Services (OCS) hotline, which assists American citizens traveling or residing abroad who require emergency support.

Consider the numerical identifier `1202501444` that represents the OCS hotline number. In base-256 representation, this number can be expressed as [2, 204, 191, 40, 172] or, equivalently, [(0, 2), (204, 191), (40, 172)]. Using the predefined lookup table, this representation can be further mapped into its corresponding bisociated form, yielding the sequence *[(aardvark, adapter), (pomelo, net), (cabbage, lantern)]* which can be converted to a visual mnemonic as shown in Fig. 3.

4.4 Digital-Currency Keys

The challenge of securely recalling complex numeric codes becomes particularly salient in the context of cryptocurrency, where the security of private keys is paramount. Private keys are typically stored on computers or printed, both of which present security risks. System-generated keys used for digital asset

Fig. 3. Picture mnemonic that encodes the OCS hotline number.

wallets—often consisting of lengthy, random alphanumeric strings—pose significant memorization challenges. Storing these keys in written form or on a computer system not only increases vulnerability to security breaches but also risks permanent loss [17,22,23]. The loss of a Bitcoin private key implies that the associated funds become impossible to withdraw.

Individuals have reportedly lost access to millions of dollars in Bitcoin due to forgotten passwords or misplaced private keys. In 2021, the Canadian Broadcasting Corporation (CBC) reported that Stefan Thomas, a Bitcoin millionaire, was unable to access $321 million in bitcoins because he forgot the password to his encrypted wallet [6]. Similarly, in 2011, Gabriel Abed, founder of Abed Group and co-founder of Bitt, lost around 800 Bitcoins when a colleague accidentally reformatted the laptop containing the wallet's private keys [21].

Current industry standards, such as the *Bitcoin Improvement Proposal 39 (BIP39)*, already acknowledge the need for more human-centric approaches [19]. BIP39 converts long binary strings into sequences of standardized words, making them easier to record and recall. However, many of these words remain abstract, and not all users find them intuitively memorable. By contrast, the proposed generative image mnemonic system builds on these principles and potentially exceeds their efficacy by integrating strong visual and conceptual cues.

The concept of using picture mnemonics with conceptual blending to memorize numeric codes can significantly enhance the usability and security of digital wallets and cryptocurrencies. The given 12-word mnemonic directly corresponds to a specific base-2048 number (and thus a specific 132-bit binary string), ensuring a standardized and interoperable way to convert human-readable seed phrases into the underlying entropy and vice versa.

Consider the following 12-word mnemonic: *(music, rural, under, antique, story, diamond, kit, arrow, main, potato, loan, service)*. Using the BIP39 mapping, this sequence is represented in base-2048 as [1167, 1516, 1894, 0079, 1716, 0489, 0983, 0101, 1074, 1350, 1048, 1569], which can then be converted into the base-256 code [9, 31, 123, 59, 24, 79, 214, 177, 233, 122, 225, 150, 25, 84, 104, 99, 1]. This base-256 sequence may be further chunked into nine pairs: [(9, 31), (123, 59), (24, 79), (214, 177), (233, 122), (225, 150), (25, 84), (104, 99), (1)].

Fig. 4. Picture mnemonic for a 132-bit private key using bisociated images.

These pairs can then be used to generate nine bisociated mnemonic images by mapping them onto the object-organism codes, as shown in Fig. 4.

5 Implementation Guidelines

To implement this system effectively, designers should use culturally familiar and visually distinct objects, organisms, and cities to build a robust lookup table that supports clear and memorable mnemonics. Care must also be taken to protect mnemonic images and their mappings from unauthorized access.

Future research should evaluate recall performance across user groups and scenarios, making this approach a scalable, inclusive, and secure method for managing digital numeric codes. Controlled user studies are needed to evaluate the mnemonic effectiveness across demographic groups and use cases. Variables such as recall accuracy, time to recall, and subjective memorability should be measured. Longitudinal studies can assess durability over time, particularly in high-stress environments such as emergency response or financial recovery.

References

1. Adams, A., Sasse, M.A.: Users are not the enemy. Commun. ACM **42**(1), 40–46 (1999)
2. Apple Support Webpage. https://support.apple.com/en-au/guide/iphone/iph14a867ae/ios. Accessed 13 Oct 2024
3. Bellezza, F.S.: Mnemonic devices: classification, characteristics, and criteria. Rev. Educ. Res. **51**(2), 247–275 (1981)
4. Bellezza, F.S.: Mnemonic methods to enhance storage and retrieval. In: Memory, pp. 345–380. Academic Press (1996)
5. Brown, A.S., et al.: Generating and remembering passwords. Appl. Cogn. Psychol. **18**(6), 641–651 (2004)
6. CBC Radio: This man owns $321M in bitcoin—but he can't access it because he lost his password. In: As It Happens (2021)
7. Cowan, N.: The magical number four in short-term memory. Behav. Brain Sci. **24**(1), 87–114 (2001)
8. Dickel, M.J.: Principles of encoding mnemonics. Percept. Mot. Skills **51**(1), 111–118 (1983)
9. Diffie, W., Woods, W.A.: Method for generating mnemonic random passcodes. U.S. Patent 7,552,469 (2009)
10. Einstein, G.O., McDaniel, M.A., Lackey, S.: Bizarre imagery, interference, and distinctiveness. J. Exp. Psychol.: Learn. Mem. Cogn. **15**(1), 137–146 (1989)
11. Eapen, T.T., Finkenstadt, D.J., Folk, J., Venkataswamy, L.: How generative AI can augment human creativity: use it to promote divergent thinking. Harv. Bus. Rev. **101**(4), 56–64 (2023)
12. Fiorentini, V., Shao, M., Medero, J.: Generating memorable mnemonic encodings of numbers. arXiv:1705.02700 (2017)
13. Horky, E.A.: 1-800-I-AM-VAIN: should telephone mnemonics be protected as trademarks? J. Intell. Prop. L. **3**, 213–235 (1995)
14. Huh, J.H., et al.: On the memorability of system-generated PINs: can chunking help? In: SOUPS 2015, pp. 197–209 (2015)
15. Juang, K.A., Ranganayakulu, S., Greenstein, J.S.: Using system-generated mnemonics to improve password usability. In: HFES Annual Meeting, pp. 506–510 (2012)
16. Juang, K., Greenstein, J.: Integrating visual mnemonics with passphrases. Hum. Factors **60**(5), 658–668 (2018)
17. Lindqvist, G., et al.: How do Bitcoin users manage their private keys? In: STPIS 2021, pp. 11–21 (2021)
18. OpenAI, *DALL·E 2* [Text-to-image model]. https://openai.com/dall-e-2. Accessed 13 Oct 2024/10/13
19. Palatinus, M., et al.: BIP39: mnemonic code for generating deterministic keys (2013). https://github.com/bitcoin/bips/blob/master/bip-0039.mediawiki
20. Papanek, V.: Design for the Real World, 2nd. edn. Academy Chicago (1985)
21. Popper, N.: Lost passwords lock millionaires out of their bitcoin fortunes. In: The New York Times (2021). https://www.nytimes.com/2021/01/12/technology/bitcoin-passwords-wallets-fortunes.html
22. Vasek, M., et. al.: The bitcoin brain drain: examining brain wallets. In: Financial Cryptography 2016, pp. 609–618. Springer, Cham (2016)
23. Voas, J., Kshetri, N.: Lost and never found. Computer **54**(7), 12–13 (2021)

Intelligent Design and Innovative Inheritance of Baoxiang Floral Motif Through LoRA Technology

Yixiao Gong[1(✉)], Shiqi Tang[1], Yan Gan[1], and Haoran Xu[2]

[1] School of Mechanical Science and Engineering, Huazhong University of Science and Technology, Wuhan, Hubei, China
{m202370454,ganyan}@hust.edu.cn

[2] School of Civil and Hydraulic Engineering, Huazhong University of Science and Technology, Wuhan, Hubei, China

Abstract. As a classic of Chinese traditional decorative art blending Buddhist culture, has been extensively utilized across various domains, the Baoxiang floral motif faces challenges in intelligent generation, style modernization, and design efficiency in modern applications. This study uses deep learning algorithms and semantic annotation to decode its cultural genes, employs LoRA lightweight training technology for controllable feature generation, and establishes a "traditional inheritance-modern application" evaluation framework with digital tools (EMD, ResNet-50, LPIPS, YOLOv5, etc.) and manual scoring to validate its effectiveness. Design practice shows human-AI collaboration makes the motif align with modern aesthetics, enhances designer efficiency, and boosts traditional culture preservation. The research offers a viable approach for traditional motif modernization and introduces a new paradigm for intelligent human-computer collaborative design and cultural heritage computing, facilitating the innovative transmission of intangible cultural heritage.

Keywords: Baoxiang floral motif · Low-Rank Adaptation (LoRA) · Human-Computer Collaboration · Design Innovation · Cultural Heritage

1 Introduction

The Baoxiang floral motif, a classic of Chinese decorative art, blends Buddhist symbolism and indigenous aesthetics with distinctive forms and craftsmanship, carrying auspicious meanings across historical and modern designs. However, adapting it to modern contexts faces challenges: limited digitalization hinders resource accessibility; its intricate style clashes with minimalist trends, reducing versatility; and traditional manual design processes rely on static reinterpretation, limiting innovation and efficiency. These issues demand new solutions.

In an era of tech-culture integration, AIGC (Artificial Intelligence Generated Content) has emerged as a catalyst for reimagining cultural heritage. China's 2023 Digital China plan emphasizes "cultural digitization," providing strategic guidance for such

C. Stephanidis et al. (Eds.): HCII 2025, CCIS 2773, pp. 33–44, 2026.
https://doi.org/10.1007/978-3-032-12773-0_4

efforts. The Baoxiang motif's unique structure and symbolism make it an ideal case for AIGC exploration, offering significant value in AI-assisted generative design.

This study focuses on AIGC-driven innovative design of Baoxiang motifs, via human-AI collaboration to tackle cultural transformation challenges. It analyzes visual structure, integrates algorithms and annotation to boost AI decoding, and uses LoRA for controllable feature generation. A dual evaluation framework balances tradition and innovation, aiming to innovate designs, construct a technical framework, and establish a reusable AIGC paradigm for cultural heritage in the Digital China context.

2 Related Research

2.1 Baoxiang Floral Motif

Cultural Origins and Research Development of the Baoxiang Floral Motif. Rooted in Buddhist culture, the Baoxiang motif blends Eastern and Western art. Emerging in the Wei-Jin-Northern and Southern Dynasties, it evolved from a sacred symbol to a mainstream pattern in *Yingzao Fashi* [1, 2]. With radial symmetry of lotus, honeysuckle, beads, etc., it formed unique traits. As Buddhism secularized, its meaning shifted to auspiciousness, absorbing folk motifs in the Ming-Qing [3].

Under China's cultural confidence initiative, the Baoxiang motif's heritage and charm drive its widespread modern use, reflecting market demand and commercial value. Their wide application across architecture, fashion, brands, and entertainment reflects cultural confidence and commercial value (see Fig. 1) [4].

Fig. 1. Multifield Applications of Baoxiang floral motif in Contemporary Market

Artistic Structure Analysis of the Baoxiang Floral Motif. The Baoxiang floral motif has developed unique artistic features over a long historical evolution, specifically reflected in the following three aspects:

Element Integration: Centered on the Buddhist lotus, incorporating elements such as the Indian eight-petaled lotus, Greek honeysuckle motifs, Persian bead and pomegranate motifs [2], resulting in three main petal types: Side-Curled Petal, Hook-Shaped Petal and Cloud-Curved Petal (see Fig. 2).

Compositional Principles: Each motif exhibits circular radial symmetry with multilayered overlapping petals; combination motifs include single motif symmetry, two-way repeats, four directions consecutive and surrounded in eight directions (in Table 1), embodying the unity of geometric order and natural rhythm.

Color Application: Exemplified by Dunhuang cases, blue, green, and gold serve as the base tones, with contrasting warm and cool colors and gradient rendering techniques. Black, white, and gold outlines are used for harmony, creating a model of classical color aesthetics [3].

Fig. 2. Schematics of Side-Curled Petal (a), Hook-Shaped Petal (b), and Cloud-Curved Petal (c) in Baoxiang floral motif.

Table 1. Combinatorial arrangement methods of Baoxiang floral motif

Apply style	Motif
Single motif symmetry	
Two-way repeats	
Four directions consecutive	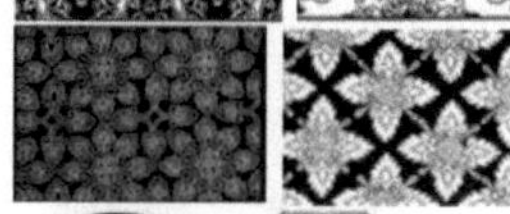
Surrounded in eight directions	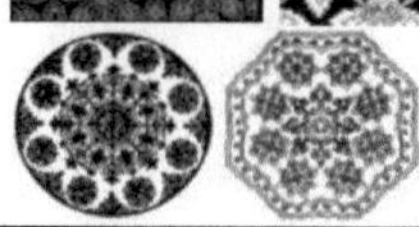

2.2 AIGC-Based Image Generation Technology

AIGC image generation technology has evolved through GANs and diffusion models. However, as most existing training data is sourced from Western contexts, generating Chinese traditional motifs often results in cultural discontinuity. Stable Diffusion, widely used since 2022, enables Baoxiang motif generation. LoRA fine-tuning overcomes scarce Chinese data, promoting cultural continuity [5–7].

Stable Diffusion, an efficient image generation technique based on latent diffusion models (LDM), features a diffusion-denoising process in latent space. Stable Diffusion uses VAE, U-Net, and CLIP to generate images via latent-space denoising. It enables efficient, multimodal, and lightweight fine-tuning, making it widely used in artistic creation (see Fig. 3) [8, 9].

LoRA fine-tunes pre-trained models by introducing low-rank matrices A and B to the original weight matrix W_0, updating only 0.1%–1% of parameters [10, 11]. It operates via an "original transformation + low-rank correction" approach: after input features are linearly transformed by W_0, the low-rank increment BA adjusts the generation of queries (Q), keys (K), and values (V), enabling targeted optimization of task-specific feature correlations through lightweight training of A and B [12]. This achieves efficient adaptation to new tasks with minimal data while preserving general generative ability (see Fig. 4).

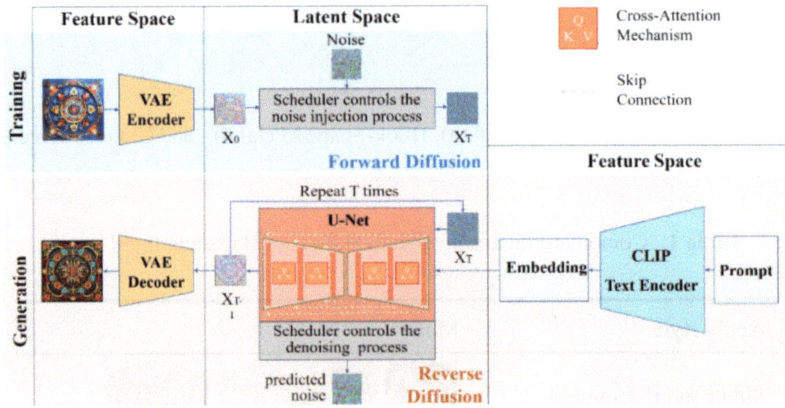

Fig. 3. Schematic Diagram of Stable Diffusion Model Training and Generation Workflow

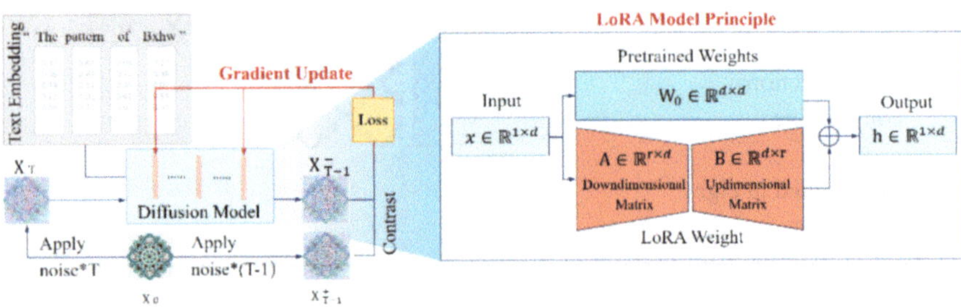

Fig. 4. Diffusion Model Fine-Tuning with LoRA Technology

3 Research Design and Experiment

3.1 Method

This study develops an AI-powered image generation framework (Fig. 5) for intelligent, automated Baoxiang motif design. The workflow includes data collection and preprocessing for input consistency, cloud-based LoRA model training utilizing robust computing resources, AI-assisted creative design generation, and iterative optimization where the model is evaluated and adjusted at each stage at each stage to ensure high-quality, innovative outcomes.

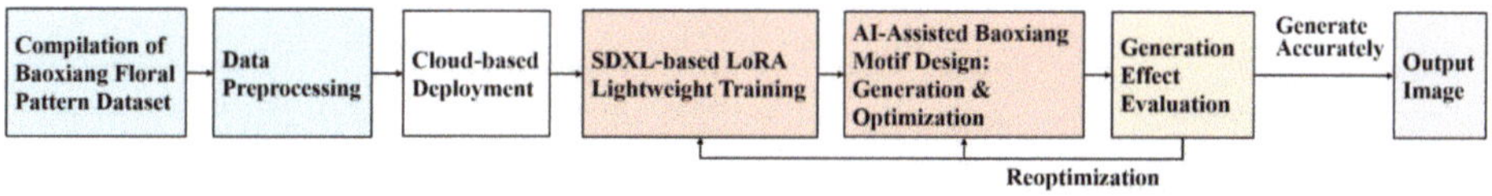

Fig. 5. AIGC-Based Baoxiang Motif Design Generation and Evaluation Framework

3.2 Training Data Collection and Processing

The Baoxiang floral motif dataset in this study is based on the "Wenzang-Motif Database" with internet, academic, museum supplements and covers Dunhuang Caisson Ceiling, ethnic costumes, bronzeware, porcelain, and ancient architecture, forming a 200-sample set (Fig. 6). Preprocessing includes: (1) cleaning invalid data (resolution < 300dpi, defects, distortion); (2) resizing to 1024 × 1024; (3) feature screening by integrity, typicality, representativeness, with multi-dimensional labeling by material, period, composition, and tagged "Bxhw".

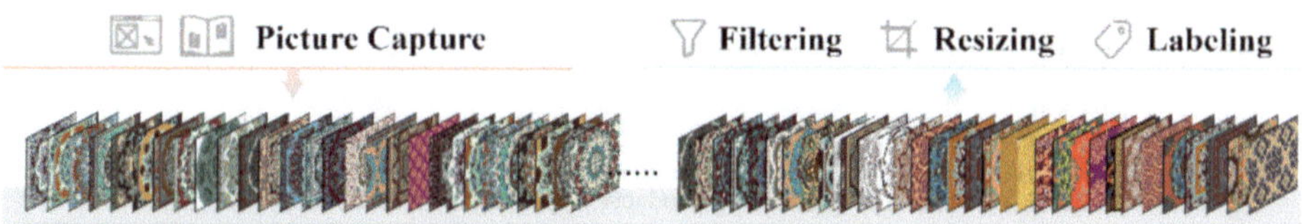

Fig. 6. Baoxiang Floral Motif Dataset Construction

3.3 LoRA Model Training

The study performed cloud-based model training with real-time metrics monitoring and parameter tuning on an environment with Xeon 8474C, RTX 4090D, Win10, Python 3.8, PyTorch 2.0.1, CUDA 11.8, and cuDNN 8.6.0.

A LoRA model was trained on SDXL using a Baoxiang motif dataset. SDXL's two-stage process enhances resolution and coherence. Training involved initializing the base model as "SDXL-LoRA", bucket-sorting 1024 × 1024 images, saving every 2 epochs over 10 epochs (batch size 4, 6 repetitions). Gradient checkpointing reduced memory. Unet lr was 1e−4 (text encoder lr lower), with cosine-restarts scheduling, warm-up, and LoRA settings (network_dim 128, network_alpha 64).

3.4 Generation and Selection of Creative Baoxiang Floral Motif Designs

This study uses Stable Diffusion Web UI with the SDXL framework and a self-trained Baoxiang LoRA model (weight 0.8–1.0), generating via txt2img with positive prompts like "Bxhw" (incorporating 8-petal symmetry, Dunhuang style, and cinnabar-lapis color semantics) and negative prompts. Key parameters include DPM++2M Karras sampler, 1024 × 1024 resolution, 30 steps, optimized by R-ESRGAN 4x+ Anime6B. Two groups of experiments on Baoxiang motifs and product applications explore design principles and LoRA's innovation potential, verifying the balance of cultural expression and commercial use. The generation process is shown in Fig. 7, and results are in Table 2.

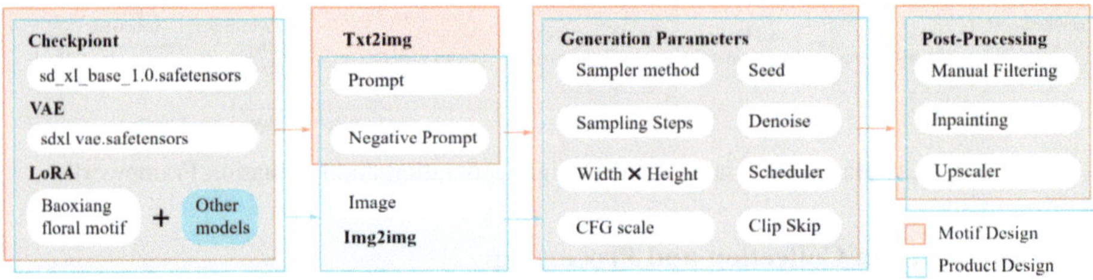

Fig. 7. Baoxiang Floral Motif and Product Design Generation Framework

Table 2. The Generation Results of the Baoxiang floral motif and Product Design

Design focus	Generation Results							
Baoxiang floral motif design	 motif 1	 motif 2	 motif 3	 motif 4	 motif 5	 motif 6	 motif 7	 motif 8
Product Design	 product1	 Product2	 product3	 product4	 product5	 Product6		

3.5 Construction of the Design Evaluation System

To verify LoRA fine-tuning's efficacy in enabling AIGC to generate culturally authentic and innovatively modern Baoxiang motifs and products, this study introduced the "Traditional Gene Inheritance–Modern Innovation Application" (TGI-MIA) dual-dimensional evaluation system. It assesses both cultural fidelity and innovative value in AIGC outputs.

For the two types of test sets, independent motif design and product application, differentiation indicators are set in terms of TGI and MIA dimensions respectively. A combination of digital algorithms and human evaluation is used, with normalization and weighting for comprehensive evaluation (see Fig. 8).

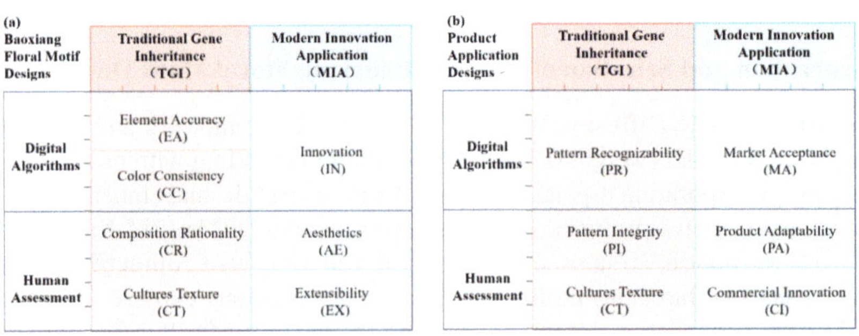

Fig. 8. Diagram of the Two-Dimensional Evaluation System for Baoxiang Floral Motif (a) and Its Product Application Designs (b) Based on Digital Algorithms and Manual Evaluation

In the evaluation of Baoxiang floral motif design:

Traditional dimension: Focuses on element morphology accuracy and cultural symbol continuity. (1) Element Accuracy (EA): Measured via ResNet-50 model extracting features and calculating cosine similarity with traditional samples. (2) Color Consistency (CC): Quantified by EMD distance between generated and traditional color schemes. (3) Composition Rationality (CR): Assessed by designers using a five - point Likert scale to evaluate layout regularity. (4) Cultural Texture (CT): Scored by experts using a five - point Likert scale to assess the motif's capacity to convey religious or symbolic meaning.

Innovation dimension: Emphasizes stylistic breakthroughs and extensibility. (1) Aesthetics (AE): Rated by designers using a five - point Likert scale to reflect visual appeal. (2) Innovation (IN): Measured by the LPIPS model to calculate perceptual difference between generated and traditional motifs. (3) Extensibility (EX): Evaluated by designers using a five - point Likert scale regarding the motif's applicability to derivative scenarios.

In the evaluation of product designs with Baoxiang motifs:

Traditional dimension: Focuses on symbol recognizability and cultural integration. (1) Motif Recognizability (PR): Determined by YOLOv5 detecting the class probability of core Baoxiang floral motif features (such as roundel structures) in the product. (2) Pattern Integrity (PI): Scored by designers using a five - point Likert scale to assess the completeness of traditional composition on the product surface. (3) Cultural Texture (CT): Scored by experts using a five - point Likert scale to verify the coordination of traditional meaning and modern function.

Innovation dimension: Emphasizes functional adaptation and commercial potential. (1) Market Acceptance (MA): Examined by Package Design AI for product design. (2) Product Adaptability (PA): Scored by designers using a five - point Likert scale to measure the degree of coordination and matching between the Baoxiang floral motifs and the product's functional characteristics, style positioning and usage scenarios. (3) Commercial Innovation (CI): Scored by designers and users using a five - point Likert scale to measure the responsiveness of the design to the industry trends.

In the evaluation data processing, all indicators were normalised to the [0, 1] interval to eliminate scale differences. Positive indicators (e.g., EA, IN, PR.) in the [0, 1] interval were used as raw values as in Eq. (1), negative indicators (e.g., CC) in the $[0, +\infty)$ were converted to positive values by Eq. (2), scoring indicators (e.g., CR, CT, AE, EX, PI, MA, PA, CI.) in the [1, 5] interval were linearly mapped by Eq. (3):

$$X = S \tag{1}$$

$$X = \frac{1}{1 + D} \tag{2}$$

$$X = \frac{S - 1}{4} \tag{3}$$

Where: S is the original evaluation data; D is the original EMD value of color difference; X is the normalized indicator.

The total score adopts a dual-weight mechanism: traditional and modern dimensions each account for 50%, and within each dimension, digital evaluation accounts for 50%

and human evaluation for 50%. Therefore, for motifs, the total score is composed of element accuracy (12.5%), color consistency (12.5%), composition rationality (12.5%), and cultures texture (12.5%) for the traditional dimension, and aesthetics (12.5%), innovation (25%), and extensibility (12.5%) for the modern dimension. The final 100-point score is synthesized by formula (4):

$$Total\ Score_{Motif} = (0.125X_{EA} + 0.125X_{CC} + 0.125X_{CR} + 0.125X_{CT} + 0.25X_{IN} + 0.125X_{AE} + 0.125X_{EX}) \times 100 \tag{4}$$

Where: $Total\ Score_{Motif}$ is the total evaluation score for Baoxiang floral motif design; X is the normalized indicator.

For product applications, the total score is constructed from pattern recognizability (25%), pattern integrity (12.5%), and cultures texture (12.5%) for the traditional dimension, and product adaptability (25%), commercial innovation (12.5%), and market acceptance (12.5%) for the modern dimension. The final 100-point score is synthesized by formula (5):

$$Total\ Score_{Product} = (0.25X_{PR} + 0.125X_{PI} + 0.125X_{CT} + 0.25X_{MA} + 0.125X_{PA} + 0.125X_{CI}) \times 100 \tag{5}$$

Where: $Total\ Score_{product}$ is the total evaluation score for Baoxiang floral motif product application; X is the normalized indicator.

This system, through the synergy of algorithmic validation and humanistic evaluation, balances the objective transmission of cultural genes and the subjective perception of innovation value, providing a quantifiable evaluation pathway for AIGC design (Tables 3 and 4).

Table 3. AIGC - assisted Generation of Baoxiang Floral Motif Design Evaluation Indicators

Dimension	Indicator	Evaluation method	Range	Evaluation criteria	Weight	Normalization
TGI	EA	ResNet-50 feature cosine similarity	[0, 1]	The higher the better	12.5%	$X_{EA} = S_{EA}$
	CC	EMD color distance	[0, +∞)	The lower the better	12.5%	$X_{CC} = \frac{1}{1+D_{CC}}$
	CR	Designer rating (Level 5 scale)	[1, 5]	The higher the better	12.5%	$X_{CR} = \frac{S_{CR}-1}{4}$
	CT	Expert rating (Level 5 scale)	[1, 5]	The higher the better	12.5%	$X_{CT} = \frac{S_{CT}-1}{4}$
MIA	AE	Designer rating (Level 5 scale)	[1, 5]	The higher the better	12.5%	$X_{AE} = \frac{S_{AE}-1}{4}$

(continued)

Table 3. (*continued*)

Dimension	Indicator	Evaluation method	Range	Evaluation criteria	Weight	Normalization
	IN	LPIPS Style distance	[0, 1]	The higher the better	25%	$X_{IN} = S_{IN}$
	EX	Designer rating (Level 5 scale)	[1, 5]	The higher the better	12.5%	$X_{EX} = \frac{S_{EX}-1}{4}$

Table 4. AIGC - assisted Generated Floral Motif Product Design Evaluation Indicators

Dimension	Indicator	Evaluation method	Range	Evaluation criteria	Weight	Normalization
TGI	PR	YOLOv5 Category probability	[0, 1]	The higher the better	25%	$X_{PR} = S_{PR}$
	PI	Designer rating (Level 5 scale)	[1, 5]	The higher the better	12.5%	$X_{PI} = \frac{S_{PI}-1}{4}$
	CT	expert rating (Level 5 scale)	[1, 5]	The higher the better	12.5%	$X_{CT} = \frac{S_{CT}-1}{4}$
MIA	MA	AI rating (Level 5 scale)	[1, 5]	The higher the better	25%	$X_{MA} = \frac{S_{MA}-1}{4}$
	PA	Designer Rating (Level 5 scale)	[1, 5]	The higher the better	12.5%	$X_{PA} = \frac{S_{PA}-1}{4}$
	CI	Designer Rating (Level 5 scale)	[1, 5]	The higher the better	12.5%	$X_{CI} = \frac{S_{CI}-1}{4}$

4 Evaluation and Analysis of Design Results

This study used Python to build algorithmic models (ResNet-50, YOLOv5, etc.) for feature extraction, object detection, and quantitative analysis, and business value is validated by Package Design AI with market survey data. A 30-member team (20 designers, 10 experts) evaluated via online scoring and interviews. Results are in Tables 5, 6.

Table 5. AIGC-assisted Generated Baoxiang Floral Motif Design Evaluation Results

Image number	S_{EA}	D_{CC}	S_{CR}	S_{CT}	S_{AE}	S_{IN}	S_{EX}	Total score
motif 1	0.9071	0.0021	4.75	4.8	4.85	0.7864	4.90	91.29
motif 2	0.9131	0.0021	4.80	4.9	4.80	0.7632	4.75	90.63
motif 3	0.9450	0.0021	4.45	4.6	4.85	0.7267	4.45	87.33
motif 4	0.9361	0.0015	4.80	4.7	4.55	0.8112	4.70	90.56
motif 5	0.9349	0.0023	5.00	4.8	4.85	0.7873	4.85	92.29
motif 6	0.9283	0.0020	4.80	4.6	4.75	0.7765	4.70	89.91
motif 7	0.9096	0.0023	5.00	5	4.65	0.7503	4.90	91.20
motif 8	0.8694	0.0019	4.85	4.6	4.6	0.8422	5.00	91.43

Table 6. AIGC-assisted Generated Baoxiang Floral Product Design Evaluation Results

Results	S_{PR}	S_{PI}	S_{CT}	S_{MA}	S_{PA}	S_{CI}	Total score
product 1	0.512	4.85	4.8	3.017	4.55	4.70	71.98
product 2	0.389	4.70	4.9	3.361	4.65	4.85	71.68
product 3	0.673	4.65	4.7	3.395	4.60	4.80	77.89
product 4	0.698	4.60	4.7	3.409	4.65	4.80	78.60
product 5	0.725	4.85	4.8	3.493	4.85	4.85	81.69
product 6	0.718	4.85	4.9	3.422	4.70	4.85	80.91

In the evaluation of 8 Baoxiang floral motifs, traditional-dimension indicators (Element Accuracy is 0.8694–0.9450, Color Consistency is 0.0015–0.0023, Composition Rationality is 4.45–5.0, Cultural Texture is 4.6–5.0) show strong heritage. Innovation-dimension indicators (Aesthetics is 4.55–4.85, Innovation is 0.7503–0.8422, Extensibility is 4.45–5.00) balance tradition with novelty. Motifs 1 and 5 excel overall, Motif 8 leads in innovation, while Motif 3 lags in details and extensibility.

In evaluating six Baoxiang motif product designs, traditional - dimension scores (Motif Recognizability: 0.389–0.725; Pattern Integrity: 4.60–4.85; Cultural Texture: 4.7–4.9) show all have clear motifs, three hit perfect Pattern Integrity, and most harmonize tradition with modernity. Innovation-dimension scores (Market Acceptance: 3.017–3.493; Product Adaptability: 4.55–4.85; Commercial Innovation: 4.70–4.85) reveal half have high market potential, all fit usage scenarios, four lead in trend - responsiveness, and two lag. Most balance tradition and innovation, with Product 5 excelling and Product 2 trailing (lowest Motif Recognizability).

In exploring LoRA-based intelligent generation of Baoxiang motifs, quantitative evaluation has shown its design and product application potential. Further multidimensional analysis via interviews with designers, experts, and consumers (summarized in Fig. 9) clarifies its practical value. All groups affirmed that LoRA: streamlines design for efficiency, integrates tradition-modernity for innovative styles, ensures high-fidelity cultural inheritance through limited-data training, and delivers market-appealing designs that enhance cultural identity and expand audience reach.

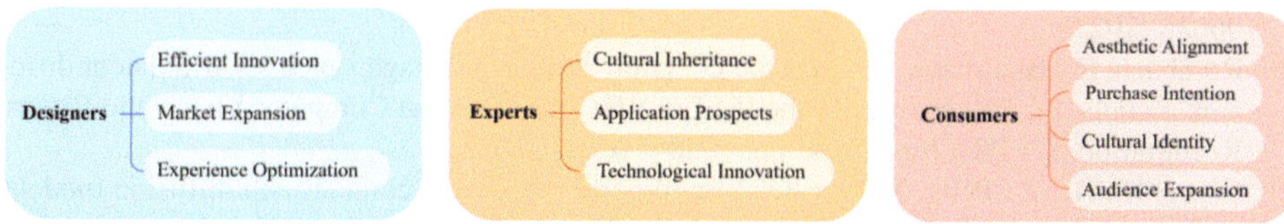

Fig. 9. Sorting of Interviews on the Design of Baoxiang Floral Motif and Their Product Applications

5 Conclusion

This study integrates generative AI with traditional Chinese Baoxiang floral motif design, achieving controllable generation via LoRA-tuned SDXL models trained on cultural and artistic analyses and large dataset. Stable Diffusion-generated motifs blending tradition and modernity were applied to packaging, enabling digital revitalization. Quantitative and qualitative validation confirms the LoRA method preserves motif essence while driving design and market innovation through its "decoding → innovation → adaptation" pathway.

Core innovations include: (1) a "bidirectional cultural bridge" empowering designers with AI tools, regenerating motifs for modern use, and connecting consumers to cultural textures via design; (2) a closed-loop system quantifying cultural inheritance through interdisciplinary metrics; (3) standardized processes balancing heritage preservation and technological innovation for intangible cultural heritage digitization. This framework advances human-AI design and cultural computing, fostering dynamic heritage transmission. Future focus: enhancing tech inclusivity across cultures and scaling traditional motif value generation.

Disclosure of Interests. The authors have no competing interests relevant to the content of this article.

References

1. Liu, R.: The Application of Tang Dynasty Lotus Flower Patterns in Modern Jewelry Design. Shanghai University of Engineering Science, Shanghai (2021)
2. Qin, S.: Application of the Baoxiang flowers patterns in Dunhuang grottoes of tang dynasty in decorative art design. Green Packag. **8**, 114–117 (2022)
3. Zhang, Y.: The Basic Characteristics of Baoxiang Flower and Its Application in Modern Design: Taking Baoxiang Flower in Dunhuang Grottoes of Tang Dynasty as an Example. China Academy of Art, Zhejiang (2018)
4. Zhang, K.: A review of the research status of flower pattern in the field of design — based on the search results of knowledge network and WOS database. West Leather **46**(1), 47–49 (2024)

5. Cao, Y., Li, S., Liu, Y.: A comprehensive survey of AI-generated content (AIGC): a history of generative AI from GAN to ChatGPT. arXiv preprint arXiv:2303.04226 (2023)
6. Ran, C.: Exploring the opportunities and challenges of developing large AI models and their commercialization. Adv. Eng. Technol. Res. **6**, 611 (2023)
7. Wu, J., Gan, W., Chen, Z.: AI-generated content (AIGC): a survey. arXiv preprint arXiv:2304.06638 (2023)
8. Rombach, R., Blattmann, A., Lorenz, D.: High-resolution image synthesis with latent diffusion models. In: Proceedings of the IEEE/CVF Conference on Computer Vision and Pattern Recognition (CVPR), New York, pp. 10684–10695 (2022)
9. Wang, X., He, Z., Peng, X.: Artificial-intelligence-generated content with diffusion models: a literature review. IEEE Trans. Pattern Anal. **12**(7), 977 (2024)
10. Hu, E., Shen, Y., Wallis, P.: LoRA: low-rank adaptation of large language models. arXiv preprint arXiv:2106.09685 (2021)
11. Ruiz, N., Li, Y., Jampani, V.: DreamBooth: fine tuning text-to-image diffusion models for subject-driven generation. In: Proceedings of the IEEE/CVF Conference on Computer Vision and Pattern Recognition (CVPR), Vancouver, pp. 22500–22510 (2023)
12. Wu, X., Sun, K., Zhu, F.: Human preference score: better aligning text-to-image models with human preference. In: Proceedings of the IEEE/CVF International Conference on Computer Vision (ICCV), Paris, pp. 2096–2105 (2023)

Empowering Educators: A Framework for Maintaining Course Integrity in the Age of Artificial Intelligence

Alekzander Green and Jay Dee Johns III(✉)

Purdue University, Fort Wayne, IN 46805, USA
{greead04,jdjohns}@pfw.edu

Abstract. As Artificial Intelligence (AI) becomes more popular and more students adopt these technologies into their studies, educators must face new challenges. These tools are handy but have many limitations and bring with them several ethical concerns, especially when it comes to the topic of academic and course integrity. Research into these tools, their role in higher education, their limitations, ethical concerns, and how they are used and viewed by students and educators is studied. From these studies, a flexible framework was developed that can be used to empower educators and safeguard academic integrity in a world rich with AI. This framework consists of four (4) parts: integration, AI education, AI resistant assignments, and AI detection and monitoring. This framework should help create an environment rich with academic integrity that encourages students to explore AI tools without worry.

Keywords: Education · Academic Integrity · Artificial Intelligence (AI) · Ethical AI Engagement · Assessments · Planning · Progress Measurements · Course Evaluation Framework

1 Introduction

As Artificial Intelligence (AI) and Large Language Models (LLMs) become more popular, many students are taking notice and adopting these technologies into their academic workflows. However, there is a growing concern regarding the impact of AI tools on course and academic integrity. There is a clear need for educators and Human Computer Interaction (HCI) professionals to seriously consider how students will interact with AI tools like ChatGPT, Copilot, and more.

It may be tempting to prohibit or avoid interacting with AI and AI policies, but this is a futile effort. AI technology will continue to exist and students will not simply stop acknowledging the existence of these tools because their instructors may want to avoid them. Instead, this paper intends to provide educators and HCI professionals with the tools and insights necessary to maintain course integrity and adapt to the current AI-rich environment with the knowledge that the persistence of these tools is inevitable.

C. Stephanidis et al. (Eds.): HCII 2025, CCIS 2773, pp. 45–56, 2026.
https://doi.org/10.1007/978-3-032-12773-0_5

2 Background

2.1 AI and LLMs

AI has a history of being difficult to define due to the very nature of the technology. Sheikh, et al. [1] thoroughly examined how AI is defined and have come to define it as, "Systems that display intelligent behavior by analyzing their environment and taking actions—with some degree of autonomy—to achieve specific goals." This definition can be broadly applied to many algorithms and systems that professionals consider AI.

LLMs are a specific category of AI models. These models rely on a field of computation called Natural Language Processing (NLP) which studies how computers can effectively process human language. LLMs are models trained using extensive amounts of text data with the intent to generate human-like answers in response to questions or other language-related tasks [2]. AI chatbots like ChatGPT or Copilot use LLMs at their core [3].

2.2 Academic and Course Integrity

The International Center for Academic Integrity (ICAI) defines academic integrity as a commitment to six core values: honesty, trust, fairness, respect, and courage. These values should inspire students and educators to be truthful, avoid plagiarism, be objective, be transparent, take accountability, follow codes of conduct, and so on. Without integrity, much of academia becomes devalued [4].

It is essential to recognize how we talk about academic integrity if we want to cultivate a culture of integrity. These values need support at an institutional level, but educators can also take steps to implement these values at a course level. Unfortunately, institutions and educators tend to address academic and course integrity by taking prohibitive actions against behaviors that are considered to lack integrity [4]. Many educators took steps towards banning AI use [5] when it became clear that it could lead to problematic behaviors that threatened academic integrity. This may have been suitable during the early adoption of AI tools, but their wide adoption means that this is no longer viable. Long-term success depends on how we teach students about the use of AI tools, instruct lecturers on integrating or working in an age of AI tools, and study how we, as a society, interact with these tools.

3 Relevant Research

3.1 Role of AI in Education

The following is a summary of the many places where tools like ChatGPT can have positive impacts in an educational setting. The use of these tools for the following purposes is well-documented, highly encouraged, or already implemented.

Personalized Learning and Diversity Support. Most studies agree that AI chat bots are excellent tools for developing tailored learning experiences. This is because AI can use input text and other contextual information to generate personalized learning materials. Moreover, AI can enhance and support diversity in higher education settings by providing real-time services such as translation for multilingual students or live transcriptions for the visually impaired [2,3,7].

Studying and Tutoring Help. Generative AI tools can help with studying and tutoring in several different ways. ChatGPT can provide study plans, assist with testing strategies, and generate practice problems. These tools can help tutor students without making them feel inadequate for asking "dumb" questions. Multilingual AI tools could also assist students studying new languages by conversing with students in their language of study [3,7,11,14].

Research and Writing Help. LLMs are built to process large amounts of text data. This makes these tools great for research and writing tasks. ChatGPT and similar models can quickly summarize and outline text for research purposes. Not only that, but AI can also be used to push students and researchers towards unexplored topics. Then, when it comes time to write reports and papers, AI can also help find and iron out any editing mistakes like grammatical and syntactical errors or simple typos [2].

Instructor Support. Generative AI can also be used to empower educators. It can help develop lesson plans, analyze learning outcomes, generate engaging or accessible learning materials, simplify complex concepts, generate simple syllabi, and more. The most prevalent use is to help generate and evaluate examinations and other kinds of test content [2,3,11].

3.2 AI Challenges, Limitations, and Concerns in Education

The following is a summary of many challenges, limitations, and concerns that LLM chat tools like ChatGPT currently pose. Note that this list is not extensive, but instead focuses on academic integrity and AI interaction in higher education settings.

Reliability and Accuracy Concerns. The nature of LLMs means that they can never be completely reliable or accurate. This leads to situations where chat bots generate misleading or incorrect information, often called "hallucinations." This unreliability is not ideal in academia [3,8].

Implicit Biases and Unfairness. Models are trained on lots of data that may contain inherent biases. The AI can integrate these biases into the model when trained on biased data. This could lead to general biases, stereotypes, prejudices, and unfairness being propagated by the AI. This could cause any information obtained from the models to contain unjust biases, obscure lesser-known or local knowledge, and be problematic if we want to use AI to help with academic determinations like grading [2,3,7].

Generalization and Lack of Domain Depth. Models like ChatGPT will try to find the best answer to a given input based on all of the text on which it was trained. This often leads the model to output very general or basic responses (generalization or overfitting). This is generally fine until more complex or domain-specific responses are requested. This could lead to confusion when students or researchers are provided with details that lack depth [3,7].

Privacy and Security Concerns. LLMs are trained on massive amounts of user data and must process data provided by users. This could be problematic in an educational setting where personal data is protected by HIPAA or FERPA laws [2,3,7].

Complexity and Lack of Explainability. The model underlying ChatGPT and other generative AI chat bots is complex. This makes the model nearly impossible to explain, making it difficult to see how or why it chooses what to output [3].

Accountability and Authorship Due to the nature of AI, it can be hard to determine who the generated content belongs to or how to attribute authorship to AI sources. It is also difficult to identify who is responsible for the model's outputs. This lack of accountability goes against ideas of integrity [3,7].

Limited Knowledge or Expertise in Using AI. Many educators, students, and institutions may not be aware of the limitations or capabilities of AI tools. Without this knowledge, it can be easy to blindly rely on or give undue trust to the model [2,7,8].

Overreliance on AI and Autonomy Concerns. As models become more advanced, adopted, and culturally accepted, we risk developing an overreliance on them. The simplification of acquisition can negatively impact essential academic skills like critical thinking, problem-solving, creativity, originality, and analytical thinking. Studies have also shown that dependence on AI models can influence behavior, decision-making, and agency. The ease of generating answers may inhibit users from investigating further or coming to their own conclusions and solutions [2,3,7,8].

Misuse, Abuse, Plagiarism, and Cheating. AI models can be misused as easily as they can be used correctly. In an educational setting, these models can be used for plagiarism and cheating, threatening academic integrity [2,3,7,11].

Difficulty Distinguishing Between AI and Human-Generated Content. As models become more developed, differentiating AI from human-generated content is becoming more challenging. Models often outperform the average student on many activities. Ironically, they also fail at tasks that children can easily accomplish [2,7,9].

Lack of Regulation or Inconsistent Practices. The adoption of AI is only now becoming commonplace. This means that there is often a lack of regulations surrounding the use of AI at many institutions. Even when clear regulations are present, acceptable use and instructions on use are often inconsistent between courses [11].

Increased Workloads As instructors adapt to these new technologies, they are likely to incur an increased workload as they work to adapt to an AI-rich landscape. Once they have adapted their courses, they must still take additional steps to safeguard against AI-related academic misconduct [11].

3.3 AI Interaction and Perspectives in Educational Environments

A German study from 2023 found that nearly two-thirds of students use or have used AI tools [12]. A year later, a survey by HEPI found that 64% of students were using AI tools in 2024. Then, a follow-up survey by HEPI in 2025 found that 92% of students, from a survey of 1,041 students, were using generative AI tools [15]. It is evident that the mass adoption of AI tools into curricula and academia is inevitable.

Exact attitudes toward AI are mixed. Many instructors have positive outlook but do not have much experience with AI tools and fear the consequences of misuse [2]. Many students share similar attitudes, with one study finding that more than 80% of students surveyed enjoyed using the technology and found it helpful for completing assignments quickly [12]. However, 10–35% of students in another survey feared that AI threatened the integrity of higher education [13].

These fears may be justified. One survey found that 30% of students surveyed believed that using AI on exams was okay[14]. Another study found that 88% of students admitted to using generative AI to complete assessments, and as many as 18% of students admitted to including AI-generated content directly into their work [15]. Despite this, most students agree that the majority of submitted work should be original [14].

4 A Four-Part Framework for Academic Integrity

Based on research on AI and its role in higher education, the following section aims to provide a flexible framework that can empower educators to maintain course integrity in an AI-rich environment or develop their own strategies. This framework is not prescriptive but instead provides a set of ideas that can help educators develop integrity policies suited to their unique course objectives, disciplinary needs, and teaching methodologies.

This framework consists of four (4) parts, each helping to build an environment that promotes integrity, transparency, critical thinking, engagement with AI, and ethical AI use.

4.1 Integration

Educators must accept that students will be using AI tools. The only questions is on how much the instructor wishes to integrate these tools into their courses. Here, the term "integration" is used to talk about creating learning materials, assignments, or other course content that directly references, displays, encourages, or requires the use of generative AI tools like ChatGPT. Creating an environment that acknowledges the existence of these tools and works with or around them creates a better environment of academic integrity than prohibiting these tools outright [4].

Low Integration. While educators must accept that students will be engaging with these tools, not all educators need to integrate the tools directly into their courses. In this case, following the rest of the framework, is still recommended.

High Integration. Educators who wish to integrate AI directly into their courses may find pleasing results. However, AI should not be used as a substitution for human expertise. Educators should ensure that AI is being integrated as an aid, not as their replacement [11].

4.2 AI Education

Educators must educate students on the existence, functionality, limitations, and concerns surrounding generative AI tools and how to properly use these tools in safe and academically honest ways.

Recognition. Educators should help students recognize the existence of generative AI tools and models that can help them with domain-specific tasks, such as recommending Copilot or Codex for code review or DALL-E and Midjourney for image generation [2,9,12,14].

Functionality. Educators should consider that many students are unfamiliar with how AI models work. To avoid confusion on what AI models are, it should be made clear that these AI tools are simply computer programs. These programs use complex algorithms and statistics to learn from training data so that they can produce a statistical "best" output for any given input. These tools do not "think" and cannot create novel outputs without basis in their training data [2,3,6,8,11].

Applications. Educators should consider how students might use AI tools within a given discipline or course. For instance, we could consider using AI to debug code or generate images during artistic exploration [2,3,10,11,14]. These different application spaces should be shared with students so that they know how they might be expected to use these tools effectively.

Limitations. Because of the way that these generative AI models work, they have many limitations that students should be educated on. Students should be made aware of the following:

- AI models are not entirely reliable or accurate.
- AI models often "hallucine" incorrect or misleading information.
- AI models may produce content with implicit biases or prejudices.
- AI models may give incomplete, simple, or common answers instead of complex or specific answers that may be more appropriate.
- AI models may not have up-to-date information.
- AI models may not securely handle personal information.
- AI models cannot create original or novel ideas.
- AI models lack common sense and can fail at simple tasks.
- AI models cannot take accountability for errors, judgments, or user actions.

Knowledge of these limitations should be reinforced to ensure that students understand how much to trust the model and the additional responsibilities that come with AI tools [2,3,6,8,11].

Concerns. Students should be made aware that overreliance on tools like ChatGPT can have negative consequences on core academic skills. This includes problem-solving, critical thinking, analytical thinking, decision-making, creativity, originality, and agency [2,3,7,8].

Mitigations. To mitigate the concerns and limitations surrounding AI use, students should be recommended to take the following mitigation steps:

- Cross-reference all information against authoritative sources [2,6].
- Do not use these tools to generate answers, only ideas or perspectives [2,6].
- Thoroughly review all updates that the model suggests [2,6].
- Students should be given insights on how to address biases in results [2].
- Students should be told to never share personal information.
- Encourage students to be highly critical of generated content [8].
- Enforce citing, crediting, or acknowledging AI tools on submitted work [6].
- Consider requiring students to submit AI interactions as supplemental materials [6].
- Educate students on how directly using content generated from AI tools in writing or code is plagiarism [3,8,10].
- Educate students on how using AI tools to complete examinations or assignments without express permission is cheating [3,8,10].
- Encourage students to practice using AI to learn to use it effectively [11].
- Set concrete regulations and guidelines around the acceptable use of AI [10].

Implementation. To help students understand these tools, educators might consider integrating one or more of the following items into their courses:

- Handouts to help educate students on the use of AI models [11].
- Explicit mention of AI usage and knowledge in syllabi, learning materials, and assignments.
- Live or recorded lectures and demonstrations using AI models.
- Exploratory assignments that require students to understand and work with AI models directly.

4.3 AI Resistant Assignments

The third part of this framework is intended to introduce educators to ways that they might safeguard academic integrity by updating assignments to be more AI-resistant. These updates or changes are intended to test and reinforce critical thinking, problem-solving, creativity, and communication skills. This should not only help prevent overreliance but also ensure that students are being properly graded on their own understanding rather than the "understanding" of a machine [2,10,11].

Draft Assignments. Consider requiring students to document their design process for large projects or research papers [10,11].

Pre-reviewed Submissions. Consider requiring students to submit their assignments for review before a Finally submission [7].

Oral Examinations. Consider conducting oral examinations to test understanding and the student's ability to communicate about complex topics. These examinations could cover regular course topics or the student's own submissions [10,11].

Presentations. Consider requiring students to present on topics or submissions to test understanding and communication skills[10,11].

Open-Ended Assessments. Consider developing open-ended assessments that require students to develop research questions and defend arguments to encourage creativity and originality.

Real-Time Assessments. Consider proctoring exams in person rather than online to ensure integrity [10].

AI Usage Self-reflections. Consider requiring students to submit a self-reflection of how they used AI on their assignment in addition to the submission.

Live Group Discussions/Peer-Reviews. Consider requiring students to participate in live group discussions or peer reviews to develop their communication and critical thinking skills [10].

4.4 AI Detection and Monitoring

The fourth part of this framework is intended to help introduce educators to ways to detect AI-assisted plagiarism and cheating. Educators must be able to distinguish between AI and human-generated content so that they can monitor how and where students are using these technologies and safeguard course integrity in cases where these tools are being used unethically [2,3,7,10,11].

Surveying. Surveying is a simple way to see how students use AI tools in coursework. These surveys could be questionnaires or feedback on how students feel about AI tools [2].

Identifying AI Predictors. Due to the nature of AI, many identifying features can be used to help identify signs of plagiarism and cheating. These include:

- Lack of proper citations. The AI may not cite any sources or hallucinate sources that seem viable but do not exist [2,7,10,11].
- Inconsistencies in language. The AI can have trouble being consistent when writing extensive responses, leading to irregular language patterns and inconsistencies [7].
- Factual errors. AI tools often hallucinate misinformation which will come across as factual errors in writing [7,10].
- Poor context awareness. Because AI lacks any understanding of the real world or human communication, it may generate responses that lack context or awareness of nuances [7,10].
- Lack of originality. Due to the way AI is trained, it cannot create truly novel or original ideas [10].
- Ambiguity. AI may not be trained on data to sufficiently answer a question, leading it to create ambiguous responses, especially on complex topics [10].
- Lack of personality. AI-generated text often comes off as very basic or bland in personality due to generalization [7].

AI and Plagiarism Detection Tools. The rise of AI has also come with an increase in AI detection tools that can detect if text was generated with AI in the same way that plagiarism detection tools can detect recycled work. While these tools should not be used in isolation or to determine plagiarism or cheating, they can help educators identify which works they may need to examine more closely [10,11].

5 Conclusion

Background information was reviewed, and relevant research was done to corroborate information related to the role of AI in education, limitations and concerns related to AI use, and how students and educators currently think about and use AI. With this research in mind, a framework was developed to help educators safeguard course integrity and navigate an educational landscape rich with AI use.

The framework comprises four (4) parts: integration, AI education, AI resistant assignments, and AI detection and monitoring. Integration should help educators consider how much they wish to integrate AI into their courses with the knowledge that students will inevitably use the tools alongside their studies. AI education should help create a knowledgeable and understanding environment where educators and students both recognize the existence of AI tools, understand how they function, can identify applications for AI tools, recognize the limitations and concerns of these tools, and can see how to mitigate problems and work around constraints; as well as providing ways that educators can reasonably impart this knowledge onto their students. AI-resistant assignments should help maintain course integrity by pushing students to complete tasks that test critical thinking, problem-solving, creativity, originality, and communication skills which may not be as developed if students relied on AI for their assignments. Finally, AI detection and monitoring should help educators keep track of where and how students are using AI, allowing them to find instances of plagiarism and cheating early and deal with these actions accordingly.

All together, these pieces should make a flexible framework that educators can use to protect against academic misconduct or otherwise empower educators to develop strategies to bolster the integrity of their courses and students.

6 Discussion

Further research is necessary to see how we can alter or create new types of assignments that are AI-resistant. This framework attempts to provide some ideas for implementing these kinds of assignments, but exact implementations are left for the educator to develop.

In addition, further support from institutions and regulatory bodies is needed to make the integration of AI tools more consistent across disciplines and institutions. This framework could potentially serve as an adaptable basis for these regulations to build on top of.

Disclosure of Interests. The authors have no competing interests to declare that are relevant to the content of this article.

References

1. Sheikh, H., Prins, C., Schrijvers, E.: Artificial intelligence: definition and background. In: Sheikh, H., Prins, C., Schrijvers, E. (eds.) Mission AI. Research for Policy. Springer, Cham. (2023). https://doi.org/10.1007/978-3-031-21448-6_2
2. Kasneci, E., et al.: ChatGPT for good? On opportunities and challenges of large language models for education. Learn. Individ. Differ. **103** (2023). https://doi.org/10.1016/j.lindif.2023.102274
3. Ray, P.: ChatGPT: a comprehensive review on background, applications, key challenges, bias, ethics, limitations and future scope. Internet Things Cyber-Phys. Syst. **3**, 121–154 (2023). https://doi.org/10.1016/j.iotcps.2023.04.003
4. International Center for Academic Integrity [ICAI]. The Fundamental Values of Academic Integrity, 3rd edn (2021). https://academicintegrity.org/aws/ICAI/pt/sp/values
5. Sam, L., Philip, G.: From "Ban It Till We Understand It" to "Resistance is Futile": how university programming instructors plan to adapt as more students use AI code generation and explanation tools such as ChatGPT and GitHub copilot. In: Proceedings of the 2023 ACM Conference on International Computing Education Research - Volume 1 (ICER '23), vol. 1, pp. 106–121. Association for Computing Machinery, New York, NY, USA (2023). https://doi.org/10.1145/3568813.3600138
6. Almarie, B., Teixeira, P.E.P., Pacheco-Barrios, K., Rossetti, C.A., Fregni, F.: Editorial - the use of large language models in science: opportunities and challenges. Principles Pract. Clin. Res. (2015) **9**(1), 1–4 (2023). https://doi.org/10.21801/ppcrj.2023.91.1
7. Rahman, M.M., Watanobe, Y.: ChatGPT for education and research: opportunities, threats, and strategies. Appl. Sci. **13**(9), 5783 (2023). https://doi.org/10.3390/app13095783
8. Zhai, C., Wibowo, S., Li, L.D.: The effects of over-reliance on AI dialogue systems on students' cognitive abilities: a systematic review. Smart Learn. Environ. **11**, 28 (2024). https://doi.org/10.1186/s40561-024-00316-7
9. Finnie-Ansley, J., Denny, P., Becker, B., Luxton-Reilly, A., Prather, J.: The robots are coming: exploring the implications of OpenAI codex on introductory programming. In Proceedings of the 24th Australasian Computing Education Conference (ACE '22), pp. 10–19. Association for Computing Machinery, New York, NY, USA (2022). https://doi.org/10.1145/3511861.3511863
10. Cotton, D.R.E., Cotton, P.A., Shipway, J.R.: Chatting and cheating: ensuring academic integrity in the era of ChatGPT. Innov. Educ. Teach. Int. **61**(2), 228–239 (2023). https://doi.org/10.1080/14703297.2023.2190148
11. Neumann, M., Rauschenberger, M., Schön, E.M.: "We Need To Talk About ChatGPT": the future of ai and higher education. In: IEEE/ACM 5th International Workshop on Software Engineering Education for the Next Generation (SEENG), pp. 29–32 (2023). https://doi.org/10.1109/SEENG59157.2023.00010
12. von Garrel, J., Mayer, J.: Artificial Intelligence in studies–use of ChatGPT and AI-based tools among students in Germany. Humanit. Soc. Sci. Commun. **10**, 799 (2023). https://doi.org/10.1057/s41599-023-02304-7
13. Okulich-Kazarin, V., Artyukhov, A., Skowron, Ł, Artyukhova, N., Wołowiec, T.: Will AI become a threat to higher education sustainability? A study of students' views. Sustainability **16**(11), 4596 (2024). https://doi.org/10.3390/su16114596

14. Balabdaoui, F., Dittmann-Domenichini, N., Grosse, H., et al.: A survey on students' use of AI at a technical university. Discov. Educ. **3**, 51 (2024). https://doi.org/10.1007/s44217-024-00136-4
15. Freeman, J.: Student Generative AI Survey 2025. Technical report, HEPI (2025). https://www.hepi.ac.uk/2025/02/26/student-generative-ai-survey-2025

Application of Generative Artificial Intelligence Combined with the Morphological Chart Method in Product Design

Shih-Wen Hsiao and Yu-Chien Wu(✉)

Industrial Design Department Faculty, National Cheng Kung University, Tainan, ROC
swhsiao@mail.ncku.edu.tw, p36121138@gs.ncku.edu.tw

Abstract. In the modern era of diverse design tools, designers not only use computer-aided design (CAD) for product development but also incorporate generative artificial intelligence (AI) in recent times to assist in idea generation and iteration. Therefore, this study aims to develop a design method that integrates generative AI—primarily using ChatGPT—with the morphological chart method to create an AI-assisted design approach. Through practical case demonstrations, the study illustrates the application process of this method and gathers feedback from approximately five professional designers and other stakeholders (informed consent forms will be provided beforehand). The goal is to evaluate the rationality and practicality of the method and examine the pros and cons of empowering generative AI as a participant in design teams.

The morphological chart [1] is a long-established divergent technique, commonly used in product design as a tool for expanding ideas. However, traditional methods like brainstorming or mind mapping, while effective in stimulating creativity, are often constrained by the designers' personal experiences or cultural backgrounds, potentially missing out on more innovative solutions. This study employs the morphological chart by defining the parameters of individual components in the first column and using focus group discussions or brainstorming sessions within the design team to generate various possibilities in subsequent columns. Ultimately, the design team selects one option from each category for the final decision.

In this research, ChatGPT is employed to generate possibilities for components by inputting instructions to produce related visual proposals (based on product definitions and the conditions set in the first column). These generated visuals serve as design suggestions, thereby improving efficiency and mitigating the influence of the design team's backgrounds and experiences on idea generation.

After creating the morphological chart with the assistance of generative AI, the design team will exclude components with potential patent or plagiarism risks during the analysis phase. They will then select ten feasible options for final decision-making, which will lead to the production of a product—a dumbbell storage rack.

The study collects approximately ten valid questionnaires through a survey (with informed consent forms provided in advance) and uses fuzzy comprehensive evaluation [2] to analyze and consolidate the results. The findings aim to confirm that the products developed using generative AI integrated with the morphological chart method meet public expectations and avoid infringement issues.

C. Stephanidis et al. (Eds.): HCII 2025, CCIS 2773, pp. 57–64, 2026.
https://doi.org/10.1007/978-3-032-12773-0_6

In summary, this study will be conducted in three stages of analysis and discussion:

1. Development and Discussion of the Generative AI Integrated with the Morphological Chart Method
2. Benefits and Key Points of Using the AI-Enhanced Morphological Chart Design Method for Participatory Design
3. Practical Case Development and Result Analysis.

Keywords: Generative Artificial Intelligence · Morphological Chart Method · AI-Assisted Design

1 Introduction

1.1 Research Motivation

In the early stages of product design, designers employ various methods for data collection, brainstorming, image generation, and modeling. Although design teams benefit from collaborative discussions and mutual inspiration, leading to novel designs, practical constraints exist. Factors such as designers' cultural and personal backgrounds can limit creative possibilities. In many design projects, innovative ideas may not emerge quickly enough, resulting in products that lack differentiation from competitors or fail to better meet user needs due to time constraints. Therefore, this study aims to integrate traditional design methodologies, specifically the morphological chart method, with AI-generated images and design insights from ChatGPT. This approach seeks to overcome time and cognitive limitations in product design projects, ultimately optimizing the final product.

1.2 Research Background

With the rapid advancement of artificial intelligence, OpenAI's ChatGPT has demonstrated powerful natural language processing capabilities. In recent years, its applications have expanded to include image processing, making it increasingly relevant to creative and design-related industries. Leveraging GPT-4's multimodal capabilities, ChatGPT can now understand and generate images, broadening its scope of application. This study explores the development and application of ChatGPT in image processing, integrating its image-generation capabilities with the traditional morphological chart method to evaluate and refine dumbbell rack designs.

1.3 Research Objectives

This study utilizes the morphological chart method in conjunction with AI-generated images to analyze and compare design outcomes. The final design solutions will be evaluated through surveys collecting feedback from industrial designers and end-users. The study aims to assess design outcomes based on user perception and compare the innovation level with existing products. By doing so, it seeks to determine whether this research process effectively breaks conventional design constraints and enables more optimized design results within a shorter timeframe.

2 Theoretical Background

2.1 Morphological Analysis Method

Morphological analysis is a commonly used analytical tool in form design, widely applied across various fields, from product design to problem-solving. The core concept of this method lies in systematically and comprehensively analyzing the structure of an object to identify its fundamental components, characteristics, and interrelationships. This approach enhances understanding and facilitates problem-solving. The fundamental principle of morphological analysis involves deconstructing a complex object or system into its basic elements and then systematically studying the interactions between these elements. This process consists of multiple steps, including decomposition, description, definition, combination, and validation. Morphological analysis is a highly influential tool in the field of product design.

Designers can break down a product into different components, analyze their interactions, and create designs that better meet user needs and expectations. This method helps determine the optimal functional combinations, improving the product's usability and market competitiveness. Furthermore, morphological analysis is widely used for solving complex problems. By deconstructing a problem into different aspects, analyzing possible solutions for each aspect, and then combining and validating them, the most suitable solution can be found. This systematic approach ensures the comprehensiveness and effectiveness of the solutions.

In the innovation process, morphological analysis stimulates new ideas. By exploring and combining different elements, creative teams can discover new concepts and possibilities, which drive continuous advancements in products and services. Additionally, morphological analysis is applicable in project management, particularly in complex and dynamic environments. By decomposing a project and identifying relationships between different elements, project managers can better understand and address challenges, developing more effective plans.

The strengths of morphological analysis lie in its systematic, comprehensive, and innovative nature. It provides a powerful methodology for solving complex problems, enhancing design efficiency, and fostering innovation. However, it may become overly cumbersome when dealing with extremely complex systems and may be influenced by subjective factors during decomposition and description. Overall, morphological analysis is a robust analytical tool that demonstrates its value and practicality across various applications, making it an indispensable tool in many fields.

2.2 Fuzzy Comprehensive Evaluation Theory

Fuzzy comprehensive evaluation theory was proposed in 1965 by Professor Lotfi A. Zadeh at the University of California, Berkeley. It explores the quantitative processing of human subjective thinking and reasoning, introducing the concept of "fuzzy sets" as a new branch of mathematics. In practice, phenomena can generally be categorized into three types: deterministic phenomena, stochastic phenomena, and fuzzy phenomena. To address deterministic objects, mathematical tools such as geometry, algebra, differential equations, and numerical analysis are applied. Probability theory and mathematical statistics are used to study stochastic objects, whereas fuzzy mathematics serves as the analytical tool for studying fuzzy phenomena. [1].

Since a single object often possesses multiple attributes and is influenced by various factors, a comprehensive and holistic evaluation of multiple related factors is necessary when assessing an object. Fuzzy comprehensive evaluation mainly consists of six steps.[3].

1. Establishing the Factor Set

The factor set represents the set of evaluation criteria affecting the evaluation process. It is defined as:

$$U = \{u_1, u_2, \ldots, u_m\}$$

2. Establishing the Weight Set

The weight set represents the relative importance of each factor in the evaluation. It is defined as:

$$\underset{\sim}{A} = \{a_1, a_2, \ldots, a_m\}$$

3. Establishing the Evaluation Set

The evaluation set represents the possible evaluation outcomes. It is defined as:

$$V = \{V_1, V_2, \ldots, V_n\}$$

4. Single-Factor Fuzzy Evaluation

$$\underset{\sim i}{R} = (\frac{r_{i1}}{V_1} + \frac{r_{i2}}{V_2}, + \cdots + \frac{r_{in}}{V_n})$$

$$\underset{\sim}{R} = \begin{pmatrix} r_{11} & r_{12} & \ldots & r_{1n} \\ r_{21} & r_{22} & & r_{2n} \\ \vdots & & \ddots & \vdots \\ r_{m1} & r_{m2} & \cdots & r_{mn} \end{pmatrix}$$

5. Fuzzy Comprehensive Evaluation

$$\underset{\sim}{B} = \underset{\sim}{A} \circ \underset{\sim}{R}$$

$$\underset{\sim}{B} = (a_1, a_2, \ldots, a_m) \circ \begin{pmatrix} r_{11} & r_{12} & \ldots & r_{1n} \\ r_{21} & r_{22} & & r_{2n} \\ \vdots & & \ddots & \vdots \\ r_{m1} & r_{m2} & \cdots & r_{mn} \end{pmatrix} = (b_1, b_2, \ldots, b_n)$$

where each $b_j = \bigvee_{i=1}^{m} (a_i \wedge r_{ij}), j = 1,2, \ldots, n$

3 Implementation Procedures

First, the morphological chart classification for the dumbbell storage rack is established, divided into three categories: panel design, side frame design, and additional functions. Then, ChatGPT is used to generate the morphological chart, followed by a focus group discussion to produce the final design outcomes.

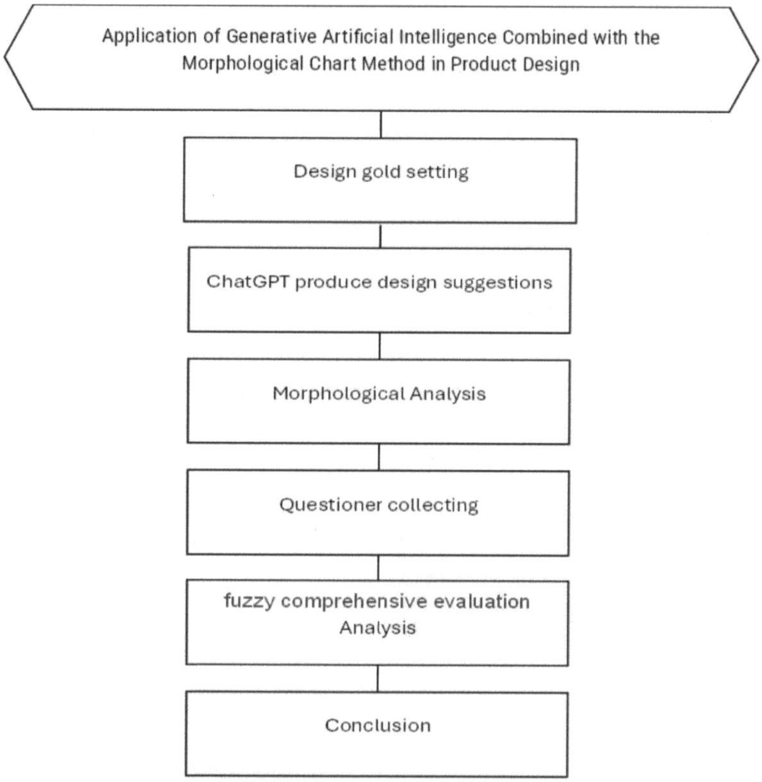

3.1 Application Process of ChatGPT

This study formulates a language template based on ChatGPT's linguistic characteristics to guide AI-assisted design, which can serve as a reference for readers. First, a set of multifunctional storage rack design images for commercial gyms is generated based on the following requirements: the design concept targets fitness professionals in large gyms (ages 18–60) and focuses on a three-tier dumbbell storage rack. The design emphasizes weight reduction through hollow structures and lightweight metal, space efficiency by minimizing footprint for easy storage and movement, ease of movement with ergonomic handles or mobility features, and ease of manufacturing using laser-cut metal and welding. The structural design incorporates polygonal frames, such as triangles, pentagons, and trapezoids for structural support, and streamlined elements to enhance modern aesthetics and stability. The material and appearance feature black powder-coated metal for durability and a modern look, using high-strength yet lightweight steel, with dimensions of approximately 120 cm wide and 90 cm high.

Based on these design requirements, 10 different geometric variations of the design are generated, ensuring each image includes: a triangle-based structure emphasizing stability and an industrial aesthetic, a pentagon-based structure creating a unique and modern design, a trapezoid-based structure showcasing a simple yet supportive design, a mixed polygonal structure (e.g., triangle + trapezoid) to enhance visual diversity and strength, and a combination of streamlined and polygonal elements offering an aesthetic and futuristic appeal. Each design image should feature distinct structural variations while maintaining feasibility for real-world production, ensuring users can clearly distinguish different design concepts. ChatGPT's outputs may vary based on language versions, prior training, or user-specific prompts. Designers should refine the language or generate additional variations to ensure that the morphological chart aligns better with practical needs.

3.2 Establishing the Morphological Chart

After ChatGPT generates the images, designers extract valuable reference elements and systematically organize them into the morphological chart. A focus group is then conducted to analyze and refine the designs, leading to the final optimized results. After selection by designers outcome below.

	bord	side	Other(X)
5			
9			

4 Results and Discussion

After evaluation by the design team, the selected results retain the panel design from option five and the side frame design from option nine. The panel design primarily adopts an iron mesh structure, while the side frame incorporates a hollow structure with a triangular shape. Additional functions were not adopted as they were deemed less suitable for practical use. Following further refinement of the structural design and layout by the designers, the final design images were generated for participant feedback through a survey.

4.1 Questionnaire Feedback

This study conducts a fuzzy comprehensive analysis based on user feedback regarding the originality and usability of the dumbbell storage rack.

	0Mismatch	2.5	0.5	0.75	1Match
This study demonstrates greater originality compared to competing products. ($\boldsymbol{X}_1$)	0.077	0.077	0.154	0.231	0.308
This study out come is user-friendly. ($\boldsymbol{X}_2$)	0.077	0.231	0.231	0.231	0.231

This study conducts a fuzzy comprehensive analysis based on user feedback regarding the originality and usability of the dumbbell storage rack.

1. Factor Set $U_1 = \{X_1, X_2\}$
2. Weight Set $\underset{\sim}{A}1 = \{0.6, 0.4\}$
3. Evaluation Set

$$V_1 = \{\text{Mismatch}\ ,\ \text{Slightly Mismatch}\ ,\ \text{Average}\ ,\ \text{Slightly Matches, Matches}\}$$

4. Single-Factor Fuzzy Evaluation

$$\underset{\sim}{R}(X_1) = \begin{pmatrix} 0.077\ 0.077\ 0.154\ 0.231\ 0.308 \end{pmatrix}$$

$$\underset{\sim}{R}(X_2) = \begin{pmatrix} 0.077\ 0.231\ 0.231\ 0.231\ 0.231 \end{pmatrix}$$

Thus, the single-factor evaluation matrix is obtained as:

$$\underset{\sim}{R} = \begin{pmatrix} 0.077\ 0.077\ 0.154\ 0.231\ 0.308 \\ 0.077\ 0.231\ 0.231\ 0.231\ 0.231 \end{pmatrix}$$

5. Fuzzy Comprehensive Evaluation

$$B = \underset{\sim}{A} \circ \underset{\sim}{R} = (0.60.4) \circ \begin{pmatrix} 0.077 & 0.077 & 0.154 & 0.231 & 0.308 \\ 0.077 & 0.231 & 0.231 & 0.231 & 0.231 \end{pmatrix}$$

$$= (0.077, 0.1386, 0.1848, 0.231, 0.2772)$$

The result after normalization is: (0.0847, 0.1525, 0.2034, 0.2542, 0.3051).

5 Conclusions

30.5% of the participants considered the study results to meet the criteria of originality and usability, while 25.4% found them to be somewhat aligned. This indicates that 55.9% of the participants held a positive attitude toward the study results. However, this outcome does not exhibit a high level of significance.

During the research process, it was also observed that when using ChatGPT's AI model to assist in product design, a common issue arises where many generated design possibilities are impractical for real-world implementation. As a result, multiple iterations are required, and designers must evaluate feasibility and select appropriate images. Therefore, for product design and industrial design, there is a need for AI models that better understand the product design and manufacturing process, or additional human intervention to ensure the development of more complete and practical products.

References

1. Zwicky, F.: Morphological astronomy. Observatory **68**, 121–143 (1948)
2. Tian, Q.M.: The result analysis of fuzzy comprehensive evaluation. J. Dalian Fish. Coll. **5**, 61–65 (1990)
3. Li, H., Wu, Q., Xing, B., Wang, W.: Exploration of the intelligent-auxiliary design of architectural space using artificial intelligence model. PLoS ONE **18**(3), e0282158 (2023)
4. Tang, S.-C. (2024). Generative artificial intelligence, newsroom automation, and the changing landscape of journalism. Culture: Policy, Management, and Innovation, 3(1), 9–27
5. Li, Y.: [Retracted] intelligent environmental art design combining big data and artificial intelligence. Complexity **2021**(1), 1606262 (2021)
6. Wu, F., Hsiao, S.W., Lu, P.: An AIGC-empowered methodology to product color matching design. Displays **81**, 102623 (2024)
7. Lu, P., Hsiao, S.W., Wu, F.: A product shape design and evaluation model based on morphology preference and macroscopic shape information. Entropy **23**(6), 639 (2021)

Using Design Thinking in Alternate Reality Games to Explore Rural Experience Design

Jui-Hsiang Lee[1](✉) and Chien-Yao Wang[2]

[1] Department of Digital Multimedia Design, China University of Technology, Taipei, Taiwan
leockmail@gmail.com

[2] Department and Graduate Institute of Visual Communication Design, China University of Technology, Taipei, Taiwan

Abstract. This study investigates the integration of Design Thinking within Alternate Reality Game (ARG) research to explore and enhance the design of rural experiences within the context of place-based education. Recognizing the potential of ARGs to foster engagement and understanding of local contexts, and addressing challenges in their development and implementation, this research proposes a five-step Design Thinking framework (Empathize, Define, Ideate, Prototype, Test) as a theoretical and practical approach for ARG development in rural settings. A case study was conducted in the Shibachongxi riverside community in Shiding District, New Taipei City, Taiwan, involving teachers, and local cultural workers. Focus group discussions and a mixed-methods approach, including qualitative feedback and quantitative questionnaire analysis (Cronbach's Alpha = 0.928), were employed to evaluate the feasibility and educational potential of this framework. Preliminary findings indicate that the integration of Design Thinking and ARG effectively promoted cognitive learning outcomes and enhanced learning motivation and attitude change towards local culture. The study also highlighted areas for improvement in user interface design and the integration of historical content. The study concludes by emphasizing the potential of this integrated approach to create innovative and participatory learning experiences in place-based education and provides recommendations for future ARG design in rural contexts.

Keywords: Alternate Reality Game (ARG) · Design Thinking · Place-Based Education · Rural Experience · Educational Innovation · Game-Based Learning

1 Introduction

A fundamental challenge in contemporary higher education lies in effectively guiding students to acquire practical and applicable knowledge, thereby enabling them to demonstrate autonomy, responsibility, and critical thinking in authentic real-world scenarios (Ferreras, Pineda, & Hunt 2020). In response to this imperative, educators are increasingly exploring innovative and alternative pedagogical approaches to empower students as active citizens who can contribute meaningfully to social progress and ecological sustainability (Santisteban 2019). Achieving this necessitates grounding teaching and learning within genuine community contexts, fostering a vision of education that actively engages in a dialogue with the specific characteristics of a place (Tu 2021).

C. Stephanidis et al. (Eds.): HCII 2025, CCIS 2773, pp. 65–72, 2026.
https://doi.org/10.1007/978-3-032-12773-0_7

In recent years, Alternate Reality Games (ARGs), characterized by their immersive gameplay interwoven with real-world environments, have emerged as a promising tool for community cultural exploration and place-based education. ARGs leverage engaging, gamified mechanisms to facilitate participants' understanding of local history and cultural nuances through interactive puzzle-solving and collaborative engagement. For instance, research has highlighted the efficacy of ARGs, through carefully structured learning designs, in enhancing students' comprehension and appreciation of historical and cultural heritage (Lin, Lu, & Lu 2024). Furthermore, ARGs possess the unique ability to expand the learning landscape, adding both depth and heightened engagement to real-world exploration (Lee & Wang 2024).

Despite the acknowledged potential of ARGs in educational settings, their practical implementation is not without significant hurdles. The development of ARGs often demands considerable resources and can be constrained by logistical and financial limitations (Delaney 2022; Blomé 2025; Poplin 2013). Moreover, the inherent complexity of ARG systems can restrict their adaptability across diverse learning contexts (Koivisto & Hamari 2019). While gamification aims to boost motivation, an over-reliance on extrinsic rewards may paradoxically diminish learners' intrinsic drive (Kohn 1999) and could even elicit resistance or discomfort due to perceived manipulation (Thiel & Fröhlich 2017). Gamification has also been applied across multiple domains, including sports and professional training, workflow optimization, education, and entertainment products (Deterding, Dixon, Khaled, & Nacke, 2011). Extending this perspective, Huotari and Hamari conceptualize gamification as the enhancement of services with gameful experiences for value creation, emphasizing its experiential nature and service marketing context (Huotari & Hamari, 2016). In higher education, empirical research has further shown that well-designed gamified online learning environments can strengthen students' motivation and engagement, although outcomes remain sensitive to contextual and design factors (Torrado & Díaz Lage, 2022).

Although numerous ARG examples demonstrate their capacity to enhance players' motivation for real-world exploration, a critical challenge persists in effectively balancing the design of local experiences with the transmission of cultural knowledge. Questions remain regarding how newcomers can rapidly immerse themselves in a place's context and how to avoid superficial or commercialized portrayals of local culture within the gameplay (Hamari & Koivisto 2015). Recognizing the potential of ARGs for rural revitalization and cultural learning within place-based education, this study addresses the existing gap in systematic research concerning the specific design elements and practical strategies for their effective implementation in such contexts. In response to the core tenets of place-based education—emphasizing the grounding of learning in local culture, natural environments, and social contexts (Sobel 2004)—this research proposes the application of the five-step model of Design Thinking as both a theoretical and a practical framework for the development of ARGs tailored for rural educational settings. Design Thinking, with its emphasis on human-centered, iterative innovation, is particularly well-suited for student-centered learning design in educational contexts (Razzouk & Shute 2012).

2 Literature Review

2.1 The Concept and Development of Place-Based Education

Place-based education emphasizes the connection between learning and place. It cultivates students' understanding and identification with their living environment through local knowledge, community resources, and cultural context. According to Gruenewald's (2003) theory of Place-based Education (PBE), education should not be detached from the geographical and social contexts of learners. Instead, it should function as a practical tool that responds to local needs and promotes sustainable development. This perspective suggests that learning environments extend beyond classrooms into neighborhoods, fields, and local communities.

In Taiwan, the promotion of the 12-Year Basic Education policy and curriculum guidelines has gradually emphasized localization and real-life relevance in education. Many schools integrate local culture, industry, and ecology into thematic teaching and project-based learning, aiming to increase students' motivation and sense of participation in their communities. The development of place-based education serves as a counter-response to standardized, decontextualized school education by encouraging teaching content and experiences that are closely tied to everyday life. This approach guides students to develop a sense of place and responsibility.

2.2 Integrating Place-Based Education with Innovative Pedagogies: The Potential of Design Thinking and ARGs

The Application of Design Thinking in Education. Originating from the field of design, Design Thinking emphasizes a user-centered approach characterized by empathy, interdisciplinary collaboration, prototyping, and iterative processes. Brown (2009) argues that design thinking is not only a method for solving problems but also a way to cultivate innovative thinking. In educational contexts, design thinking is increasingly being adopted to promote active learning and creative problem-solving. It is especially suited to interdisciplinary learning, project-based inquiry, and simulations of real-world scenarios.

Integrating design thinking into place-based education can help teachers and students collaboratively explore local issues, define problems, conduct research, and co-create solutions. This design-driven learning model empowers students to become not just observers of their community but potential change agents who take part in local transformation.

The Educational Potential of ARGs (Alternate Reality Games). Alternate Reality Games (ARGs) are a form of game that blends physical and digital worlds through cross-media storytelling. Participants advance the narrative by solving puzzles, searching for clues, and working collaboratively (McGonigal 2011). ARGs emphasize realism and participatory storytelling, blurring the boundaries between games and reality, allowing players to engage as themselves in the experience.

In educational settings, ARGs are seen as innovative tools that offer high levels of immersion and learner motivation. Research has shown that ARGs can enhance learners' engagement, problem-solving abilities, and critical thinking (Dede 2009). As a narrative-driven learning strategy, ARGs facilitate multisensory and multi-path knowledge construction. Their cross-platform, story-based, and collaborative features are particularly suitable for simulating complex scenarios or exploring local issues, inspiring students to understand and engage with place from multiple perspectives.

2.3 ARGs as a Catalyst for Innovation in Place-Based Education

Both design thinking and ARGs emphasize participant agency, realistic contexts, and problem-based learning processes—aligning with the core principles of place-based education. Integrating ARGs into place-based education enhances learners' immersion in and perception of their environment. Through game-based design and narrative structures, local knowledge can be presented in concrete and engaging ways.

Furthermore, ARGs can serve as a bridge connecting local memories, community roles, and environmental issues. As students assume roles and complete tasks, they engage in field exploration, interview residents, and interpret the cultural context of the place. This helps construct a deeper sense of identity—answering questions like "Who am I?" and "Where am I?" Through such learning experiences, place-based education becomes not just the transmission of knowledge but the creation and transformation of place-based experiences.

3 Research Methodology

3.1 Research Framework and Participants

This study adopts **Design Thinking** as the core framework for research and development. Following the five-stage model proposed by Stanford d.school (Plattner, Meinel, & Leifer 2010), the study develops and implements a curriculum that integrates the concepts of place-based education and alternate reality games (ARGs). Design Thinking emphasizes human-centeredness, iterative innovation, and cross-disciplinary collaboration, making it particularly suitable for educational innovation and the development of teaching tools.

The research was conducted in the Shibachongxi riverside community in Shiding District of New Taipei City. This rural area is rich in natural landscapes and local cultural resources, offering strong potential for place-based educational practices. The research subjects included teachers from local primary schools as well as cultural workers actively involved in preserving and promoting local cultural heritage. The project aimed to create an experiential learning environment that combines education with entertainment and features games through cross-border collaboration.

3.2 Research Procedure

The research followed the five stages of the Design Thinking process, with specific operations detailed as follows:

Empathize – Exploring Local Needs and Cultural Contexts. The study began with qualitative data collection, primarily through semi-structured interviews with local stakeholders such as: Ye XX (a returning youth), local volunteers, ecological tour guides, students, and parents. Field observations were also undertaken by participating in community activities, documenting cultural contexts, spatial characteristics, and patterns of human-place interaction. Key insights: Students' lack of awareness about Shiding's history and ecology; fading community culture; youth outmigration. Fireflies as metaphors for illuminating the mountain town—evoking imagery of return and guardianship. "Roads can take people away, but they can also bring urbanites back home."

Define – Focusing Learning Goals and Design Challenges. Data from the empathize stage were synthesized to identify learners' needs and key educational pain points. The central design challenge was extracted: "How can we use a game to help players understand Shiding's local culture and ecological resources, and inspire a sense of action to protect their hometown?" Learning objectives: Understand Shiding's historical landscapes and cultural transformations. Learn about mushroom ecology and environmental conservation concepts. Experience the agency and values of returning youth.

Ideate – Co-creating Game Scenarios and Learning Tasks. Through creative ideation and collaborative design, a series of design workshops were held with teachers, students, and local cultural workers. Techniques such as brainstorming, scenario mapping, and task design were used to generate the initial game framework and content components. These included the main storyline, task formats, character roles, and route planning. The game was designed around three axes: map navigation, narrative puzzle-solving, and challenge-based tasks, resulting in the following elements: immersive learning tasks, gamified mechanisms rooted in local sites, and a story-driven structure incorporating ecological and cultural themes.

Prototype – Developing a Preliminary Game Model. Based on the outcomes of the ideation stage, a low-fidelity prototype was created. This included: Paper-based game flowcharts. Story scripts. Scene layout sketches. Interactive task designs. A basic website platform was also developed to guide the gameplay and serve as an interactive interface for testing and feedback. Narrative Setup: The protagonist returns to their hometown to recover from illness. While tidying up the old family house, they discover an ancient medicine pouch, triggering memories of their grandfather and a realization of how little they know about him and the bygone era. Seeking answers, the protagonist turns to the internet to uncover the truth. Physical task cards and a local color swatch tool ("place-based color cards") allowed students to record observations in real time. Each location featured a "task card prototype" and a "story fragment prototype".

Test – Conducting Implementation Tests and Iterative Optimization. The game was tested in collaboration with teachers and community members. A focus group of 15 participants—including local elementary school teachers and community residents—was invited to take part in the test session. During the small-scale implementation: Participants completed feedback forms regarding their experience. Researchers observed engagement levels and comprehension. Interviews were conducted with community residents to assess their sense of identification with the game scenarios and local interpretations.

4 Research Findings

This study adopted a mixed-methods approach that integrates both qualitative and quantitative techniques to comprehensively assess the effectiveness of the game design and implementation of learning activities.

4.1 Preliminary Thematic Summary of Qualitative Data

Based on participant feedback, preliminary open coding and thematic categorization were conducted. The following themes and representative quotations were identified and are used for further analysis in subsequent sections of the paper:

Positive Affirmation and Emotional Connection-The integration of game design and local culture received high recognition. *A4: "An intellectual journey, filled with valuable insights." A5: "A well-curated tour, sincerely commendable." A10: "Thoughtfully designed—truly admirable." A7: "Extremely thoughtful; it definitely benefits local development." A11: "Appreciation for the farm's commitment to environmental conservation and community development." A12: "Nutritious and delicious meals, fun and intellectually stimulating games—truly rewarding."*

Content Suggestions and Future Development-Recommendations to enhance the ecological features of the farm and further utilize local resources. *A13: "The farm's ecological environment is excellent, and the lingzhi industry could be further highlighted..." A8: "Consider collecting more historical and cultural materials and producing infographic posters..." A14: "Offer educational travel courses during holidays targeting preschool and elementary school groups."*

Interface and Usability Adjustments-Suggestions to adapt the interface for different age groups. *A6: "The game is fun, but the font is too small." A9: "For older participants, I recommend enlarging the font." A16: "The intention is great—simplifying the game would make it more accessible to visitors." A15: "Game instructions could be customized for different age groups."*

Optimization of Spatial Design and Environmental Setup-Suggestions to improve space layout and guided experiences. A15 (continued): "Enhance the farm's thematic decorations and signage along the tour path." "Install interpretive signs for plant species." "Add interactive art installations for social media promotion." "Introduce DIY projects to create memorable experiences."

4.2 Quantitative Data Analysis

Questionnaire data were primarily analyzed using descriptive statistics to assess their perceptions and evaluations across various dimensions, including learning content, game enjoyment, understanding of local culture, and changes in learning motivation and attitudes. Quantitative data served to supplement qualitative findings and enhance the overall validity and reliability of the study. The 15 questionnaire items yielded a Cronbach's alpha $= 0.928$ (> 0.7), indicating high reliability. Each item showed a p-value of less than 0.05, demonstrating statistical significance.

Based on the quantitative results, the 15 items were grouped into three analytical categories: Cognitive Learning Outcomes, User Experience and Usability, and Learning Motivation and Attitude Change. These were used to evaluate the overall effectiveness of the game. Cognitive Learning Outcomes (Items 1–6): All six items exceeded an average score of 4.25, suggesting that the game was effective in knowledge transfer. Content related to Lingzhi and the farm showed the strongest results, while items related to historical knowledge showed more room for improvement. User Experience and Usability (Items 7–9): Interface design and user interaction emerged as the main areas needing improvement. Although overall clarity was adequate, the high standard deviations indicate a wide range of user experiences, likely influenced by age or digital literacy. Learning Motivation and Attitude Change (Items 10–15): The location-based game effectively enhanced learning motivation and awareness of cultural values. Participants demonstrated a significant willingness to explore and respect local and rural cultures, indicating a meaningful shift in attitudes and affective engagement.

5 Conclusion and Recommendations

In conclusion, the integration of place-based education with Design Thinking and ARGs demonstrably promises more innovative and deeply engaging learning experiences. This study illuminates their powerful synergy, offering practical strategies focused on participant experience and immersive storytelling within local contexts. By providing a concrete framework centered on iterative design, this study successfully integrated local culture, history, and natural features into gameplay. Regarding knowledge transfer, the game could further enhance interaction depth concerning historical and mining content. Most participants reported gaining intellectual and cultural insights, and their local development interest increased. Regarding interface usability, older participants desired adjustable font sizes and simpler operation, suggesting more real-world instructional prompts for elder navigation—an important design consideration given real-world distractions affecting user experience. Consequently, we advocate for wider adoption of this integrated framework to revolutionize place-based education and forge stronger learner-community connections.

References

Barab, S., Gresalfi, M., Ingram-Goble, A.: Transformational play: using games to position person, content, and context. Educ. Res. **39**(7), 525–536 (2010). https://doi.org/10.3102/0013189X10386593

Blomé, O.: Gameful participation: the use of gamification in citizen participation within the public space planning process. Second cycle, A2E. Alnarp: SLU, Dept. of Landscape Architecture, Planning and Management (from 130101) (2025)

Brown, T.: Change by Design: How Design Thinking Creates New Alternatives for Business and Society. Harvard Business Press (2009)

Dede, C.: Immersive interfaces for engagement and learning. Science **323**, 66–69 (2009). https://doi.org/10.1126/science.1167311

Delaney, J.: Minecraft and playful public participation in urban design. Urban Plan. **7**(2), 330–342 (2022). https://doi.org/10.17645/up.v7i2.5229

Deterding, S., Dixon, D., Khaled, R., Nacke, L.: From game design elements to gamefulness: defining "gamification". In: Proceedings of the 15th International Academic MindTrek Conference: Envisioning Future Media Environments, pp. 9–15. ACM (2011)

Ferreras, M., Pineda, J.A., Hunt, C.I.: Heritage education as a tool for creating critical citizens: analysis of conceptions of teachers in training. In: Delgado-Algarra, E.J., Cuenca, J.M. (eds.) Handbook of Research on Citizenship and Heritage Education, pp. 199–218. IGI Global, London (2020)

Gruenewald, D.A.: The best of both worlds: a critical pedagogy of place. Educ. Res. **32**(4), 3–12 (2003). https://doi.org/10.3102/0013189X032004003

Huotari, K., Hamari, J.: A definition for gamification: anchoring gamification in the service marketing literature. Electron. Mark. **27**(1), 21–31 (2016). https://doi.org/10.1007/s12525-015-0212-z

Hamari, J., Koivisto, J.: Why do people use gamification services? Int. J. Inf. Manag. **35**, 419–431 (2015). https://doi.org/10.1016/j.ijinfomgt.2015.04.006

Kohn, A.: Punished by Rewards: The Trouble with Gold Stars, Incentive Plans, A's, Praise, and Other Bribes. Houghton Mifflin (1999)

Koivisto, J., Hamari, J.: The rise of motivational information systems: a review of gamification research. Int. J. Inf. Manag. **45**, 191–210 (2019)

Lin, H.-C.K., Lu, L.-W., Lu, R.-S.: Integrating digital technologies and alternate reality games for sustainable education: enhancing cultural heritage awareness and learning engagement. Sustainability **16**, 9451 (2024). https://doi.org/10.3390/su16219451

Lee, J.H., Wang, C.Y.: Applying alternate reality games to strengthen place-based recreation: a rural village case study. In: 2024 The Information Technology and Application Conference Proceedings, Taipei, Taiwan, 11 April 2024, pp. 118–126. Publisher: China University of Technology (2024)

McGonigal, J.: Reality Is Broken: Why Games Make Us Better and How They Can Change the World. Penguin, London (2011)

Plattner, H., Meinel, C., Leifer, L.: Design Thinking: Understand – Improve – Apply. Springer, Heidelberg (2010). https://doi.org/10.1007/978-3-642-13757-0

Poplin, A.: Digital serious game for urban planning "B3 - design your marketplace!" Environ. Plan. B Urban Anal. City Sci. **40**, 1–19 (2013). https://doi.org/10.1068/b39032

Razzouk, R., Shute, V.: What is design thinking and why is it important? Rev. Educ. Res. **82**(3), 330–348 (2012). https://doi.org/10.3102/0034654312457429

Santisteban, A.L.: Enseñanza de las ciencias sociales a partir de problemas sociales o temas controvertidos: Estado de la cuestión y resultados de una investigación. El Futuro Del Pasado **10**, 57–79 (2019)

Sobel, D.: Place-Based Education: Connecting Classrooms & Communities. Orion Society (2004)

Torrado, M., Maria Diaz Lage, J.: Gamification, online learning and motivation: a quantitative and qualitative analysis in higher education. Contemp. Educ. Technol. **14**(4), 1–18 (2022)

Tu, M.-F.: Becoming a service designer: pedagogic practices in adopting design thinking for developing alternate reality game in place. J. Teach. Pract. Res. High. Educ. **5**(2), 1–32. https://doi.org/10.6870/JTPRHE.202112_5(2).0001

Thiel, S.-K., Fröhlich, P.: Gamification as motivation to engage in location-based public participation? In: G. Gartner & H. Huang (Eds.), Progress in Location-Based Services 2016, Lecture Notes in Geoinformation and Cartography, pp. 399–421. Cham: Springer International Publishing (2017)

When Ideas Meet AI: Exploring Human-AI Interactions of Design Students Through the Lens of TAM and HCAI

Haleema Mujeeb, Zeynep G. Karapars(✉), and Atanur Andiç(✉)

Özyegin University, İstanbul 34794, Turkey
haleemamujeeb22@gmail.com, {zeynep.karapars,atanur.andic}@ozyegin.edu.tr

Abstract. This work-in-progress study examines how undergraduate design students interact with AI-powered large language models (LLMs) such as ChatGPT and Gemini during the design process. Using a mixed-methods approach grounded in Technology Acceptance Model, Human Centred AI framework, and Emotional Design theory, we combined surveys (n = 51) with semi-structured interviews. Findings show that while students find LLMs useful and easy to use, their experiences involve ethical concerns, emotional motivations, and creative tensions. Students used LLMs not just for ideation, but also as collaborators and cognitive supports. Some expressed discomfort with originality, memory limitations, or ideological values of LLM providers. These insights highlight the need for more adaptive, emotionally aware AI tools in education. Data collection is ongoing, with additional interviews planned.

Keywords: Large Language Models (LLMs) · Human-AI Interaction (HAI) · Design Education · Technology Acceptance Model (TAM) · UX

1 Introduction

LLMs such as ChatGPT, Gemini, and Deepseek are reshaping how we engage with digital tools, offering unprecedented accessibility and versatility across all domains [3,10].

In design education, AI tools are beginning to influence how students conceptualize, iterate, and reflect—especially during open-ended, creative tasks [1,6,8,21,24]. Yet most existing studies emphasize visual tools or advanced users, leaving a critical gap in our understanding of how design students engage with text-based LLMs during their formative learning experiences [7].

2 Literature Review

The intersection of AI and design has become an important area of inquiry following the rise of LLMs such as ChatGPT [11]. A review by Ge and Fan (2024)

C. Stephanidis et al. (Eds.): HCII 2025, CCIS 2773, pp. 73–85, 2026.
https://doi.org/10.1007/978-3-032-12773-0_8

identified a clear shift toward exploring how these models integrate into design programs [7]. LLMs are becoming essential parts of creative workflows, shaping how students and professionals ideate, reflect, and iterate across design stages [14,18,25]. They have been shown to scaffold ideation [14,18], support reflective thinking [25], function as collaborative partners during conceptual development [4,21], and enhance creativity, personalization and learning outcomes more broadly [8,15]. These text-based LLMs introduced a more conversational and reflective engagement, prompting students to brainstorm, critique, and refine ideas in real-time [2,12].

However, the unpredictable nature of AI systems complicates their role in traditional design workflows such as sketching, prototyping, and user testing [23]. New design approaches are needed that prioritize transparency, user control, and system reliability [19,22]. Frameworks like ISO 9241-210 and Norman's Emotional Design Theory are already being studied to account for emerging concerns in AI-mediated processes [16,20] and people are integrating different versions of TAM scale to evaluate PEOU Aand PU of ChatGPT among students [9,13].

Technology Acceptance Model. The TAM scale was developed by Fred D Davis in 1989. It explains users' acceptance of technology based on two key factors: Perceived Usefulness and Perceived Ease of Use [5]. It is particularly suitable here as it helps assess whether design students find AI-powered LLMs valuable and easy to integrate into their creative workflows. Using TAM will provide a structured way to screen participants based on their actual engagement and attitudes toward LLM tools before deeper qualitative exploration.

Human Centered AI Framework. Human-Centered AI (HCAI) is a framework proposed by Ben Shneiderman to guide the design of AI systems that empower users, support human agency, and promote trust, accountability, and ethical use. Shneiderman's goal was to shift AI development away from full automation toward systems that augment human capabilities while respecting core human values like control, fairness, and transparency [19]. We chose the HCAI framework because it helps us examine whether AI-powered LLMs support users' agency, trust, and ethical concerns during creative tasks. It's especially relevant to our study, as we're exploring how design students interact with these tools in ways that go beyond just functionality.

Norman's Emotional Design Theory. Norman's emotional design theory is used to capture the emotional aspects of user experience of students [17] We included Norman's Emotional Design framework to understand what design students experience when interacting with AI-powered LLMs—beyond just how well the tools work. Norman's three layers of emotional design—visceral, behavioral, and reflective—describe how users respond to products: instinctively-visceral, through usability and function- behavioral, and through meaning and personal value- reflective. These are especially important in creative contexts where emotion and engagement play an important role.

To the best of our knowledge, very few studies have examined how undergraduate design students use and interact with text-based LLMs throughout the entire design process. There is also limited data on design students perceived ease of use and perceived usefulness for LLMs. To address this empirical gap, our study adopts a mixed-methods approach. We wanted to study and understand the UX of LLMs for design students by combining TAM scale, HCAI Framework and Norman's Emotional design Framework. Together, the 2 theoretical frameworks and 1 model form a multidimensional lens which can help us to understand not just how and why design students use LLMs, but also how these tools can be ethically and emotionally optimized for better UX and thus giving valuable insights into Designer-LLM interactions. After in depth analysis and observation, the following research questions were drafted to capture insights in user experience.

- RQ1: How do design students interact with AI-powered LLM chat bots during the design process?
- RQ2: What are the pain points experienced by students while using LLM chat bots?
- RQ3: What improvements do students recommend for enhancing LLM UX in design education?

3 Methodology

This study employs a mixed-methods approach. The methodology integrates both quantitative and qualitative data to provide a comprehensive understanding of user acceptance and experience of design students with LLMs. The survey was used as a screening tool grounded in TAM constructs (usefulness and ease of use) to identify participants with varying engagement levels with LLMs. Emotional and ethical dimensions were intentionally reserved for the in-depth interviews to allow for richer and more contextual insights.

Early observations from our data suggested that student interaction with LLMs extended well beyond ideation into entire design thinking process. As a result, we expanded the study's scope to encompass the entire design process. This shift allowed for a more holistic and contextually relevant understanding of LLMs' evolving role in creative education.

3.1 Research Context and Sampling Strategy

Students from the undergraduate Communication Design program at Ozyegin University were selected as a focused case for participant sampling. This choice was made to ensure contextual relevance, as Communication Design students regularly engage in ideation, iteration, and digital tool use within project-based studio courses, making them especially suited to exploring interactions with LLMs.

3.2 Ethical Considerations

All participants were briefed on their rights, including voluntary participation and the option to withdraw at any time. All data was anonymized and stored securely. Ethical approval for the study was obtained from Ozyegin's University Research Ethics Committee, ensuring adherence to academic and participant welfare standards.

3.3 Quantitative Phase: Survey Instrument

A structured online survey was distributed using Google Forms. The survey was divided into three sections:

Demographic and Consent Information: Participants indicated their academic year, major, and if they were willing to participate in follow-up interviews. Explicit consent was obtained for academic research purposes, with clear assurances of anonymity and confidentiality.

LLM Usage Patterns: This section captured how students engage with LLM during different stages of the design process, including frequency of use, preferred tools and task types (e.g., ideation, development, refinement, presentation).

Acceptance Measures Based on TAM: Questions measured Perceived Usefulness (PU) and Perceived Ease of Use (PEOU), adapted from Davis (1989) and contextualized for creative design tasks. A target sample of 50–80 students was set. As of submission, 51 valid responses had been collected and analyzed.

3.4 Qualitative Phase: Semi-structured Interviews

Interviews were conducted online via zoom and recorded with participant permission. As of this writing, four interviews have been completed, with a planned range of 10–15 interviews. Open-ended interview questions were designed to align with TAM constructs and supplemented by HCI and UX concerns—such as adaptability, trust, and user control as well as emotional experience aspects. The semi-structured interviews explored areas like:

- *How students decide to use LLMs*
- *Challenges and limitations encountered*
- *Emotional and cognitive reactions during interaction*
- *Recommendations for future AI design assistants*

4 Results

4.1 Survey

A total of n = 51 students participated. Students responded to each item using a 7-point Likert scale (1 = Strongly Disagree, 7 = Strongly Agree). Mean values and standard deviations were calculated to evaluate overall trends. High average scores in both PU and PEOU confirm student acceptance of LLMs. Students found LLMs helpful for brainstorming, copywriting, and conceptual development. The study showed that 90% of students are using LLMs for design tasks showed in Fig. 1 and Fig. 2. 98% of them are using Chat GPT, Leaving Gemini and Deep seek as secondary options- Fig. 3. When asked when they turn to LLM usage during a task, majority agreed that they start using it during the ideation phase, as Fig. 4 shows. However it is important to note that in depth interviews showed their consistent use of LLMs throughout the process.

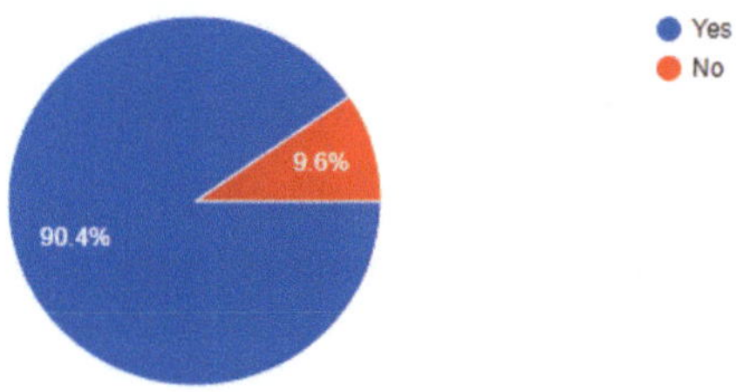

Fig. 1. Students response when asked if they have used LLM for design tasks.

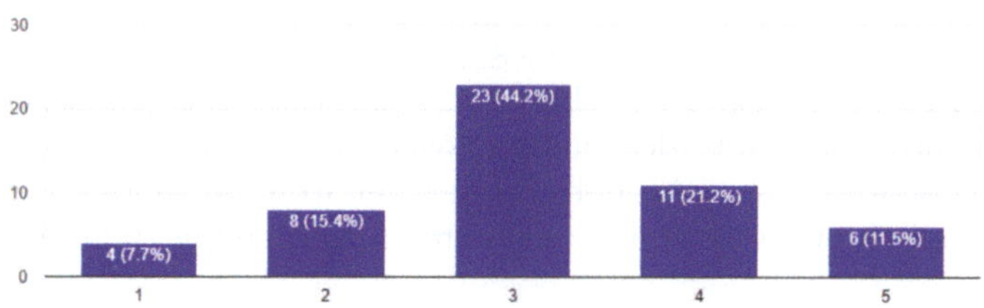

Fig. 2. students response to how frequently they used LLM for design tasks, with 1 being never and 5 being always

Perceived Usefulness (PU). This construct evaluated how much students believed LLMs improved their design performance, productivity, and task effectiveness. As shown in Table 1, the students perceived LLMs generally useful.

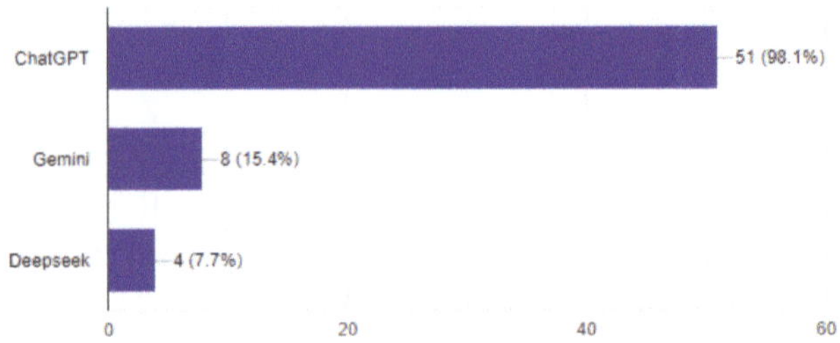

Fig. 3. LLMs mostly used by students

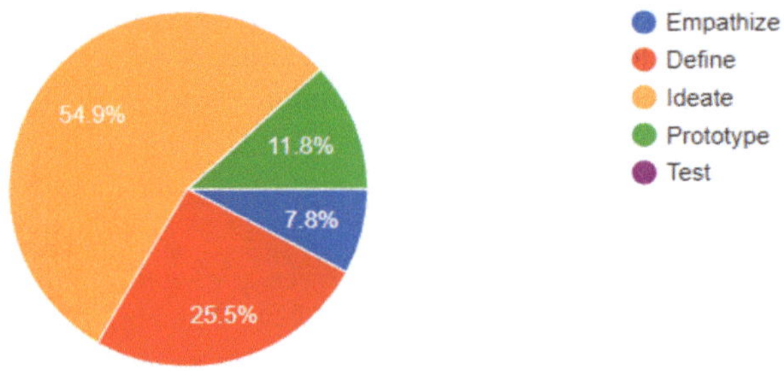

Fig. 4. Pie chart showing when students typically turn to LLMs during the design process

Interpretation: The Perceived Usefulness (PU) results indicate that design students generally find AI-powered LLMs beneficial in improving their design performance, productivity, and task effectiveness. With mean scores above 4.3 on all PU items, students perceive these tools as making design work easier and faster, which aligns strongly with the Technology Acceptance Model (TAM). According to TAM, higher perceived usefulness is a key predictor of users' intention to adopt and continue using a technology, suggesting that LLMs have strong potential for integration into design workflows.

These PU scores reflect the behavioral layer from Norman's theory, focusing on how well the LLMs support users' tasks by making them easier, useful,

Table 1. Perceived Usefulness (PU)—Descriptive Statistical Analysis

PU Item	Mean	Std. Dev.
Overall easier design work	4.84	1.59
Useful for design process/tasks	4.96	1.59
Quick task accomplishment	4.71	1.54
Enhanced effectiveness on job	4.67	1.48
Increased productivity	4.51	1.50
Improved task performance	4.39	1.47

efficient, effective etc. We can say that the students' perceptions of usefulness likely contribute to a more emotionally engaging experience with the AI tools, enhancing overall user acceptance.

In the light of Shneiderman's framework, the students' belief that LLMs increase productivity and effectiveness supports the notion that these tools enhance human performance rather than replace it. However, while PU questions captured functional benefits, and further research was needed to explore other HCAI aspects like trust and ethical considerations.

4.2 Perceived Ease of Use (PEOU)

This construct assessed how intuitive, accessible, and learnable students found LLMs when used in design workflows. As shown in Table 2, students percieved LLMs generally ease to use.

Table 2: Perceived Ease of Use (PEOU)—Descriptive Statistics

Table 2. Perceived Ease of Use (PEOU)—Descriptive Statistical Analysis

PEOU Item	Mean	Std. Dev.
Easy to use	5.29	1.62
Clear and understandable interaction	5.04	1.48
Easy to learn operating	4.98	1.58
Flexible interaction	4.80	1.63
Ease of Mastery in LLMs for design	4.71	1.75
Output Alignment	4.61	1.74

Interpretation: The data suggests that design students generally find AI-powered LLM chatbots easy to use and learn. The highest mean score (5.29) on "Easy to use" indicates strong user perception of accessibility, while scores on "Clear and understandable interaction" and "Flexibility" reinforce this positive usability impression. TAM posits that such perceptions of low effort significantly enhance users' willingness to adopt and continue using technology, implying that ease of use is a key facilitator for integrating LLMs into design workflows.

These PEOU items correspond closely to the behavioral layer of Norman's Emotional Design framework, which emphasizes effective and efficient usability. Clear and flexible interactions reduce user frustration and cognitive strain, leading to smoother task completion. The confidence gained through ease of mastery also relates to Norman's reflective layer, where users form positive emotional connections based on successful experiences. It was important to note that relatively lower score for "Output alignment" suggests some mismatch between user expectations and LLM responses, highlighting an area that could disrupt emotional satisfaction and trust.

These quantitative insights provide a foundation for interpreting the richer, more nuanced findings that emerged from the qualitative interviews in the following section.

4.3 Qualitative Analysis

Semi-structured interviews explored how students used LLMs during design thinking process. Themes were analyzed using Braun and Clarke's (2006) approach. Braun and Clarke's Thematic Analysis is used to identify and interpret patterns or themes within data. It involves familiarizing with the data, coding it, grouping codes into themes, reviewing and refining those themes, and then reporting them. It's flexible and well-suited for exploring user experiences and perceptions. A total of 4 participants have been interviewed as of yet and we are still in process. The interviewees will be referred as Participant 1, Participant 2 and so on in the following section. This section presents a thematic analysis of four semi-structured interviews with Communication Design students.

The analysis followed a theoretical thematic framework, drawing from the Technology Acceptance Model (TAM), Shneiderman's Human-Centered AI (HCAI), and Norman's Emotional Design Theory, while remaining open to emergent, participant-driven insights. Analyzing qualitative data with survey responses revealed how these students relate to large language models (LLMs) not just functionally, but emotionally, ethically, and reflectively.

Theme 1: LLMs Help Start Ideas Faster. All participants reported using LLMs to initiate their creative process. They described the tools as useful for breaking creative blocks, generating prompts, and organizing ideas in early stages. One participant shared, "I mostly use ChatGPT when I don't know where to start. It gives me something to build on." Another mentioned, "It helps bring my ideas together when I'm too tired to think clearly."

This theme supports TAM's Perceived Usefulness (PU): students feel these tools genuinely improve their efficiency. It also shows alignment with HCAI, as students retain control over where and how to use the AI in their workflow.

Theme 2: Ethical Concerns and Creative Identity. A significant tension appeared around ethics and originality. One participant voiced discomfort with other students using AI to submit unedited work: "It's unfair when someone just pastes a ChatGPT answer and we're graded the same." Another participant said, "I don't like using ChatGPT because of Sam Altman and what he stands for. I prefer Gemini—Google feels safer to me."

These responses reflect HCAI's concerns about trust, agency, and value alignment, and highlight gaps in TAM, which does not account for ideological or ethical factors in tool adoption. They also connect to Norman's reflective layer, where users evaluate how technologies shape their self-image and principles.

Theme 3: Easy to Start, But Not Always Easy to Use. Participants rated LLMs highly on learnability in the survey, and interviews supported this. However, they revealed that meaningful output often required careful prompting. "You need to know how to ask. It took me time to figure out how to get exactly what I want," one participant explained. It was also reported that getting useful and specific results often required a lot of effort and multiple prompt adjustments.

This supports TAM's Perceived Ease of Use (PEOU) only partially. While starting is easy, using LLMs well for design requires skill and effort in prompting, which was not covered in the TAM scale questions.

Theme 4: Emotional and Motivational Support. Several participants described LLMs as emotionally supportive. LLMs were not just seen as tools, but also as motivators and companions during stressful tasks. One student said, "Sometimes I just type to it like it's my bestie. It hypes me up when I'm stuck." Another appreciated that Gemini felt more casual and "less robotic" when speaking aloud.

This aligns with Norman's emotional design theory. Students aren't just using AI for tasks—they're forming affective relationships with it. These emotional experiences are not addressed by TAM but are crucial for design education.

Theme 5: Desire for Personalized and Memory-Based AI. All participants desired better personalization and continuity. One noted, "I wish it remembered my past projects, like a creative partner." Another said, "I'm using Cursor now—it lets me switch models without losing what I'm working on."

This theme supports HCAI's call for user-aligned, memory-aware AI, and touches on Norman's reflective level, where users want tools that grow with them and support their personal identity and workflow.

5 Discussion

While the survey confirmed students found LLMs useful and easy to adopt, the interviews revealed deeper layers—ethical reflections, emotional reliance, identity tensions, and expectations for smarter tools. These experiences show that while TAM helps explain acceptance, HCAI and Norman's Emotional Design Theory are critical to understanding how students actually feel and behave with AI in creative settings. This is a work in progress, and more interviews are being conducted to refine these themes. This section discusses the results in relation to the original research questions and the theoretical frameworks guiding this study.

5.1 RQ:1

How do design students interact with AI-powered LLM chatbots during the design process?

Design students interact with AI-powered large language models (LLMs) such as ChatGPT and Gemini in multifaceted ways that go beyond basic task automation. The data reveals that these tools are primarily used during the early stages of the design process—namely, ideation, research, and planning. Students treat LLMs as cognitive supports that help them initiate ideas, clarify thoughts, and organize creative directions. For instance, one participant described the chatbot as a "launchpad" that helped them break creative blocks and generate starting points for design projects.

Students often engage in prompt-based iteration, where they test and refine their queries to extract more relevant, contextual, or divergent outputs. Some have developed multi-agent strategies, switching between LLMs like ChatGPT and Gemini depending on the task—for example, using ChatGPT for idea generation and Gemini for planning or outlining.

Interactions are not purely functional; students also form emotional connections with these tools. One participant likened ChatGPT to a "motivational bestie," highlighting how the AI's tone and responsiveness helped reduce anxiety during creative blocks. Another participant used LLMs in mobile, voice-enabled formats while sketching or walking, indicating a shift toward more casual, integrated use in their workflow.

However, interactions are shaped by personal values and ethical considerations. One student intentionally avoided ChatGPT due to ideological disagreements with OpenAI leadership and preferred using Gemini, which they perceived as more aligned with their values. This points to a reflective and critical engagement with AI, rather than blind acceptance.

In summary, design students use LLMs not just as assistants, but as co-creators, motivators, and personalized thinking partners. Their interaction is fluid and strategic, shaped by tool capabilities, personal ideologies, creative needs, and emotional states. These findings suggest that AI tools are becoming embedded not only in the mechanics of design but also in the identity and emotional experience of student designers.

5.2 RQ:2

What are the pain points experienced by students while using LLM chat bots?

While students found LLMs useful and easy to begin with, several pain points emerged during deeper interaction. One major issue was prompting difficulty—students had to rephrase and iterate frequently to get relevant, specific responses. As one noted, "You need to know how to ask."

Another frustration was the lack of memory and personalization. Students wished the AI could retain previous context, with one saying, "I have to re-explain everything every time." Repetitive or generic outputs also caused concern, especially when peers produced similar results using the same model, raising issues around originality and fairness.

Some experienced information overload from long responses, particularly in voice-based formats. Lastly, one participant avoided ChatGPT entirely due to ethical concerns, showing that ideological discomfort can also be a barrier.

These pain points go beyond usability and highlight the need for more adaptive, transparent, and emotionally attuned AI tools.

5.3 RQ:3

What improvements do students recommend for enhancing LLM UX in design education?

Students suggested several improvements to make LLMs more useful, personalized, and supportive in creative workflows. A key recommendation was contextual memory—the ability for AI to remember previous projects, user preferences, or ongoing tasks. One participant explained, "I wish it remembered how I usually design, or what I've already done."

They also wanted adaptive output control, including shorter, more focused responses and the ability to guide the tone or complexity of replies. Long, verbose answers were seen as mentally tiring and time-wasting, especially in voice formats.

Another recurring suggestion was better style and aesthetic alignment, such as training AI on a student's own sketches or design history. This reflects a desire for AI that acts more like a personalized creative partner.

Lastly, one student requested tools that are ethically transparent, with clear information about data use and system values—especially for those who base tool choices on ideology or trust.

These recommendations emphasize a need for LLMs that are not only usable, but also adaptive, emotionally aware, and values-aligned, aligning with HCAI principles and Norman's reflective-level design.

Preliminary Implications of the Study: The findings contribute to the evolving discourse in human-AI interaction, particularly within creative domains. As LLMs become embedded in academic and professional workflows, future research must look beyond task completion and begin assessing how these tools reshape students' relationships with originality, authorship, and self-expression.

It is important to note that the findings of this study, considering a small sample size, are preliminary and might evolve. We plan to conduct further interviews in next 3 months and produce more comprehensive insights.

6 Conclusion

This work-in-progress study provides early insights into how design students interact with AI-powered LLMs during their creative processes. While the survey confirms strong acceptance based on usefulness and ease of use, the interviews reveal deeper dimensions of emotional engagement, ethical reflection, and evolving expectations around personalization. These findings highlight the limitations of relying solely on models like TAM and emphasize the value of integrating frameworks like HCAI and Norman's Emotional Design Theory for a more holistic understanding. As more data is collected and analyzed, we expect to refine these themes and uncover additional patterns that can inform the development of more supportive, adaptive, and ethically aligned AI tools for design education. Early results suggest that LLMs hold strong potential as co-creative partners—but only when designed with users' values, emotions, and agency in mind.

References

1. Agkathidis, A., Song, Y., Symeonidou, I.: AI-assisted design: utilising artificial intelligence as a generative form-finding tool in architectural design studio teaching. In: eCAADe Proceedings, vol. 2, pp. 619–628 (2024). https://doi.org/10.52842/conf.ecaade.2024.2.619
2. Albaugh, L., Hudson, S., Yao, L.: An augmented knitting machine for operational assistance and guided improvisation. In: Proceedings of the 2023 CHI Conference on Human Factors in Computing Systems, pp. 1–15 (2023). https://doi.org/10.1145/3544548.3581549
3. Amershi, S., et al.: Guidelines for human-AI interaction. In: Proceedings of the 2019 CHI Conference on Human Factors in Computing Systems (2019). https://doi.org/10.1145/3290605.3300233, [Preprint]
4. Asadi, A.: LLMs in design thinking: autoethnographic insights and design implications. In: 2023 The 5th World Symposium on Software Engineering (WSSE), pp. 55–60 (2023). https://doi.org/10.1145/3631991.3631999
5. Davis, F.: Perceived usefulness, perceived ease of use, and user acceptance of information technology. MIS Q. **13**(3), 319 (1989). https://doi.org/10.2307/249008
6. Flechtner, R., Stankowski, A.: AI is not a wildcard: challenges for integrating AI into the design curriculum. In: Proceedings of the 5th Annual Symposium on HCI Education, pp. 72–77 (2023). https://doi.org/10.1145/3587399.3587410
7. Ge, P., Fan, F.: A systematic review of the role of AI artificial intelligence in design education. In: Proceedings of the International Conference on Engineering and Product Design Education, EPDE 2024, pp. 103–108 (2024). https://doi.org/10.35199/epde.2024.18
8. Hashem, O., Hakeem, M.: Design education methodology using AI. J. Art Des. Music **3**(1) (2024). https://doi.org/10.55554/2785-9649.1030
9. Ishengoma, F.: Revisiting the tam: adapting the model to advanced technologies and evolving user behaviours. Electron. Libr. **42**(6), 1055–1073 (2024). https://doi.org/10.1108/el-06-2024-0166
10. Ivancie, M.: The best AI chatbots & LLMs of q1 2025: rankings & data. UpMarket (2025). https://www.upmarket.co/blog/the-best-ai-chatbots-llms-of-q1-2025-complete-comparison-guide-and-research-firm-ranks/#top-3-ai-chatbots-and-models-overall-by-intelligence-and-reasoning. Accessed 24 May 2025
11. Kerner, S.: 25 of the best large language models in 2025. WhatIs (2025). https://www.techtarget.com/whatis/feature/12-of-the-best-large-language-models. Accessed 24 May 2025
12. Kudina, O., Ballsun-Stanton, B., Alfano, M.: The use of large language models as scaffolds for proleptic reasoning. Asian J. Philos. **4**(1) (2025). https://doi.org/10.1007/s44204-025-00247-1
13. Liu, F., et al.: Assessing clinical medicine students' acceptance of large language model: based on technology acceptance model. BMC Med. Educ. **24**(1) (2024). https://doi.org/10.1186/s12909-024-06232-1

14. Luckin, R., Cukurova, M.: Designing educational technologies in the age of AI: a learning sciences-driven approach. Br. J. Edu. Technol. **50**(6), 2824–2838 (2019). https://doi.org/10.1111/bjet.12861
15. McCardle, J.: The challenge of integrating AI & smart technology in design education. Int. J. Technol. Des. Educ. **12**(1), 59–76 (2002). https://doi.org/10.1023/a:1013089404168
16. Mishra, T., et al.: Use of large language models as artificial intelligence tools in academic research and publishing among global clinical researchers. Sci. Rep. **14**(1) (2024). https://doi.org/10.1038/s41598-024-81370-6
17. Norman, D.: Emotional Design: Why We Love (or Hate) Everyday Things. Basic Books (2007)
18. Shaer, O., et al.: AI-augmented brainwriting: Investigating the use of LLMs in group ideation. In: Proceedings of the CHI Conference on Human Factors in Computing Systems, pp. 1–17 (2024). https://doi.org/10.1145/3613904.3642414
19. Shneiderman, B.: Human-centered artificial intelligence: reliable, safe & trustworthy. Int. J. Hum.-Comput. Interact. **36**(6), 495–504 (2020). https://doi.org/10.1080/10447318.2020.1741118
20. Tsiakas, K., Murray-Rust, D.: Unpacking human-AI interactions: from interaction primitives to a design space. ACM Trans. Interact. Intell. Syst. **14**(3), 1–51 (2024). https://doi.org/10.1145/3664522
21. Wang, W.F., et al.: AIdeation: designing a human-AI collaborative ideation system for concept designers. In: Proceedings of the 2025 CHI Conference on Human Factors in Computing Systems, pp. 1–28 (2025). https://doi.org/10.1145/3706598.3714148
22. Weisz, J., et al.: Design principles for generative AI applications. In: Proceedings of the CHI Conference on Human Factors in Computing Systems, pp. 1–22 (2024). https://doi.org/10.1145/3613904.3642466
23. Yang, Q., et al.: Re-examining whether, why, and how human-AI interaction is uniquely difficult to design. In: Proceedings of the 2020 CHI Conference on Human Factors in Computing Systems, pp. 1–13 (2020). https://doi.org/10.1145/3313831.3376301
24. Yu, W.: Ai as a co-creator and a design material: transforming the design process. Des. Stud. **97**, 101303 (2025). https://doi.org/10.1016/j.destud.2025.101303
25. Yuan, B., Hu, J.: Generative AI as a tool for enhancing reflective learning in students (2024). https://doi.org/10.36227/techrxiv.173324189.99227671/v1, [Preprint]

Students' Reliance on AI in Higher Education: Identifying Contributing Factors

Griffin Pitts(✉), Neha Rani, Weedguet Mildort, and Eva-Marie Cook

University of Florida, Gainesville 32611, FL, USA
{w.pitts,neharani,weedguet.mildort,evamariecook}@ufl.edu

Abstract. The increasing availability and use of artificial intelligence (AI) tools in educational settings has raised concerns about students' overreliance on these technologies. Overreliance occurs when individuals accept incorrect AI-generated recommendations, often without critical evaluation, leading to flawed problem solutions and undermining learning outcomes. This study investigates potential factors contributing to patterns of AI reliance among undergraduate students, examining not only overreliance but also appropriate reliance (correctly accepting helpful and rejecting harmful recommendations) and underreliance (incorrectly rejecting helpful recommendations). Our approach combined pre- and post-surveys with a controlled experimental task where participants solved programming problems with an AI assistant that provided both accurate and deliberately incorrect suggestions, allowing direct observation of students' reliance patterns when faced with varying AI reliability. We find that appropriate reliance is significantly related to students' programming self-efficacy, programming literacy, and need for cognition, while showing negative correlations with post-task trust and satisfaction. Overreliance showed significant correlations with post-task trust and satisfaction with the AI assistant. Underreliance was negatively correlated with programming literacy, programming self-efficacy, and need for cognition. Overall, the findings provide insights for developing targeted interventions that promote appropriate reliance on AI tools, with implications for the integration of AI in curriculum and educational technologies.

Keywords: Appropriate Reliance · Overreliance · Underreliance · Programming Self-Efficacy · Need for Cognition · AI in Education · Human-AI trust

1 Introduction

The use of artificial intelligence (AI) in higher education has increased dramatically with the development of large language models such as OpenAI's ChatGPT, Anthropic's Claude, and Microsoft's Copilot. These AI assistants offer students easy to access, and often times, free support in tasks through instant feedback,

C. Stephanidis et al. (Eds.): HCII 2025, CCIS 2773, pp. 86–97, 2026.
https://doi.org/10.1007/978-3-032-12773-0_9

explanations, and problem-solving assistance. Students' adoption of these technologies has been substantial, with recent research finding that 64.5% of surveyed undergraduate students use AI chatbots at least once a week, with 90.4% reporting prior experience with these systems [22]. While prior research has examined why students initially adopt AI tools, focusing on factors like perceived usefulness and ease of use [5,13,17,21,27], the widespread adoption of these tools has introduced a new challenge that remains understudied: students' reliance on AI. Following the framework outlined by [28], we distinguish between three primary forms of reliance: appropriate reliance, overreliance, and underreliance (see Fig. 1). Appropriate reliance occurs when students correctly accept helpful AI recommendations and reject flawed ones, demonstrating calibrated trust and critical evaluation; overreliance occurs when users accept flawed or incorrect AI-generated recommendations without verification; and underreliance occurs when students reject accurate AI recommendations.

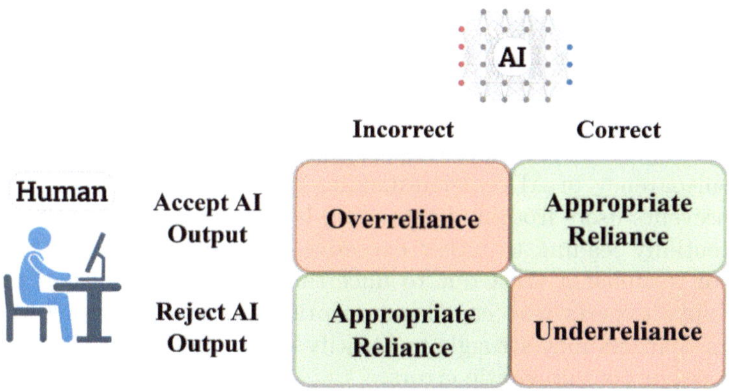

Fig. 1. Human-AI reliance framework

When students overrely on AI outputs, it can undermine learning outcomes and reduce their development of critical thinking skills. AI hallucinations can introduce "inaccuracies or fabrications" that can propagate through academic work [30]. Students themselves express concerns about peers using AI "as a crutch" and losing the ability to "think for themselves" [22]. These concerns are particularly salient in education, where students face competing pressures: the immediate need to complete assignments efficiently versus the long-term objective of developing domain expertise and critical thinking skills. When students turn to AI tools for assistance, they risk bypassing the very processes through which such expertise is built.

The tendency to accept or reject AI outputs reflects broader patterns in human information processing and decision-making, particularly when engaging with intelligent systems. Vasconcelos et al. [28] proposed that users engage in an unconscious cognitive cost-benefit calculation when deciding whether to verify

AI outputs or accept them uncritically. This framework aligns with dual process theory outlined in [12], which distinguishes between fast, intuitive "System 1" thinking and slow, analytical "System 2" thinking. This framework helps explain why users might accept AI outputs through quick judgments (System 1) rather than analytically evaluating them (System 2) when the effort of verification outweighs its perceived value [11,28]. In educational settings, these cognitive tendencies may be amplified as students face time pressures and potentially develop what has been characterized as cognitive laziness [1,26,30].

The cognitive processes involved in accepting and rejecting AI output are influenced by automation bias, which can lead users to favor automated suggestions over other sources of information or their own judgment [10,20]. In educational contexts, this bias poses an added risk of developing an under-skilled workforce. Students with limited domain expertise are more vulnerable to uncritically accepting inaccurate AI-generated content [8,16], potentially undermining their autonomy and decision-making abilities [6]. While our understanding of human-AI trust is still developing [9,23], research shows that students' trust levels significantly affect their engagement patterns and willingness to accept AI recommendations [18,24,25], with excessive trust potentially leading to complacency effects where users reduce their vigilance and passively accept AI outputs [19].

The challenge of appropriate trust calibration is further complicated by the lack of transparency in AI decision-making processes [7,29]. This "black box" problem prevents users from understanding how systems arrive at their conclusions, potentially leading to either excessive trust based on surface-level performance or insufficient trust due to uncertainty about the system's reasoning [14,28]. Unlike experts who can draw on prior domain experience to evaluate AI outputs, learners may struggle to identify when AI suggestions deviate from best practices or contain subtle errors.

The tendency to rely on AI systems varies considerably across individuals, suggesting that individual differences play a significant role in determining reliance patterns. Among these differences, need for cognition (NFC), defined as an individual's tendency to engage in and enjoy effortful cognitive activities, has been identified as a significant predictor of AI reliance behaviors [3,4,11,28]. NFC represents a personality trait that captures intrinsic motivation for analytical thinking rather than domain expertise itself, with research showing that individuals with higher NFC tend to exhibit lower overreliance on incorrect AI recommendations [3,4,11,28]. Beyond NFC, other individual characteristics have been investigated in relation to AI reliance patterns: students with higher self-efficacy in domain-specific abilities tend to work more independently, while those with lower confidence lean more on AI support [2], and trust propensity influences how readily individuals conform to AI advice, with more trusting students showing greater adherence to AI recommendations [15]. Toward system design interventions, cognitive forcing functions [3] have shown promise in reducing overreliance, while other approaches like partial explanations [11,31] have yielded mixed results. Despite these insights, our understanding of how individual psychological factors predict different patterns of AI reliance in educational settings remains limited.

1.1 Research Questions

Our study aims to identify predictors of students' appropriate reliance, overreliance, and underreliance on AI to inform educational interventions and guide responsible use of AI in education. We designed a controlled experiment where students solve Python programming problems with an AI assistant that provides both accurate and misleading recommendations. Through this approach, we examined factors measured before students interacted with the AI system (pre-task) and after they completed the programming tasks (post-task) to understand what influences their reliance patterns. Pre-task factors include programming self-efficacy, programming literacy, need for cognition, AI literacy, and concerns about trust in AI. Post-task factors include students' self-assessment of their reliance on AI, trust in the specific chatbot used, satisfaction with the AI, and their decision-making process while using AI recommendations. Based on these factors, we investigate the following research questions:

- **RQ1:** What factors are associated with students' appropriate reliance on AI tools (correctly following helpful recommendations and rejecting misleading ones)?
- **RQ2:** What factors are associated with students' overreliance on AI tools (incorrectly following misleading recommendations)?
- **RQ3:** What factors are associated with students' underreliance on AI tools (incorrectly rejecting helpful recommendations)?

2 Methodology

2.1 Participants and Study Design

Fifty undergraduate students enrolled in computing-related courses participated in this study, all with prior programming experience in Python. Participants were recruited through course announcements and received extra credit for participation. We employed a controlled experiment combining pre- and post-survey instruments with a programming task. The programming task involved an AI chatbot that provided both accurate recommendations (8 problems) and misleading recommendations (6 problems) in randomized order, allowing us to observe participants' reliance patterns under varying AI reliability conditions.

2.2 Task Description

Participants completed 14 Python programming problems of varying difficulty, designed to test their knowledge of programming concepts including loops, conditionals, data structures, and basic algorithms. Each problem presented a coding challenge followed by an AI-generated recommendation for solving it. Six of the 14 problems included intentionally flawed AI recommendations containing either logical errors (e.g., incorrect loop conditions) or syntax mistakes (e.g., missing parentheses), while eight contained accurate and helpful recommendations. Problem order was randomized to control for ordering effects.

We developed the web-based platform for this study using Python Flask as the backend framework, with an HTML/CSS frontend interface. The platform implemented a "Wizard of Oz" approach, where initial AI responses were pre-programmed rather than generated in real-time to ensure consistent experimental conditions across participants. While initial recommendations were predetermined, the platform integrated OpenAI's API (gpt-3.5-turbo-0125) to handle follow-up interactions, allowing participants to ask clarifying questions and receive contextually relevant responses based on their specific queries (see Fig. 2).

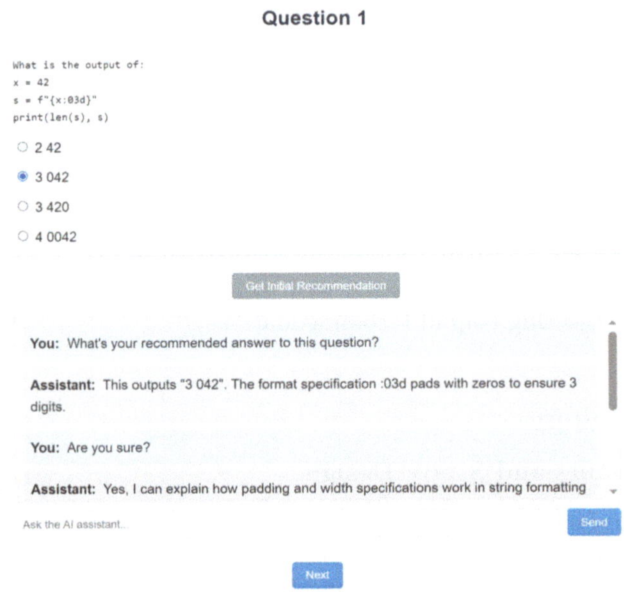

Fig. 2. Experimental interface with AI chatbot recommendation

2.3 Measures

Pre-task Measures. The pre-survey included six multi-item scales, with items rated on 7-point Likert scales (1 = Strongly Disagree, 7 = Strongly Agree). Composite scores were created by averaging related items.

- *Programming Self-Efficacy* was measured using a 3-item scale assessing students' confidence in their programming abilities, including their perceived ability to program independently, learn new programming languages, and identify when their code needs improvement.

- *Programming Literacy* was assessed through a 6-item scale evaluating students' knowledge of fundamental programming concepts, ability to read and comprehend code written by others, identify appropriate data structures, understand object-oriented programming principles, explain programming concepts to others, and proficiency in one or more programming languages.
- *AI Literacy* was measured using a 4-item scale examining knowledge about AI systems, including understanding of basic AI principles, identifying appropriate use cases for AI in programming, understanding the risks and biases of AI assistants, and effectively prompting AI tools to get desired results.
- *General Trust in AI* was measured using a 3-item scale assessing participants' baseline trust in AI technology for programming tasks, including perceived dependability, reliability for coding assistance, and clarity in explaining programming concepts.
- *Concerns for Trust* was assessed using a 4-item scale that measured worries about becoming too dependent on AI, concerns about incorrect advice, uncertainty about blindly trusting AI's suggestions, and concerns that AI might hinder learning.
- *Need for Cognition* was measured using a 5-item scale assessing participants' tendency to engage in and enjoy thinking about programming problems, including understanding how code works, exploring different solutions, understanding underlying concepts, figuring out solutions before asking for help.

Task and Behavioral Measures. Participants completed 14 programming problems. For each problem, they received a recommendation from an AI chatbot on how to approach or solve the problem as outlined in Sect. 2.2. Participants could choose to follow or disregard each recommendation. Through this procedure, we collected behavioral data relating to three measures:

- The percentage of cases where the participant correctly followed helpful recommendations and rejected misleading ones (**Appropriate Reliance**)
- The percentage of misleading recommendations incorrectly followed (**Overreliance**)
- The percentage of helpful recommendations incorrectly rejected (**Underreliance**)

Post-task Measures. After completing the programming task, participants completed a post-survey with scales measuring:

- *Overreliance Self-Assessment:* A 4-item self-assessment scale measuring participants' perceptions of their own reliance on AI recommendations, including accepting suggestions without understanding them, questioning recommendations before accepting them, habitually using AI suggestions immediately, and verifying AI answers with their own knowledge.

- *Trust in Chatbot:* A 4-item scale assessing trust in the AI chatbot used in the study, including reliability of advice, trustworthiness of explanations, dependability of recommendations, and helpfulness in problem-solving.
- *Satisfaction:* A 4-item scale measuring overall satisfaction with the AI assistance provided, including helpfulness of recommendations, clarity of explanations, appropriateness of responses, and overall quality of assistance.
- *Decision-Making Process:* A 5-item scale examining approaches to using AI recommendations, including careful consideration before acceptance, combining personal knowledge with AI suggestions, maintaining independence in decision-making, critically evaluating AI reasoning, and maintaining problem-solving independence.

2.4 Data Analysis

We conducted correlational analyses to examine relationships among pre-task, behavioral, and post-task measures in this pilot study. Using Pearson's correlation coefficients, we identified factors associated with students' appropriate reliance, overreliance, and underreliance on an AI chatbot.

3 Results

3.1 RQ1: Factors Associated with Appropriate Reliance on AI

Our analysis revealed several pre-survey factors significantly associated with students' appropriate reliance on AI systems. Programming self-efficacy showed a positive correlation with appropriate reliance ($r = 0.333$, $p = .018$), indicating that students with higher confidence in their programming abilities were more likely to rely on AI appropriately. Similarly, programming literacy demonstrated a significant positive correlation with appropriate reliance ($r = 0.370$, $p = .008$), suggesting that higher domain knowledge helps students discern when to trust AI recommendations. Need for cognition was positively correlated with appropriate reliance ($r = 0.371$, $p = .008$) as well.

Post-task measures had significant relationships with appropriate reliance. Students' decision-making processes were positively correlated with appropriate reliance ($r = 0.312$, $p = .027$), suggesting that specific approaches to problem-solving support more effective AI use. Trust-related outcomes showed negative correlations with appropriate reliance. Final trust in the chatbot was negatively correlated with appropriate reliance ($r = -0.303$, $p = .032$), as was satisfaction ($r = -0.292$, $p = .040$). This suggests that students who developed a more skeptical stance toward the AI system were more likely to use it appropriately.

3.2 RQ2: Factors Associated with Overreliance on AI

None of the pre-survey measures (programming self-efficacy, general trust in AI, concerns for trust, need for cognition, programming literacy, and AI literacy) showed significant correlations with overreliance. This contrasts with our findings for appropriate reliance, where several pre-survey factors showed significant relationships. One possible explanation is that overreliance is more dependent on the interaction experience itself rather than from pre-existing traits or knowledge. Participants may approach AI recommendations with initial caution, but their decision to overrely develops during the interaction process.

However, post-task measures showed significant relationships with overreliance. Final trust in the chatbot demonstrated a strong positive correlation with overreliance ($r = 0.441$, $p = .001$), as did satisfaction ($r = 0.348$, $p = .013$). Students' self-assessment was somewhat accurate, as post-task overreliance self-assessment positively correlated with students' measured overreliance behavior ($r = 0.355$, $p = .011$). Additionally, students' decision-making processes showed a negative correlation with overreliance ($r = -0.265$, $p = .063$), though this relationship fell just short of statistical significance at the $p < .05$ threshold.

3.3 RQ3: Factors Associated with Underreliance on AI

Our analysis of factors related to underreliance on AI revealed several significant relationships. Among pre-survey measures, programming self-efficacy showed a negative correlation with underreliance ($r = -0.308$, $p = .030$), indicating that students with higher confidence in their programming abilities were less likely to reject helpful AI recommendations. Similarly, need for cognition was negatively correlated with underreliance ($r = -0.312$, $p = .027$), suggesting that students who enjoy thinking deeply about problems were more likely to recognize helpful AI recommendations. The strongest negative correlation with underreliance was observed for programming literacy ($r = -0.439$, $p = .001$), indicating that students with stronger programming knowledge were significantly less likely to dismiss helpful AI recommendations. Other pre-survey measures, including general trust in AI, concerns for trust, and AI literacy, did not show significant correlations with underreliance. Similarly, none of the post-task measures (final overreliance assessment, final trust in chatbot, satisfaction with AI, and decision-making process) were significantly correlated with underreliance.

4 Discussion

This study sought to understand what individual characteristics predict different patterns of AI reliance among undergraduate students. Our findings reveal several factors associated with appropriate reliance, overreliance, and underreliance behaviors. We discuss three insights relating to the findings and their implications.

First, our findings identify a clear profile of students who use AI effectively: those with higher programming self-efficacy (r = 0.333), programming literacy (r = 0.370), and need for cognition (r = 0.371). These students demonstrated the ability to correctly accept helpful AI recommendations while rejecting misleading ones, indicating calibrated trust and thoughtful evaluation. This finding aligns with Gaube et al. [8] and Li and Little's [16] observations, where professionals with domain expertise are less vulnerable to uncritically accepting flawed AI recommendations. In our educational context, programming literacy functions as this protective factor. Students with higher programming literacy appear to leverage their understanding of coding concepts to evaluate the AI recommendations in the study. The role of need for cognition complements this domain expertise by ensuring students actively scrutinize rather than passively accept AI suggestions, as was found in [3,11,28]. Similarly, self-efficacy provides students the confidence necessary to trust one's own judgment when AI recommendations seem questionable. These factors distinguish students who appropriately rely on AI, suggesting that educational interventions should focus on developing domain expertise, critical thinking skills, and the confidence to question AI outputs.

Second, our analysis reveals a concerning relationship between trust, satisfaction, and overreliance during students' interactions with AI. While no pre-task measures predicted overreliance, post-task trust ($r = 0.441$) and satisfaction ($r = 0.348$) in the AI chatbot showed strong positive correlations with overreliance. These correlations indicate that overreliant students trusted the system, felt satisfied with its assistance, yet unknowingly accepted errors that undermined their performance. This finding provides evidence for a potential "false-confidence loop" in human-AI interactions. Unlike human advisors, whose errors might trigger skepticism through behavioral cues or inconsistencies, AI systems can deliver incorrect information with confidence.

Students who develop trust through initial positive experiences appear to generalize this trust inappropriately, leading them to accept subsequent recommendations with less scrutiny. Each uncritically accepted suggestion reinforces their satisfaction with the AI, which in turn strengthens their trust, creating a self-perpetuating cycle. This extends automation bias research by demonstrating how the very features that make AI appealing (consistency, availability, and authoritative presentation) not only prevent users from recognizing limitations but actively reinforce overreliant behavior patterns, creating a feedback loop where each accepted recommendation deepens trust in the system.

Third, our finding that students can partially recognize their own overreliance ($r = 0.355$, $p = .011$) represents an important opportunity for intervention design. This significant correlation suggests students possess some metacognitive awareness of when they're accepting AI recommendations too readily. While this self-awareness isn't perfect, it provides a foundation that educational interventions can build upon. For instance, interventions could prompt students to predict their own reliance patterns during AI interactions and reflect on how they engage with the outputs, helping calibrate self-perception with reality. This aligns with cognitive forcing functions research [3], which found that prompting users to think before accepting AI recommendations reduces overreliance. Our finding that students possess partial self-awareness suggests they would be receptive to such interventions that make their reliance patterns explicit. By leveraging students' existing metacognitive awareness through reflection prompts, acceptance rate feedback, or required justifications for following AI suggestions, we can strengthen their ability to recognize and correct overreliant behaviors.

5 Limitations and Future Work

This pilot study has several limitations that suggest directions for future research. Our sample of computer science students may not generalize to other disciplines where domain expertise operates differently. Students in fields like humanities or social sciences might show different reliance patterns when using AI for writing or analysis tasks. Additionally, our experimental design using pre-programmed AI responses, while ensuring consistency, may not capture the variability of real-world AI systems that students encounter.

Our measurement of AI literacy may also require refinement. The lack of correlation between AI literacy and reliance patterns could indicate that students' self-reported AI knowledge reflects personal experience and technical understanding rather than their ability to critically assess AI recommendations. Students may feel knowledgeable about AI while lacking skills to identify unreliable outputs. Future work should develop AI literacy assessments and educational curriculum focused on practical competencies (e.g. recognizing hallucinations, understanding when AI presents uncertain information as fact, and identifying when AI assistance may be harmful to learning).

Furthermore, examining reliance patterns within a single session prevented us from understanding how these behaviors develop and solidify over time. The "false-confidence loop" we identified may strengthen or weaken with extended use. Future research should employ longitudinal designs to track how reliance patterns change over time, test intervention strategies like embedded reflection prompts, and examine whether the related factors we identified remain stable across extended AI use.

6 Conclusion

This study investigated factors contributing to different patterns of AI reliance among undergraduate students. Through a controlled experiment where students solved programming problems with an AI assistant providing both accurate and misleading recommendations, we identified distinct predictors for appropriate reliance, overreliance, and underreliance behaviors. Students who demonstrated appropriate reliance possessed higher programming self-efficacy, domain expertise, and need for cognition. In contrast, overreliance showed no correlation with pre-task measures but was strongly associated with high post-task trust and satisfaction. Underreliance was negatively associated with domain expertise and need for cognition. These findings highlight the need for educational approaches that build domain expertise, foster critical thinking skills, and incorporate reflection mechanisms to help students calibrate their trust in AI systems. The partial self-awareness students demonstrated about their reliance patterns in the post-survey provides an opportunity for interventions that make inappropriately reliant behaviors known and correctable. As AI becomes increasingly integrated in education, understanding and addressing patterns of under- and overreliance will be necessary for helping students develop the judgment to leverage these tools effectively without compromising their ability to learn and think independently.

References

1. Ahmad, S.F., et al.: Impact of artificial intelligence on human loss in decision making, laziness and safety in education. Humanit. Soc. Sci. Commun. **10**(1), 1–14 (2023)
2. Bernabei, M., Colabianchi, S., Falegnami, A., Costantino, F.: Students' use of large language models in engineering education: a case study on technology acceptance, perceptions, efficacy, and detection chances. Comput. Educ. Artif. Intell. **5**, 100172 (2023)
3. Buçinca, Z., Malaya, M.B., Gajos, K.Z.: To trust or to think: cognitive forcing functions can reduce overreliance on AI in AI-assisted decision-making. Proc. ACM Hum. Comput. Interact. **5**(CSCW1), 1–21 (2021)
4. Cacioppo, J.T., Petty, R.E.: The need for cognition. J. Pers. Soc. Psychol. **42**(1), 116 (1982)
5. Dahri, N.A., et al.: Extended tam based acceptance of AI-powered ChatGPT for supporting metacognitive self-regulated learning in education: a mixed-methods study. Heliyon **10**(8) (2024)
6. Duhaylungsod, A.V., Chavez, J.V.: ChatGPT and other AI users: innovative and creative utilitarian value and mindset shift. J. Namibian Stud. **33**(2023), 4367–4378 (2023)
7. Ehsan, U., Liao, Q.V., Muller, M., Riedl, M.O., Weisz, J.D.: Expanding explainability: towards social transparency in ai systems. In: Proceedings of the 2021 CHI Conference on Human Factors in Computing Systems, pp. 1–19 (2021)
8. Gaube, S., et al.: Do as AI say: susceptibility in deployment of clinical decision-aids. NPJ Digit. Med. **4**(1), 31 (2021)
9. Glikson, E., Woolley, A.W.: Human trust in artificial intelligence: review of empirical research. Acad. Manag. Ann. **14**(2), 627–660 (2020)
10. Goddard, K., Roudsari, A., Wyatt, J.C.: Automation bias: a systematic review of frequency, effect mediators, and mitigators. J. Am. Med. Inform. Assoc. **19**(1), 121–127 (2012)
11. de Jong, S., Paananen, V., Tag, B., van Berkel, N.: Cognitive forcing for better decision-making: reducing overreliance on ai systems through partial explanations. Proc. ACM Hum. Comput. Interact. **9**(2), 1–30 (2025)
12. Kahneman, D.: Thinking, fast and slow. Macmillan (2011)
13. Kanont, K., et al.: Generative-ai, a learning assistant? Factors influencing higher-ed students' technology acceptance. Electron. J. e-Learn. **22**(6), 18–33 (2024)
14. Kizilcec, R.F.: How much information? Effects of transparency on trust in an algorithmic interface. In: Proceedings of the 2016 CHI Conference on Human Factors in Computing Systems, pp. 2390–2395 (2016)
15. Klingbeil, A., Grützner, C., Schreck, P.: Trust and reliance on AI–an experimental study on the extent and costs of overreliance on AI. Comput. Hum. Behav. **160**, 108352 (2024)

16. Li, M.D., Little, B.P.: Appropriate reliance on artificial intelligence in radiology education. J. Am. Coll. Radiol. **20**(11), 1126–1130 (2023)
17. Lin, X.: Factors influencing college students' use of ai chatbots for learning–empirical study based on tam extended model. In: 2024 5th International Conference on Artificial Intelligence and Electromechanical Automation (AIEA), pp. 151–159. IEEE (2024)
18. Nazaretsky, T., Mejia-Domenzain, P., Swamy, V., Frej, J., Käser, T.: The critical role of trust in adopting ai-powered educational technology for learning: an instrument for measuring student perceptions. Comput. Educ. Artif. Intell., 100368 (2025)
19. Parasuraman, R., Manzey, D.H.: Complacency and bias in human use of automation: an attentional integration. Hum. Factors **52**(3), 381–410 (2010)
20. Parasuraman, R., Riley, V.: Humans and automation: use, misuse, disuse, abuse. Hum. Factors **39**(2), 230–253 (1997)
21. Pitts, G., Marcus, V., Motamedi, S.: A proposed model of learners' acceptance and trust of pedagogical conversational ai. In: Proceedings of the Eleventh ACM Conference on Learning@ Scale, pp. 427–432 (2024). https://doi.org/10.1145/3657604.3664682
22. Pitts, G., Marcus, V., Motamedi, S.: Student perspectives on the benefits and risks of ai in education. arXiv preprint arXiv:2505.02198 (2025)
23. Pitts, G., Motamedi, S.: Understanding human-AI trust in education. arXiv preprint arXiv:2506.09160 (2025)
24. Ranalli, J.: L2 student engagement with automated feedback on writing: Potential for learning and issues of trust. J. Second. Lang. Writ. **52**, 100816 (2021)
25. Rani, N.: Investigating user trust in context-aware recommender systems in search as learning. University of Florida (2023)
26. Sabharwal, D., Kabha, R., Srivastava, K.: Artificial intelligence (ai)-powered virtual assistants and their effect on human productivity and laziness: study on students of delhi-ncr (india) & fujairah (uae). J. Content Commun. Commun. **17**(9), 162–174 (2023)
27. Sánchez-Prieto, J.C., Cruz-Benito, J., Therón Sánchez, R., García-Peñalvo, F.J., et al.: Assessed by machines: development of a tam-based tool to measure ai-based assessment acceptance among students. Int. J. Interact. Multimedia Artif. Intell. **6**(4), 80 (2020)
28. Vasconcelos, H., Jörke, M., Grunde-McLaughlin, M., Gerstenberg, T., Bernstein, M.S., Krishna, R.: Explanations can reduce overreliance on ai systems during decision-making. Proc. ACM Hum. Comput. Interact. **7**(CSCW1), 1–38 (2023)
29. Von Eschenbach, W.J.: Transparency and the black box problem: why we do not trust AI. Philos. Technol. **34**(4), 1607–1622 (2021)
30. Zhai, C., Wibowo, S., Li, L.D.: The effects of over-reliance on ai dialogue systems on students' cognitive abilities: a systematic review. Smart Learn. Environ. **11**(1), 28 (2024)
31. Zhang, Y., Liao, Q.V., Bellamy, R.K.: Effect of confidence and explanation on accuracy and trust calibration in ai-assisted decision making. In: Proceedings of the 2020 Conference on Fairness, Accountability, and Transparency, pp. 295–305 (2020)

Aesthetic Preference Patterns in Chinese-Style Digital Human Design: An Eye-Tracking Study with AIGC-Driven Cultural Innovation Implications

Yuxin Sheng(✉), Feifei Chen, Luyu Jiang, and Huinan Liu

Southeast University, Nanjing 211189, Jiangsu, China
220234600@seu.edu.cn

Abstract. This study investigates aesthetic preferences and visual attention patterns toward Chinese-style digital humans in the context of AI-generated content (AIGC). Combining a questionnaire (N = 136), semi-structured interviews, and eye-tracking experiments, the research identifies key design elements preferred by young consumers. Results show a strong preference for young female digital humans with extroverted personality traits, rendered in 3D cartoon-style and featuring hybrid cultural symbolism that blend traditional and modern elements. Based on this result, 12 participants were selected for semi-structured interviews to extract key visual elements, which were then used to construct prompts for generating a Chinese-style digital human using AIGC techniques. Eye-tracking data (N = 21) reveal that participants focused primarily on facial region and culturally symbolic costume details, such as jewelry, embroidery, and ornamental fastenings. The findings highlight the potential of integrating user insight with AIGC to create culturally expressive digital humans aligned with contemporary youth aesthetics. The study offers empirical evidence and design strategies for the innovative digital expression and dissemination of traditional Chinese culture.

Keywords: Digital Human · Chinese-Style · HCI-AI · Aesthetic Preference · Eye-Tracking Experiment

1 Introduction

For decades, designers have pursued increasingly realistic digital humans. In AI-mediated interactions, artificial intelligence can embody digital humans to enable more natural and socially intuitive communication. Such embodiments transform human–machine interaction from mere clicking to relational dialogue [1]. The visual appearance of digital humans plays a critical role in shaping users' perceptions of emotional capability [2]. While some studies have shown that realistic avatars enhance users' sense of social presence and interaction quality [3], others suggest that anthropomorphism alone does not significantly influence behavioral trust, which instead depends on the quality of the agent's suggestions [4]. These discrepancies may partly arise from differences in

C. Stephanidis et al. (Eds.): HCII 2025, CCIS 2773, pp. 98–111, 2026.
https://doi.org/10.1007/978-3-032-12773-0_10

users' aesthetic preferences regarding avatar appearance. Digital humans that align with user expectations can enhance engagement and perceived efficacy, while mismatched designs may evoke discomfort and negative attitudes [5].

In recent years, China's rich cultural heritage has been revitalized through digital media, with Chinese-style digital humans emerging as a new medium for cultural expression. "Chinese-style" refers to the contemporary integration of traditional Chinese aesthetics and cultural symbols into fashion, entertainment, and lifestyle [6]. These digital avatars incorporate classical elements such as traditional costumes, ornamental patterns, and cultural motifs, positioning them as virtual ambassadors of Chinese heritage. This study explores user preferences for key design dimensions—including gender, personality, visual style, and cultural symbolism—to guide the development of visually appealing and culturally meaningful digital humans.

2 Literature Review

2.1 Digital Humans as Embodied AI Agents

Digital humans are virtual characters created through a combination of computer graphics, motion capture, artificial intelligence, and virtual reality technologies. These agents possess near-human appearances and behavioral capabilities, such as speech, facial expressions, and body movements, enabling them to perceive external environments and interact with users [7]. With rapid advancements in AI and dynamic motion technologies, digital humans are becoming increasingly interactive and socially expressive. As embodied representations of AI systems, digital humans are now widely used in marketing, virtual social platforms, intelligent customer service, and digital broadcasting [8]. Beyond facilitating information exchange and task execution, their human-like appearance reshapes user cognition and trust mechanisms toward AI [4]. Under the trend of "AI personification," digital humans are evolving toward possessing autonomous speech, emotional feedback, and cultural identity construction capabilities.

As visual embodiments of AI, digital humans have moved beyond purely technical artifacts to become symbols with cultural and aesthetic significance. Their design increasingly reflects values of empathy, recognition, and aesthetic appeal. However, current studies predominantly focus on performance metrics, speech interaction, and system acceptance, while overlooking the visual aesthetic construction of digital humans and users' aesthetic reception. Research on aesthetic preferences from a cultural and perceptual perspective remains limited.

2.2 Aesthetic Preference Dimensions of Digital Human Design

As visual design objects, users' aesthetic preferences for digital humans are shaped by multiple factors. Current literature identifies five key dimensions that shape the perceived appeal of digital human design: gender identity, age identity, personality traits, visual style, and cultural symbols.

In terms of gender identity, user trust and affinity often vary based on the digital human's assigned gender. For instance, users tend to prefer female avatars for roles such as sales assistants or game guides, while male avatars are preferred for medical or professional advisory roles. These preferences may stem from users' gender orientation, cultural norms, or stereotypes [1, 9]. Regarding age, youthful avatars are often perceived as energetic and trendy, whereas older avatars convey authority and reliability [10]. Personality traits are expressed through voice, facial expressions, language style, and costume, directly influencing user engagement and emotional investment [11]. Characters perceived as cute and lively often have large eyes, small chins and noses, fuller cheeks, and short midfaces. These features evoke impressions of warmth and trustworthiness, though also sometimes manipulation. In contrast, mature characters are associated with elongated, symmetrical features and firm facial structures, such as defined jaws and long midfaces, projecting steadiness and dependability [12]. Zheng et al. found that cute female and mature male faces attract visual attention more quickly and sustain user interest [10].

Aesthetic judgments of AI-generated images still follow traditional cognitive evaluation frameworks, involving both formal analysis and semantic interpretation. Visual style is a crucial determinant of user preference, including 2D vs. 3D format and realism vs. stylization. While some studies argue that more human-like avatars foster trust and likability [5], others highlight the risk of the "uncanny valley" effect with overly realistic avatars, showing greater acceptance of moderately stylized meta-human designs [2]. The cultural symbolism dimension refers to design elements such as language, attire, color schemes, and motifs that evoke cultural identity and emotional resonance [6].

Although each of these five dimensions has been discussed in isolation, there remains a lack of integrated analysis of how they interact to shape aesthetic preferences. Most prior studies rely on surveys or interviews, with limited use of objective physiological measures like eye-tracking to explore deeper perceptual mechanisms.

2.3 Aesthetic Preferences in AI-Generated Chinese-Style Digital Design

Humans possess an innate ability to judge visual stimuli aesthetically across everyday experiences, including photos, artworks, environments, architecture, bodies, and faces [13]. The external appearance of digital humans' influences user perceptions of their intended roles and functions. Facial features, demeanor, and attire can suggest an avatar's profession or use context, thereby guiding user behavior [14]. Although visual traits are not always reliable indicators of function, they can trigger aesthetic pleasure or aversion, influencing user attitudes [15].

Chinese-style visual design, which integrates traditional aesthetic elements such as ethnic costumes, classical makeup, and ink-inspired color schemes, has become a prominent trend in digital innovation. These features not only enrich digital human design with cultural depth but also strengthen users' sense of identity and emotional connection [16]. With the advancement of AI-driven image generation and style transfer technologies, the creation of Chinese-style digital humans has become more efficient and diverse, allowing for highly personalized visual expressions [17]. However, AI-generated aesthetics often deviate from traditional beauty standards such as neoclassical proportions and the golden ratio. This suggests AI models are integrating contemporary preferences, cultural biases, or emerging trends that reflect evolving human aesthetics [18].

Despite growing interest, existing studies on Chinese-style digital humans remain focused on technical implementation and visual effect evaluations. There is a clear gap in research examining how users perceive and emotionally respond to different Chinese-style designs. In particular, empirical studies exploring users' visual attention patterns, emotional engagement, and cultural resonance are still lacking, necessitating interdisciplinary approaches that integrate design and cognitive psychology.

2.4 Overview of Eye-Tracking Technology

Eye-tracking is a powerful tool for measuring visual attention and cognitive load, widely applied in human-computer interaction, advertising, and interface design [19]. By capturing gaze patterns, fixation points, and pupil dilation, eye-tracking offers objective data on how users perceive visual stimuli and where their interest is focused.

In aesthetic research, eye-tracking can reveal subconscious responses to different visual designs, such as fixation durations, initial gaze locations, and attention heatmaps. These metrics help determine which features of a digital human (e.g., facial features, attire, gaze) draw the most attention. When comparing visual and cultural styles, eye-tracking can also indicate potential cognitive overload or shifts in interest.

Although eye-tracking has been well developed in advertising and branding studies, its application in the study of digital human aesthetics—particularly for Chinese-style digital humans—is still emerging. There is a need for systematic studies linking eye-tracking data with design dimensions and cultural perception to uncover nuanced user responses, offering both theoretical and methodological innovation.

3 Empirical Study

3.1 Research Design

This study aimed to investigate user aesthetic preferences for Chinese-style digital humans and to identify key design elements influencing visual preference. The experiment was conducted in two stages.

In the first stage, we explored participants' aesthetic preferences across five design dimensions of Chinese-style digital humans: gender identity, age identity, personality traits, visual style, and cultural symbolism. Based on aggregated preferences, the most favored digital human profile was identified. Participants who selected this profile were then invited to participate in semi-structured interviews to uncover the underlying reasons for their choices, including expectations, detailed visual requirements, and emotional associations. These interview transcripts were thematically analyzed to extract grounded keywords, which were used as prompts in an AIGC tools to create digital human representations aligned with participants' aesthetic expectations.

The second stage investigated which visual elements most influenced participants' preferences using eye-tracking technology. The most favored digital human from the first stage was used as the experimental stimulus. Eye-tracking data were collected to quantify participants' visual attention and emotional responses to various design attributes of the Chinese-style digital human.

3.2 Participants

This study received ethical approval from the School of Art at Southeast University. In the first stage, 136 valid responses were collected via a questionnaire. According to the Internet Society of China [20], individuals aged 18–30 represent the core user group for digital humans in China. Among our respondents, 125 fell within this age range, making the sample demographically representative. Of these, 65 were male and 71 female; 66 participants had academic or professional backgrounds in art, design, or related fields, while the remaining participants came from other disciplines.

Twelve participants were invited for semi-structured interviews—six male and six female. In the second stage, 21 participants (9 male, 12 female) aged 18–30 took part in the eye-tracking experiment. All had normal or corrected-to-normal vision (within -2.00 diopters). The stimulus images were presented in randomized order to avoid visual inertia, and each was displayed for 12 s. Following the eye-tracking session, brief semi-structured interviews were conducted.

3.3 Materials

In the first stage, the five aesthetic dimensions used to construct the experimental materials are shown in Table 1. The gender identity dimension was defined as male, female, or non-binary based on Ribeiro et al. [12]. Age identity followed Ebner et al. [21], categorized as young, middle-aged, or older. Personality traits were divided into extroversion and agreeableness, based on Lin [22]. Visual style followed the typology proposed by Song [23]: 2D illustration, 3D cartoon-style, 3D realistic, and digital twin. Using an AIGC tool, male and female digital humans were created for each visual style. To ensure experimental control, only the visual style was manipulated, while other factors—such as hairstyle and visible facial structure—were held constant. All generated images were reviewed and validated by an expert panel to confirm stylistic consistency. Additionally, post-processing was applied using image editing software to ensure uniformity in size, background, and resolution across all stimuli. The cultural symbolism dimension followed the classification of Wei [24], distinguishing between traditional and hybrid styles.

In the second stage, eye-tracking data were collected using the Tobii Pro Nano device, with Tobii Pro Lab as the associated data analysis platform. Participants viewed the representative images of the most preferred Chinese-style digital human from the first stage. These images were presented against a 16:9 blank background and displayed for 12 s each. Eye-tracking data—including fixation time, fixation counts, and heatmaps—were collected to assess visual attention toward various elements such as facial features, attire, and hairstyle. Statistical analysis was conducted to identify significant differences and correlations among eye-tracking metrics and aesthetic preference indicators (Fig. 1).

Table 1. Aesthetic preference dimensions of Chinese-style digital human.

Dimension	Items	Reference
Gender Identity	1.male;2. Female;3. non-binary	[12]
Age Identity	1.young(21-31); 2.middle-aged(45-55); 3.older(70-81)	[21]
Personality Traits	1.Agreeableness: Refers to a calm, composed, and introverted demeanor; 2. Extroversion：Refers to a lively, cute, and outgoing personality	[22]
Visual Style	 1. 2D Stylized; 2. 3D cartoon-style; 3. 3D Realistic; 4. Digital Twin	[23]

Fig. 1. Eye-tracking experiment equipment and experimental process.

4 Research Result

4.1 Chinese-Style Digital Human Image Style Preference

The data analysis was conducted using SPSS 24.0. Table 2 presents the distribution of aesthetic preference dimensions for digital humans across two participant groups: professionals ($n = 66$) and non-professionals ($n = 70$). Overall, no statistically significant differences were found between the groups in terms of gender identity, age identity, personality traits, or preference for cultural symbolism styles (all $p > 0.05$). However, a significant difference was observed in the visual style dimension ($\chi2\ (3) = 12.119$, $p = 0.007$).

Professionals showed a higher preference for 3D cartoon-style (37.9%) and 2D stylized (33.3%) compared to non-professionals. In contrast, non-professionals expressed a stronger preference for digital twin (35.7%), which may reflect a greater appreciation for hyper-realistic and lifelike representations among general users.

With respect to cultural symbolism, both groups showed a clear preference for hybrid styles (professional: 62.1%; non-professional: 65.7%), indicating that the integration of traditional Chinese motifs within modern fashion contexts is widely favored, regardless of professional background.

These results suggest that while aesthetic preferences for cultural symbols and identity traits remain stable across groups, professional users tend to favor more stylized and visually interpreted forms, whereas non-professionals lean toward realism and digital twin in digital human design.

Table 2. Statistical data of aesthetic preferences of Chinese-style digital human.

Dimension	Professional Background			χ^2(df)	p
	Professional (66)	Non-professional (70)	Total (136)		
Gender Identity				1.923 (1)	0.166
Male	19.7% (13)	30% (21)	25% (34)		
Female	**80.3% (53)**	**70% (49)**	**75% (102)**		
Non-binary	—	—	—		
Age Identity				0.060 (1)	0.806
Young (21–31)	**65.2% (43)**	**67.1% (47)**	**66.2% (90)**		
Middle-aged (45–55)	34.8% (23)	32.9% (23)	33.8% (46)		
Older (70–81)	—	—	—		
Personality Traits				1.409 (1)	0.235
Agreeableness	53% (35)	42.9% (30)	47.8% (65)		
Extroversion	47% (31)	57.1% (40)	52.2% (71)		
Visual Style				12.119 (3)	0.007
2D Stylized	33.3% (22)	21.4% (15)	27.2% (37)		
3D Cartoon-style	**37.9% (25)**	**30% (21)**	**33.8% (46)**		
3D Realistic	18.2% (12)	12.9% (9)	15.4% (21)		
Digital Twin	10.6% (7)	35.7% (25)	23.5% (32)		
Cultural Symbolism				0.190 (1)	0.663
Traditional style	37.9% (25)	34.3% (24)	36% (49)		
Hybrid style	**62.1% (41)**	**65.7% (46)**	**64% (87)**		

To gain a deeper understanding of participants' expectations, detailed preferences, and emotional connections associated with the most favored Chinese-style digital human configuration— young female, extroversion, 3D cartoon-style, and hybrid cultural aesthetic—we conducted a semi-structured interview study (N = 12). The aim was to extract rich, precise linguistic cues that could inform prompt engineering for Gen AI image tools.

Table 3. Analysis of User Preferences for Chinese-style Digital Human Design (Lively & Cute Style, N = 12).

Core User Preference Description	Representative Quotes	AI Prompt Keywords (partial)
3D cartoon style with refined details; moderate proportion exaggeration avoiding low-quality appearance	"Q7: Like the 3D rendering in animated movies, with cute cartoon charm yet premium texture – not childish animation" "Q3: Eyes can be larger but facial contour should be girlish, no chubby cheeks, maybe with twin braids"	3D cartoon style, Pixar-level details, anime-inspired proportions, large expressive eyes (15–18% face ratio), twin braids, smooth shading, anti-aliasing
Dynamic vitality with natural affinity; enhancing liveliness through body language	"Q5: Need lively micro-expressions! Like tilting head when smiling or higher blink frequency" "Q9: Richer hand gestures to convey cheerfulness"	energetic posture, playful head tilt (15°), lively and cute, sparkling eye effect
Traditional carriers: Modernized Hanfu, ICH elements, traditional features Modern carriers: Tech accessories, fashion items	"Q2: Hanfu skirt shortened to knee-length with glowing hair accessories – classical yet trendy" "Q1: Design modern Hanfu: short-sleeved vest with brocade patterns, frog closures, tassels" "Q11: Light-colored Nanjing velvet flowers for hairpin, pixel-art jade pendant"	modern Hanfu: cropped vest + knee-length skirt, intricate brocade patterns on vest, stand collar with closures, pixel jade pendant, transparent cyber-earpiece, luxury stiletto heels, brocade patterns, silk tassels
Dominant: Macaron-toned traditional colors Accent: Fluorescent hues	"Q4: Morandi color base with school-uniform inspired accents for cute contrast" "Q8: Main outfit in elegant sky-blue and grey with neon belt for pop"	color scheme: Morandi base (moon white, grey, aqua) + fluorescent accents (neon belt, electric blue trim), gradient ombré hair tips

After transcribing the interview recordings, a thematic analysis was performed. The process involved iterative reading, open coding, and thematic categorization to identify salient patterns. Core preference features were distilled and subsequently translated into structured keywords and prompt elements for generative AI tools (see Table 3). The interviews provided concrete, user-centered vocabulary, helping to avoid ambiguity in the design process and enhancing alignment with audience expectations.

Based on the derived prompts, a series of Chinese-style digital human portraits were generated and refined using AI image tools. The final output included four representative visuals (Fig. 2): (a) front-facing modern Chinese fashion portrait, (b) front-facing traditional Chinese attire, (c) front-facing half-body with gesture, and (d) full-body side view.

These AI-generated visuals served as stimulus materials in the subsequent eye-tracking experiment.

Fig. 2. The most favored Chinese-style digital human configuration.

4.2 Visual Hotspot Visualization

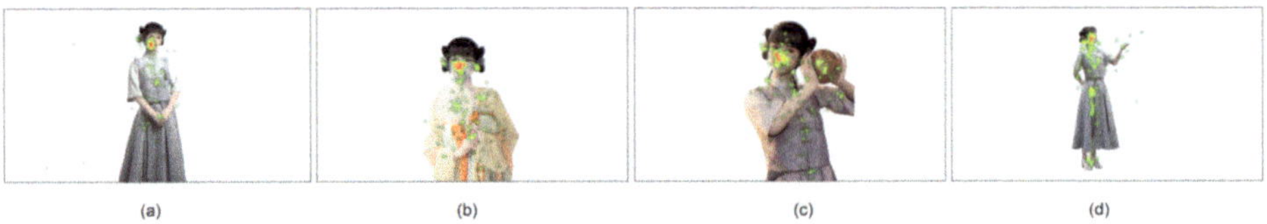

Fig. 3. Visual heatmaps of subjects.

Participants' fixation points and gaze paths across four subjects were visualized using Tobii Pro Lab, resulting in heatmaps (Fig. 3) and gaze trajectory plots (Fig. 4). Heatmaps indicate fixation duration through a warm color scale, where warmer areas represent longer attention and higher visual attraction.

The facial region consistently attracted the longest fixation durations, confirming it as the primary focus. Within the face, the eyes and nose, especially on the left side, drew the most attention. In hairstyles, gaze hotspots were concentrated on hair accessories, highlighting their role in conveying character distinctiveness. For costume elements, attention focused on culturally significant details such as frog buttons, waistbands, and footwear, while plain cuffs and collars received less attention. These refined elements, as condensed carriers of traditional aesthetics, naturally act as visually dense information zones that trigger cultural identity verification (Fu & Luo, 2023). This may also be explained by participants' sensitivity to cultural distortion in AI-generated details. When pattern structures appear distorted, historically inaccurate, or rendered inappropriately, participants experience discomfort—activating a realism validation mechanism. This heightened vigilance renders detailed areas critical in assessing image authenticity.

Fig. 4. Gaze trajectory plots of subjects.

To avoid excessive overlap, data from five participants were overlaid, each represented by a distinct color and sequentially numbered to indicate fixation order. Trajectory plots (Fig. 4) show that initial gaze typically landed at the geometric center of the image, then dispersed to surrounding areas before focusing on visual attractors. Motion and props influenced gaze shifts, with participants often following the direction of movement or gesture. Overall, participants displayed a vertical scanning pattern, moving predominantly from top to bottom or vice versa.

4.3 Analysis of Visual Element Division in AOI Indicators

The eye tracking experiment aims to objectively identify the visual focus of users when viewing Chinese-style digital human images, in order to quantify the visual attractiveness of different design elements and provide empirical evidence for subsequent image design optimization and cultural symbol embedding. The image materials were divided into three visual elements: clothing, hairstyle, and face. AOI regions of interest were divided using Tobii Pro Lab, and the visual element division results of the subjects are shown in Fig. 5.

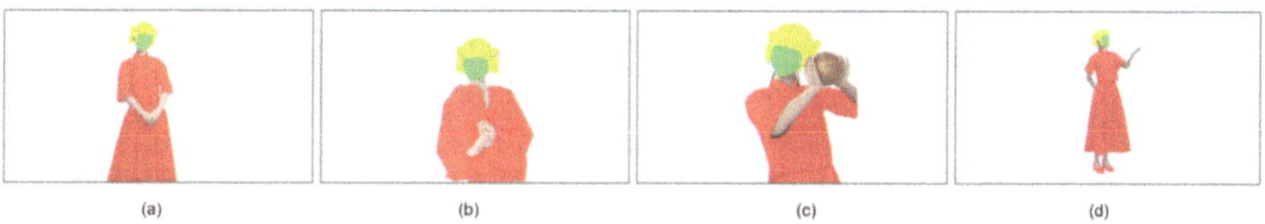

Fig. 5. AOI region

As shown in Table 4, visual attention was measured across three key Areas of Interest (AOIs)—hairstyle, costume, and face—using a comprehensive set of eye-movement indices: Total Dwell Fixation (TDF), Number of Fixations (NF), Fixation Frequency (FF), and Pupil Fixation Duration (PFD), along with Average Fixation Duration (AFD), Number of Entry Sequences (NES), Average Entry Sequence (AES), and Saccade Frequency (SF).

The statistical analysis revealed significant differences in gaze behavior across AOIs, with p-values reaching significance levels of $p < 0.001$ or $p < 0.05$ in all cases.

Among the three AOIs, costume emerged as the most visually engaging element. It consistently recorded the highest mean values across several metrics, including TDF (AVE = 5.66), NF (AVE = 17.4), and NES (AVE = 10.8), suggesting that clothing elements play a central role in attracting and maintaining viewer attention. The face was the second most frequently fixated area, particularly notable in TDF (AVE = 6.139) and NF (AVE = 9.35), reinforcing its importance in conveying personality, identity, and emotional cues in digital human design. In contrast, hairstyle attracted relatively lower levels of visual attention across all indices, especially in AFD (AVE = 0.035) and AES (AVE = 0.035), suggesting it functions more as a background or complementary feature rather than a primary focus.

These findings indicate that participants are predominantly drawn to costume and facial features when viewing Chinese-style digital humans. The statistical significance of differences across AOIs confirms the hierarchical nature of visual salience in such culturally themed digital humans, where costume design stands out as the key driver of aesthetic engagement.

Table 4. Of variance analysis of indicators.

Index	TDF		NF		FF		PFD	
Variance test	F=32.852 P=0.000***		F=34.148 P=0.000***		F=3.278 P=0.045**		F=33 P=0.000***	
AOI	AVE	SD	AVE	SD	AVE	SD	AVE	SD
Hairstyle	1.161	0.882	2.75	1.943	3.011	1.949	0.057	0.044
Costume	5.66	2.507	17.4	7.769	3.146	0.787	0.283	0.125
Face	6.139	2.591	9.35	5.518	1.914	1.986	0.307	0.131
Index	AFD		NES		AES		SF	
Variance test	F=8.973 P=0.000***		F=34.13 P=0.000***		F=34.13 P=0.000***		F=20.829 P=0.000***	
AOI	AVE	SD	AVE	SD	AVE	SD	AVE	SD
Hairstyle	0.434	0.372	0.7	1.129	0.035	0.056	0.621	1.127
Costume	0.339	0.085	10.8	5.709	0.54	0.285	1.894	0.566
Face	0.779	0.462	3.35	3.787	0.168	0.189	0.444	0.486

4.4 Discussion

This study employed a combination of empirical and eye-tracking methods to explore aesthetic preferences regarding the design elements of Chinese-style digital humans. The results reveal distinct consumer preferences, showing that digital humans characterized by young female attributes, extroverted personality traits, 3D cartoon-style, and a hybrid cultural aesthetic are particularly favored. Eye-tracking data further illuminate patterns of visual attention, providing scientific evidence for optimizing visual design in this domain.

1. The findings indicate a significant gender and age preference among consumers, with the vast majority of participants showing a strong inclination toward young female digital human representations. Personality trait analysis revealed a relatively balanced distribution between extroversion and agreeableness, with extroversion slightly more favored. Regarding visual style, the 3D cartoon-style emerged as the most popular across participants. However, preferences varied notably based on professional background: professional users tend to favor more stylized and visually interpreted forms, whereas non-professionals lean toward realism and digital twin in digital human design. In terms of cultural expression, hybrid styles that integrate traditional and modern elements received overwhelming support, far surpassing purely traditional approaches. This reflects a strong consumer demand for contemporary reinterpretations of traditional culture.
2. Eye-tracking results further revealed the distribution of visual attention when participants viewed Chinese-style digital humans. The facial region, especially the eyes

and other facial features, attracted the most attention, aligning with humans' innate focus on faces during social interactions. In addition, clothing details with Chinese cultural elements—such as frog buttons, traditional accessories, and footwear—also drew notable attention. This suggests that culturally rich and visually intricate costume elements play a crucial role in capturing viewers' visual interest and should be prioritized in design.

3. The results highlight the differential impact of design elements in attracting consumer attention, offering valuable insights for future digital human design. Designers should carefully consider user aesthetic preferences, especially in facial characteristics, costume design, and behavioral expressions, to enhance both appeal and cultural resonance. Additionally, when using AI tools for visual creation, designers should pay particular attention to fine-grained visual details, as these are focal points of user attention. These visual preference patterns offer three key implications for AI-assisted design: First, prompt engineering should emphasize detail-specific descriptors to enhance AI's ability to accurately regenerate cultural elements; Second, detail-first validation procedures should be integrated into the iterative design workflow—post-generation refinement should focus on the semantic accuracy and visual salience of key patterns using targeted editing tools; Third, cultural translation must strike a balance between authenticity and contemporary legibility—for instance, transforming ancient motifs into modular design data to retain cultural essence while improving digital media adaptability.

As AI becomes increasingly central to the design process, the human designer's core value will shift toward translating cultural codes and managing cognitive thresholds. Only by mastering the cognitive processing mechanisms of traditional elements in modern visual contexts can designers effectively utilize technological tools to ensure accurate cultural regeneration. This will enable traditional aesthetics to be meaningfully revived within digital media platforms.

5 Conclusion

This study explored the aesthetic preferences, design elements and visual attention mechanisms associated with Chinese-style digital humans in an AI-generated context, employing a mixed-methods approach including questionnaire surveys, semi-structured interviews, AIGC image generation, and eye-tracking experiments. The findings reveal that young female digital humans with extroverted personality traits, presented in a 3D cartoon-style and incorporating hybrid cultural symbolism, are most favored by young consumers. Eye-tracking data further confirmed that participants' visual attention was primarily concentrated on facial features and culturally rich costume details, emphasizing the significance of both emotional expression and cultural elements in digital human design.

While these findings contribute valuable insights into user-centered cultural digital human design, the study has several limitations. First, the sample size was relatively small and skewed toward younger demographics, which may limit the generalizability of the results. Second, although AIGC technology was employed to generate stimuli, its current level of nuance in rendering subtle cultural cues or personality expression still lags behind human artistry. Third, the study focused mainly on static portrait-style visuals, without considering motion or interactive behaviors, which are also crucial to digital human engagement.

Future research should expand the participant pool across diverse age groups and cultural backgrounds to validate the universality of these aesthetic preferences. In addition, integrating dynamic and interactive elements into the experimental stimuli may offer a more comprehensive understanding of user perception. Further exploration of real-time generative AI tools and personalization algorithms could also enhance the precision and cultural resonance of digital human design. Ultimately, this study provides an empirical foundation and practical reference for

References

1. Yao, R., Qi, G., Wu, Z., Sun, H., Sheng, D.: Digital human calls you dear: How do customers respond to virtual streamers' social-oriented language in e-commerce livestreaming? A stereotyping perspective. J. Retail. Consum. Serv. **79**, 103872 (2024)
2. Sung, E., Danny Han, D.-I., Bae, S., Kwon, O.: What drives technology-enhanced storytelling immersion? The role of digital humans. Comput. Hum. Behav. **132**, 107246 (2022)
3. Ashrafi, N., Neuhaus, V., Vona, F., Peperkorn, N.L., Shiban, Y., Voigt-Antons, J.-N.: Effect of external characteristics of a virtual human being during the use of a computer-assisted therapy tool. In: Kurosu, M., Hashizume, A. (eds.) HCII 2024. LNCS, vol. 14686, pp. 3–21. Springer, Cham (2024). https://doi.org/10.1007/978-3-031-60428-7_1
4. Kulms, P., Kopp, S.: More human-likeness, more trust? The effect of anthropomorphism on self-reported and behavioral trust in continued and interdependent human-agent cooperation. In: Proceedings of Mensch und Computer 2019, pp. 31–42 (2019)
5. Seymour, M.Y., Lingyao (Ivy), Dennis, A., Riemer, K.: Have we crossed the uncanny valley? Understanding affinity, trustworthiness, and preference for realistic digital humans in immersive environments. J. Assoc. Inf. Syst. **22** (2021)
6. Song, C., Zhao, H., Men, A., Liang, X.: Design expression of "Chinese-style" costumes in the context of globalization. Fibres Text. East. Eur. **31** (2023)
7. Sagar, M., et al.: A neurobehavioural framework for autonomous animation of virtual human faces. In: SIGGRAPH Asia 2014 Autonomous Virtual Humans and Social Robot for Telepresence, pp. 1–10 (2014)
8. Silva, E.S., Bonetti, F.: Digital humans in fashion: will consumers interact? J. Retail. Consum. Serv. **60**, 102430 (2021)
9. Sharma, M., Vemuri, K.: Accepting human-like avatars in social and professional roles. ACM Trans. Hum. Robot Interact. (THRI) **11**, 1–19 (2022)
10. Zheng, W., Luo, T., Hu, C.-P., Peng, K.: Glued to which face? Attentional priority effect of female babyface and male mature face. Front. Psychol. **9**, 286 (2018)
11. Isbister, K.: Better Game Characters by Design: A Psychological Approach. CRC Press (2022)
12. Ribeiro, T., Mendes, R., Veloso, A.I.: Playable characters in digital games: aesthetics and gender identity in digital game player's preferences. In: Fang, X. (ed.) HCII 2023. LNCS, vol. 14047, pp. 285–300. Springer, Cham (2023). https://doi.org/10.1007/978-3-031-35979-8_23
13. Blijlevens, J., Carbon, C.C., Mugge, R., Schoormans, J.P.: Aesthetic appraisal of product designs: independent effects of typicality and arousal. Br. J. Psychol. **103**, 44–57 (2012)
14. Legde, K., Cunningham, D.W.: Evaluating the effect of clothing and environment on the perceived personality of virtual avatars. In: Proceedings of the 19th ACM International Conference on Intelligent Virtual Agents, pp. 206–208

15. Iigaya, K., Yi, S., Wahle, I.A., Tanwisuth, K., O'Doherty, J.P.: Aesthetic preference for art can be predicted from a mixture of low-and high-level visual features. Nat. Hum. Behav. **5**, 743–755 (2021)
16. Li, H.X., et al.: Robotic Xiangsheng theater: designing audio-animatronics with cartoon-style facial expression for Chinese intangible cultural heritage exhibition. In: 2023 11th International Symposium of Chinese CHI, Chinese CHI2023, pp. 331–343 (2023)
17. Li, F.Z.: Mengchen: innovation of Chinese traditional culture from the perspective of digital cultural industries. Theor. Stud. Lit. Art **42**, 12–19 (2022)
18. Bernal, I.C., Andre, J., Patel, M., Newman, M.I.: Beauty re-defined: a comparative analysis of artificial intelligence-generated ideals and traditional standards. Cureus **16**, e71026 (2024)
19. Novák, J.S., Masner, J., Benda, P., Simek, P., Merunka, V.: Eye tracking, usability, and user experience: a systematic review. Int. J. Hum. Comput. Interact. **40**, 4484–4500 (2024)
20. Internet Society of China: China Digital Human Development Report (2024). Internet Society of China (2024)
21. Ebner, N.C., Riediger, M., Lindenberger, U.: FACES—a database of facial expressions in young, middle-aged, and older women and men: development and validation. Behav. Res. Methods **42**, 351–362 (2010)
22. Lin, L.Y.: The relationship of consumer personality trait, brand personality and brand loyalty: an empirical study of toys and video games buyers. J. Prod. Brand. Manag. **19**, 4–17 (2010)
23. Song, Z.Z., Yongqiong; Fang, H.: Aesthetic preferences of AI avatar visual style: moderating role of situational factors. Packag. Eng. **45**, 332–338 (2024)
24. Wei, S.L.J.: Grey relation analysis and evaluation of improved Hanfu based on Kansei engineering. Wool Text. J. **50**, 94–100 (2022)

MetaCQ: An Etextbook Platform with an Open Learner Model to Support Metacognition

Beier Wang[1] and Xueting Huang[2(✉)]

[1] University of Sydney, Sydney, NSW, Australia
[2] Swinburne University of Technology, Melbourne, VIC, Australia
xuetinghuang@swin.edu.au

Abstract. This study has proposed an E-textbook platform, MetaCQ, which integrates ITS and OLM to enable users to monitor their study progress. The platform adopts a chatbot to generate MCQs and manage learners' study data and their learning model. Additionally, it regulates help-seeking behaviour and provides immediate feedback tailored to users' learning processes. Three adaptive feedback methods have been implemented to construct chatbots, examining the MCQs' relevancy and difficulty through the ThinkAloud study to evaluate the most effective method of measuring the user's study performance. However, no valid result demonstrates which method can significantly assess learners' study outcomes based on the current experiment, which requires further studies to improve it.

Keywords: E-textbook platform · Open Learner Model · Metacognition · Chatbot · Multiple Choice Questions

1 Introduction

Since the development of artificial intelligence and its extension of application in the educational field, along with the shifting study mode into online study due to the pandemic, E-textbooks have become an essential component within the educational technology field from their accessibility and adaptability to assist students' learning process and teachers' teaching procedure being personalisation and convenience.

Intelligent Tutoring System (ITS) is a core feature to support E-textbook functionalities, which has been defined by Nwana [9] as made up of computer programs to support the tutoring process by integrating the teaching materials and guiding the teaching instruction, composing with expert knowledge module, student model module, tutoring module and user interface module. Bull [2] has also suggested that embedding ITS with the E-textbook platform enables the system to adapt learner interaction to educational needs and support learners' study outcomes, and can further result in the composition of the Open Learner

C. Stephanidis et al. (Eds.): HCII 2025, CCIS 2773, pp. 112–122, 2026.
https://doi.org/10.1007/978-3-032-12773-0_11

Model (OLM) when the learners' learning progresses are visible and accessible since OLM is a learner model that is externalised in a form that users can interpret.

Metacognition has been recognised as "higher-order cognition about cognition" stated from Veenman et al. [13], deploying the OLM into the E-textbook platform will facilitate learners' metacognition activity by supporting long-term learning outcomes mentioned by Bull and Kay [3], and reversely providing immediate metacognitive feedback through the OLMs can improve learners' metacognition skills and benefit with their learning process indicated by Roll et al. [10].

Technology's improvement has further accelerated artificial intelligence's implementation. Chatbot, as a significant product, has been identified as a bridge to connect technology and education, contributing to learners' personalised learning and interactive learning experience with its capability, as stated by Clarizia et al. [6]. Applying the chatbot to generate multiple choice questions (MCQs) can accurately measure users' study outcomes, covering a wide knowledge range with broad ranges of difficulty, while enhancing their metacognitive ability as suggested by Simkin and Kuechler [11].

Under the background driven and benefits of the E-textbook platform, this paper introduces an E-textbook platform, MetaCQ, consisting of the ITS and consolidating the OLM and the metacognition strategy, allowing the user to interact with the chatbot and answering the practice questions in the form of MCQs to improve study outcome.

2 Design and Implementations

2.1 Design Architecture

MetaCQ's architecture design references PUMPT's structure [7], deployed Sphinx and reStructured Text to build the E-Textbook platform, and uses HTML and JavaScript to support its functions. Similar to PUMPT, MetaCQ also runs locally to support the web page. However, instead of collecting the learning data from the local PC and updating it to the cloud storage, it communicates to the chatbot to allow it to handle the learning data and enable it to respond to the download request to update the OLM of the current topic knowledge mastery level. Content and the code have been uploaded on GitHub.

The MetaCQ consists of three components: **Chatbot**, **OLM** and **Metacognition strategy**. According to the ITS framework, MetaCQ, as the platform, handles the function of the user interface module to provide the interface and interactions; OLM, in the role of student model, maintains students' learning progress and outcomes; chatbot delivers the generated MCQs to represent the expert module, cooperating with metacognition strategy with guidance to serve tutoring module. The components within MetaCQ corresponding to the ITS framework have been displayed in Fig. 1.

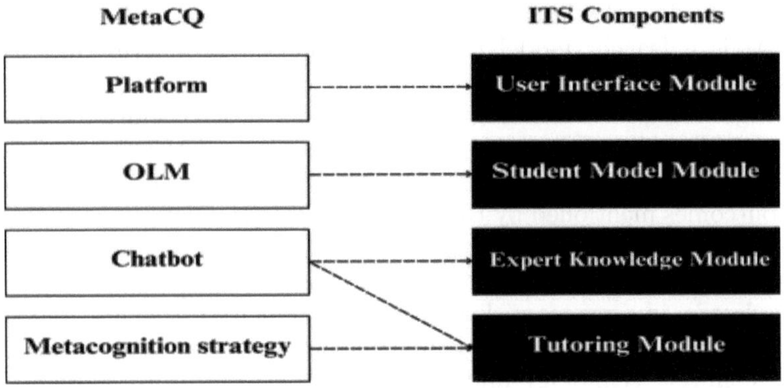

Fig. 1. The MetaCQ components and the ITS framework

2.2 Implementations

MetaCQ was designed to instruct users' general data privacy knowledge under the content and developed from the University of Sydney's unit, **DATA3406: Human-in-the-Loop Data Analytics**, which covered the topics of Data privacy principles, Data privacy laws and Data privacy management. Each topic contains clear and corresponding learning objectives for users to reach study expectations and guide the content writing by applying relevant resources to explain theories with simple explanations. To deploy the MetaCQ, users need to read through the content of each topic, answer the MCQs generated from the chatbot and award a satisfied mark to process the next topic's study.

Chatbot. MetaCQ has applied the chatbot innovated by the University of Sydney, which deployed the GPT-4 large language model to operate the MCQs generation and user's study performance evaluation. Cogniti.ai allows users to create chatbot-based agents that can be steered with specific instructions and resourced with specific contextual information from units of study, as Liu [8] explained. Implementing the on-time chatbot has constituted ELM-ART's limitation of delayed discussion responses [14], which are available with instant interactions to boost user engagement.

MetaCQ has developed three different adaptive feedback method chatbots based on the number of chapter topics. Each topic has assigned a unique adaptive method chatbot to generate the content-aligned questions, minimising each chatbot's content-loading, focusing on the current topic to ensure the question's content quality, and avoiding questions accidentally encountered with other topics. Each practice session offers the user five questions in total, with two marks worth each question. Final scores correspond to different knowledge mastery rankings, as shown in Fig. 2.

Considering the purpose of allowing chatbots to generate effective MCQs, particularly from Butler's six requirements [5] of designing MCQ, chatbots' con-

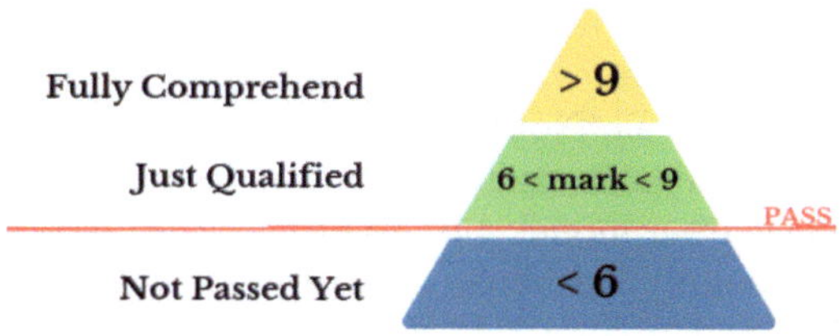

Fig. 2. Final mark and knowledge mastery level ranking

figuration regarding generating MCQs has focused on: (1) Provide three potential answers to balance the difficulty level with the ideally intermediate level. (2) The evaluation will deliver concise feedback on each question and overall performance. (3) Question options will avoid the terms of "None-of-the-Above" and "All-of-the-Above". (4) Implement the metacognition strategy, help-seeking, to allow users to reflect in depth on their knowledge.

To maintain the intermediate level of the MCQ difficulty level, motivated by ELM-ART's weighting strategy [14], each question's default difficulty level has been set at 0.5, ranging from 0 (minimum) to 1 (maximum). Three adaptive feedback methods have been differentiated from the approach of calculating the practice questions' difficulty level: (1) **all-in-all:** The newly generated MCQs practice difficulty level will be based on the previous performance. (2) **1-after-1:** Each newly generated MCQ will be based on the previous MCQ's performance. (3) **No extra settings.** The mechanism behind the adaptive feedback methods can be refined into the Fig. 3.

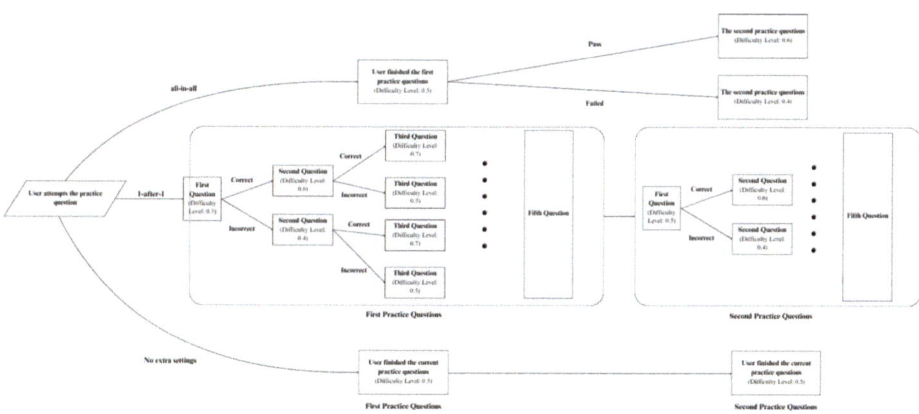

Fig. 3. Three adapative feedback methods

OLM. Within the MetaCQ, there is a table on the homepage that displays the user's current study performance in Fig. 4. All the chapters' knowledge-mastery levels have been initially set as "Not Qualified" to stimulate users to proceed with their study progress and enable users to update their learner models regarding ELM-ART's editable learner model [14]. To update the OLM knowledge mastery levels, users must manually download the practice test conversation between them and ChatGPT and upload the conversation file to the current chapter performance box locally. Users can intuitively visualise their knowledge mastery levels at each topic, be aware of their knowledge mastery status and adjust their study plans. Users can also make reasonable arguments to request the chatbot re-evaluate their knowledge mastery levels by requesting to redo the practice test within the chat. This negotiation process has referred to Bull's persuadable model in the SMIL framework [4], but they do not have access to modify their learner models directly.

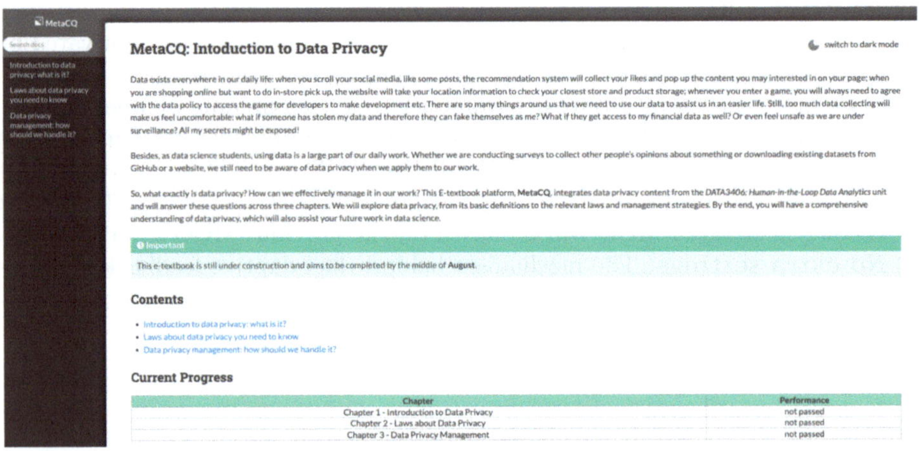

Fig. 4. MetaCQ Homepage with OLM

Metacognition. Research has shown that immediate metacognitive feedback through OLM enhances users' metacognitive skills and supports learning [1], leading to its integration into E-textbook platforms. Building on this, MetaCQ incorporates a help-seeking strategy inspired by Help Tutor. It combines with the question-answering process to provide hints while applying a proportional penalty to marks for assistance. Users can seek help anytime during the answering process by typing "?tips" illustrated as Fig. 5.

The restriction boundary has been claimed to minimise help-seeking errors: users can seek help up to three times per question, with each request revealing additional hints and reducing the attainable marks accordingly. The help-seeking mechanism is illustrated in Fig. 6. Limiting help-seeking opportunities minimises

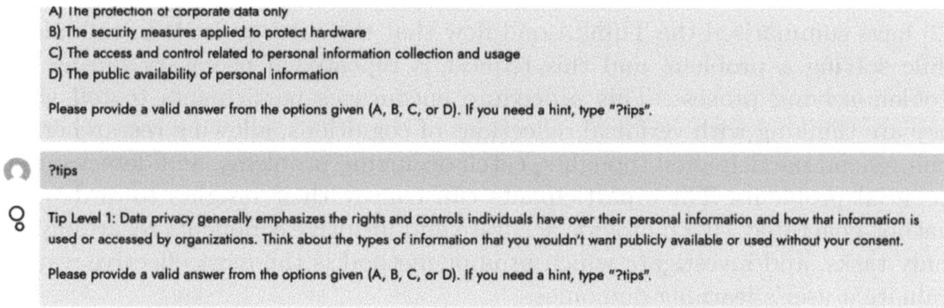

Fig. 5. Applying hints during the answering process

the risk of over-reliance on hints while encouraging users to reflect on knowledge gaps, remain aware of mark deductions, and make informed decisions.

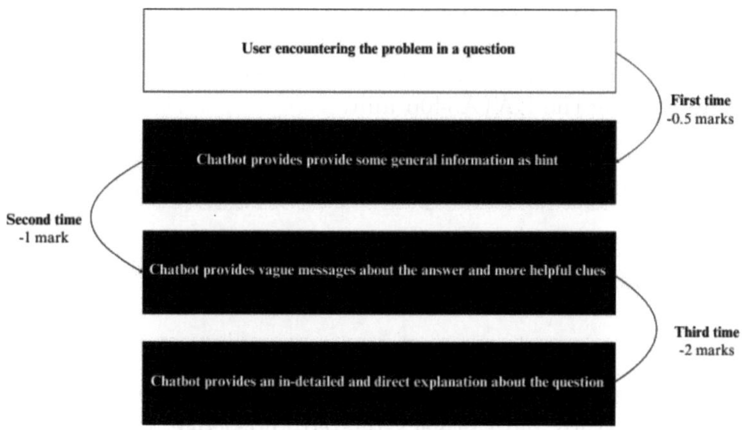

Fig. 6. Help-seeking mechanism

3 User Study

To examine which adaptive feedback method can more effectively evaluate a user's study performance, a ThinkAloud session was constructed since considering the difficulty level can appropriate tailoring the question based on the user's current knowledge level and enabling the user's learning motivation. Additionally, the dynamic difficulty level mechanism that generates MCQs with varied difficulty level points from the chatbot's prompt can further assess the user's depth of understanding.

ThinkAloud is a technique that collects participants' perspectives from verbal communication through tasks that align with the research purpose. Researches

[12] have summarised the ThinkAloud flow that the subject needs to talk aloud while solving a problem, and this request is repeated if necessary during the problem-solving process. This procedure encourages participants to tell what they are thinking with veridical reflections of cognitions, allowing researchers to comprehend participants' thoughts, catch occurring problems, and detect minor potential problems. Thus, participants can convey their insights towards each chatbot-generated MCQ, provide accurate and intuitive comments regarding the study tasks, and investigate which prompt method is the most effective way to evaluate a user's learning outcomes.

The ThinkAloud session has been conceptualised into four parts. The "Introduction" aims to guide the participants with the study purpose and grant them the persona of "the student who is currently taking DATA3406 unit's study" and provides a short demonstration to display MetaCQ's workflow in "Demonstration". "Tasks" outlined what participants need to accomplish, and the "Demographic" gathered participants' background knowledge and DATA3406 study status.

Ten participants from the the University of Sydney has been selected to support the study's validity, regarding to their relevant backgrounds and data privacy understandings, particularly those participants have accomplished or are currently undertaking the DATA3406 unit.

Table 1. Chatbot allocations on each chapter

Chap. 1	Chap. 2	Chap. 3
1-after-1	No extra settings	all-in-all

There are two scenarios within the tasks: (1) a student currently working on this material to study data privacy-related knowledge; (2) preparing for the upcoming quiz and reviewing this material as revision. For each task, participants need to evaluate each MCQ's difficulty level after they finish the current practice questions for each chapter, with a Likert scale measurement from 1 to 5, and then explain the rationale behind it. 1 represents very easy, and 5 means very hard. Each chatbot's allocation to each chapter remains unrevealed to reduce the bias within the feedback. The chatbot allocations are demonstrated in Table 1. The repeated tasks allow participants to reach out to more generated MCQs and provide more extensive information to evaluate the generated MCQs' qualities under the different knowledge familiarity scenarios. It also ensures fairness among the adaptive methods examination as "all-in-all" requires the previous test results. During the ThinkAloud session, the conversation pattern has been adhered to as below:

Host: How would you rate this question's difficulty level with the scale from 1 to 5? While 1 stands for ...
Participant: I will rate this question as ...

Host: Would you like to explain why you would rate this question as ...?
Participant: I think ...

4 Results and Discussion

The difficulty level results have been retrieved from participants' Likert scales and their clarified rating reasons. This scale can intuitively measure participants' degrees of opinion and offers comprehensive insight with flexibility from their rationale in the analysis of the results.

Figure 7 has recorded each participant's difficulty score for each question in two tasks, while Table 2 and Table 3 have calculated each chatbot's difficulty ratings among all the participants with mean, median, and mode scores for each task.

		User 1	User 2	User 3	User 4	User 5	User 6	User 7	User 8	User 9	User 10
	First Task										
	C1Q1	1	1	4	2	1	1	1	2	1	1
	C1Q2	1	1	4	2	2	1	4	2	1	1
	C1Q3	1	1	3	1	1	1	2	1	1	3
	C1Q4	5	3	2	2	1	1	1	5	3	3
1-after-1	C1Q5	4	1	2	1	4	4	1	2	2	1
	C2Q1	1	2	3	4	2	4	3	1	1	3
	C2Q2	4	2	2	3	1	2	1	3	1	4
	C2Q3	1	2	3	1	2	1	3	2	2	1
	C2Q4	1	1	2	1	2	2	2	1	1	3
No Extra Settings	C2Q5	1	1	2	1	3	1	2	2	1	3
	C3Q1	1	1	4	1	1	5	1	2	4	1
	C3Q2	2	1	5	1	2	1	1	4	2	1
	C3Q3	1	1	1	1	3	1	2	1	1	4
	C3Q4	1	1	3	2	3	3	4	2	4	1
all-in-all	C3Q5	4	1	4	1	3	1	1	3	1	4
	SecondTask										
	C1Q1	1	1	2	1	2	2	2	1	1	1
	C1Q2	1	1	1	1	2	2	1	1	2	1
	C1Q3	1	1	2	1	2	1	2	1	1	2
	C1Q4	1	1	1	1	1	1	1	2	1	1
1-after-1	C1Q5	1	2	3	2	4	1	2	4	3	2
	C2Q1	1	1	2	1	1	2	2	2	1	1
	C2Q2	1	1	1	1	3	4	2	1	1	3
	C2Q3	1	1	2	1	3	1	1	3	2	3
	C2Q4	1	1	3	2	3	2	3	1	3	1
No Extra Settings	C2Q5	1	1	1	3	3	1	2	3	1	2
	C3Q1	1	1	1	1	2	2	1	2	1	1
	C3Q2	1	1	1	2	1	2	1	2	4	2
	C3Q3	4	1	3	1	2	1	1	3	2	4
	C3Q4	1	1	2	3	2	3	2	1	5	1
all-in-all	C3Q5	4	1	2	1	3	1	3	2	1	4

Fig. 7. Difficult Scores Table

Table 2. Each chatbot's difficulty ratings among all the participants in terms of mean, median, and mode in the first task

Factor	Mean	Median	Mode
1-after-1	1.9	1	1
No extra settings	2.0	2	1
all-in-all	2.1	1	1

Table 3. Each chatbot's difficulty ratings among all the participants in terms of mean, median, and mode in the second task

Factor	Mean	Median	Mode
1-after-1	1.5	1	1
No extra settings	1.8	1	1
all-in-all	1.9	2	1

Between Table 2 and Table 3, 4 out of 6 median scores are 1 (very easy), and two median scores have been quantified in 2 (easy); one is allocated in the first task's "No extra settings" chatbot, another one is allocated in the second task's "all-in-all" chatbot. The two different median scores occurred in different tasks that happened on different chatbots, along with the mode values for those two special cases are all equivalent to 1 (very easy), implicating the right skewness occurs in two tasks score distributions, resulting in the median being affected and raised up to 2 (easy). Considering participants' experiences, this categorical analysis suggests that chatbots can generate very easy MCQs.

Table 4 has calculated the mean score of each chatbot's capability of generating difficult level's MCQ between two tasks. Even though the average scores that measure the difficulty capability among the chatbots are slightly different, with a maximum marginal variation of 0.3, the results are close to each other as 1.7 and 1.9 can be rounded up to 2 (easy) to interpret the scale rating. The Mean Average Deviation scores are no larger than 0.4, demonstrating each chatbot has a relatively stable capability to generate similar difficulty MCQs for each task. Therefore, all three chatbots have the similar stable capability of generating "easy" difficulty-level MCQs. Based on the previous analysis, there is a contradiction between the difficulty level generated by chatbots and participation perception. Three chatbots can stably generate "easy" level MCQs, while the participation standard view illustrates that questions difficulty-level are "very easy". This has further led to Table 5, which synthesised participants' feedback with respect to their scores to reflect the conflicts. Participants mentioned that "very easy" difficulty levels are too straightforward and basic, consisting of the stable generated "easy" difficulty level scaled from the chatbots. This indicates the chatbot prompts required further refinement about its difficulty-level scales. Additionally, the "very hard" difficulty level is out of the content, which is supposed to stay in the content but requires critical thinking and logical judgement from Bloom's taxonomy model as Simkin and Kuechler [11] discussed.

In summary, three chatbots performed similarly in MCQs difficulty generations, with the participants' group common views for three chatbots on difficulty level rated in "1" (very easy), and the average difficulty level scores from each task are close to "2" (easy), which resulted in the conclusion that there's no significant difference among these three discussed adaptive MCQs generating methods to evaluate users' study performance, and they all can measure users' study performance in some extent. However, three chatbots cannot accurately

Table 4. The average of difficulty level scores among the chatbots between two tasks

Factor	Mean
1-after-1	1.7
No extra settings	1.9
all-in-all	2

Table 5. Participants comment summarisation on difficulty level

1	Intuitive questions and have been asked general definition questions, the correct option is obvious.
2	Questions are relevant and straightforward with the content of knowledge memorisation, the correct option is quite easy to tell.
3	Questions require basic knowledge comprehension, and options are able to differentiate, but some terms are quite related.
4	Questions are mixed up with concepts, require knowledge reflection, options contain distractions that are hard to differentiate.
5	Questions have covered the content not mentioned, requires in-depth thinking and knowledge application, options contain too many distractions.

generate stable MCQs with a score of 3 (intermediate level) in expectation and contain the Definition-Perception gap with the defined difficulty level, which requires adjusting the difficulty level to improve.

5 Conclusion and Further Improvements

This study presents MetaCQ, an E-Textbook platform designed to facilitate data privacy learning by integrating adaptive chatbots, OLM-based self-assessment, and metacognitive help-seeking strategies. The platform employs three adaptive feedback mechanisms, evaluated through a user study with the Think-Aloud method. Findings indicate that while the system shows potential, limitations arise from the small participant pool and an imbalance in question difficulty, with most items rated as "very easy." Future work will refine question design by enhancing difficulty differentiation and adjusting adaptive difficulty ranges from 0.1 to 0.3. Moreover, expanding participant involvement for question difficulty annotation and adopting reinforcement learning techniques are suggested to improve the generation of higher-difficulty MCQs. Further studies will also apply more robust statistical methods, including hypothesis testing, ANOVA, and t-tests, to validate the adaptive mechanisms' impact across different demographic groups and explore correlations between perceived difficulty, performance, and user engagement.

Disclosure of Interests. The authors have no competing interests to declare that are relevant to the content of this article.

References

1. Aleven, V., Mclaren, B., Roll, I., Koedinger, K.: Toward meta-cognitive tutoring: a model of help seeking with a cognitive tutor. Int. J. Artif. Intell. Educ. **16**(2), 101–128 (2006)
2. Bull, S.: There are open learner models about! IEEE Trans. Learn. Technol. **13**(2), 425–448 (2020)
3. Bull, S., Kay, J.: Open learner models as drivers for metacognitive processes. In: Azevedo, R., Aleven, V. (eds.) International Handbook of Metacognition and Learning Technologies. SIHE, vol. 28, pp. 349–365. Springer, New York (2013). https://doi.org/10.1007/978-1-4419-5546-3_23
4. Bull, S., Kay, J.: Smili:): a framework for interfaces to learning data in open learner models, learning analytics and related fields. Int. J. Artif. Intell. Educ. **26**, 293–331 (2016)
5. Butler, A.C.: Multiple-choice testing in education: Are the best practices for assessment also good for learning? J. Appl. Res. Mem. Cogn. **7**(3), 323–331 (2018)
6. Clarizia, F., Colace, F., Lombardi, M., Pascale, F., Santaniello, D.: Chatbot: an education support system for student. In: Castiglione, A., Pop, F., Ficco, M., Palmieri, F. (eds.) CSS 2018. LNCS, vol. 11161, pp. 291–302. Springer, Cham (2018). https://doi.org/10.1007/978-3-030-01689-0_23
7. Kay, J., Kummerfeld, B.: PUMPT: an e-textbook platform based on a personal user model for learning. In: Proceedings of the Third International Workshop on Intelligent Textbooks, pp. 27–34 (2021)
8. Liu, D.: Letting educators take control of generative ai to improve learning, teaching, and assessment (2023)
9. Nwana, H.S.: Intelligent tutoring systems: an overview. Artif. Intell. Rev. **4**(4), 251–277 (1990)
10. Roll, I., Aleven, V., McLaren, B.M., Koedinger, K.R.: Improving students' help-seeking skills using metacognitive feedback in an intelligent tutoring system. Learn. Instr. **21**(2), 267–280 (2011)
11. Simkin, M.G., Kuechler, W.L.: Multiple-choice tests and student understanding: what is the connection? Decis. Sci. J. Innov. Educ. **3**(1), 73–98 (2005)
12. Van Someren, M.W., Barnard, Y.F., Sandberg, J.A.: The Think Aloud Method: A Practical Approach to Modelling Cognitive Processes, p. 208, Academic Press, London (1994)
13. Veenman, M.V., Van Hout-Wolters, B.H., Afflerbach, P.: Metacognition and learning: conceptual and methodological considerations. Metacogn. Learn. **1**, 3–14 (2006)
14. Weber, G., Brusilovsky, P.: ELM-ART: an adaptive versatile system for web-based instruction. Int. J. Artif. Intell. Educ. **12**, 351–384 (2001)

Analogy-Based Learning Approach for Teaching AI Fundamentals to Teens

Yi Yang [1,2,3](✉), Hao Feng[1,2,3], Beichen Lu[1,2,3], and Jiasong Sun[1,2,3]

[1] Department of Electronic Engineering, Tsinghua University, Beijing, China
{yangyy,sunjiasong}@tsinghua.edu.cn, {fh20, lubc23}@mails.tsinghua.edu.cn
[2] School of Software, Tsinghua University, Beijing, China
[3] School of Public Policy and Management, Tsinghua University, Beijing, China

Abstract. Mastering AI technology skills is becoming a major talent for employees in the industry. It has become a common phenomenon in the world's famous universities to widely offer AI courses in computer and non-computer majors. Outside the scope of higher education campuses, teachers and students in grades K9–K12 have also realized the advent of the AI era. As candidates for higher education, these teenagers have many ambitions on learning AI technologies, they lack the mathematics, physics and programming knowledge required to develop AI technology, so they cannot jump directly into the development stage to produce creative contents. This paper proposes an Analogies-Based Learning Approach to teach teenagers fundamental AI concepts and knowledge. Although teenagers lack the basic knowledge of mathematics and physics required to understand AI, teenagers connect the common sense in their minds with specific technologies in AI through the teacher's analogies. At the same time, the learners' hobbies are also discovered and connected with these analogies, such as using basketball terms to describe the decision tree in machine learning. Some youth volunteers were selected to participate our research between K9 to K12 grade from different cities and schools over a three-year period. The preliminary findings based on the questionnaire show that compared with ordinary teaching methods, the analogy-based method can alleviate the anxiety and fear of young volunteers about AI learning and their acceptance of learning AI has improved.

Keywords: Analogies-Based Learning · Artificial Intelligence · AI Education for Teenagers · Learners' Hobbies

1 Introduction

Artificial Intelligence and machine learning are the most sought-after technical skills by employers in the 2024 market [1]. In addition to the computer and internet industries, the healthcare, finance, and energy industries are also increasingly relying on AI tools to automate their processes, make complex business decisions, and predict the future. The reason is that companies need AI more than ever as a competitive driver to realize their vision of digital transformation and automated business. Even just having simple

C. Stephanidis et al. (Eds.): HCII 2025, CCIS 2773, pp. 123–134, 2026.
https://doi.org/10.1007/978-3-032-12773-0_12

practical experience with AI programming languages like Python and artificial intelligence platforms like TensorFlow can help most college students achieve better career development.

Hence, the education field and educators need to quickly shift their focus and teaching methods to keep up with the explosive growth of AI technology and cultivate qualified employees with AI capabilities in all professions. The young people with higher education need to adapt to AI technology and applications in work and life more quickly. Therefore, well-known universities such as MIT or Stanford University have begun to offer AI courses to students majoring in other fields besides computer science [2], which could help students cope with a series of challenges and problems brought by AI and ensure that they remain competitive globally.

The urgent need for AI education is not only happening on college campuses. Even high school education has begun to call for more AI courses and related tutoring. Some middle schools have already started using the programming language Scratch as a tool, integrating "computational thinking" and "maker spirit" to solve practical problems such as puzzles and games [3, 4]. With the emergence of foundation models such as ChatGPT, young people can also use AI tools to understand, process and analyze data. As candidates for colleges and universities, young people are not satisfied with using AI tools, but are eager to develop new AI applications, improve existing AI algorithms, and create popular AI games.

Although young people who are interested in AI technology are full of desire for knowledge and motivation to learn, in fact, most young people do not have basic knowledge related to AI, such as calculus, linear algebra or signal processing [5], so they can only use the developed platforms or applications for operation, and it is difficult to modify them or propose new applications.

Analogy learning is an effective educational method that organically links learners' existing knowledge or concepts with the knowledge or concepts to be learned. When this teaching method is used to educate teenagers to learn AI knowledge, it can reduce their unfamiliarity and fear of AI, attract their interest and attention, and express AI-related ideas with the vocabulary and language they have mastered.

This paper proposes an Analogies-Based Learning Approach to teach high school teenagers fundamental AI concepts and knowledge. This Analogies-Based Learning method attempts to link a set of common sense and knowledge structures that high school students already have with the specific AI key concepts. In their experience with high school students, teachers understand and refine some concepts that teenagers are familiar with during this period, such as what happens in daily life or their favorite literary works and games, and use these concepts to explain some obscure terms and processes in AI technology. Furthermore, teachers can use language and communication methods consistent with teenagers in terms of language to make learning more attractive.

Through the teacher's analogy, an interesting connection is formed between students and difficult basic knowledge, encouraging teenagers not to be frightened by difficult special terms. For example, when teaching the structure of CNNs (Convolutional Neural Networks), which is described by analogy as a jigsaw puzzle game often played by teenagers. Each piece of the puzzle is similar to the CNNs weight. Players need to observe with their eyes and constantly try to change the combination of puzzle pieces.

The adjustment method of CNNs weights is similar to this puzzle game. The value of the weight is adjusted by constantly passing information in the opposite direction, and finally the puzzle is complete and correct. Another example is the pooling operation in CNNs, which is likened to a map treasure hunt in Analogies-Based Learning, where players need to find the highest value item on the map and can only take one item. In the pooling operation, the pooling layer selects the maximum value and discards the other values. In this case, we use the method of asking students to find the highest value number in a 9-square grid to imitate the work of the pooling layer.

At the same time, we try to connect learners' hobbies with the analogies given by teachers, such as using basketball terms to describe the decision tree in machine learning, comparing this algorithm to a classification tree with the probability of wins and losses during the women's basketball tournament games. This specific analogy can sometimes unexpectedly improve the learning enthusiasm of teenagers.

We selected 20 youth volunteers between K9 to K12 grade from different cities and schools for this study over a three-year period. The preliminary findings based on the questionnaire show that compared with ordinary teaching methods, the analogy-based method can alleviate the anxiety and fear of young volunteers about AI learning. When they can use relatively simple vocabulary instead of AI-specific terms to express their ideas, their acceptance of learning AI has improved. And it is easy to understand that boys have a better learning experience using sports terms such as basketball or tennis to describe AI terms.

2 The Analogies-Based Learning for AI Youth Education

Students in high school are often in adolescence, a unique mental stage during which rapid physiological and psychological changes often occur. Compared with undergraduates who are a few years older, high school students are often unable to concentrate for long periods of time. This phenomenon is often explained by the fact that brain areas related to impulse control and attention control are not fully developed, resulting in tasks that require long-term concentration, such as learning difficult unfamiliar content, being more difficult for adolescents than for undergraduates. Second, because high school students' brains are still developing, they are unable to directly relate abstract content, such as formulas or theorems, to the real world or experience. Therefore, it is more difficult for high school students to understand or remember abstract information than for undergraduates. Finally, high school students are already capable of forming some complex thought pathways in their minds, but it is still a challenge to convey these thoughts to others through mature language expression, which is much more capable for college students [6–9].

In response to these three phenomena, we adopt one kind of analogy learning educational method to teach AI technology for high school students. The term analogy refers to a structural comparison between two fields, which principle is shown in Fig. 1 [10]. Analogy teaching used in education can be seen as multiple comparisons of two groups of objects in terms of structure or function and other characteristics. It is applied in basic disciplines, science and engineering, and economics, enabling students to form a correspondence between old and new knowledge [11].

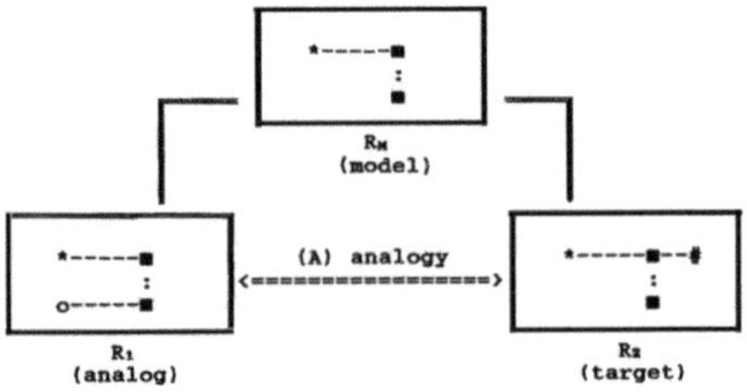

Fig. 1. The meaning of Analogy [10].

First of all, with the Analogies-Based Learning for AI teaching, the high school students could recall their common sense or familiar knowledge with the help of analogy cases of AI terms. Students usually feel relaxed and can complete brain activities for a longer time when they meet very familiar content. Second, this teaching approach will reduce the fear of middle school students about the abstract concepts of AI technology and make concepts easier to form long-term memory. Finally, if teachers can use simpler words rather than professional terms to introduce it, high school students can be more proactive and actively participate in asking questions and interacting.

2.1 Analogy Learning with Attention Control in Teenagers

Research into differences in teenagers and adult brains that lead to behavioral differences has been ongoing for years. Research shows that during adolescence, cognitive and attentional abilities continue to improve along with physical brain development. Using fMRI, researchers studied the developmental changes in neural networks associated with cognitive and attentional tasks in adolescents and adults and found that brain areas associated with these tasks, such as frontocortical networks, continue to develop. As they get older, teenagers' ability to use metaphors and analogies improves. However, if teenagers can't be engaged in class, their chances of learning anything are still slim. Some researchers have used analogies in music lyrics to improve teenagers' decision-making abilities [12–14].

Analogies-based learning helps teachers break down AI concepts that are too obscure and complex for teenagers who lack basic knowledge into simple and continuous learning steps. Through the teacher's analogy, an interesting connection is formed between students and difficult basic knowledge, encouraging teenagers not to be intimidated by difficult special terms. For example, as shown in Fig. 2, when teaching the structure of convolutional neural networks, CNN is described by analogy as a jigsaw puzzle game often played by teenagers. Each piece of the puzzle is similar to the CNN weight. Players need to observe with their eyes and constantly try to change the combination of puzzle pieces. The adjustment method of CNN weights is similar to this puzzle game. The value of the weight is adjusted by constantly passing information in the opposite direction, and finally the puzzle is complete and correct. Another example is the pooling operation in CNN, which is likened to a map treasure hunt in Analogies-Based Learning, where players need to find the highest value item on the map and can only take one item. In the pooling operation, the pooling layer selects the maximum value and discards the other values. In this case, we use the method of asking students to find the highest value number in a 9-square grid to imitate the work of the pooling layer.

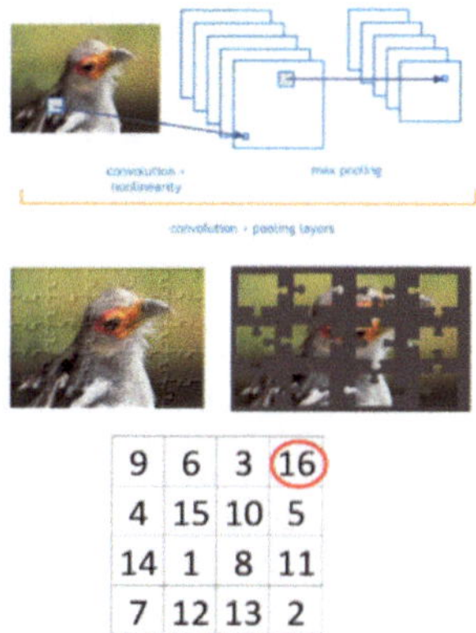

Fig. 2. The Analogies-based learning on Convolutional Neural Networks [15].

2.2 Analogy Learning with Personal Interest of Teenagers

In addition to analogizing professional terms with daily life and games, we also introduced the interest-based teaching [18] that has been implemented before into AI education for teenagers. Teachers carefully explore the learners' interests and hobbies, such as sports or music, and explore the analogy between these interests and AI teaching. For example, as shown in Fig. 3, we analogize the decision tree in machine learning with the probability of scoring in a basketball tournament. This specific analogy can sometimes unexpectedly increase the learning enthusiasm of teenagers.

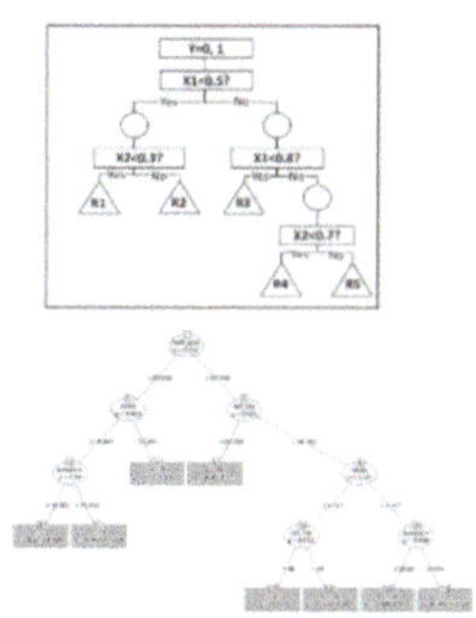

Fig. 3. The decision tree with the probability of scoring in a basketball tournament [16, 17].

In this analogy teaching method based on personal interests, we summarized some comparative cases that are popular among teenagers during the teaching process, as shown in Table 1.

Table 1. Algorithms/Terms with Analogy Cases.

Category	Algorithm/Term	Teenagers' Interests	Analogy Case
Machine Learning	Decision Tree	Basketball	decision tree vs. the probability of scoring in a basketball tournament
	SVM Maximize Margin	Fencing	maximize the SVM margin vs. maximizing the safety distance a fencer maintains to reduces the risk of being hit
	Clustering	Poker	clustering vs. grouping poker players by styles (aggressive, conservative, balanced)
	Training/Validation	Competing in Sports	training a model vs. the practice phase and the competition phase in the sports
Deep Learning	Gradient Descent	Mountain Climbing	minimizing the loss function vs. Whether the direction of going down the mountain is correct and how far each step is taken
	Learning Rate	Piano	learning rate vs. everyday piano practice intensity. A higher intensity might lead to faster improvement but also to potential mistakes
	Overfitting	Marathon	overfitting vs. athletes become dependent on running on single type of terrain
	CNNs	Gaming	CNNs weights and pooling vs. jigsaw puzzle game and map treasure hunt
Foundation Model	Multi-Agent System	Video Games	multi-agent vs. multiple players with different strategies interacting in a shared environment

(continued)

Table 1. (*continued*)

Category	Algorithm/Term	Teenagers' Interests	Analogy Case
	Pre-training	Skiing	Pre-training vs. ski lessons where beginners practice on various terrains and conditions are like the pre-training phase
	Transfer Learning	Writing	transfer learning vs. An author hones their writing abilities by writing various types of content before specializing in a specific genre or story
	Fine-Tuning	Sculpture	Fine-Tuning vs. refining the features of the sculpture and polishing the final piece

2.3 Analogy Learning with Appropriate Terminology for Teenagers

Colloquial language is a social language used to build group identity and social cohesion. The reasons why teenagers use colloquial language include group belonging, creativity and social differentiation. Researchers at the University of Bergen have created The Bergen Corpus of London Teenage Language specifically for teenage slang [19, 20]. Research suggests that adolescents may communicate differently when they talk to adults than when they talk to their peers, such as using more figurative language and abrupt topic changes with their peers [21].

For example, in Chinese teenagers' colloquial language, "Er ci yuan" means the 2D world, often referring to anime and manga culture. Teachers can use "Er ci yuan" to describe some concepts related to two-dimensional space in AI technology. Another colloquialism commonly used by Chinese teenagers is "Keng", which means to deceive or disappoint others. In the communication process, teachers can use this colloquialism to describe the data bias in machine learning that induces the model to generate wrong results. When teachers use colloquialisms commonly used by teenagers in teaching AI, it helps promote an open communication atmosphere, reduce the generation gap between students and teachers, and encourage them to actively express their ideas. This approach also makes teenagers feel that teachers respect the unique culture of students, which helps to cultivate a sense of trust between teachers and students.

3 The Statistical Results

3.1 Data Collection

We invited 20 (half male and half female) high school students from K9 to K12 to participate in our Analogies-based teaching class. In the class, we designed a series of AI teaching courses involving machine learning, deep learning and foundation model as shown in Table 1. The content includes basic concepts related to algorithms such as decision tree, support vector machine (SVM), clustering, CNNs, multi-agent system and simplified mathematical and physical principles. These courses usually last for one week, with students learning for 4 h in class and practicing for 4 h every day. After the course, students will propose some interesting topics to implement. Students proposed many interesting topics, such as using indoor robots for garbage collection or using drones for cargo delivery. After the course, we asked students to answer a questionnaire. The content of the questionnaire is shown as:

Section 1: Personal

a) Gender: Male/Female
b) Grade Level: K9/K10/K11/K12

Section 2: Experience

a) Before this course, how would you rate your fear or anxiety about AI terms and algorithms? Very High/High/Moderate/Low/Very Low
b) After this course, how would you rate your fear or anxiety about AI terms and algorithms? Very High/High/Moderate/Low/Very Low
c) On average, how long could you concentrate during the classroom learning sessions? Full times/30–40 min/20–30 min/10–20 min/ Less than 10 min
d) On average, how long could you concentrate during the hands-on practice sessions? Full times/30–40 min/20–30 min/10–20 min/ Less than 10 min

Section 3: Course Content

a) How clear were the explanations of AI concepts and algorithms in our class? Very clear/Clear/Neutral/Unclear/Very unclear
b) How helpful were the analogies in making difficult concepts easier to understand? Extremely helpful/Very helpful/Somewhat helpful/Not very helpful/Not helpful at all
c) Did you like the hands-on part? Very much/Like/Fairly/Not very/Not at all
d) What was the most impressive analogy case you learned in this course? (Open-ended response)
e) Describe your understanding of an algorithm (such as SVM) with your own words. (Open-ended response)

Section 4: Impressions

a) Which project topic proposed by the students is most interesting? (Open-ended response)

b) Compared to the courses you have studied in the past, how would you rate the friendliness and approachability of our teacher? Much friendlier/Friendlier/About the same/Less friendly/Much less friendly
c) Did this course inspire you to think of new ways to use AI in everyday life? Yes, definitely/Yes, somewhat/Neutral/Not really/Not at all
d) How confident are you in your ability to work in AI in the future? Very Confident/Confident/Neutral/Not very confident/Not confident at all

Section 5: Feedback and Suggestions

a) What feature did you enjoy most in our class? (Open-ended response)
b) What improvements would you suggest for future courses? (Open-ended response)
c) Do you have any additional comments or feedback? (Open-ended response)

3.2 Analysis and Results

We collected and analyzed the questionnaires from all students. Excluding personal and open-ended questions, there were 10 multiple choice questions, all with 5 optional answers. The 5-score format is adopted to record students' answer choices.

First of all, we try to analyze whether there is a relationship between fear or fear of AI technology and gender. The Chi-square test was used to determine whether there was a significant association between gender and levels of fear or anxiety about AI before and after the course.

$$\chi^2 = \sum \frac{(O_i - E_i)^2}{E_i} \tag{1}$$

Where O_i represents the observed frequency in each category. E_i represents the expected frequency in each category, calculated under the assumption of independence. The p values obtained in the Chi-square test are all greater than 0.05, indicating that there is no significant association or difference between gender and the level of fear or anxiety about AI technology.

Next, we use T-test to analyze the relationship between grade and fear or anxiety about artificial intelligence. The T-test statistical method, which is shown in Eq. 2, is chosen here to compare the means of the two groups to determine whether there is a significant difference between them.

$$t = \frac{\overline{X}_1 - \overline{X}_2}{\sqrt{\frac{s_1^2}{n_1} + \frac{s_2^2}{n_2}}} \tag{2}$$

Where $\overline{X}_1$ represents mean of the first sample. $\overline{X}_2$ represents the second sample. s_1^2 is variance of the first sample. s_2^2 is variance of the second sample. n_1 represents size of the first sample. n_2 is size of the second sample. The results showed that the anxiety level in Grade 9 before the start of this course was significantly different from other grades (p value < 0.05). After the course, there was still a significant difference in anxiety levels between Grade 9 and Grade 12 (p-value < 0.05), and the difference from other grades was not significant. Therefore, we speculate that this course has the best effect on reducing the fear or anxiety of artificial intelligence among ninth-grade students.

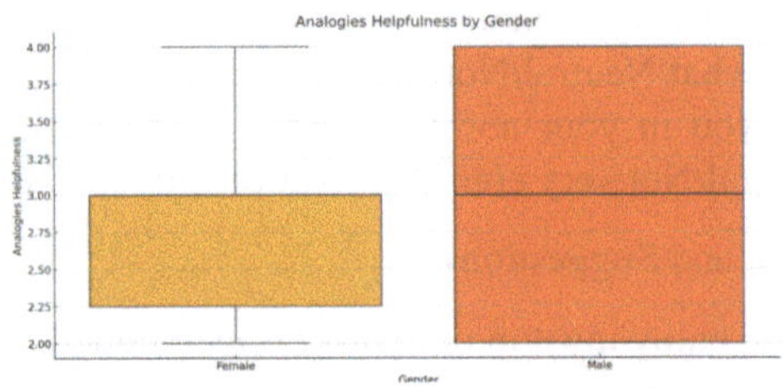

Fig. 4. The box plot of the relationship between gender and how helpful the analogies-based teaching.

Figure 4 shows the relationship between gender and analogy teaching. When analyzing the relationship between gender and analogy learning methods, the statistical method used was the Mann-Whitney U Test [22]. The results showed that there were no statistically significant differences between different gender and grade level in their endorsement of the analogical learning method (p-value = 0.658).

As shown in Fig. 5, the confidence levels of students in different grades in their future AI careers are shown. The correlation analysis shows that there is a moderate positive correlation between the extent to which students are inspired to engage in AI innovation and the extent to which they use analogy learning to enhance understanding. That is, using analogies is more likely to lead students to find new applications of AI in daily life.

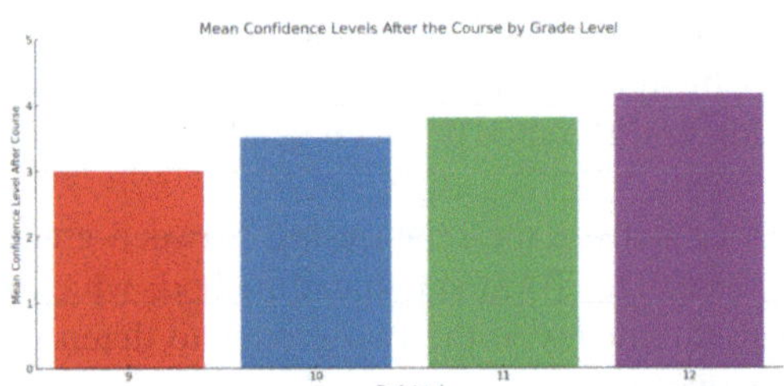

Fig. 5. The confidence levels of students in different grades in their future AI careers.

Besides these multiple choice questions, regarding the Open-ended question of what was the most impressive analogy case, one student wrote, "I remember the teacher using the marathon race to explain overfitting in class. Because I am a marathon enthusiast myself, I need to hone my running ability on different tracks". Regarding the understanding of an algorithm, one student wrote, "In my mind, SVM is a classification method, just like setting up an electric fence for the cat and dog at home to keep them as far away from each other as possible so that they don't fight". Regarding the question of which project topic proposed by the students is most interesting, a student wrote, "My favorite is a smart factory system that can reduce energy consumption, because I am very concerned about global warming, and I think AI technology is an important technology to mitigate global warming". Regarding "What feature did you enjoy most in our class?", one of the responses was, "I really like the analogy method used in class. It feels like I am listening to and learning a story without too many abstract definitions, and I am not distracted".

4 Conclusion

Learning AI is becoming important for students of any age. For college students, there are already a lot of courses and competitions to increase their level of learning and applying AI. But for middle school students, they may be afraid of learning AI due to lack of basic knowledge and problems such as attention and language expression, or the existing courses have too many terms for them.

This paper proposed an Analogies-Based Learning Approach to provide AI concepts to teenagers. By comparing AI terms or algorithms to familiar content such as jigsaw puzzles or marathon competitions, and using colloquialisms that middle school students like, such as "Er ci yuan", middle school students are less intimidated by AI courses and more confident in working in AI. Statistical analysis based on the questionnaire showed that gender had no correlation with whether initial students had fear of AI courses, and that teaching using analogies was most effective in reducing ninth-grade students' fear or anxiety about AI, and that students were more confident in discovering new applications of AI in daily life. Next, we will continue to study whether learning AI can help improve high school students' learning ability in other courses.

References

1. https://www.pluralsight.com/resources/blog/it-ops/top-tech-skills-2024-with-tests. 01 June 2024
2. Rodriguez, C.O.: MOOCs and the AI-Stanford like courses: two successful and distinct course formats for massive open online courses. Eur. J. Open Distance E-Learn. (2012)
3. Tsai, C.C., Chung, C.C., Cheng, Y.M., et al.: Deep learning course development and evaluation of artificial intelligence in vocational senior high schools. Front. Psychol. **13**, 965926 (2022)
4. Sperling, A., Lickerman, D.: Integrating AI and machine learning in software engineering course for high school students. In: Proceedings of the 17th ACM Annual Conference on Innovation and Technology in Computer Science Education, pp. 244–249 (2012)
5. Karaali, G.: Artificial intelligence, basic skills, and quantitative literacy. Numeracy **16**(1), 9 (2023)
6. Alderman, E.M., Breuner, C.C., Grubb, L.K., et al.: Unique needs of the adolescent. Pediatrics **144**(6) (2019)
7. Rathunde, K., Csikszentmihalyi, M.: Undivided interest and the growth of talent: a longitudinal study of adolescents. J. Youth Adolesc. **22**(4), 385–405 (1993)
8. Hazen, E., Schlozman, S., Beresin, E.: Adolescent psychological development: a review. Pediatr. Rev. **29**(5), 161–168 (2008)
9. Loschert, K.: Science of learning: what educators need to know about adolescent development. Alliance Excell. Educ. (2019)

10. Duit, R.: On the role of analogies and metaphors in learning science. Sci. Educ. **75**(6), 649–672 (1991)
11. Newby, T.J., Ertmer, P.A., Stepich, D.A.: Instructional analogies and the learning of concepts. Educ. Technol. Res. Dev. **43**(1), 5–18 (1995)
12. Feinstein, S.G.: Secrets of the Teenage Brain: Research-Based Strategies for Reaching and Teaching Today's Adolescents. Corwin Press (2009)
13. Clark, S.S.: Improving analogical reasoning skills in adolescence through figurative music lyric exposure: towards better decision-making skills. Australian Catholic University (2018)
14. Rubia, K., Smith, A.B., Woolley, J., et al.: Progressive increase of frontostriatal brain activation from childhood to adulthood during event-related tasks of cognitive control. Hum. Brain Mapp. **27**(12), 973–993 (2006)
15. Siva Krishna, P., Mariam Bee, M.K.: Automatic medicinal plant recognition using random forest classifier. In: Hassanien, A.E., Bhattacharyya, S., Chakrabati, S., Bhattacharya, A., Dutta, S. (eds.) Emerging Technologies in Data Mining and Information Security. AISC, vol. 1300, pp. 869–881. Springer, Singapore (2021). https://doi.org/10.1007/978-981-33-4367-2_83
16. Song, Y.Y., Ying, L.U.: Decision tree methods: applications for classification and prediction. Shanghai Arch. Psychiatry **27**(2), 130 (2015)
17. Leicht, A.S., Gomez, M.A., Woods, C.T.: Team performance indicators explain outcome during women's basketball matches at the Olympic Games. Sports **5**(4), 96 (2017)
18. Yi, Y., Shengjin, W., Jiasong, S., et al.: Interest-based learning for teaching a human-computer interaction course: media and cognition course. In: Proceedings of the International Conference on Frontiers in Education: Computer Science and Computer Engineering (FECS), pp: 62–67 (2017)
19. http://korpus.uib.no/icame/colt/. 01 June 2024
20. Stenström, A.B.: From slang to slanguage: a description based on teenage talk. In: Mi a szleng, pp. 89–108 (2000)
21. Larson, V.L., McKinley, N.L.: Characteristics of adolescents' conversations: a longitudinal study. Clin. Linguist. Phon. **12**(3), 183–203 (1998)
22. McKnight, P.E., Najab, J.: Mann-Whitney U test. In: The Corsini Encyclopedia of Psychology, p. 1 (2010)

Security, Privacy, and Social Impact

BERT-Based Fine-Tuning for Automated Tagging of Robbery Crime Narratives

Lenin G. Falconi(✉), Myriam Hernandez-Alvarez, and Ángel Leonardo Valdivieso Caraguay

Departamento de Informática y Ciencias de la Computación (DICC), Escuela Politécnica Nacional, Quito 170525, Ecuador
{lenin.falconi,myriam.hernandez,angel.valdivieso}@epn.edu.ec
https://www.epn.edu.ec

Abstract. Accurate classification of crime narratives is vital for reliable public safety statistics. In Ecuador, the Comisión Especial de Estadística de Seguridad, Justicia, Crimen y Transparencia (CEESJCT) manually categorizes robbery incident reports, which is a time-consuming process. While transformer-based models have shown success in natural language processing tasks, their application to Ecuadorian legal and security texts in the Spanish language remains underexplored. This study addresses this gap by developing an automated classification system using a BERT model tailored to Spanish robbery narratives. Utilizing transfer learning and subsequent fine-tuning on an expanded labeled dataset, the system significantly improves classification performance. Initial transfer learning achieved moderate accuracy (80.5%) but faced difficulties with semantically similar categories. Fine-tuning notably increased minority-class recall (up to 30%) with an improved accuracy (90.3%). The final implementation, which increased the number of categories to 11, achieved 95.5% accuracy with robust and consistent results on both police and judicial narratives. Collaboration with Ecuadorian institutions, including the Fiscalía General del Estado (FGE) and Instituto Nacional de Estadística y Censos (INEC), ensures model credibility.

Keywords: Legal Natural Language Processing · NLP · Natural Language Processing · transformers · fine-tuning · transfer learning

1 Introduction

Deep learning (DL) has achieved remarkable success in text classification (TC), often outperforming traditional Machine Learning (ML) methods [11]. However, DL models typically require vast amounts of data and computational resources. For specialized domains with limited data, such as legal text processing, *Transfer Learning (TL)* and *Fine-Tuning (FT)* offer a viable path to adapt large pre-trained models to niche tasks [7,22].

The legal domain poses distinct challenges for Natural Language Processing (NLP), characterized by complex terminology, lengthy documents, and intricate

C. Stephanidis et al. (Eds.): HCII 2025, CCIS 2773, pp. 137–147, 2026.
https://doi.org/10.1007/978-3-032-12773-0_13

structural features. These factors have fostered the emergence of Legal NLP (LNLP) as a specialized subfield [2,23]. Although there has been increasing interest in judicial outcome prediction [9,12,20], legal article prediction from text, and document classification [4,21], available benchmark datasets such as LexGlue primarily target English, thereby neglecting other languages. While transformer models such as mBERT have facilitated cross-lingual transfer, the unique characteristics of legal terminologies and system-level differences underscore the need for domain-specific pretraining (e.g., LegalBERT [3]) or hybrid approaches [10], especially in the context of low-resource languages [14].

In Ecuador, the national penal code (COIP) defines robbery broadly, but for public security analytics, it must be sub-classified into types like home, street, or vehicle robbery. This classification is manually performed by the CEESJCT from crime incident reports. To automate this, we propose a classifier based on the distilbert-base-multilingual-cased transformer model [13], which is well-suited for multilingual applications. Our development involved three phases: (1) Initial TL using the transformer as a feature extractor, which yielded 80.5% accuracy; (2) Full model FT, which improved accuracy to 90.3%; and (3) a final FT phase on a large-scale dataset of 1.1 million narratives, expanding from 6 to 11 categories and achieving a final accuracy of 95.5%.

This research makes three key contributions: (1) a novel large-scale dataset of over one million annotated Spanish-language robbery narratives from Ecuadorian police reports; (2) an effective three-phase FT approach that adapts a pre-trained BERT model to the Ecuadorian legal context, achieving 95.5% accuracy; and (3) the successful deployment of our model in Ecuador's FGE, automating a critical manual classification process. This represents, to our knowledge, the first application of transformer models for crime narrative analysis in Ecuadorian Spanish.

The remainder of this article is structured as follows: Related works are presented in Sect. 2. The proposed methodology, including dataset generation, is detailed in Sect. 3. Section 4 presents the experimental results. Finally, Sect. 5 discusses the main findings, conclusions, and directions for future work.

2 Related Works

Legal Text Classification (LTC) refers to the task of categorizing legal documents into predefined juridical categories. Research has increasingly adopted transformer architectures, which use a self-attention mechanism to capture long-range dependencies in text more effectively than prior architectures [17,18] and are considered state-of-the-art in NLP tasks. BERT [5], a notable application of the Transformer encoder, generates deeply bidirectional contextual representations through an exclusively encoder-based architecture.

A review of LTC research, as summarized in Table 1, reveals a predominant focus on English corpora, whereas the present work constitutes a novel application to Spanish legal documents from Ecuador. Transformer architectures, notably BERT, have been shown to outperform LSTM-based models on large, multi-label legal datasets by employing strategies such as gradual layer unfreezing and domain-specific pretraining, as demonstrated in prior studies [15]. Furthermore, research has extended these findings by exploring zero-shot cross-lingual transfer; for instance, models fine-tuned exclusively on English data have achieved strong performance on French and German texts [16]. Additional validation of transformer superiority over traditional machine learning methods, even when limited data is available, has been provided for Turkish legal texts [1]. Moreover, domain-adapted transformer models, including Legal-LongFormer and Legal-BERT, have demonstrated superior performance compared to their general-domain counterparts when applied to lengthy legal documents, such as U.S. Supreme Court decisions [19].

Table 1. Comparative analysis of legal text classification approaches

Ref	Model	Task	Dataset	Language	Key Results
[15]	BERT, RoBERTa, DistilBERT, XLNet, M-BERT	Multi-label classification	JRC-Acquis, EURLEX57K	Multilingual, English	0.661 (F1) on JRC-Acquis
[16]	M-BERT, M-DistilBERT	Cross-lingual transfer	EURLEX57K Extended	Models pretrained in Multilingual. FT in English	34% improvement on French, 87% improvement on German
[1]	Transformer-based	Document classification	Turkish Legal Corpus	Turkish	DL models improve over traditional ML
[19]	BERT, RoBERTa, Legal-BERT, LongFormer, Legal-LongFormer	Long document classification	SCDB	English	80.1% accuracy (15 categories), 60.9% accuracy (279 categories) with Legal-BERT
This work	DistilBERT	Multi-label classification	CEESJCT robbery reports	Spanish	95.5% accuracy (11 categories)

The reviewed literature indicates that BERT models are widely utilized for LTC. Transformer-based architectures consistently outperform traditional ML methods in this domain [1]. FT pre-trained BERT's weights to the target task is a standard approach. Also, our methodology is comparable to that of [19], wherein models are trained for both broader and fine-grained legal categories. A recurrent challenge with BERT-based approaches concerns the processing of lengthy documents, due to BERT's tokenization limits.

Distinct from previous works, our study specifically addresses the classification of robbery types. Most literature focuses on broader legal categories, and while some studies may implicitly include robbery within categories such as "criminal law" or "property offenses", explicit attention to robbery classification is absent, marking our focus as potentially novel and expanding the exploration in the application of transformer-based models in the legal domain.

An additional distinguishing aspect of this study lies in the nature of its data. Our dataset consists of narratives drawn from citizen crime reports, police accounts, and prosecutor's office documents. As a result, it features a rich combination of technical language and non-technical descriptions provided by victims. The deployment of the model at the FGE, utilizing the proposed methodology, demonstrates significant potential for generating innovative solutions within the legal domain of governmental institutions.

3 Methodology

This section details the development of a transformer-based robbery classification model. The process involved three stages: dataset generation, initial TL on a 6-category dataset ($D_{\kappa=6}$) followed by FT, and concluding with FT on an expanded 11-category dataset ($D_{\kappa=11}$).

3.1 Dataset Generation

The initial target dataset, $D^T_{\kappa=6,N}$, comprises six crime categories from 671,146 robbery records provided by CEESJCT. After standard text pre-processing, including the removal of non-alphanumeric characters and conversion to lowercase, we analyzed statistical characteristics of the narrative length. To comply with DistilBERT's [13]) 512-token limit, we filtered narratives to be between 35 and 300 words, resulting in a dataset of $N = 431,669$ samples. This was stratified into training (63.32%), validation (15.83%), and test (20.85%) subsets.

Extended Taxonomy *($D_{\kappa=11}$)* Dataset. We constructed a larger dataset of 11 categories by integrating police reports with prosecutor's office records from 2014-2022. This process involved extracting, filtering, and merging narratives, followed by quality control, including text length filtering (50-400 words) and label standardization. The final dataset contained 1,109,335 records, partitioned into training (807,468 samples, approximately 72%), validation (201,867 samples, approximately 18%), and test (100,000 samples, approximately 10%) sets (Table 2).

Table 2. Extended Taxonomy Dataset

Basic Taxonomy	Extended Labels	Total
HOME ROBBERY	HOME ROBBERY	172,264
STREET ROBBERY	STREET ROBBERY	421,497
BUSINESS ROBBERY	BUSINESS ROBBERY	74,088
VEHICLE PARTS AND ACCESSORIES THEFT	VEHICLE PARTS AND ACCESSORIES THEFT	154,546
CAR THEFT	CAR THEFT	90,038
MOTORCYCLE THEFT	MOTORCYCLE THEFT	119,128
NO INFORMATION	OTHER ROBBERIES	43,468
	WATER VESSEL ROBBERY	9,407
	SOCIAL ORGANIZATION ROBBERY	3,087
	EDUCATIONAL INSTITUTION ROBBERY	17,252
	PUBLIC INSTITUTION ROBBERY	4,560
Total		1,109,335

3.2 Model Training

Problem Formulation. We address the problem of classifying crime report narratives of robbery into k predefined categories. Since a language model estimates the conditional probability of the next token given a preceding sequence of tokens, TC can be formalized as shown in (1). Training a TC model thus implies learning a function f that maps a target dataset D^T, consisting of text sequences $X_i \in D = \{X_1, X_2, \ldots, X_N\}$ to one of k categories (2).

For this work, we selected the distilbert-base-multilingual-casedmodel [13], a distilled version of BERT, which retains 97% of BERT's language understanding capabilities while significantly reducing the number of parameters. Moreover, it supports multilingual tasks, including Spanish, aligning well with the linguistic requirements of our dataset.

$$\hat{y} = \operatorname*{argmax}_{y \in \{1,\ldots,k\}} P(y \mid w_1, w_2, \ldots, w_i) \tag{1}$$

$$f : D \longrightarrow \mathbb{Z}^k \tag{2}$$

To enable processing by a transformer-based language model, textual sequences must first undergo tokenization and be transformed into numerical representations. This involves segmenting the text into discrete tokens and subsequently mapping these tokens to vector embeddings. Let Tokenize : $\mathcal{X} \to \mathbb{Z}^\lambda$ be the tokenization function that maps text sequences to token IDs, where $\mathcal{X}$ is the text space and λ is the maximum sequence length. For each input sequence $X_i \in D_N^T$, the tokenizer produces:

$$(\boldsymbol{\nu}_i, \boldsymbol{\tau}_i) = \text{Tokenize}(X_i) \tag{3}$$

where:

- $\boldsymbol{\nu}_i \in \mathbb{Z}^\lambda$ are the token IDs
- $\boldsymbol{\tau}_i \in \{0,1\}^\lambda$ is the attention mask
- $\lambda = 512$ for distilbert-base-multilingual-cased

The token IDs are passed through the embedding layer, which maps each token to a $d = 768$ dimensional vector representation. The embedding matrix $W_{embedding} \in \mathbb{R}^{119,547 \times 768}$ uses a $V = 119,547$ vocabulary, where each row corresponds to a unique token, thereby providing dense vector representations.

$$\mathbf{E} = \text{Embedding}(\boldsymbol{\nu}_i) \in \mathbb{R}^{\lambda \times d} \tag{4}$$

The encoded numerical representations of the text are then processed by distilbert-base-multilingual-cased:

$$\mathbf{H} = \text{BERT}(\mathbf{E}, \boldsymbol{\tau}_i) \in \mathbb{R}^{\lambda \times d} \tag{5}$$

The classification layer comprises a feedforward layer that maps the hidden state vector output from the encoder (or CLS embedding) $\mathbf{h}_{[\text{CLS}]}$ to the k categories:

$$\hat{\boldsymbol{y}}_i = \text{softmax}(\mathbf{W}\mathbf{h}_{[\text{CLS}]} + \mathbf{b}) \in \mathbb{R}^k \tag{6}$$

where:

- $\mathbf{h}_{[\text{CLS}]} \in \mathbb{R}^d$ is the input feature vector of $d = 768$
- $\mathbf{W} \in \mathbb{R}^{k \times d}$ is the classification weight matrix, mapping from embedding space to k classes.
- $\mathbf{b} \in \mathbb{R}^k$ is the bias vector
- k is the number of target categories
- A softmax activation to obtain probabilities $p_i = \frac{\exp(y_i)}{\sum_{j=1}^{k} \exp(y_j)}$, where p_i is the probability of class i

In this work, we experiment with TL and FT to adapt the weights of a pre-trained model from a large source dataset D^S to the characteristics of a target dataset D^T. We adopt the TL definition provided by [6]:

Definition 1 (Transfer Learning). *Given an original domain $\mathcal{D}^S$ with an original learning task $\mathcal{T}^S$, a target domain $\mathcal{D}^T$, with a target task $\mathcal{T}^T$, the TL operation seeks to improve the learning of a prediction function $\phi^{\mathrm{T}}(\cdot)$ in $\mathcal{D}^T$ using the knowledge acquired in $\phi^{\mathrm{S}}(\cdot)$ in $\mathcal{T}^S$, through ϕ^S; where $\mathcal{D}^S \neq \mathcal{D}^T$ or $\mathcal{T}^S \neq \mathcal{T}^T$.*

Considering the mentioned definition of TL, (7) represents the TL operation applied to the text classification problem, starting from a pre-trained natural language model; where L is the number of layers of the pre-trained model.

$$\mathbb{T}_{\mathbb{L}} \left\langle \phi^{\mathrm{S}}(\mathcal{D}^S), \mathcal{D}^T \right\rangle = \mathcal{A}\left(\phi^{\mathrm{S}}(\mathcal{D}^T)\Big|_0^L \right) \tag{7}$$

Consequently, the prediction generation is represented by Eq. (8)

$$\mathcal{Y}^T = \mathbb{T}_{\mathbb{L}} \left\langle \phi^{\mathrm{S}}(D^S), \mathcal{D}^T \right\rangle = \phi^{\mathrm{T}}(D^T) \tag{8}$$

Similarly, we use the definition of FT as presented in [6]:

Definition 2 (Fine Tuning). *Given an original domain $\mathcal{D}^S$ with an original learning task $\mathcal{T}^S$, a target domain $\mathcal{D}^T$, with a target task $\mathcal{T}^T$, the FT procedure enhances the learning of a target function $\mathcal{Y}^T = \phi^{\mathrm{T}}(\mathcal{I}^T)$ by retraining r layers of the original model $\mathcal{Y}^S = \phi^{\mathrm{S}}(\mathcal{I}^S)$ with L layers and $\gamma = L - r$.*

The definition for FT is provided in (9), whereas the special case $\gamma = 0$, where $L = r$, is given in (10) and corresponds to full model tuning.

$$\mathbb{F}_{\mathbb{T}} \left\langle \phi^{\mathrm{S}}(\mathcal{D}^S), \mathcal{D}^T \right\rangle = \mathcal{A}\left(\phi^{\mathrm{S}} \left(\phi^{\mathrm{S}}(\mathcal{D}^T)\Big|_0^{\gamma-1} \right)\Big|_\gamma^L \right) \tag{9}$$

$$\mathbb{F}_{\mathbb{T}} \left\langle \phi^{\mathrm{S}}(\mathcal{D}^S), \mathcal{D}^T \right\rangle = \mathcal{A}\left(\phi^{\mathrm{S}}(\mathcal{D}^T) \right) \tag{10}$$

Phase 1: Baseline Transfer Learning. At this stage, transfer learning is employed to adapt a pre-trained *distilbert-base-multilingual-cased* model, denoted as $\phi^{\mathrm{S}}(\cdot)$, to the target task, represented by $\phi^{\mathrm{T}}(\cdot)$. This adaptation is performed by applying a set of transformations $\mathcal{A}$ to its outputs, while keeping the original weights, $\mathcal{W}^S = 134,735,616$, frozen.

The feature extractor encodes input samples as tensors of dimension $\mathbb{R}^{N\times\lambda\times d}$. Subsequently, Global Max Pooling (GMP) reduces these tensors to $\mathbb{R}^{N\times d}$. The adaptation block consists of $\mathcal{W}^T = 104,294$ trainable parameters. It incorporates Batch Normalization (BN), a fully connected layer with 512 units (FC_{512}), Dropout with a probability of 0.1 ($\mathrm{Dro}_{0.1}$), two consecutive fully connected layers with 128 units each (FC_{128}), an additional Dropout layer, and an output layer with $\kappa = 6$ units (FC_{κ}), as detailed in Eqs. (7), (8), and (11).

$$\mathcal{A} = FC_6 \circ Dro_{0.1} \circ FC_{128} \circ Dro_{0.1} \circ FC_{128} \circ Dro_{0.1} \circ FC_{512} \circ BN \circ GMP \quad (11)$$

Due to hardware constraints, a reduced subset of the data was employed in this phase: $d^T_{\mathrm{train}} : 20,000 \subset D^T_{\mathrm{train}}$, $d^T_{\mathrm{valid}} : 4,000 \subset D^T_{\mathrm{valid}}$, and $d^T_{\mathrm{test}} : 4,000 \subset D^T_{\mathrm{test}}$. The training parameters utilized in this stage are summarized in Table 3 Phase 1.

Phase 2: Fine-Tuning on Dataset $D_{\kappa=6}$. In this phase, we adopt FT for all the pre-trained model's weights, as represented in (10), leveraging the inherent advantage that full FT does not necessitate supplementary output layers. As stated in [17], this procedure reduces loss and increases classification performance on the new task. Table 3 details the training hyperparameters utilized to FT the model in the basic taxonomy dataset in the Phase 2 column.

Phase 3: Scaling to Dataset $D_{\kappa=11}$. In this phase, we extend the scope of the FT model to the $D_{\kappa=11}$ dataset, which expands to a total of 11 categories. Procedures for building the aforementioned dataset were described in Sect. 3.1. The dataset was split into training, validation, and testing sets with 807,468, 201,867, and 100,000 samples, respectively. To FT the model using such a large dataset, we used a TPU v2 [8]. The hyperparameters settings for this phase are presented in Phase 3 of Table 3.

Table 3. Training Parameters Across Phases

Parameter	Phase 1 (TL)	Phase 2 (FT)	Phase 3 (FT-extended)
Loss	Categorical Cross Entropy	Sparse Categorical Cross Entropy	Sparse Categorical Cross Entropy
Metrics	Categorical Accuracy	Sparse Categorical Accuracy	Sparse Categorical Accuracy
Optimizer	Adam	Adam	Adam
Learning rate	2×10^{-4}	3×10^{-6}	3×10^{-6}
Epochs	20	10	12
Early stopping	5 epochs	10 epochs	10 epochs
Batch size	16	16	128

4 Experimental Results

Tables 4, 5, and 6 report the model's performance across Phases 1, 2, and 3, respectively. FT the model on the extended dataset with TPU acceleration led to improved performance and enabled the prediction of a broader range of robbery categories. The observed discrepancies in support counts between Phase 1 and Phase 2 are attributed to changes in category labeling introduced by CEESJCT. It is also evident that the distribution of samples across categories is imbalanced, reflecting the underlying social circumstances surrounding criminal activity. Consequently, we opted not to employ synthetic data augmentation for this study. The results further suggest that the *Public Institution Robbery* category should be merged into the *Other Robberies* category, due to the limited number of available samples.

Table 4. Phase 1 TL Classifier Performance on $D_{\kappa=6}$

class	precision	recall	f1-score	support
Car Theft	0.58	0.36	0.45	285
Motorcycle Theft	0.90	0.84	0.87	457
Vehicle Parts And Accessories Theft	0.79	0.79	0.79	613
Street Robbery	0.82	0.91	0.86	1,666
Business Robbery	0.82	0.70	0.75	328
Home Robbery	0.76	0.77	0.77	651
micro avg	0.80	0.80	0.80	4,000
macro avg	0.78	0.73	0.75	4,000
weighted avg	0.80	0.80	0.80	4,000

Table 5. Phase 2 FT Classifier Performance on $D_{\kappa=6}$

class	precision	recall	f1-score	support
Business Robbery	0.78	0.79	0.78	297
Car Theft	0.95	0.88	0.92	363
Motorcycle Theft	0.95	0.93	0.94	392
Vehicle Parts & Accessories	0.85	0.92	0.88	663
Home Robbery	0.87	0.89	0.88	663
Street Robbery	0.94	0.92	0.93	1,671
Accuracy			0.90	4,000
Macro Avg	0.89	0.89	0.89	4,000
Weighted Avg	0.90	0.90	0.90	4,000

Table 6. Phase 3 FT Classifier Performance on $D_{\kappa=11}$

	precision	recall	f1-score	support
Educational Institution Robbery	0.925995	0.946599	0.936184	1,573
Motorcycle Theft	0.985211	0.988317	0.986762	10,785
Public Institution Robbery	0.724528	0.474074	0.573134	405
Car Theft	0.967669	0.980198	0.973893	7,878
Social Organization Robbery	0.750000	0.752688	0.751342	279
Street Robbery	0.969847	0.972298	0.971071	37,976
Business Robbery	0.878871	0.893877	0.886311	6,794
Home Robbery	0.944779	0.952335	0.948542	15,504
Vehicle Parts & Accessories Theft	0.977752	0.968340	0.973023	14,024
Water Vessel Robbery	0.965197	0.983452	0.974239	846
Other Robberies	0.817738	0.766006	0.791027	3,936
accuracy			0.954610	100,000
macro avg	0.900690	0.879835	0.887775	100,000
weighted avg	0.954050	0.954610	0.954175	100,000

5 Conclusions and Future Works

Transformer-based models have achieved state-of-the-art performance across a range of NLP tasks. In this work, we employed FT to address text classification for legal documents. The proposed methodology, based on FT, demonstrates that transformer architectures can be effectively adapted to the legal domain. Notably, our model demonstrates substantial robustness to class imbalance, with the exception of the *Public Institution Robbery* category. Due to the limited number of instances associated with this particular type of robbery, it may be advisable to consolidate it within the broader *Other Robberies* category. The utilization of TPU hardware was pivotal for processing the expanded dataset, enabling both an increase in the number of target categories and overall model performance. These results highlight the practical potential of deploying ML solutions within legal institutions such as the FGE, where automated narrative classification may facilitate more efficient resource allocation and optimized operational workflows. Future research should prioritize the adaptation of novel NLP tasks, as addressed by transformer-based models, to LNLP. Such tasks encompass, but are not limited to, legal question answering, legal named entity recognition, and legal judgment prediction. The latter, in particular, necessitates an increased emphasis on model explainability, given the importance of interpretability for legal stakeholders.

Acknowledgments. The authors would like to thank to the Faculty of Systems Engineering at Escuela Politécnica Nacional in Quito, Ecuador, for providing both academic guidance and financial support. We are equally indebted to the Fiscalía General del Estado and INEC for their cooperation in the development of this research.

Disclosure of Interests. The authors have no competing interests to declare that are relevant to the content of this article.

References

1. Akca, O., Bayrak, G., Issifu, A.M., Ganiz, M.C.: Traditional machine learning and deep learning-based text classification for Turkish law documents using transformers and domain adaptation. In: 16th International Conference on INnovations in Intelligent SysTems and Applications, INISTA 2022 (2022). https://doi.org/10.1109/INISTA55318.2022.9894051
2. Ariai, F., Demartini, G.: Natural language processing for the legal domain: a survey of tasks, datasets, models, and challenges. ACM Comput. Surv. **1** (2024). https://doi.org/10.1145/nnnnnnn.nnnnnnn, https://arxiv.org/abs/2410.21306v2
3. Chalkidis, I., Fergadiotis, M., Androutsopoulos, I.: Legal-BERT: the muppets straight out of law school. arXiv preprint arXiv:2010.02559 (2020)
4. Clavié, B., Alphonsus, M., Clavié, C., Mundi, J.: The unreasonable effectiveness of the baseline: Discussing SVMs in legal text classification (2021). https://gitlab.com/jusmundi-group/public/Legal-svm-baselines
5. Devlin, J., Chang, M.W., Lee, K., Toutanova, K.: BERT: pre-training of deep bidirectional transformers for language understanding. In: Burstein, J., Doran, C., Solorio, T. (eds.) Proceedings of the 2019 Conference of the North American Chapter of the Association for Computational Linguistics: Human Language Technologies, Volume 1 (Long and Short Papers), pp. 4171–4186. Association for Computational Linguistics, Minneapolis, Minnesota (2019). https://doi.org/10.18653/v1/N19-1423, https://aclanthology.org/N19-1423/
6. Falconí, L.G.: Transfer and ensemble learning models in breast mammogram pathology classification. Master's thesis, Quito (2020)
7. Howard, J., Ruder, S.: Universal language model fine-tuning for text classification arXiv:1801.06146 (2018)
8. Jouppi, N.P., Yoon, D.H., Kurian, G., Li, S., Patil, N., Laudon, J., Young, C., Patterson, D.: A domain-specific supercomputer for training deep neural networks. Commun. ACM **63**(7), 67–78 (2020)
9. Kalia, A., Kumar, N., Namdev, N.: Classifying case facts and predicting legal decisions of the Indian central information commission: a natural language processing approach. In: Advances in Deep Learning, Artificial Intelligence and Robotics, pp. 35–45. Springer (2022). https://doi.org/10.1007/978-3-030-85365-5_4
10. Liu, Z., Li, Z., Zhang, H.: Legal knowledge-enhanced language models for legal text processing. ICAIL (2022)
11. Minaee, S., Kalchbrenner, N., Cambria, E., Nikzad, N., Chenaghlu, M., Gao, J.: Deep learning–based text classification. ACM Comput. Surv. (CSUR) **54** (2021). https://doi.org/10.1145/3439726
12. Mumcuoğlu, E., Öztürk, C.E., Ozaktas, H.M., Koç, A.: Natural language processing in law: prediction of outcomes in the higher courts of turkey. Inf. Process. Manag. **58**(5), 102684 (2021)
13. Sanh, V., Debut, L., Chaumond, J., Wolf, T.: Distilbert, a distilled version of BERT: smaller, faster, cheaper and lighter. arXiv:1910.01108 (2019)
14. Savelka, J., Ashley, K.D.: Cross-domain generalization and knowledge transfer in transformers for legal text. ICAIL (2021)
15. Shaheen, Z., Wohlgenannt, G., Filtz, E.: Large scale legal text classification using transformer models. arXiv:2010.12871v1 (2020)
16. Shaheen, Z., Wohlgenannt, G., Mouromtsev, D.: Zero-shot cross-lingual transfer in legal domain using transformer models. In: Proceedings - 2021 International Conference on Computational Science and Computational Intelligence,

CSCI 2021, pp. 450–456 (2021). https://doi.org/10.1109/CSCI54926.2021.00145, https://arxiv.org/abs/2111.14192v2
17. Tunstall, L., von Werra, L., Wolf, T.: Natural Language Processing with Transformers. O'Reilly Media, Inc. (2022)
18. Vaswani, A., Shazeer, N., Parmar, N., et al.: Attention is all you need. In: Advances in Neural Information Processing Systems, vol. 30 (2017)
19. Vatsal, S., Meyers, A., Ortega, J.E.: Classification of us supreme court cases using BERT-based techniques (2023). https://huggingface.co/saibo/
20. Wang, Y., Gao, J., Chen, J.: Deep learning algorithm for judicial judgment prediction based on BERT. In: 2020 5th International Conference on Computing, Communication and Security (ICCCS), pp. 1–6. IEEE (2020)
21. Yan, G., Li, Y., Shen, S., Zhang, S., Liu, J.: Law article prediction based on deep learning. In: 2019 IEEE 19th International Conference on Software Quality, Reliability and Security Companion (QRS-C), pp. 281–284. IEEE (2019)
22. Yosinski, J., Clune, J., Bengio, Y., Lipson, H.: How transferable are features in deep neural networks? In: Advances in Neural Information Processing Systems, vol. 27 (2014)
23. Zhong, H., et al.: How does NLP benefit legal system: a summary of legal artificial intelligence. In: Proceedings of the Annual Meeting of the Association for Computational Linguistics, pp. 5218–5230 (2020). https://doi.org/10.18653/V1/2020.ACL-MAIN.466, https://aclanthology.org/2020.acl-main.466/

Security and Privacy Research on Muslim Communities: A Literature Review

Yousra Javed[1(✉)] and Elham Al Qahtani[2]

[1] Illinois State University, Normal, IL, USA
yjaved@ilstu.edu
[2] University of Jeddah, Jeddah, SA, Saudi Arabia
eaalqahtani@uj.edu.sa

Abstract. Security and privacy research on marginalized population such as Muslim communities is an emerging topic. The cultural context and religious norms of these communities emphasize the need for studying security and privacy on this population. This paper provides an overview of the existing literature on this topic by summarizing findings from 28 papers focused on studying the security and privacy perceptions, practices, and comprehension of this population. It discusses the unique challenges faced by researchers when investigating this population both for general HCI research as well as for security and privacy.

Keywords: Muslim communities · user studies · security · privacy · literature review

1 Introduction

Human-Computer Interaction (HCI) and usable security/privacy are connected by their shared aim of enhancing the way users interact with technology. HCI provides the framework for user-friendly technology design, while usable security/privacy applies these principles to ensure effective, accessible, and practical security and privacy measures for users. Together, they aim to create secure and user-friendly systems, balancing protection and user experience.

There is a perception that humans are the weakest link in the security chain [35]. Security and privacy researchers have, therefore, focused on devising strategies for communicating security and privacy risks to the end-users and evaluating the usability of existing security and privacy tools. However, certain users, such as those in marginalized populations have been relatively less explored. One such population is users in conservative societies as Muslim communities.

Religions define people's identities, beliefs, and constraints, which have an impact on their security and privacy perceptions as well as their technology practices [27]. Many users in these communities perceive the usage of smart-home technologies for religious reasons (e.g., when the smart lights turn off, the religious meeting should end) [39]. Various themes (refugees and Islamophobia, Muslim feminism, and digital financial services) identify how technology

C. Stephanidis et al. (Eds.): HCII 2025, CCIS 2773, pp. 148–160, 2026.
https://doi.org/10.1007/978-3-032-12773-0_14

is consumed or perceived by Muslim communities. For example, most Western financial sectors offer interest rates on savings, which is prohibited according to the Islamic guidelines on finances [27]. Similarly, cultural norms, such as gender segregation, add challenges (such as participant recruitment) to studying this population [8]. Therefore, the cultural context of these communities emphasizes the need for studying digital security and privacy on this population.

In this paper, we take the first step to summarize findings from 28 papers focused on studying the security and privacy perceptions, practices, and comprehension of this population. We conclude with a discussion on the unique challenges faced when investigating HCI and security and privacy in Muslim communities.

2 Dataset Description

To collect papers focused on studying aspects of security and privacy in the Muslim communities, we used the search string "security+privacy+muslim+islam" on Google Scholar and selected papers that were published in the past 20 years. Any papers not written in English language, whose full-text was unavailable, or which mentioned security and privacy in Muslim communities but did not investigate this population were excluded. We selected a total of 28 papers from the search results based on this criteria. A larger percentage of these papers were published at peer-reviewed conferences (67.85%, N=19) compared to peer-reviewed journals (32.14%, N=9). Table 1 shows the distribution of papers across publication years. A majority of the papers in our dataset were published between 2016 and 2023.

Table 1. Distribution of papers published on usable security and privacy in Muslim communities from years 2003–2023

2006	2010	2012	2014	2015	2016	2017	2018	2019	2020	2021	2022	2023
1	1	2	1	1	3	3	2	3	4	1	3	3

The most investigated topic was privacy perceptions, concerns, and strategies (57.14%, N=16) whereas topics, such as risk communication, security behavior, and sources of security advice were least investigated (14.28%, N=4). Table 2 provides a distribution of investigated topics in the selected papers.

Table 2. Distribution of investigated topics in the selected papers

Topic	No. of Papers
Security comprehension/education	4
Security behavior	2
Risk communication	1
Source of security advice	1
Privacy perceptions, concerns, and strategies	16
Privacy compliance	4

3 Security and Privacy Studies on Muslim Communities

In this section, we present the security and privacy studies on the Muslim population. Table 3 summarizes the focus and design, demographics, and sample size of each study.

Security Comprehension and Education. The regions within the Gulf and the Middle East have become the hotspots aimed for Internet crimes like cyber-attacks over recent years ([16]). Therefore, governments in Muslim countries should provide training to all stakeholders and the public to empower the masses and help raise awareness on cyber-attack issues. Jawad et al. [24] developed a gamification-based mobile app in the Arabic language to educate Arab-speaking people in the Middle East and North Africa about cybersecurity topics such as Two-Factor Authentication, social engineering, DDOS attacks, and malware. Multiple choice questions were incoporated throughout the app to track user comprehension. However, the app was not tested on users.

Cultural upbringing and lower awareness in the Muslim world can increase the vulnerability of the Muslim population to phishing attacks as compared to users in the western world. Al-Hamar et al. [7] investigated Qatar citizens' vulnerability to e-mail phishing. They found that Qatari citizens put too much trust in technology and their ability to detect email phishing, making them an easy target of phishing. Similarly, Aloul [15] conducted a fake-university website based controlled phishing audit on 11000 students, faculty, and staff in American University of Sharjah. The participants who fell for the phishing email underwent a security awareness training. The researchers demonstrated the effectiveness of their training, as the number of participants who fell for phishing decreased from 954 down to 220 when the phishing email was resent 2 weeks later. Similarly, Hashmi et al. [22] developed a WhatsApp chatbot to train users to recognize voice-based phishing attacks by identifying the persuasion principles used by the scammer. They also conducted an online experiment and interviews with 50 university students in Pakistan to show the effectiveness of this training.

Security Behavior/Perceptions. The aspect of trust and family-oriented culture in the Muslim world has an impact on this population's security behavior

Table 3. Summary of security and privacy studies on Muslim communities

Focus	Design	Demographics	Sample Size	Source
Security comprehension	Online experiment	Students,faculty,staff of uni. in Sharjah	11k	[15]
Security comprehension	Online experiment	Employees in Qatari organization	NA	[7]
Security education	NA	Arabic users in Middle East& Africa	NA	[24]
Security education	Online experiment	WhatsApp users in Pakistani university	100	[22]
Security behavior	Semi-structured interview	Bank customers in Saudi Arabia	29	[13]
Security behavior	Structured interview	Women in SA & Pakistan	156	[9]
Risk communication	Replication experiment	Smartphone users in Saudi Arabia	200	[10]
Source of security advice	Structured interview	Stayhome women in SA & Pakistan	156	[9]
Privacy perceptions	Mixed methods analysis	Twitter users in Qatar	2587	[2]
Privacy strategies	Structured interview	Social media users in Qatar and SA	42	[3]
Privacy strategies	Semi-structured interview	Social media users in Qatar and SA	32	[1]
Privacy perceptions	Online survey	High/low SES in SA,Egypt,Germany	156	[33]
Privacy strategies	Focus group	Women in India,Pakistan,Bangladesh	199	[34]
Privacy strategies	Online survey	WhatsApp users in Saudi Arabia	626	[31]
Privacy strategies	Online survey	WhatsApp users in SA and India	820	[18]
Privacy perceptions/strategies	Semi-structured interview	Islamic communities in Bangladesh	23	[32]
Privacy perceptions	Ethnography + online survey	Mobile users in Bangladesh	606	[6]
Privacy risk perception	Semi-structured interview	Muslim women in United States	21	[4]
Privacy perceptions/strategies	Semi-structured interview	Low literacy/income users in Pakistan	40	[29]
Privacy perceptions/strategies	Survey and case studies	Terrace housing residents in Malaysia	441	[26]
Privacy perceptions/strategies	Interview	Smart device owners in Jordan	30	[12]
Privacy perceptions/strategies	Semi-structured interview	Shared phone users in Bangladesh	72	[5]
Privacy strategies	Focus group & interview	Muslim children in Belgium	NA	[17]
Privacy risk perception	Online survey	Social media users in Malaysia	200	[30]
Privacy compliance	Manual evaluation	Mobile apps for Hajj & Umrah	471	[37]
Privacy compliance	Manual evaluation	e-commerce websites in Gulf	183	[36]
Privacy compliance	Manual evaluation	e-govenment websites in SA	54	[14]
Privacy compliance	Manual evaluation	Websites in India,Pakistan,Bangladesh	284	[23]

and perceptions. A survey of Wireless access points in 2007 showed a significant number of un-secure wireless networks among residents of Dubai and Sharjah ([25]). Alghamdi et al. [13] investigated the security practices of 29 household bank customers in Saudi Arabia and the reasons behind their behavior. Based on their responses, the participants were categorized into those who share their bank authentication credentials with family members and those who do not. So, 86% of the participants perceived that sharing their bank credentials with family members is safe and involves no risks. In contrast, those who do not share their credentials perceive its importance for privacy reasons (e.g., to keep their balance confidential).

In another study, Al Qahtani et al. [9] re-validated the rational decision model ([19]) on women from Saudi Arabia and Pakistan to understand their perceptions of (not) following four smartphone security measures, namely enabling a screen lock, updating the software, deleting suspicious text messages, and using a secure WIFI. They found that the participants' reasons for (not) following these four pieces of smartphone security advice were grouped into four categories: 1) those who were security/privacy related, 2) those where participants saw the risk but their need outweighed it, 3) those where participants did not see the risk and 4) others related to convenience.

Risk Communication. It is important to study strategies tailored for Muslim communities to communicate security risks to incur behavior change. For instance, using culturally relevant vocabulary seems to help address the risks and fears of this population. Al Qahtani et al. [10] conducted a study to examine the effectiveness of fear appeal (through Arabic dubbed video, video with Arabic captions, and Saudi-customized video) in changing Saudi Arabians' risk perception and behavior for adopting screen locks on their smartphones. They found that the Saudi-customized video was extremely effective in changing participants' locking behavior (72.5% of the participants enabled the screen lock). The dubbed video was the second-most effective (62.5%) in impacting their screen lock behavior.

Source of Security Advice. The channels (e.g., Internet Service Providers (ISPs) and government) through which the Muslim population receives security advice can be different from that in the western world. Al Qahtani et al. [9] performed an investigation on the sources of receiving smartphone security advice (e.g., enabling a screen lock, deleting suspicious text messages, using secure WIFI, and updating the device software) by Muslim women outside the workforce in Saudi Arabia and Pakistan. They found that a majority of the participants (53.7% from Pakistan and 24.5% from Saudi Arabia) use their family/friends' past negative experiences of security threats to receive such information. Also, 16.7% of Saudi participants and 14.8% of Pakistani participants reported Internet and ISPs as the second source. ISPs send text messages to inform their customers about the security risks and how to prevent them. Additionally, 19.6% of the Saudi participants mentioned that they obtain security advice from the government through their messages, emails, and websites.

Privacy Perceptions, Concerns, and Strategies. Unlike the western world, the need for privacy (e.g., data ownership and photo sharing) in the Muslim world is strongly affected by religion and family-oriented cultural restrictions. Issues such as data ownership and photo sharing are influenced by cultural and religious norms, which may require different privacy practices than Western standards. analyzed Twitter posts to understand the meaning of privacy in Qatar [2]. They found that the need for privacy in this community is often supported by Quranic text, advice on how to protect privacy is frequently discussed, and the use of paternalistic language by men when discussing women's privacy is common. Above all, privacy is framed as a communal attribute, including not only the individual but the behavior of those around them; it even extends beyond one's lifespan. For example, women's photos can only be seen by men who are blood-related and non-marriageable. It is important to understand the privacy norms in public places. Abokhodair et al. [1,3] identified the collective vs autonomous aspect of photo sharing in the Arab context (e.g., Saudi Arabia and Qatar) as well as the privacy perspective of using social media in the Middle East.

Another study by Saleh et al. [33] investigated privacy invasion perceptions in various scenarios, such as hacking, shoulder surfing, and change of privacy perception after an attack, among three user groups in Egypt, Saudi Arabia, and Germany. These groups belonged to high socioeconomic groups in Arab countries (HSA), medium to low socioeconomic groups in Arab countries (LSA), and high socioeconomic groups in Germany (HSG), respectively. They found similarities and differences among these groups for each privacy invasion scenario. For example, authors found that HSA and HSG accepted situations of privacy invasion in case of death or parents invading a child's privacy. In contrast, LSA did not accept them for any reason.

Sambasivan et al. [34] conducted a qualitative study in India, Pakistan, and Bangladesh about how women perceive, manage and control their personal privacy on shared phones. The participants employed five performative practices to maintain individuality and privacy, namely management of phone and app locks, content deletion, technology avoidance, and use of private modes.

Rashidi et al. [31] investigated how Saudi users manage their privacy preferences when they use WhatsApp. They found that the majority of Saudis are aware of the privacy settings and control the visibility of profile information to be limited to specific WhatsApp users. In addition, they want to be asked before being added to a public group chat in WhatsApp. An extension of this study was performed by Dev et al. [18]. They investigated how demographics (e.g., gender, education, age) impact WhatsApp users in Saudi Arabia and India in terms of privacy concerns and security practices (e.g., information sharing and feature use). They found that gender and age of both populations have a strong impact on the blocking feature and profile information sharing on WhatsApp.

Rifat et al. [32] conducted an eight-month-long ethnographically informed study in Bangladeshi Islamic communities to understand how the Islamic spirits of Purdah, Amanah, Gheebat, Riya, and Buhtan represent the notion of privacy and guide privacy practices among observant Bangladeshi Muslims. They discuss how sacred values generate norms and customs associated with privacy and surveillance. Another ethnographic study focused on biometric registration for mobile users in Bangladesh revealed users' privacy and safety concerns regarding identity, ownership, and trust [6].

Afnan et al. [4] conducted 21 semi-structured interviews to understand how Muslim-American women perceive digital privacy risks related to three contexts: government surveillance, Islamophobia, and social surveillance. They found that privacy concerns held by Muslim-American women unfolded with respect to three dimensions of identity: as a result of their identity as Muslim-Americans broadly (e.g., Islamophobic online harassment), as Muslim-American women more specifically (e.g., reputational harms within one's cultural community for posting taboo content), and as a product of their own individual practices of Islam (e.g., constructing female-only spaces to share photos of oneself without a hijab).

Naveed et al. [29] conducted a qualitative study with 40 participants to explore the privacy perceptions, beliefs, and practices of low-literate, low-income users in Pakistan. They examined the cultural, religious, and familial structures that impact users' perceptions, management, and control of their personal privacy. Their findings show significant gendered differences in privacy understandings, privacy-preserving practices, and access to privacy-related knowledge.

Norwawi et al. [30] conducted a survey with 200 social network users from Malaysia to understand their awareness of privacy and security issues on Social Media from the Islamic perspective. Their findings show that a majority of users are not aware of or bothered by security and privacy issues. Another survey-based study [26] with 441 terrace housing residents in Malaysia indicated that Muslim families required a balance between visual exposure and visual access which influences the four identified factors influencing Muslim visual privacy which are protection of aurat, security, community interaction and hospitality to guest.

Albayaydh et al. [12] conducted interviews with 30 smart device users and bystanders (households, and domestic workers), policy makers, and human and civil rights activists to explore smart home power dynamics in the Muslim Arab Middle Eastern (MAME) context of Jordan. Their show that asymmetric socio-economic power dynamics between households and domestic workers influence smart technology privacy concerns, practices, and rights perceptions.

De Wolf et al. [17] conducted focus groups and interviews with Muslim children in the northern Dutch-speaking region of Belgium to understand the privacy management strategies they use to manage and hide Islam-related information.

Privacy Compliance. It is equally important to study the privacy compliance of organizations in the Muslim world and how transparent these organizations are about protecting their customer's data e.g., by providing a clear privacy policy statement on their website/app. However, limited studies exist on this topic. The privacy policy availability by e-commerce and e-government websites in the Middle East is low. shalhoub et al. [36] evaluated the privacy policies of 183 e-commerce websites in Gulf Cooperation Council countries against the Federal Trade Commission's Fair Information Practice Principles (FIPPs). They found that 73.2% of these websites had no privacy policy available. Similarly, Alhomod et al. [14] evaluated the privacy policies of 54 e-government websites in Saudi Arabia against FIPPs and found that 72% of websites did not have a privacy policy. Also, 40% of the websites that had a privacy policy complied with two or fewer of the 5 privacy principles. Shambour et al. [37] investigated the confidentiality and disclosure measures of mobile apps for Hajj & Umrah in Saudi Arabia, by studying the privacy practices before and after these apps are downloaded. Javed et al. [23] investigated the website privacy policies from 10 sectors in the three largest South Asian economies, namely India, Pakistan, and Bangladesh. They found that compliance with GDPR principles in sectors, such as education, healthcare, and government, was low. Additionally, the content of privacy statements scored low on readability.

4 Challenges to HCI and Usable Security and Privacy Research in Muslim Communities

Running an HCI-based study in Muslim communities has unique challenges as identified in our dataset. Moreover, there are some added challenges specific to studying security and privacy in this population.

Religious and Cultural Norms. There are many cultural norms in Muslim communities that can impact HCI research in this population and have security and privacy implications. In many Muslim communities, traditions and beliefs shape their approach to privacy in distinctive ways. One example is the principle of "tahara", which emphasizes purity, and the profound value placed on respecting family privacy. Recognizing and honoring these cultural practices is crucial when devising security solutions to ensure that they not only align with the community's values but also seamlessly integrate into their existing way of life. Living in a shared household may impact the way data is shared and handled within the community. For instance, cultural expectations in Bangladesh and Pakistan dictate that women should share mobile phones with family members and that their digital activities be open to scrutiny by family members [34]. Users might be less cautious about data security when sharing information with family members, contrasting with more individualistic security practices common in Western contexts. Gender segregation is another factor. Two researchers [8] mentioned challenges in conducting user experiments and usability studies in Saudi Arabia at a segregated female campus. Sultana et al. [38] investigated how to design technologies to empower women in low-income rural societies in Bangladesh. Additionally, individuals in conservative societies present themselves in a good light, for example, by sharing appropriate photos that will reflect upon collectivist (e.g., users' families) [3]. With the new Saudi Arabia policies of modernization, this should warrant studying these effects.

Participant Recruitment. Participant recruitment from these communities for both short experiments and long-term studies is another challenge [20]. This challenge can be faced while engaging users during any phase of the need-finding and user-centered design process. For instance, the strong enforcement of male/female segregation in Arab and Southeast Asian countries mandates that data collection from men be done by male researchers and from women by female researchers. The recruitment problem is intensified by the lack of a proper ethics approval process, the lack of incentive for participation [11], and the unavailability of online crowdsourcing platforms, such as Amazon Mechanical Turk. To overcome the challenges of recruiting participants from Muslim communities, researchers should prioritize understanding and respecting cultural and religious norms, obtaining local ethical approvals, offering suitable incentives, leveraging local networks, and ensuring accessibility. By implementing these strategies, researchers can enhance engagement and participation in studies while upholding cultural sensitivity and ethical integrity.

User Evaluation. The security and privacy perceptions in Muslim communities significantly impact technology usage and security feature adoption (e.g., using password managers and two-factor authentication). The low awareness plays a vital role in the interaction between users and security features/tools. Moreover, the inference of security and privacy behaviors from user studies rely on users' self-report and observations. Formulating design committees for user-centered and participatory design to test the usability and user experience of projects in industries, governmental organizations, ministries, and business sectors could improve the user experience and participation approaches [21].

Ecological Validity. Since users consider security as a secondary task, the ecological validity of experiments is a challenge. Replicating user studies conducted in the Western world (both HCI focused and security focused) can present new challenges since researchers need to ensure that the scenarios simulate what users in Muslim communities see and hear in real-life. Security measures and user interfaces should align with the actual experiences and priorities of users, rather than just theoretical models. For users in Muslim communities, a lack of culturally sensitive research leads to less effective security solutions. Many existing studies are based on a Western perspective and may not fully understand the unique needs of non-Western audiences. Few studies [1,3] have provided solutions to improve the cultural design implications for non-western audiences and enhance their user experience towards these technologies. Nasruddin et al. [28] proposed a framework of Muslim Centered User interface Design (MCUID) considering the Islamic culture and the interface design perspectives.

5 Conclusion and Future Work

There is a need for efforts by HCI and usable security and privacy researchers to address the challenges faced when investigating Muslim communities. In this paper, we provided an overview of the existing literature on usable security and privacy in Muslim communities and the associated challenges.

In-depth research focusing on security and privacy within Muslim communities has revealed significant gaps that need to be addressed. These gaps encompass a lack of comprehensive understanding and specialized education regarding security practices, which are heavily influenced by cultural and family-centric values. These cultural and familial influences have a profound impact on the security behaviors and perceptions of users within these communities. Additionally, the reliance on family trust can often result in more relaxed attitudes towards data security. Moreover, traditional media and community-based channels have proven to be more effective for disseminating security advice compared to digital-only strategies. This highlights the importance of leveraging these traditional communication channels in addition to digital platforms. Furthermore, privacy requirements deeply rooted in religious and cultural norms necessitate different approaches as compared to Western standards, particularly when it comes to aspects such as data ownership and photo sharing. Furthermore, limited research exists on how organizations in the Muslim world handle privacy compliance and transparency. This scarcity of research underscores the need for clearer privacy policies and culturally relevant communication strategies. These measures can play a significant role in enhancing security behaviors and fostering trust within these communities.

Based on our findings, the potential future directions of this research are as follows:

- Develop approaches for designing, and implementing systems that can address Muslim communities' needs. Understanding how religious values and cultural context shape privacy expectations in Muslim communities helps in designing systems that align with religious principles, such as ensuring that data collection and sharing practices respect these norms.
- Highlight the main factors contributing to the implementation of Western security/privacy approaches in the Muslim communities. Studying Muslim communities alongside other cultural groups can reveal unique security and privacy challenges faced by Muslim users. This research may help identify cultural factors influencing security practices and contribute to globally applicable solutions.
- Examine the factors that impact the security and privacy practices/perceptions of different user groups in Muslim communities (e.g., women, users with disabilities, low-income users etc.) Studying the influences on security and privacy practices among different user groups in Muslim communities requires a detailed analysis of how cultural, social, and economic factors affect their interactions with technology. For example, women may have unique privacy concerns due to cultural norms around modesty and family reputation, which impact their online behavior and security practices. Users with disabilities might face accessibility barriers that make it difficult for them to use standard security tools effectively, requiring adaptive design solutions. Low-income users may struggle with limited access to security resources and education, making them more susceptible to online threats. Research should concentrate on understanding these diverse needs and challenges, developing tailored educational programs, and designing inclusive security tools that meet the specific requirements of each group. This will ensure that all users within the community can navigate the digital landscape securely and confidently.
- Future studies could evaluate the efficacy of privacy policies in terms of clarity, cultural sensitivity, and alignment with religious principles. Additionally, research could explore user trust and satisfaction related to organizational privacy measures and identify best practices for organizations to enhance their privacy compliance in culturally sensitive ways.

By researching these directions, scholars and practitioners can better understand security and privacy needs in Muslim communities and create more effective, and culturally sensitive solutions.

References

1. Abokhodair, N.: Privacy and social media in the context of the Arab gulf. In: Proceedings of the 2016 ACM Conference on Designing Interactive Systems, pp. 672–683 (2016)
2. Abokhodair, N., Abbar, S., Vieweg, S., Mejova, Y.: Privacy and twitter in Qatar: traditional values in the digital world. In: Proceedings of the 8th ACM Conference on Web Science, pp. 66–77. WebSci '16, Association for Computing Machinery, New York, NY, USA (2016). https://doi.org/10.1145/2908131.2908146
3. Abokhodair, N., Hodges, A., Vieweg, S.: Photo sharing in the Arab gulf: expressing the collective and autonomous selves. In: Proceedings of the 2017 ACM Conference on Computer Supported Cooperative Work and Social Computing, pp. 696–711 (2017)
4. Afnan, T., Zou, Y., Mustafa, M., Naseem, M., Schaub, F.: Aunties, strangers, and the FBI: online privacy concerns and experiences of Muslim-American women. In: Eighteenth Symposium on Usable Privacy and Security (SOUPS 2022), pp. 387–406 (2022)
5. Ahmed, I., Haque, M.R., Chen, J., Dell, N.: Digital privacy challenges with shared mobile phone use in Bangladesh. Proc. ACM Hum.-Comput. Interact. **1**(CSCW) (2017). https://doi.org/10.1145/3134652
6. Ahmed, S.I., Haque, M.R., Guha, S., Rifat, M.R., Dell, N.: Privacy, security, and surveillance in the global south: A study of biometric mobile sim registration in Bangladesh. In: Proceedings of the 2017 CHI Conference on Human Factors in Computing Systems, pp. 906–918. CHI '17, Association for Computing Machinery, New York, NY, USA (2017). https://doi.org/10.1145/3025453.3025961
7. Al-Hamar, M., Dawson, R., Guan, L.: A culture of trust threatens security and privacy in Qatar. In: 2010 10th IEEE International Conference on Computer and Information Technology, pp. 991–995. IEEE (2010)
8. Al-Megren, S., Alghamdi, N.: Working Towards Culturally Sensitive Predictive Models. HCI Research and Practice in the Arab World, With an Eye to the Future (2019)
9. Al Qahtani, E., Javed, Y., Lipford, H., Shehab, M.: Do women in conservative societies (not) follow smartphone security advice? A case study of Saudi Arabia and Pakistan. In: 2020 IEEE European Symposium on Security and Privacy Workshops (EuroS&PW), pp. 150–159 (2020). https://doi.org/10.1109/EuroSPW51379.2020.00028
10. Al Qahtani, E., Shehab, M., Aljohani, A.: The effectiveness of fear appeals in increasing smartphone locking behavior among Saudi Arabians. In: Fourteenth Symposium on Usable Privacy and Security (SOUPS), pp. 31–46 (2018)
11. Alabdulqader, E., Abokhodair, N., Lazem, S.: Human-computer interaction across the Arab world. In: Proceedings of the 2017 CHI Conference Extended Abstracts on Human Factors in Computing Systems, pp. 1356–1359 (2017)
12. Albayaydh, W., Flechais, I., Flechais, I.: Examining power dynamics and user privacy in smart technology use among Jordanian households. In: 32nd USENIX Security Symposium (USENIX Security 23), pp. 4643–4659 (2023)
13. Alghamdi, D., Flechais, I., Jirotka, M.: Security practices for households bank customers in the kingdom of Saudi Arabia. In: Eleventh Symposium On Usable Privacy and Security (SOUPS 2015), pp. 297–308 (2015)
14. Alhomod, S.M., Shafi, M.M., Shafi, M.M.: Privacy policy in e government websites: a case study of Saudi Arabia. Comput. Info. Sci. **5**(2) (2012)

15. Aloul, F.A.: The need for effective information security awareness. J. Adv. Info. Technol. **3**(3), 176–183 (2012)
16. Basamh, S.S., Qudaih, H., Ibrahim, J.B.: An overview on cyber security awareness in Muslim countries. Int. J. Info. Commun. Technol. Res. **4**(1) (2014)
17. De Wolf, R., Van Hove, S., Robaeyst, B.: Exploring Flemish Muslim children's experiences and negotiation of offline and online group privacy. Eur. J. Cult. Stud. **25**(4), 1030–1046 (2022)
18. Dev, J., Das, S., Rashidi, Y., Camp, L.J.: Personalized Whatsapp privacy: demographic and cultural influences on Indian and Saudi users. Available at SSRN 3391021 (2019)
19. Fagan, M., Khan, M.M.H.: Why do they do what they do?: a study of what motivates users to (not) follow computer security advice. In: SOUPS, pp. 59–75 (2016)
20. Galal-Edeen, G.H., Abdrabou, Y., Elgarf, M., Hassan, H.M.: Hci of arabia: The challenges of hci research in egypt. Interactions **26**(3), 55–59 (2019). https://doi.org/10.1145/3318215
21. Giglitto, D., Lazem, S., Preston, A.: In the eye of the student: an intangible cultural heritage experience, with a human-computer interaction twist. In: Proceedings of the 2018 CHI Conference on Human Factors in Computing Systems, pp. 1–12 (2018)
22. Hashmi, S.I., et al.: Training users to recognize persuasion techniques in vishing calls. In: Extended Abstracts of the 2023 CHI Conference on Human Factors in Computing Systems, pp. 1–8 (2023)
23. Javed, Y., Salehin, K.M., Shehab, M.: A study of south Asian websites on privacy compliance. IEEE Access **8**, 156067–156083 (2020). https://doi.org/10.1109/ACCESS.2020.3019334
24. Jawad, H.M., Tout, S.: Introducing a mobile app to increase cybersecurity awareness in Mena. In: 2020 3rd International Conference on Signal Processing and Information Security (ICSPIS), pp. 1–4 (2020). https://doi.org/10.1109/ICSPIS51252.2020.9340128
25. Kalbasi, A., Alomar, O., Hajipour, M., Aloul, F.: Wireless security in UAE: a survey paper. In: Proceedings of the IEEE GCC Conference (2007)
26. Manaf, A.A., Rahim, Z.A., Majid, N.H.A., Omer, S.: A relook at visual privacy: definition and factors influencing Muslim visual privacy (MVP). Pertanika J. Soc. Sci. Hum. (2019)
27. Mustafa, M., et al.: IslamicHCI: designing with and within Muslim populations. In: Extended Abstracts of the 2020 CHI Conference on Human Factors in Computing Systems, pp. 1–8. CHI EA '20, Association for Computing Machinery, New York, NY, USA (2020). https://doi.org/10.1145/3334480.3375151
28. Nasruddin, Z.A., Hussin, H.: Towards a theoretical framework for understanding Muslim-centered user interface design. In: 2013 5th International Conference on Information and Communication Technology for the Muslim World (ICT4M), pp. 1–7 (2013)
29. Naveed, S., Naveed, H., Javed, M., Mustafa, M.: " ask this from the person who has private stuff": privacy perceptions, behaviours and beliefs beyond weird. In: Proceedings of the 2022 CHI Conference on Human Factors in Computing Systems, pp. 1–17 (2022)
30. Norwawi, N.M., Alwi, N.H.M., Ismail, R., Wahid, F., Alkaenay, N.M.: Promoting Islamic ethics on privacy in digital social network for user data protection and trust. Ulum Islamiyyah **13** (2014)

31. Rashidi, Y., Vaniea, K., Camp, L.J.: Understanding Saudis' privacy concerns when using Whatsapp. In: Proceedings of the Workshop on Usable Security (USEC'16), pp. 1–8 (2016)
32. Rifat, M.R., Jannat, M., Al-Ameen, M.N., Haque, S.T., Kabir, M.A., Ahmed, S.I.: Purdah, Amanah, and Gheebat: understanding privacy in Bangladeshi "pious" Muslim communities. In: ACM SIGCAS Conference on Computing and Sustainable Societies, pp. 199–214 (2021)
33. Saleh, M., Khamis, M., Sturm, C.: What about my privacy, Habibi? In: IFIP Conference on Human-Computer Interaction, pp. 67–87. Springer (2019)
34. Sambasivan, N., et al.: "privacy is not for me, it's for those rich women": performative privacy practices on mobile phones by women in south Asia. In: Fourteenth Symposium on Usable Privacy and Security (SOUPS 2018), pp. 127–142. USENIX Association, Baltimore, MD (2018). https://www.usenix.org/conference/soups2018/presentation/sambasivan
35. Schneier, B.: Secrets and Lies: Digital Security in a Networked World. John Wiley & Sons (2011)
36. Shalhoub, Z.K.: Content analysis of web privacy policies in the GCC countries. Inf. Secur. J. A Glob. Perspect. **15**(3), 36–45 (2006)
37. Shambour, M., Gutub, A., Gutub, A.: Personal privacy evaluation of smart devices applications serving hajj and umrah rituals. J. Eng. Res. **11**(2B) (2023)
38. Sultana, S., Guimbretière, F., Sengers, P., Dell, N.: Design within a patriarchal society: opportunities and challenges in designing for rural women in Bangladesh. In: Proceedings of the 2018 CHI Conference on Human Factors in Computing Systems, pp. 1–13. CHI '18, Association for Computing Machinery, New York, NY, USA (2018). https://doi.org/10.1145/3173574.3174110
39. Woodruff, A., Augustin, S., Foucault, B.: Sabbath day home automation: " it's like mixing technology and religion". In: Proceedings of the SIGCHI conference on Human factors in computing systems, pp. 527–536 (2007)

A User-Centered Interface Enabling Secure Multimodal Biometric Search in Cross-Border Law Enforcement Operations

Kyriaki Miniadou[1(✉)], Eirini Kyriakou[1], Asterios Leonidis[1,2], Maria Korozi[1], and Constantine Stephanidis[1,2]

[1] Institute of Computer Science (ICS), Foundation for Research and Technology - Hellas (FORTH), Heraklion, Crete, Greece
{kminiadou,leonidis,korozi,cs}@ics.forth.gr
[2] Computer Science Department, University of Crete, Heraklion, Crete, Greece

Abstract. Suspect identification is a critical task for Law Enforcement Agencies (LEAs) and biometric data —being inherently unique to in-dividuals— play a pivotal role. However, the usability and interpretability of biometric identification systems remain challenging, especially for officers with limited technical expertise. These challenges are amplified in cross-border scenarios involving multiple biometric modalities (e.g., face, fingerprint, and voice) from heterogeneous sources. This paper presents a user-centered interface designed to support multimodal biometric matching in such complex environments. The proposed User Interface extends a previously developed Large-Scale Biometric Indexer module, enabling efficient biometric comparisons across foreign collaborating LEAs. It supports incomplete input data, harmonises results from heterogeneous sources, and clearly distinguishes between local matches, which provide full identity details, and external matches, which initially provide only confidence scores due to jurisdictional constraints. This UI aims to bridge the gap between complex biometric processing and operational decision-making, ensuring that identification results are presented in an understandable and actionable manner for law enforcement personnel.

Keywords: User Interface · Biometrics · Multimodal Biometric Data · Deep Learning · Security · Cross-Border Collaboration

1 Introduction

The identification of individuals involved in criminal activities has long been a central objective of Law Enforcement Agencies (LEAs). Biometric evidence such as blood traces or fingerprints left at crime scenes along with other sources like CCTV footage and eyewitness accounts, has consistently played a pivotal

C. Stephanidis et al. (Eds.): HCII 2025, CCIS 2773, pp. 161–171, 2026.
https://doi.org/10.1007/978-3-032-12773-0_15

role in criminal investigations. Over the years, the technology used to collect, process, and match such evidence to potential suspects has undergone significant advancements in both accuracy and reliability.

In recent years, Artificial Intelligence (AI) has emerged as a transformative force in this domain, enabling faster and more accurate biometric identification. AI-powered algorithms are continuously refined to cope with real-world variability and data imperfections. A prominent example can be drawn from the COVID-19 pandemic, which highlighted a critical limitation in facial recognition systems as widespread mask usage obscured key facial features, drastically reducing system performance. This real-world disruption prompted an influx of research aimed at enhancing recognition systems under such conditions [3,4,14].

However, accurate identification alone is insufficient if results are not presented in an understandable and actionable manner to Law Enforcement personnel. In biometric identification systems, information is typically conveyed through a ranked list of potential suspects with associated confidence scores, allowing LEAs to assess the biometric evidence collected from the scene.

This process becomes more complex when multiple biometric modalities are taken into consideration, since different modalities may yield conflicting top matches making unified ranking across modalities non-trivial. The inclusion of multiple biometric types is necessary since, in real-world scenarios, not all biometric modalities are always available. For instance, a suspect may leave no fingerprints at the scene, rendering fingerprint matching ineffective; however they may have been recorded on CCTV, enabling face or voice matching. This complexity is further heightened in cross-border investigations, where results must be aggregated from LEAs across different jurisdictions. In such cases, the User Interface must manage input of varying completeness and harmonise results from heterogeneous sources.

To address these challenges, a User Interface (UI) was developed to assist LEAs in interpreting biometric identification results. The UI was designed to clearly present facial, fingerprint, and voice similarity results from disparate sources in a unified view [5] facilitating informed operational decision-making.

This paper is structured as follows: In Sect. 2, prior works related to user interfaces of biometric frameworks are discussed. Section 3, describes the motivation behind our approach as well as the Large-Scale Biometric Indexer module this work extends, Sect. 4 offers a detailed description of the User Interface. Finally, we conclude this paper in Sect. 5.

2 Related Work

The effectiveness of a User Interface directly impacts user experience (UX) and usability, which is critical in law enforcement settings where information must be delivered rapidly and accurately to support timely decision-making.

To improve the management of crime records, an Automated Fingerprint Biometric System [1] was developed. This web-based solution enables authorised personnel to register new individuals, store fingerprint data, and manage case records efficiently. By leveraging biometric data, the system ensures precise identification and reduces the risk of errors or data loss inherent in manual paper-based processes.

In addition to fingerprint-based systems, [2] explored facial recognition as a complementary or standalone biometric tool for law enforcement. An integrated Facial Recognition System was designed for real-time identification from live camera feeds or uploaded images.

Expanding on this concept, the Mobile Automated Fingerprint Identification System (MAFIS) [11] was introduced as a mobile Android-based platform for on-field operatives. It enables initial fingerprint inquiries, system dashboard access, and crime scene data collection directly from mobile devices. The UI plays a central role by presenting match results and investigation relevant data with clarity.

The system was further extended into MABIS (Mobile Automated Biometric Identification System) [12], incorporating facial recognition alongside fingerprints for enhanced identification. A follow-up study [13] evaluated MABIS in the Philippines, reporting a high System Usability Scale (SUS) score of 87.475, indicating strong usability. The User Experience Questionnaire (UEQ) highlighted improvement areas such as dependability and stimulation. Recommendations include visual enhancements, innovative features, and iterative, user-driven development to ensure continuous improvement.

3 Large-Scale Biometric Indexer Module

The proposed User Interface, as mentioned above, builds upon the Large-Scale Biometric Indexer, originally developed by the authors to facilitate suspect identification, particularly in cross-border investigations. The Indexer enables efficient and effective comparisons of biometric data, with the primary objective of identifying individuals based on their unique biometric traits. Initially introduced in [10], the Indexer applied to facial images and was later extended in [9] to incorporate additional biometric modalities, including fingerprints and voice samples. Furthermore, the Indexer operates as a core component within a broader secure ecosystem —the Biometrics Data Space— introduced in [6]. This ecosystem leverages Data Spaces technology, advanced Privacy Enhancing Technologies (PETs), and blockchain to support secure and sovereign data exchange between LEAs. In addition to interoperability and scalability, particular attention is devoted to privacy protection and ethical considerations ensuring that the handling of biometric data is aligned with principles of security, data minimisation, and accountability. The full set of technical details regarding implementation, system architecture, and privacy-preserving mechanisms are comprehensively described in our previous works [6,9,10].

The Large-Scale Biometric Indexer accepts as input any combination of biometric modalities for a given individual and performs matching against a database (referred to as the catalogue) of previously apprehended individuals—both from the initiating LEA and from external partner LEAs. Law Enforcement

Agents working on a case can upload data directly from the local storage on their operational devices. Once uploaded, the biometric samples are matched against local data and securely transmitted to external LEAs for additional matching. The underlying system architecture and technical specifications are detailed in prior work by the authors.

Matching results —both local and external— are aggregated and visualised through interactive charts that summarise key statistics. The results are organised per LEA, meaning that matches retrieved from different partner agencies' databases are grouped according to their source. This allows investigators to easily identify which agency contributed each candidate match and, if needed, follow up directly with the corresponding authority. Each candidate is further broken down by biometric modality (e.g., face, fingerprint, voice) along with its confidence score. A confidence score represents the similarity measure produced by the biometric matching algorithm, typically expressed as a percentage.

It is important to note that local matches provide full access to the biometric profiles and associated information of the identified individuals, including names, addresses, and criminal histories. This information is made available to the investigating agent, as it resides within the jurisdiction of the initiating LEA. In contrast, external matches —those retrieved from databases managed by other LEAs— only return similarity scores or confidence values. To access detailed personal or criminal information for external matches, a formal request must be submitted to the corresponding LEA. This restriction is in place to ensure compliance with data protection regulations and to prevent the irresponsible sharing of sensitive personal data across networks.

3.1 Motivational Scenario

To illustrate the practical significance of our research objectives as well as highlight the difference between local and external matches, two motivational scenarios are presented.

- **Local Case: Drug Store Burglary:**
  A burglary occurred at a drug store and investigators recovered a fingerprint from the cash register and obtained CCTV footage showing the suspect. Tom, the police officer leading the case, uploads both biometric samples into the Large-Scale Biometric Indexer. The system returns high confidence scores from the local catalogue. Tom reviews the results and confirms that the samples match those of a previously apprehended individual. Because the match is local, the full identity details are displayed —including the suspect's name, address, prior offenses, and risk assessment profile— enabling Tom to take immediate investigative action.
- **Cross-Border Case: Human Trafficking Investigation:**
  A human trafficking investigation uncovers a hideout. The only available biometric evidence contains a voice recording intercepted during a surveillance operation and a low-quality facial image extracted from a camera. Amanda,

the officer in charge, uploads the biometric data into the Large-Scale Biometric Indexer. The system finds no high confidence matches locally. However, a strong match is returned from an external LEA. Because of privacy regulations, only the confidence scores, the originating agency and a pseudonymised ID are shown. Amanda initiates a formal request to the relevant LEA to obtain the suspect's identity and background for further legal processing.

3.2 Datasets

To evaluate the performance of the Large-Scale Biometric Indexer and support realistic testing scenarios, multiple biometric datasets were employed. These datasets were selected to reflect the diversity and complexity of real-world data encountered in law enforcement operations and cover three primary biometric modalities: face, fingerprint, and voice. For facial images, the GANDiffFace dataset [8] was used, which provides high-quality synthetic faces for robust face recognition evaluation. Fingerprint data was sourced from the FVC2000 dataset [7], which contains a diverse collection of fingerprint samples from multiple participants under varying acquisition conditions. For voice samples, the VCTK Corpus developed by the Centre for Speech Technology (CSTR) [15] was utilized. This dataset includes recordings from English speakers with a wide range of regional accents, enabling the system to be tested under diverse audio input scenarios.

4 User Interface

The proposed User Interface was developed to bridge the gap between complex biometric processing and operational decision-making. It supports seamless interaction with the Large-Scale Biometric Indexer, enabling users to upload evidence, view similarity scores, and compare results across multiple biometric modalities and jurisdictions.

4.1 Initiation of Biometric Matching

To perform the biometric profile matching, three distinct biometric modalities are available, (a) Facial Images, (b) Fingerprints, and (c) Voice Samples. As illustrated in Fig. 1, the interface allows the user to upload biometric evidence by dragging and dropping files into dedicated drop boxes, each outlined with a dotted border and clearly labeled with the corresponding modality. Each box includes a visual or audio preview of the uploaded input, depending on the modality.

The user can choose a combination of query biometric data that pertain to the same individual. To account for real time conditions where not all biometric data can be made available each image is uploaded to a specific drop box and additionally a preview is available.

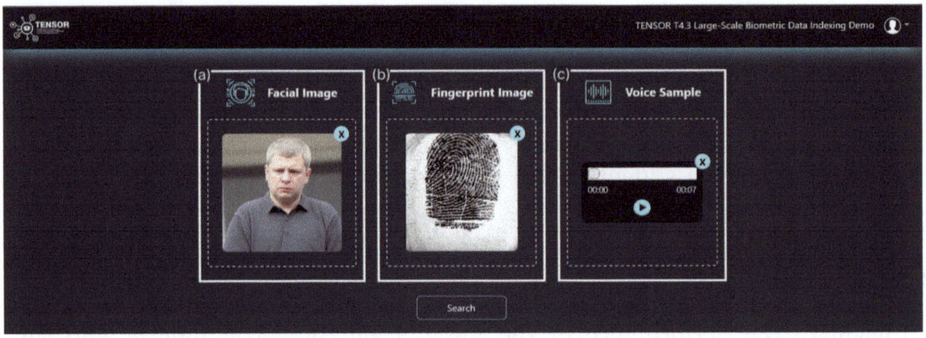

Fig. 1. Initiation of Biometric Matching

Each modality panel also includes a “X” button to remove or replace inputs, supporting error correction or changes in input before submission. This design accommodates real-world conditions, where not all biometric modalities may be available simultaneously.

Importantly, uploading biometric data does not automatically trigger a search. The user must explicitly initiate the matching process by clicking the central "Search" button, located beneath the modality panels. This deliberate action ensures that the user maintains control over the timing of the query submission.

4.2 Biometric Matching Results and Statistics

For each biometric matching request, the interface presents the detailed results along with an overview of relevant statistics, as depicted in Fig. 2.

The statistical summary, shown in Fig. 2a, provides a concise yet informative snapshot of the overall results. It includes the total number of matching entries retrieved, the number of contributing LEAs, including the requesting one, and the average matching score across all results. Two diagrams are displayed: a pie chart representing the contribution of each LEA to the total matches, and a Venn diagram showing the distribution of results across the three biometric modalities —face, fingerprint, and voice.

As shown in Fig. 3, additional information is revealed by hovering over each section of the diagrams. Specifically, Fig. 3a, in the pie chart displays the number and percentage of results contributed by each LEA, while in Fig. 3b the Venn diagram indicates how many results correspond to each individual modality or combination of modalities.

The actual matching results Fig. 2b are organised by the originator LEA. The requesting LEA, and thus the local results are displayed first by default. Users can navigate between LEAs by selecting the respective tabs at the top of the results section. Each result includes a pseudonymised identifier and displays the matching scores for the available biometric modalities, provided there is a

Fig. 2. Biometric Matching Results

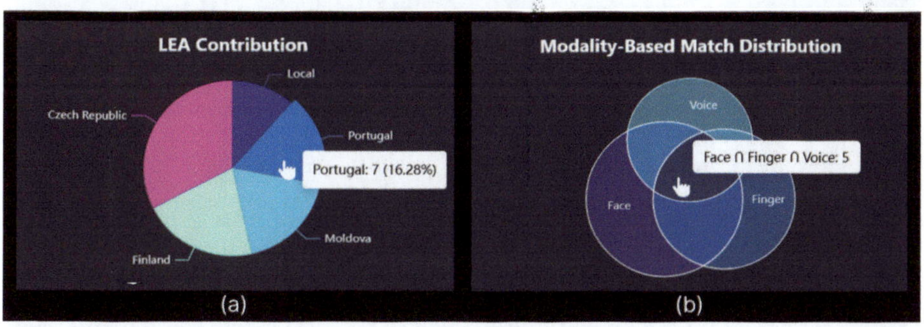

Fig. 3. Biometric Matching Statistics

match in the corresponding biometric profile. The results are initially sorted in descending order by facial matching score. Users can re-sort the table based on fingerprint or voice sample scores by clicking the sorting button next to each modality name.

4.3 Local Biometric Matches Result

For local matches, since the biometric profiles already belong to the user's LEA, full access to the associated data is granted for all possible matches. This allows the user to quickly assess whether the retrieved result corresponds to the same

Fig. 4. Local Biometric Matches Result

individual as the query. A confirmed match typically indicates that the individual has previously been apprehended by the LEA.

As shown in Fig. 4, if the matching confidence scores are relatively low, the user can manually verify the identity and confirm the match. By clicking the "View" button, the complete biometric profile becomes available. This includes the full name, personal information, and criminal background of the suspect.

Facial images and voice samples are particularly useful for manual verification, as they can be evaluated more intuitively compared to fingerprints, where differences are often more subtle. All relevant data for the individual is displayed, including biometric samples, which can be viewed and, in the case of voice, listened to. For convenience, the original query data is also shown alongside the match, enabling direct comparison by the user.

4.4 Cross-Border Biometric Matches Result

When no local match is found, the user may rely on collaborating LEAs in hopes that the individual has previously been apprehended by them. As depicted in Fig. 5, the structure of the cross-border results mirrors that of local results. However, the biometric data is not immediately available for viewing, as the profiles belong to external LEAs. In such cases, the interface presents a “Request” option, allowing the user to request permission to view the data. This decision rests with the owning LEA and is granted at their discretion. Before submitting a request, the user can examine the similarity scores for each biometric modality —face, fingerprint, and voice— to determine whether the match appears reliable. If the request is approved, the full profile becomes accessible in the same manner as a local match.

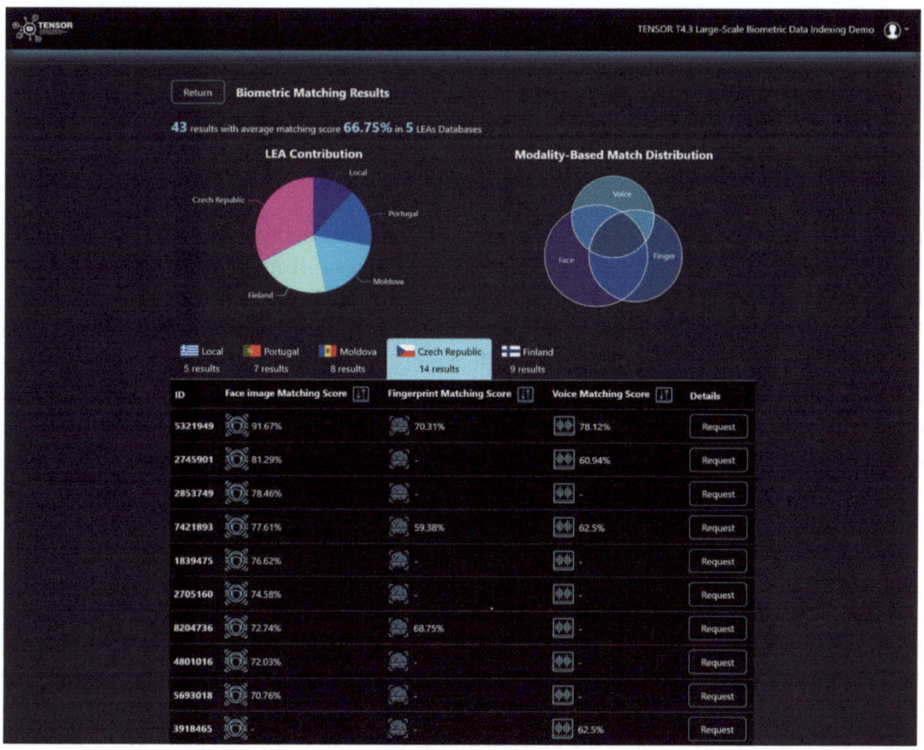

Fig. 5. Cross-border Biometric Matches Result

In the example shown in Fig. 6, the Czech Republic provides a facial image that closely matches the query, as well as corresponding fingerprints and voice samples. Once approved by the owner LEA, these materials are made available to the requesting LEA for review and verification.

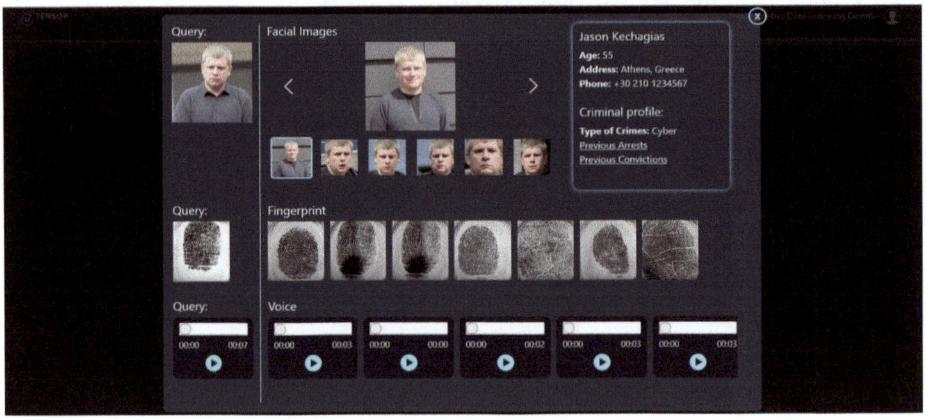

Fig. 6. Cross-border Biometric Matches Result After Request

5 Conclusion

In conclusion, this work presents a user-centered interface designed to support cross-border law enforcement investigations by streamlining multimodal biometric identification. The interface was integrated with the Large-Scale Biometric Indexer to ensure that heterogeneous biometric inputs from both local and external sources could be managed effectively, even in scenarios where data is incomplete. A clear distinction was maintained between local matches, where full identity details are accessible, and external matches from collaborating LEAs, which are presented with limited information due to privacy constraints. Complex similarity scores and match distributions were visualised interactively to aid interpretation by users without technical expertise, placing emphasis on user control and operational clarity. Through this design, a bridge was created between advanced biometric processing and practical investigative workflows.

Acknowledgment. The research leading to these results has received funding from the European Union's Horizon Europe research and innovation programme under the Grant Agreement No 101073920 (TENSOR). This publication reflects only the authors views. The European Union is not liable for any use that may be made of the information contained therein.

References

1. AbdulRaheem, M., Misra, S., Awotunde, J.B., Oladipo, I.D., Oluranti, J.: Automated fingerprint biometric system for crime record management. In: International Conference on Innovations in Bio-Inspired Computing and Applications, pp. 806–817. Springer (2021)
2. Chittibomma, S.S., Surapaneni, R.K., Maruboina, A.: Facial recognition system for law enforcement: an integrated approach using HAAR cascade classifier and LBPH algorithm. In: 2024 International Conference on Advancements in Power, Communication and Intelligent Systems (APCI), pp. 1–6. IEEE (2024)
3. Gomez-Barrero, M., et al.: Biometrics in the era of Covid-19: challenges and opportunities. IEEE Trans. Technol. Soc. **3**(4), 307–322 (2022)
4. Guo, Y.: Impact on biometric identification systems of Covid-19. Sci. Program. **2021**(1), 3225687 (2021)
5. Kim, S., Leonidis, A., Zidianakis, E.: Interaction styles. In: Interaction Techniques and Technologies in Human-Computer Interaction, pp. 1–44. CRC Press (2024)
6. Kyriakou, K., et al.: A secure and trustworthy biometric data ecosystem for cross-border suspect identification. In: 2024 IEEE International Conference on Big Data (BigData), pp. 2762–2771. IEEE (2024)
7. Maltoni, D., Maio, D., Jain, A.K., Prabhakar, S., et al.: Handbook of Fingerprint Recognition, vol. 2. Springer (2009)
8. Melzi, P., et al.: GANDiffFace: controllable generation of synthetic datasets for face recognition with realistic variations. In: Proceedings of the IEEE/CVF International Conference on Computer Vision, pp. 3086–3095 (2023)
9. Miniadou, K., Leonidis, A., Papadopoulos, G.T., Stephanidis, C.: Encrypted biometric search: a deep learning approach to scalable and secure cross-border data exchange. In: 2024 IEEE International Conference on Big Data (BigData), pp. 2794–2800. IEEE (2024)
10. Miniadou, K., Leonidis, A., Papadopoulos, G.T., Stephanidis, C.: Enhancing secure cross-border collaboration among law enforcement agencies for facial biometric search. In: 2024 5th International Conference in Electronic Engineering, Information Technology & Education (EEITE), pp. 1–6. IEEE (2024)
11. P. Rey, W., V. Rolluqui, G.: Mobile automated fingerprint identification system (MAFIS): an android-based criminal tracking system using fingerprint minutiae structure. In: 2021 5th International Conference on E-Society, E-Education and E-Technology, pp. 62–68 (2021)
12. Rey, W.P.: Face recognition (FR) integration on MABIS: a mobile automated biometric identification system for law enforcement in the Philippines. In: Proceedings of the 2023 6th International Conference on Electronics, Communications and Control Engineering, pp. 8–16 (2023)
13. Rey, W.P.: Optimizing user interaction with MABIS: an examination of usability and user experience in the mobile automated biometric identification system. In: Proceedings of the 2024 10th International Conference on Computer Technology Applications, pp. 215–222 (2024)
14. Talahua, J.S., Buele, J., Calvopiña, P., Varela-Aldás, J.: Facial recognition system for people with and without face mask in times of the Covid-19 pandemic. Sustainability **13**(12), 6900 (2021)
15. Yamagishi, J., Veaux, C., MacDonald, K.: CSTR VCTK Corpus: English Multi-speaker Corpus for CSTR Voice Cloning Toolkit (version 0.92) (2019)

A Cartography of Portuguese Feminisms: Memory as Resistance, Mapping as Mobilisation

Andreia Pinto de Sousa[1](✉), Ana Sofia Pereira[2], Célia Taborda[2], Carla Cerqueira[2], and Irina Drofa[3]

[1] HEI-Lab: Digital Human-Environment Interaction Labs, Lusófona University, Lisbon, Portugal
andreia.pinto.sousa@ulusofona.pt
[2] CICANT, Lusófona University, Porto, Portugal
[3] Porto, Portugal

Abstract. This paper introduces an interactive digital map designed to preserve and make visible feminist movements in Portugal, across both historical and contemporary contexts. While digital platforms offer unprecedented opportunities for feminist activism and visibility, they also pose significant limitations to long-term archiving and the structured representation of feminist histories due to factors such as corporate governance, algorithmic biases, impermanence, and the constraints of social media. Despite their importance for mobilisation, these platforms lack the necessary features to trace feminist historiography. Developed within the framework of the FEMglocal research project, this map addresses the absence of a unified, interactive and participatory digital resource for Portuguese feminist history. A human-centred design methodology guided the development of the platform design, ensuring accessibility, inclusivity, and user engagement. This process involved user research, co-design activities with diverse stakeholders (students, journalists, activists), and iterative prototyping supported by usability testing.

Keywords: Interactive Digital Map · Portuguese Feminist Cartography · Co-creation Design

1 Introduction

The digital era has reshaped feminist activism, offering new opportunities for visibility, engagement, and archival preservation [1, 2]. Digital platforms have been extensively studied within feminist theory as both tools of empowerment and mechanisms of control [2, 3].

Early cyberfeminists, such as Sadie Plant and the VNS Matrix collective, envisioned the internet as a space for gender liberation. Contemporary feminist scholars, however, highlight the ambivalent nature of digital platforms: while they enable the visibility, documentation and circulation of feminist movements [4], they are also shaped by significant constraints, such as corporate governance, algorithmic biases, and platform impermanence [3]. These dualities raise critical questions regarding the role of digital

C. Stephanidis et al. (Eds.): HCII 2025, CCIS 2773, pp. 172–179, 2026.
https://doi.org/10.1007/978-3-032-12773-0_16

technologies in preserving feminist histories and the sustainability of digital activism [4, 5]. While social media, for instance, are instrumental in amplifying feminist voices and mobilising communities, they are not designed for long-term preservation or for providing coherent, structured forms of archiving. In response to these limitations, but also to expand the possibilities of feminist digital memory, this research proposes a complementary approach: a purpose-built interactive digital map, conceived as a curated, participatory, and durable tool for feminist historiography.

This paper discusses a collaborative and interactive digital map design process that visualises historical and contemporary feminist movements in Portugal. The map is a central output of the research project "FEMglocal – Glocal Feminist Movements: Interactions and Contradictions", which addresses the lack of Portuguese research on the relationship between digital networked action and feminist activism. As feminist movements increasingly operate across both global and local dimensions and navigate the intersections of online mobilisation and face-to-face organising, they pose new analytical challenges that require context-specific, situated approaches. In Portugal, these dynamics remain underexplored. FEMglocal responds to this by mapping the genealogies, spatial distribution, communication strategies, and collective practices of feminist activism, aiming to recover a historical memory that has often been marginalised or rendered invisible. Many of these movements, especially informal or short-lived ones, leave behind little trace, particularly when they are organised primarily through digital means. Against this backdrop, the interactive digital map was conceived as both a research tool and a public platform for feminist historiography. Developed within the FEMglocal framework, it serves as a curated, participatory, and durable archive designed to foreground the diversity and evolution of feminist movements across the national landscape. More than a repository, the map invites users to explore, engage with, and contribute to a living cartography of feminist resistance and memory in Portugal, reflecting the project's broader commitment to recovering and representing the often-silenced histories of feminist struggles in the country [6].

Feminist scholars have long advocated collecting feminist records to ensure that the stories and History of feminist movements are preserved and accessible. This concern has been a consistent thread across what is commonly referred to as the three waves of feminism – each shaped by its own priorities and historical context [7]. More recently, a fourth wave was identified, characterised by using digital technologies and social media as key tools for activism and mobilisation [5]. This fourth wave, driven by global connectivity, has reshaped the dynamics of feminist movements by making them simultaneously more transnational and more attuned to local, historical, and cultural specificities [6]. FEMglocal's interactive map is conceived as a response to this need, functioning both as an archival tool and a means of fostering engagement, awareness, and participation in feminist activism.

2 Methodological Framework: Co-creation and Human-Centred Design in Feminist Digital Mapping

The development of a digital tool capable of communicating complex historical and social data required careful methodological consideration. Central to this challenge was the need to ensure clarity, accessibility, and visual engagement for diverse audiences. A key objective of the FEMglocal research project is to produce academic research that is both widely accessible and relevant beyond scholarly circles [6]. We adopted a human-centred design methodology to meet this goal, incorporating user research, prototyping, and usability testing [8]. Challenging technology's presumed neutrality and embracing alternative ways of knowing that centre the lived experiences of marginalised groups, our design process was grounded in feminist epistemologies and design principles, recognising that the way information is structured and presented impacts its accessibility and meaning - prompting a critical examination of whose voices are represented and who has access to them [9, 10]. By integrating these critical perspectives, the project sought to document feminist stories and co-create a digital platform grounded in feminist values of participation, inclusivity, and social justice.

Throughout the research team's co-design activities and interviews, we identified possible user profiles – students, journalists, activists, researchers and interested individuals (Fig. 1) – and design requirements (Table 1).

Fig. 1. Five different profiles of users developed in the context of the FEMglocal research project.

A central aspect of the FEMglocal research project lies in its commitment to ensuring accessibility and inclusivity. Recognising the barriers that often limit engagement with digital archives – including technological literacy, design complexity, and infrastructural limitations – we prioritised an inclusive design approach.

This involved developing mobile-friendly interfaces, intuitive navigation, and multilingual content to broaden the platform's reach. After collecting and analysing other interactive maps, we developed and refined prototypes through iterative feedback from potential users, ensuring the interface remains adaptable and responsive to user needs. The usability testing phase, with 11 participants, provided valuable insights, leading to

Table 1. Actions and Information needed requirements.

Actions
Journalist: Search by time, location, agenda, and type of movement **Activist**: Submit information about the action/event Submit information about the organisation Upload a photo and a video **Researcher, Student**: Search by time, location, agenda, and type of movement Collect information **Interested individuals**: Browse the country map and see currently active groups Find information about events
Information needed
Activist: MAP of Organisations in the country: agenda, location, type of movement, contacts, multimedia **Journalist:** Contacts or information about feminist organisations/collectives **Student:** Name, history, locations, relations, MULTIMEDIA content **Researcher:** List of all organisations/movements, organised geographically, organised chronologically, or specific actions. Relationships between organisations, events, and locations **Interested individuals:** Map of organizations that are currently active + their information: agenda, location, type of movement, members, contacts, multimedia Calendar of Events: agenda, location, members, contacts, multimedia

optimisations in navigation, content structuring, and visual hierarchy, each contributing to a more engaging user experience. Results obtained from the UEQ[1] questionnaire showed a positive reception from participants across hedonic, pragmatic, and attractiveness qualities (Fig. 2).

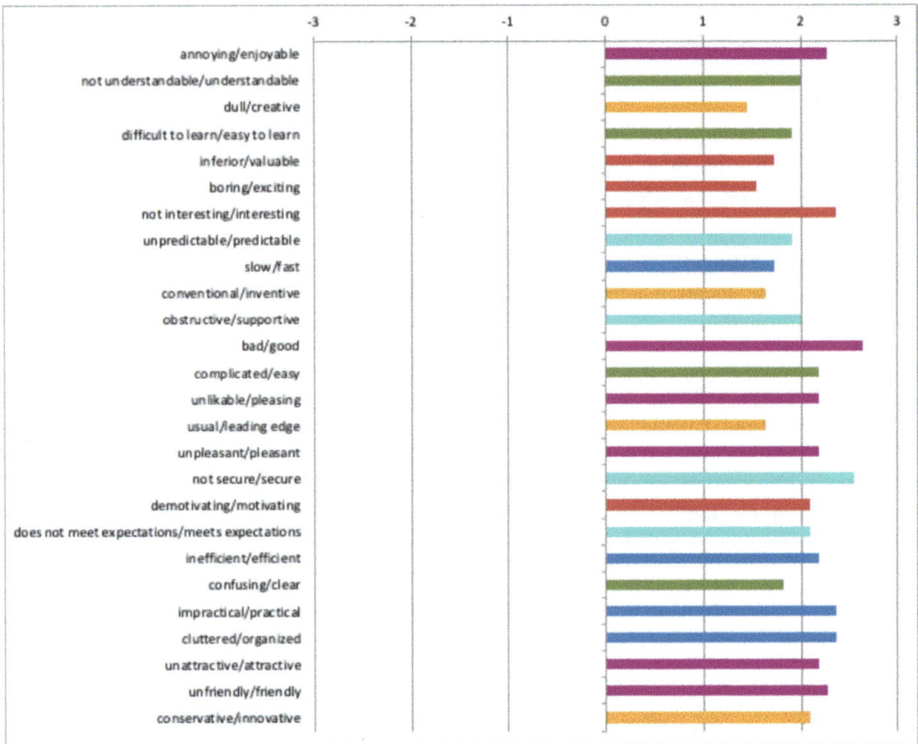

Fig. 2. Mean value per item of the UEQ used to evaluate the High-fidelity prototype.

As shown in Fig. 2, all item means exceeded the +0.8 threshold, indicating strong user satisfaction with the platform. Attractiveness received particularly high scores – for example, 2.6 on "good–bad" and 2.5 on "friendly–unfriendly" – highlighting the platform's pleasant and engaging design. Perspicuity was also rated positively, with users finding the interface understandable and easy to use (e.g., 2.2 for "complicated–easy"). Stimulation and Efficiency scored similarly well, with items such as "interesting" (2.4), "motivating" (2.1), "organized" (2.4), and "practical" (2.4) confirming the platform's clarity and usability. Dependability and Novelty were likewise positively evaluated, with no neutral or negative responses. Importantly, the data showed no significant outliers or inconsistencies across items within the same scale, suggesting a coherent and reliable pattern of user interpretation. These findings support the platform's capacity to meet

[1] User Experience questionnaire: https://www.ueq-online.org/.

its design goals of accessibility, clarity, and user engagement, in alignment with the project's feminist and participatory principles.

FEMglocal's interactive map allows users to explore feminist movements by filtering information from different categories, including non-governmental organisations, associations, collectives, and online platforms. This categorisation highlights the historical trajectories and the contemporary dynamics of feminist activism in Portugal (Fig. 3).

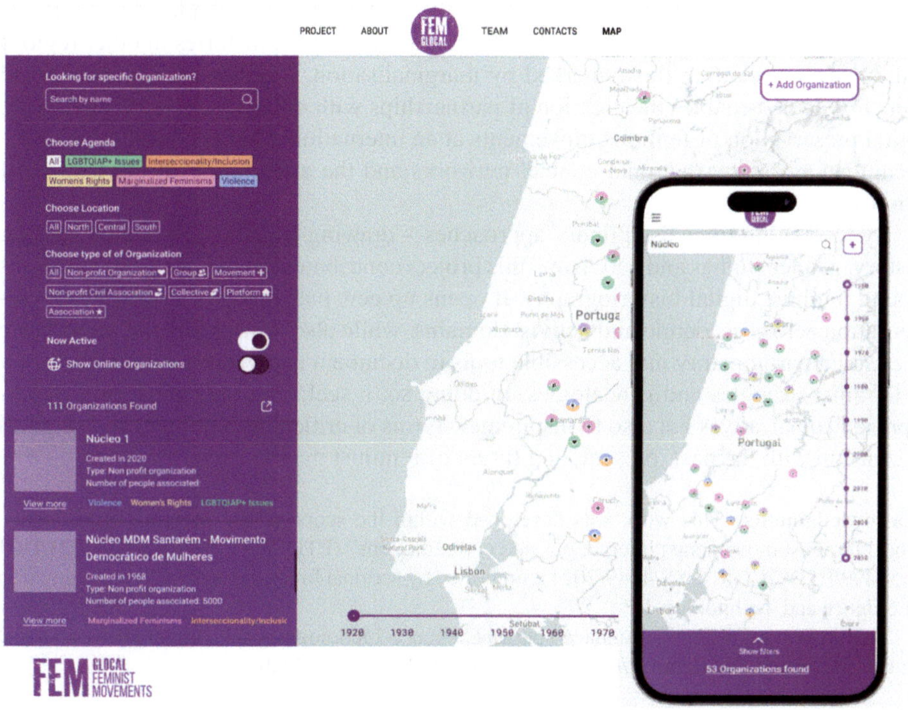

Fig. 3. High-fidelity prototype of the FEMglocal platform.

Furthermore, the research project's initiative underscores the significance of collaborative, community-driven approaches to digital feminist historiography. Unlike traditional archival projects, which often rely on institutional gatekeeping and rigid classification systems, FEMglocal seeks to foster open, participatory engagement where users can contribute to and expand the feminist historical record. This participatory ethos aligns with feminist principles of co-creation, intersectionality, and knowledge democratisation [11], reinforcing that History is not static but continuously co-created through lived experience and collective memory. In this sense, the digital archive is not only a repository of the past but a vital force for contemporary feminisms. Its accessibility, immediacy, and visibility keep feminist memories active, mobilisable, and relevant, contributing to their recovery and preservation in Portugal.

3 Final Remarks on a Work in Progress: Feminist Histories and Digital Possibilities

This paper represents a working draft of a research that is currently in progress. As such, it expresses ongoing reflections and preliminary findings that will be further deepened and refined in future stages of the project. Building on a strong commitment to accessibility, intersectionality, and the preservation of collective memory, the FEMglocal interactive map holds the potential to transcend its national context. More than a localised archive, it offers a scalable and adaptable model for mapping feminist histories in other regions and contexts, including those marked by marginalisation, fragmentation, or historical silencing. It also enables the creation of partnerships with other spaces dedicated to the digital preservation of feminist movements at an international level, contributing to the strengthening of transnational contact networks and the articulation of the history of feminisms.

By leveraging transdisciplinary approaches – drawing from design, media studies, History, gender studies and activism – this project contributes to emerging conversations around feminist digital historiography. It opens up new pathways for research and collaboration across academic and activist domains, while also reinforcing the importance of creating participatory and accessible tools to document and visualise the complexity of feminist struggles and genealogies. In doing so, it seeks not only to recover underrepresented narratives but also to inspire new forms of critical engagement and (digital) citizenship with the past, present, and future of feminist movements.

Acknowledgments. This work was developed within the scope of the project "FEMglocal - Glocal feminist movements: interactions and contradictions" (PTDC/COM-CSS/4049/2021/DOI 10.54499/PTDC/COM-CSS/4049/2021), supported by national funds through FCT — Foundation for Science and Technology, I.P.

This work was funded by Fundação para a Ciência e Tecnologia (FCT), under HEI-Lab R&D Unit (UIDB/05380/2020, https://doi.org/10.54499/UIDB/05380/2020).

Disclosure of Interests. The authors have no competing interests to declare that are relevant to the content of this article.

References

1. Cifor, M., Wood, S.: Critical feminism in the archives. J. Crit. Libr. Inf. Stud. **1**(2) (2017). https://doi.org/10.24242/jclis.v1i2.27
2. D'Ignazio, C., Klein, L.: Data Feminism. MIT Press, Cambridge (2020)
3. Umoja, S.: Algorithms of Oppression: How Search Engines Reinforce Racism. New York University Press, New York (2018)
4. Lamartine, C.: Interseccionalidade e Ciberfeminismo Construindo laços transfronteiriços nos Feminismos Contemporâneos', ontraCorrente. Revista do Programa de Pós-Graduação Interdisciplinar em Ciências Humanas **20**, 98–109 (2023). https://doi.org/10.59666/cc-ppgich.v0i20.3310
5. Wilson, N., Battershill, C., Clarkson, H., Hannah, M.N., Nokhrin, I., Willson Gordon, E.: Digital critical archives, copyright, and feminist praxis. Arch. Sci. **22**(3), 295–317 (2022). https://doi.org/10.1007/s10502-021-09384-x

6. Pereira, A.S., Ribeiro-Rodrigues, V., Cerqueira, C., Taborda, C.: Arte, ciência e ativismo em convergência: Estratégias criativas para disseminação científica feminist. In: Baptista, M.M., de Almeida, A.R.A., Ferreira, H.C.G. (eds.) Culturas, Ativismos e Mudanças Culturais, CLLC, Universidade de Aveiro, pp. 237–246 (2024). https://doi.org/10.54499/PTDC/COM-CSS/4049/2021
7. Cerqueira, C., Taborda Silva, C.: Challenges of the intergenerational feminist movement(s): some reflections. In: Gao, Q., Zhou, J. (eds.) HCII 2022. LNCS, vol. 13330, pp. 265–275. Springer, Cham (2022). https://doi.org/10.1007/978-3-031-05581-2_20
8. Conrad, J., Koehler, C., Wallach, D., Luedeke, T.: Design theory and methodology in HCI: applying CPM/PDD to UCD. In: Marcus, A., Wang, W. (eds.) DUXU 2018. LNCS, vol. 10918, pp. 27–39. Springer, Cham (2018). https://doi.org/10.1007/978-3-319-91797-9_3
9. Bardzell, S., Bardzell, J.: Towards a feminist HCI methodology: social science, feminism, and HCI. In: Proceedings of the SIGCHI Conference on Human Factors in Computing Systems, in CHI 2011, New York, NY, USA, pp. 675–684. Association for Computing Machinery (2011). https://doi.org/10.1145/1978942.1979041
10. Bellini, R., Meissner, J., Finnigan, S.M., Strohmayer, A.: Feminist human–computer interaction: struggles for past, contemporary and futuristic feminist theories in digital innovation. Fem. Theory **23**(2), 143–149 (2022). https://doi.org/10.1177/14647001221082291
11. Haraway, D.: Situated knowledges: the science question in feminism and the privilege of partial perspective. Fem. Stud. **14**, 575–599 (1988)

Leveraging Large Language Models to Address Communication and Misinformation Challenges to Enhance Information Coordination in Disaster Relief Operations

Daria Shcherbak[1](✉) and Helen Muncie[2]

[1] Easol Limited, Farnborough, UK
daria.shcherbak@easol.io
[2] Mage Insights Limited, Hove, UK

Abstract. Disaster relief operations can be chaotic and complex, often characterised by fragmented communication, conflicting information and duplicated effort across agencies. Relief workers may have to sift through large volumes of information from multiple sources to identify relevant and reliable details under time pressure, which can be a daunting task.

This poster introduces Vyron, a secure Artificial Intelligence (AI) assistant designed to streamline disaster relief coordination. Combining small language models (SLMs) for mobile devices with large language models (LLMs) and external data sources, Vyron offers a unified platform for real-time information management and decision support. Through illustrative scenarios, we demonstrate Vyron's capabilities to prioritise conflicting information, recommend safe routes based on evolving weather and road conditions and optimise the distribution of critical resources like food and medical supplies. The poster also addresses trust and transparency in AI systems, highlighting design principles that empowered users to question and verify information. This work advances the field of Human-Computer Interaction (HCI) by illustrating how AI technologies can support human teams in high-stress, real-world environments. By showcasing Vyron at HCI2025, we hope to spark discussions about the role of AI in disaster response and encourage collaboration to develop innovative systems for future crisis management.

Keywords: Human-Machine Teaming · Large Language Models · Human-Computer Interaction · User-Centred Design · Disaster Relief

1 Introduction

Disaster relief operations are inherently complex, involving communication and coordination across multiple agencies. Relief workers must operate in hazardous environments while coordinating with diverse teams and rapidly sifting through vast amounts of data from various sources to identify risks and allocate aid.

This project explored how Artificial Intelligence (AI), specifically large language models (LLMs) can address these challenges. We share our user research findings, outline

C. Stephanidis et al. (Eds.): HCII 2025, CCIS 2773, pp. 180–186, 2026.
https://doi.org/10.1007/978-3-032-12773-0_17

key design challenges and introduce Vyron—a secure AI-assistant designed to streamline information management and enhance decision-making under pressure.

2 User Research

2.1 Relief Worker's Challenges in Disaster Response

Disaster relief responders face many challenges that may hinder their ability to save lives and provide timely assistance. In sensitive interviews with experienced disaster relief workers, the following key challenges were highlighted:

- **Multi-Organisation Joint Training.** While some training exists, it is difficult to train diverse agencies, such as the emergency services, charities, hotels, media, members of the community and hospitals to work together using common operating procedures, standards and security.
- **Exposure to Hazards**. Relief workers may be exposed to a variety of hazards, which may cause illness or injury.
- **Insufficient Guidelines and Standards.** Guidance documents that provide information or interpretations of law are often not provided to relief workers in time to provide effective guidance or protection.
- **Misinformation and Conflicting Reports.** Misinformation and contradictory reports from diverse sources can make it difficult to determine the ground truth, leading to delays and potential mistakes in response efforts.
- **Managing Multiple Information Sources.** Information pours in from social media, government agencies, news outlets, and more. Filtering through these streams to determine what is relevant and reliable may overwhelm relief workers and cause them to overlook vital details.
- **Team Communication and Coordination.** Teams on the ground and in command centres often struggle to maintain communication, which is essential for managing logistics, coordinating actions and ensuring that everyone is informed and aligned.
- **Duplication of Effort Across Agencies.** A lack of communication between different agencies and organisations can lead to redundant or overlapping efforts. This wastes valuable resources and slows down response times when efficiency is required.
- **Handling Medicine and Food Distribution.** Distributing food, water and medical supplies efficiently and equitably is a complex task that requires real-time data on inventory, demand and delivery routes to prevent shortages.
- **Weather and Hazard Updates.** Sudden changes in weather, roadblocks and newly emerging hazards can disrupt planned operations and place both responders and those affected by the disaster at greater risk. Timely updates and alternative strategies are critical to ensuring the safety and effectiveness of relief workers.

2.2 Relief Worker's Needs

The user research showed that disaster relief workers need an information management system that aggregates and filters data from multiple sources (such as field reports, news feeds and social media) to provide clear, reliable and prioritised insights.

The solution must support multi-agency communication and resolve conflicting information to reduce duplicated efforts across agencies and enabling rapid and informed decision-making in chaotic and high-pressure disaster relief situations.

2.3 A Day in the Life of a Relief Worker Using Vyron

The following illustrations depict the concept of Vyron, an AI-powered assistant designed to support disaster relief efforts by enabling rapid, accurate information-sharing and decision-making (Fig. 1). The day-in-the-life comic strip showcases real-world scenarios where Vyron might helps relief workers to solve common challenges during disaster response, such as:

- Determining the most relevant and accurate information from conflicting reports.
- Locating missing people through cross-referencing social media posts and official sources.
- Coordinating the distribution of supplies
- Updating teams on the best routes based on changing conditions.

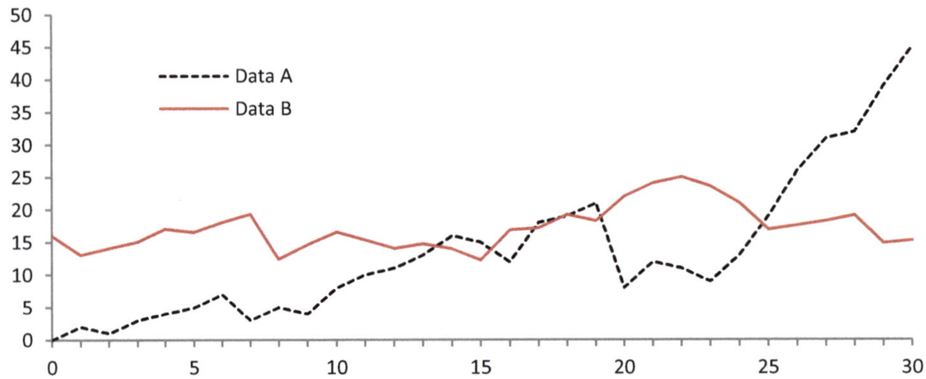

Fig. 1. A Day in the Life of a Disaster Relief Worker.

3 Design Challenges

3.1 Trust and Hallucinations

The comic strip captured real-world scenarios to highlight how Vyron might alleviate the problems that relief workers face in disaster response. It also highlighted two critical challenges in integrating AI into disaster relief operations: trust in AI-generated suggestions and AI hallucinations.

This section explores these challenges, examining their implications for system design.

3.2 Designing for Trust

Establishing and maintaining trust in AI recommendations is essential, as relief workers must rely on these insights. At the same time, AI hallucinations (instances where the system produces inaccurate or misleading outputs) may undermine decision-making effectiveness.

By addressing the following challenges, the team aimed to strengthen trust and confidence so that relief workers might use Vyron effectively and confidently in real-world situations.

- **Designing for High-Stress Environments.** In disaster scenarios, the interface must be highly intuitive and easy to navigate, even when relief workers are under intense pressure. Designers need to minimise cognitive load, reduce distractions and ensure that critical information is always visible and accessible.
- **Building Trust through Transparency.** Establishing trust between Vyron and relief workers is important, particularly when Vyron might provide conflicting or incorrect information. For relief workers to feel confident in the system, the decision-making process must be transparent, allowing them to easily query, verify and understand the AI's suggestions.
- **Balancing AI Guidance with Human Judgment.** Ensuring that Vyron's recommendations do not override human judgement and providing users with the ability to override, question, or opt-out of AI suggestions is essential for ethical and effective decision-making.
- **Familiarity and Training.** Another effective way to build trust in the system is by incorporating scenario-based training where relief workers can practice using Vyron in a controlled, low-risk environment and observe how Vyron handles different types of information to see how its suggestions align with their judgement. Through repeated exposure, relief workers can calibrate their trust in Vyron's capabilities and limitations, including understanding when to rely on the system and when to override it.

4 Prototype and User Testing

4.1 What is Vyron?

Vyron is a secure AI assistant that uses on-device Small Language Models (SLM) and high-quality server-hosted private LLMs to process and analyse data efficiently.

Built on a robust LLM architecture, Vyron has been integrated with multiple data sources, including social media feeds and weather updates, providing relief workers with a unified platform to access and interpret critical information.

Vyron's architecture currently supports versions for laptop and mobile use, using a modular design and microservices framework built with open-source technologies.

The system consists of three key components: a Flutter front-end, a Django HQ backend and a secondary Flutter HQ frontend. It uses GraphQL via Ariadne for efficient data retrieval, enabling smooth communication between web and mobile applications.

To support on-device SLM and server-hosted LLM functionalities, Vyron integrates models from the LLaMA family and leverages OpenAI's GPT-4 API for high-quality language understanding. Additional capabilities include multimodal and Retrieval-Augmented Generation (RAG), semantic search through a text-based chat interface, bidirectional speech-to-text functionality and a reinforcement learning feedback mechanism for continuous improvement based on user preferences.

4.2 Evaluation and Next Steps

In early user testing, we simulated a scenario where two teams in different locations coordinated to locate a missing person using Vyron. While Vyron was originally designed as a data aggregator, participants frequently relied on it for recommending future actions and assisting with planning. This feedback highlighted a strong need for enhanced reasoning and predictive capabilities. In response, we are currently developing these features to improve Vyron's decision-support functionality. We are keen to hear from people who may have insights, expertise or feedback on the challenges we identified in AI-driven decision support for disaster relief.

Acknowledgments. The authors would like to express their gratitude to the Coefficient team for their work in developing Vyron. The authors used OpenAI's ChatGPT for grammar checks and language editing, ensuring interpretations and final content is their own.

Disclosure of Interests. The authors have no competing interests to declare that are relevant to the content of this article.

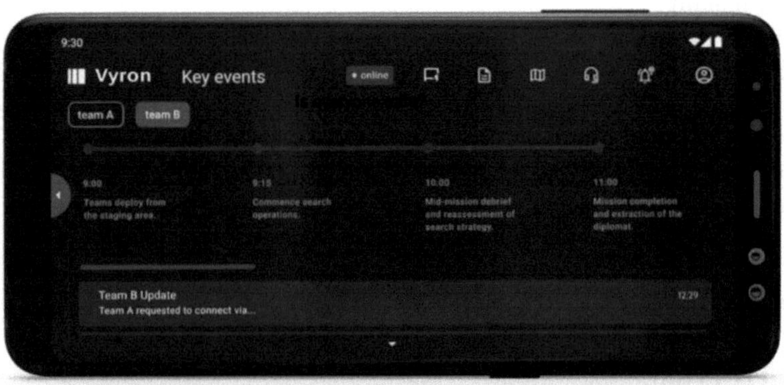

Vyron Use Cases: Developed for HCI2025. Mission timeline screen (Vyron App, version 1)

Vyron AI Use Cases: Developed for HCI Conference 2024. Illustrations designed using Adobe Firefly

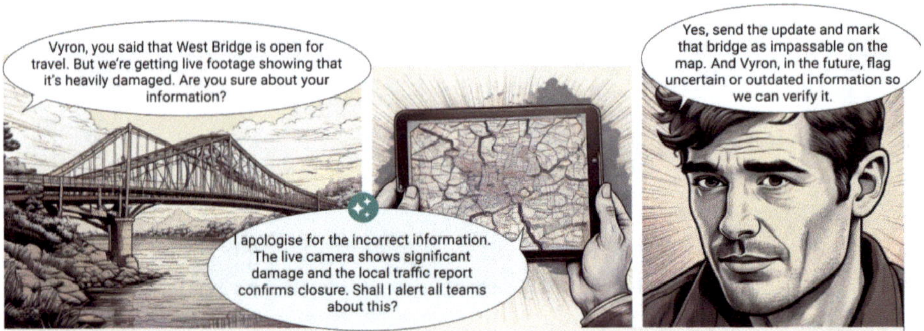

Even AI can make mistakes. In high-stress environments, it's important to ask questions and verify information. Vyron is a powerful tool but human judgement is essential to ensure decisions are safe.

We believe that Vyron may help relief workers to respond faster and more effectively to disasters, to help save lives and restore hope.

Vyron - connecting people, sharing accurate information, saving lives. If you are interested in taking this project further please get in touch robin@easol.co.uk

Vyron Use Cases: Developed for HCI2025. Illustrations designed using Adobe Firefly.

Trolled for Teaching: A Mixed-Methods Study of Internet-Facilitated Harassment among Educators

Jordyn Young(✉) and Andrea Forte

University of Michigan, Ann Arbor 48104, MI, USA
{jordyny,fortea}@umich.edu

Abstract. Academics do not typically expect their jobs to be dangerous, but they can be. As researchers seek to make their work accessible to broad audiences and leverage online platforms to share work widely, some find that visibility can expose them to harassment. This study examines the scope and nature of such harassment among educators across 12 social media platforms. We conducted exploratory semi-structured interviews with people who have encountered online harassment in their work and then used those findings to inform a large-scale survey of academics from universities in the United States to understand their experiences of harassment and of responding to harassment. Our findings identify contextual predictors and co-occurring attack types, offering recommendations for institutional strategies to better protect educators.

Keywords: internet-facilitated harassment · social media · professional support · educators · threat assessment

1 Introduction

Online communication plays a central role in how scholars do their work and engage with their communities. From sharing research on X to accepting interviews with news outlets, academics leverage technology for visibility to be successful. Public, networked scholarship is praised for generating cultural influence, but scholars may feel unsupported and unsure how to respond when that visibility invites attacks [8,20]. As Doerfler and colleagues note [8], it is important to understand the scope of harassment among academics and to explore mitigation strategies. This study examines the breadth of online harassment types experienced and witnessed among academics working at US universities (RQ1) and explores their intervention practices when such incidents occur (RQ2).

2 Related Work

Researchers in HCI and adjacent disciplines have studied the features of unwanted online behaviors under the umbrella of "online harassment," which

C. Stephanidis et al. (Eds.): HCII 2025, CCIS 2773, pp. 187–197, 2026.
https://doi.org/10.1007/978-3-032-12773-0_18

covers a wide range of actions [15,17]. As [17] found, remedy preferences vary significantly by harassment type and harm incurred. If different behaviors require different remedies, then governing bodies need to know what types of behaviors and harms are occurring to effectively support the targets experiencing them and manage the budgets necessary to do so. This leads to our first research question: (RQ1) what forms of online harassment do academics experience in the US?

Once identified, it is important to understand how to respond to attacks. Colleagues are powerful in academia. At a high level, it is a self-regulating profession where colleagues collectively shape standards and practices; peer review determines publication acceptance, collaborative decision-making guides tenure trajectories, and colleagues determine the limits of (un)acceptable behavior [5,11]. As such, scholars hold power to shape behavioral norms in their environment–to say something if they see something. A formal term for someone who sees potentially problematic behaviors unfold is a "bystander." When a bystander notices a problem and does something about it, that is referred to as "bystander intervention."

Whether or not a bystander ultimately intervenes is strongly associated with their sense of self-efficacy (i.e., their confidence in their ability to accomplish a specific task [3]) [18]. In both offline and online social situations, self-efficacy enables bystanders to take action [6,7]. Prior experience is an important factor for self-efficacy, especially if that prior experience included being the target of an online attack. Individuals with a history of victimization are more likely to notice toxic content (e.g., jokes about sexual abuse) and intervene compared to non-victims, likely because these attacks are more salient and less tolerable to people with a history of victimization [12]. To understand the extent to which academics recognize online attacks, we ask: (RQ2) How confident are academics that they can identify online harassment and intervene when it occurs?

3 Methods

3.1 Exploratory Interviews

We first conducted exploratory interviews with social media users who are in a professional position to intervene in online harassment to understand how they identify online harassment and their thoughts on intervention. Examples of such positions include analysts in law enforcement who handle instances of cybercrimes, people who work in mental health support fields, and academics who are mandatory reporters. These interviews were conducted with IRB approval from Drexel University, the authors' prior institution. Our total sample included 10 interviewees (70% female, ages 24–54).

Inductive analysis of interview transcripts suggested that participants struggled to define online harassment for themselves and often dismissed behaviors they did not think were harmful, which is a sentiment echoed in the broader literature [9]. For example, one participant referred to nonconsensually sharing secrets about others as "just drama histories" (P8). Similarly, another participant described "attacking people online" as "mean girls on steroids," then specified that "I don't know if we would call this harassment, but it's like exploitation online and trying to exploit people on their weaknesses and try to gain something from them." (P6). This equivocation suggested that a subsequent survey would benefit from clear definitions.

Whereas some participants in fields like law enforcement or mental health care could point to professional standards and norms, those who worked in academia reported wanting more guidance for proactive steps. As one participant mentioned, "In my personal opinion, there are things [institutions] could do to monitor [social media] better, even knowing the stuff that's happening, but they don't. Because again, that would be beyond the call of duty or out of our job description" (P10). To make this happen, the participant imagined creating a resource like "a school page [to] monitor [online activity]" (P10) where academics can report potential issues and/or send screenshots of problematic accounts. This request aligns with prior literature that suggests institutions could appoint a point person to handle such proactive measures and support researchers if needed [8,13]. Questions about what kind of harassment is experienced and how best to handle it in academia informed the design of the survey-based study described below.

3.2 Online Survey

The survey instrument included questions about participants' (1) experiences with various online attack types, (2) self-efficacy as digital bystanders, (3) social media use, and (4) demographic information. For (1), participants indicated whether or not they had experienced 21 different attack types identified in [2] that were condensed into the seven attack categories from [19] for analysis (content leakage, false reporting, impersonation, lockout/control, overloading, surveillance, and toxic content). For (2), we adapted questions from an existing self-efficacy scale [16] to ask, "How confident are you that you can recognize online harassment when using social media?" and "How confident are you that you know how to intervene if you see online harassment when using social media?" These questions were on a 5-point Likert scale with the answer choices not at all / slightly / moderately / very / extremely confident. For (3), we asked about the twelve most popular platforms in the United States [10]: Facebook, YouTube, Instagram, TikTok, Twitter (now X), Pinterest, Snapchat, Reddit, LinkedIn, Twitch, Tumblr, and BeReal. For each platform, participants answered a multiple choice question to indicate whether they use the platform "several times a day," "about once a day," "a few times a week," "every few weeks," "less often," or "I do not use this platform" [21]. Finally, for (4), we asked about demographic information: age, gender, whether they identify as LGBTQIA+, and race, as well as their job function.

Participants were recruited via social media and "word-of-mouth" email chains. The target population was individuals who work in a university or college setting in an academic role. The survey was hosted on Qualtrics and began with information about the study and questions to assess eligibility (18 years old, fluent in English, and currently working in a college or university setting). Participants could enter a raffle and win one of four $100 Amazon e-gift cards. Data were collected under an IRB protocol at Drexel University from June through August of 2023, and the analyses were performed under a University of Michigan IRB protocol in 2024.

After careful review and removal of incomplete data and data that failed integrity checks, the final survey sample included 277 participants. Ages ranged from 19 to 70 (M = 33.29, SD = 8.71). Participants were adjunct faculty (n = 106, 38%), graduate and undergraduate students working as TAs or RAs (graduate: n = 100, 36%; undergraduate: n = 33, 12%), tenure-track faculty (n = 21, 8%), and non-tenure track faculty (n = 17, 6%). 41% of participants identified as members of the LGBTQIA+ community and 43% identified as women. Most participants identified as white (82%).

In addition to descriptive analyses, we used stepwise regression analyses for each research question; logistic regression for RQ1 because of the binary outcome (whether or not a participant experienced each attack category) and linear regression for RQ2 because of the non-binary outcome (5-point Likert scale for bystander self-efficacy).

4 Results

4.1 Attack Occurrences

58.85% of participants (n = 163) reported experience with at least one attack category (M = 1.55, SD = 1.75); only 2 participants (0.72%) had experience with all seven. The proportion of participants who experienced each individual attack category was significant ($p < 0.05$ for the binomial test of each attack category). Toxic content was the most common (n = 106, 38.27%), followed by impersonation (n = 89, 32.13%), surveillance (n = 69, 24.91%), overloading (n = 63, 22.74%), content leakage (n = 57, 20.58%), lockout/control (n = 24, 8.66%), and false reporting was the least common category (n = 20, 7.22%).

Among participants who reported experiencing more than one attack category (n = 113, 40.79%), 37 experienced only two (which is 32.74% of those who experienced more than one attack category and 13.36% of all participants). There are 21 possible two-category combinations of the seven categories (7!(7-2)! * 2! = 21); toxic content and impersonation most frequently occurred together,

Table 1. Co-Occurrences between seven attack categories, most and least common in bold.

	falsereporting	impers-onation	lockout /control	over-loading	surve-illance	toxiccontent
content leakage	11	37	13	27	30	43
false reporting	–	13	**5**	9	13	14
impersonation	–	–	13	38	38	**63**
lockout/control	–	–	–	14	13	20
overloading	–	–	–	–	30	48
surveillance	–	–	–	–	–	46

while lockout/control and false reporting was the least frequent combination. See Table 1.

Social Media Use as Predictors of Attack Occurrences. To understand the relationship between experiencing each of the attack categories and the frequency of using different social media platforms, we used a step-wise logistic regression for each attack category (seven models total). This reveals whether people who use certain platforms more frequently are more likely to experience certain attack categories. Importantly, these analyses do not mean that the attack necessarily occurred on the platform. See Table 2.

Table 2. Results of step-wise logistic regression models for attack categories predicted by social media use showing coefficients, standard error, adjusted R2, and p-value; * <0.05.

AttackCategory	SocialMedia	Coefficient ±Standard Error	AdjustedR2	p-value
ToxicContent	Facebook	0.21 ± 0.02	0.04	0.002*
	Reddit	0.24 ± 0.02		
Impersonation	Facebook	0.06 ± 0.02	0.02	0.01*
Surveillance	TikTok	0.04 ± 0.02	0.03	0.003*
	Instagram	0.03 ± 0.02		
Overloading	Facebook	0.04 ± 0.02	0.009	0.06
ContentLeakage	Pinterest	0.04 ± 0.02	0.03	0.003*
	Instagram	0.03 ± 0.02		
Lockout /Control	Twitter	0.03 ± 0.01	0.04	0.001*
	BeReal	0.03 ± 0.01		
FalseReporting	Tumblr	0.02 ± 0.01	0.04	0.002*
	Pinterest	0.02 ± 0.01		

All coefficients were positive, meaning that using a platform more frequently was always associated with a greater likelihood of experiencing a given attack category. Most attack categories (6/7) were predicted by using one or two specific platforms; the only category that did not have a significant predictor was overloading. The strongest models (i.e., the models with the highest R2, meaning the most variance explained) were toxic content, lockout/control, and false reporting ($R2 = 0.04$ for all three models). These three attacks were predicted by Facebook/Reddit use, Twitter/BeReal use, and Tumblr/Pinterest use, respectively. Facebook and Instagram use were significant predictors of 5/7 attack categories. Facebook use predicted 3/7 attack categories (toxic content, impersonation, and overloading), while Instagram use predicted 2/7 categories (surveillance and content leakage). YouTube, LinkedIn, and Twitch did not emerge as significant predictors of any attack categories.

Demographics as Predictors of Attack Occurrences. We used a step-wise logistic regression for each attack category (seven models total) to understand whether identity characteristics (age, gender, LGBTQIA+ status, and race) predicted experiencing certain attack categories. See Table 3.

Table 3. Results of step-wise logistic regression models for attack categories predicted by demographic variables showing coefficients, standard error, adjusted R2, and p-value; * <0.05, ** <0.01. Surveillance and overloading not shown because they produced null models.

AttackCategory	DemographicVariable	Coefficient ±Standard Error	AdjustedR2	p-value
Toxic Content	LGBTQIA+	0.08 ± 0.05	0.02	0.02*
Impersonation	Black or African American	−0.35 ± 0.23	0.06	<0.01**
	Hispanic	−0.40 ± 0.23		
	Middle Eastern	0.15 ± 0.49		
	Multiple	−0.47 ± 0.23		
	Native American	−0.10 ± 0.23		
	Pacific Islander	−0.54 ± 0.25		
	White	−0.52 ± 0.19		
	Gender	0.09 ± 0.05		
Content Leakage	Gender	0.13 ± 0.04	0.03	<0.01**
Lockout /Control	Gender	0.08 ± 0.03	0.04	<0.01**
	LGBTQIA+	0.07 ± 0.03		
FalseReporting	Black or African American	−0.23 ± 0.13	0.05	<0.01**
	Hispanic	<0.00 ± 0.23		
	Middle Eastern	−0.34 ± 0.27		
	Multiple	−0.32 ± 0.13		
	Native American	−0.24 ± 0.13		
	Pacific Islander	−0.33 ± 0.14		
	White	−0.26 ± 0.11		
	Gender	0.04 ± 0.03		

None of the demographic variables meaningfully predicted surveillance and overloading. The other five attack categories were predicted by at least one demographic variable; the strongest model was impersonation ($R2 = 0.06$), which was predicted by race and gender, and the weakest was toxic content, which was predicted by whether participants identified as LGBTQIA+.

Race was a significant predictor of impersonation and false reporting; Native American and Hispanic participants reported the highest incidence of impersonation (72.73%) and false reporting (30.77%) experiences, respectively. Pacific Islanders reported the lowest incidence of impersonation experiences (28.57%) and none of the participants who identified as Pacific Islander or Middle Eastern reported experiencing false reporting. This does not imply that academics with these identities do not experience false reporting or content leakage, especially given that they were the least represented in the data (3% Pacific Islander and <1% Middle Eastern). Rather, this indicates that certain researchers may be at a heightened risk of some attack categories based on their identity.

LGBTQIA+ status significantly predicted experiencing toxic content and lockout/control. In both cases, a higher percentage of participants who identified as LGBTQIA+ experienced these attacks (toxic content: 40.35%; lockout/control: 14.04%) compared to those who did not identify as LGBTQIA+ (toxic content: 35.29%; lockout/control: 4.58%).

Lastly, gender was a significant predictor for experiencing impersonation, content leakage, lockout/control, and false reporting, which all affected a higher percentage of women (impersonation: 44.07%; content leakage: 31.36%; lockout/control: 12.71%; false reporting: 11.02%) compared to men (impersonation: 23.87%; content leakage: 12.90%; lockout/control: 5.16%; false reporting: 4.52%).

4.2 Bystander Self-Efficacy

On average, participants were more confident in their ability to identify online harassment (M = 2.25, SD = 0.87) than to intervene (M = 1.91, SD = 1.04), with a right skew to the distribution for the latter. A Welch paired t-test revealed this difference is significant ($t(276) = 4.64$, $p < 0.05$), so the regression calculations are kept for these variables separate in the following sections.

Predictors of Self-efficacy. The step-wise linear regressions did not reveal any significant predictors for confidence to identify online harassment or to intervene based on which attack categories participants had prior experience with.

Social Media Use as Predictors of Self-efficacy. The step-wise linear regression for self-efficacy based on social media use (see Table 4) indicated that using YouTube predicted both confidence to identify and intervene.

Table 4. Results of step-wise logistic regression models for self-efficacy predicted by social media use and demographic variables showing coefficients, standard error, adjusted R2, and p-value; * <0.05., ** <0.01.

Self-Efficacy	Social Media	Coefficient ±Standard Error	Adjusted R2	p-value
Identify	YouTube	-0.14 ± 0.05	0.03	<0.01**
	Facebook	0.08 ± 0.04		
	Tumblr	0.06 ± 0.04		
Intervene	Pinterest	0.09 ± 0.05	0.02	0.03*
	YouTube	-0.11 ± 0.05		
Self-Efficacy	**DemographicVariable**	**Coefficient** ± Standard Error	Adjusted R2	**p-value**
Identify	Age	0.01 ± 0.01	<0.01	0.09
Intervene	Gender	-0.25 ± 0.11	0.01	0.03*

Interestingly, spending more time on YouTube was associated with lower confidence in both identifying and intervening in online harassment. This was the only platform for which the association was negative. On the other hand, more time spent on Facebook or Tumblr was associated with higher confidence in identifying online harassment, and more time spent on Pinterest was associated with higher confidence in intervening in online harassment.

Demographics as Predictors of Self-efficacy. The only significant relationship between demographics and self-efficacy was that gender predicted confidence to intervene, where women were less confident than men (women: M = 1.81; men: M = 2.03). See Table 4.

5 Discussion

Protecting academics from online harassment requires knowing what specific behaviors to protect against. This study contributes to this goal by providing a descriptive account of online attack types experienced by people working in academic roles and the variables associated with those experiences. We build on these findings to discuss implications for institutional threat assessment and opportunities for peers to keep each other safe on social media, as well as limitations and future directions.

5.1 Implications for Institutional Threat Assessment and Transparency

Practically speaking, these findings build on previous calls for institutional resources to help academics handle online attacks [8]. While online attacks are not the norm for academics' experiences, we show that the scope of potential attacks can be broad. One way to target where help might be needed is to leverage co-occurrences; Aliapoulios and colleagues found that within online incitements to harassment that contain multiple attack types, the majority (92.3%) had only two [1]. As the results showed, the most common co-occurrence participants personally experienced was lockout/control with false reporting. As such, if we can identify the mechanisms by which these attacks happen (e.g., phishing for lockout/control), we can leverage those reports to identify other harms likely occurring simultaneously. This is useful to, for example, support targets in collecting evidence related to their experiences. Similar to the idea of collecting information related to comorbidities for diseases to strategize for intervention, co-occurrences of attacks are important for understanding overlapping needs.

Universities in the United States are required to disclose crime statistics per the Clery Act, including stalking, liquor law violations, and murder. Similar requirements are not instituted for online offenses, but informal aggregation tools do exist. For example, HeartMob created a hate and hope tracker to document experiences across the United States submitted by users and from stories online.[1] While new and possibly incomplete, such documentation is helpful for

[1] https://hateandhope.righttobe.org/.

understanding where different attacks are happening and providing a frame of reference for prospective targets. Leveraging taxonomies that specify behaviors in different attack types, as we did in the survey, is one way to organize a potential documentation tool of this nature. This information could be used to help scholars strategize about ways to protect themselves online. Building on previous calls to appoint an officer to handle harassment when it arises [8], one facet of this position could be to systematically and confidentially track harassment experiences. Doing so can allow institutions to track attacks over time, allocate resources, and improve remediation efforts.

5.2 Leveraging Peers for Safer Social Media Use

Placing responsibility on individuals to protect themselves burdens potential targets [22], and can even lead to a mindset of 'victim blaming' [14]. Social approaches may prove effective in creating protective buffers around potential targets by leveraging their existing networks. We found that academics are relatively confident in their ability to identify attacks when they use social media (see Sect. 4.1). Leveraging assemblages like departments, conferences, workshops, and symposia might allow for cohorts of academics to occupy online spaces together. For example, conference organizers could create follow lists or add the option of follow QR codes on conference badges. These relatively low-effort, contained approaches could increase the presence of knowledgeable bystanders.

Having bystanders around where they may be needed does not ensure that those who identify a risk can do something about it or feel safe doing so. Education efforts are useful to this end, but assigning additional training modules creates more work for an already busy professional community. One potential solution is to incorporate online attack types into existing bystander intervention training. Another option is to leverage the networked nature of platforms to share experiences. Previous studies have shown this is an effective strategy; for example, a study by HeartMob found that sharing victims' experiences and labeling the attacks they experienced as "online harassment" helps bystanders understand the phenomenon [4]. Furthermore, we also know that common group membership is an important factor in bystander intervention, so internal communities specifically designated to support academics in the same university and/or discipline could help provide additional support [8]. In some cases, intervention may not be safe, but a supportive network may serve other important social support purposes.

5.3 Limitations and Future Directions

Our survey population is a convenience sample, not a random, representative sample of all people working in colleges and universities across the United States so we cannot claim representativeness. The goal of these analyses is to scope relationships between variables rather than propose or measure causal effects. For example, we are not making causal claims that TikTok use is associated with an 80% increase in the likelihood of experiencing surveillance. Rather, we use coefficient trends to understand which platforms are more strongly related to certain attack types to identify opportunities for next steps. To understand specific relationships between platform use and the likelihood of attack, future studies should aim to recruit for a desired distribution based on demographic variables (e.g., race, gender, and socioeconomic status) as well as factors relevant to universities (e.g., department, seniority, and Carnegie classification). By recruiting participants online (see Sect. 3.2), we may have excluded potential participants who have left certain platforms because of harassment they experienced. Furthermore, the survey was not designed to capture experiences within a specific time frame. As such, future studies could explore how online harassment experiences change over time and whether temporal factors contribute to intervention capabilities.

Acknowledgments. Thank you to CSCAR (Consulting for Statistics, Computing and Analytics Research) at the University of Michigan, Dr. Nicole Ellison, Dr. Eric Gilbert, Dr. Sarita Schoenebeck, Lavinia Dunagan, Josh Ashkinaze, and Wells Lucas Santo for your feedback. This work was supported by the National Science Foundation #2439312.

Disclosure of Interests. The authors have no competing interests to declare that are relevant to the content of this article.

References

1. Aliapoulios, M., et al.: A large-scale characterization of online incitements to harassment across platforms. In: Proceedings of the 21st ACM Internet Measurement Conference, pp. 621–638 (2021)
2. America, P.: Online harassment field manual (2023). https://onlineharassmentfieldmanual.pen.org/defining-online-harassment-a-glossary-of-terms/
3. Bandura, A.: Self-efficacy: toward a unifying theory of behavioral change. Psychol. Rev. **84**(2), 191 (1977). publisher: American Psychological Association
4. Blackwell, L., Dimond, J., Schoenebeck, S., Lampe, C.: Classification and its consequences for online harassment: design insights from HeartMob. Proc. ACM Hum. Comput. Inter. **1**(CSCW), 1–19 (2017)
5. Braxton, J.M., Bray, N.J.: Introduction: the importance of codes of conduct for academia. New Direct. High. Educ. **2012**(160), 1–4 (2012). publisher: Wiley Online Library
6. DeSmet, A., et al.: Deciding whether to look after them, to like it, or leave it: a multidimensional analysis of predictors of positive and negative bystander behavior in cyberbullying among adolescents. Comput. Hum. Behav. **57**, 398–415 (2016)
7. DeSmet, A., Veldeman, C., Poels, K., Bastiaensens, S., Van Cleemput, K., Vandebosch, H., De Bourdeaudhuij, I.: Determinants of self-reported bystander behavior in cyberbullying incidents amongst adolescents. Cyberpsychol. Behav. Soc. Netw. **17**(4), 207–215 (2014)
8. Doerfler, P., Forte, A., De Cristofaro, E., Stringhini, G., Blackburn, J., McCoy, D.: I'm a professor, which isn't usually a dangerous job: internet-facilitated harassment and its impact on researchers. Proc. ACM Hum. Comput. Int. **5**(CSCW2), 1–32 (2021)

9. Goyal, N., Park, L., Vasserman, L.: you have to prove the threat is real: understanding the needs of female journalists and activists to document and report online harassment. In: Proceedings of the 2022 CHI Conference on Human Factors in Computing Systems, pp. 1–17 (2022)
10. Iskiev, M.: The fastest growing social media platforms of 2023 [new data] (2023). https://blog.hubspot.com/marketing/fastest-growing-social-media-platforms#:~:text=Here%20are%20a%20few%20fast,most%20popular%20social%20media%20apps
11. Keashly, L.: Workplace bullying, mobbing and harassment in academe: faculty experience. Special topics and particular occupations, professions and sectors, pp. 221–297 (2021). publisher: Springer
12. Kistler, T., Stuart, G.L., Cornelius, T.L.: Barriers to bystander interventions for sexual assault: impact of personal history of sexual victimization. J. Interp. Viol. **37**(17-18), NP16727–NP16749 (2022)
13. Marwick, A.E., Blackwell, L., Lo, K.: Best Practices for Conducting Risky Research and Protecting Yourself From Online Harassment (data & Society Guide). Data and Society Institute, New York (2016)
14. McDonald, N., Forte, A.: The politics of privacy theories: moving from norms to vulnerabilities. In: Proceedings of the 2020 CHI Conference on Human Factors in Computing Systems, pp. 1–14. ACM, New York, NY, USA (2020)
15. Pater, J.A., Kim, M.K., Mynatt, E.D., Fiesler, C.: Characterizations of online harassment: comparing policies across social media platforms. In: Proceedings of the 2016 ACM International Conference on Supporting Group Work, pp. 369–374 (2016)
16. Resnick, B., Jenkins, L.S.: Testing the reliability and validity of the self-efficacy for exercise scale. Nurs. Res. **49**(3), 154–159 (2000)
17. Schoenebeck, S., et al.: Online harassment in majority contexts: examining harms and remedies across countries, pp. 1–16 (2023)
18. Sjögren, B., Thornberg, R., Wänström, L., Gini, G.: Bystander behaviour in peer victimisation: moral disengagement, defender self-efficacy and student-teacher relationship quality. Res. Pap. Educ. **36**(5), 588–610 (2021)
19. Thomas, K., et al.: SOK: hate, harassment, and the changing landscape of online abuse, pp. 247–267. IEEE (2021)
20. Veletsianos, G.: Social Media in Academia: Networked Scholars. Routledge (2016)
21. Vogels, E.A.: The state of online harassment. Pew Res. Center **13**, 625 (2021)
22. Wei, M., Consolvo, S., Kelley, P.G., Kohno, T., Roesner, F., Thomas, K.: "there's so much responsibility on users right now:" expert advice for staying safer from hate and harassment. In: Proceedings of the 2023 CHI Conference on Human Factors in Computing Systems, pp. 1–17 (2023)

Advances in Immersive and Multimodal Interaction

Designing a Pinch Disable Mode for XR Devices

Anderson V. C. de Oliveira(✉), Pio H. F. S. Ordozgoith, Delrick N. de Oliveira, and Marcelo H. L. Cabral

Sidia Instituto de Ciência e Tecnologia - SW Solutions, Av. Darcy Vargas 654, Chapada, Manaus 69050-020, Brazil
{anderson.oliveira,pio.sobrinho,delrick.oliveira,marcelo.cabral}@sidia.com
http://www.sidia.com

Abstract. In this work, we design a pinch disable mode in order to mitigate a common user experience problem in AR/VR/MR devices: involuntary actions caused by misinterpretation of the device. Since the pinch is one of the most common actions to interact in immersive environments, being used to both select and grab and drag virtual objects, we designed a mode to disable the pinch action based on wrist rotation and taking into account that most of the pinch actions are made in a specific hand position. The aim is to avoid involuntary actions and improve the user experience. Moreover, we set up a user test to investigate how much the angle limitation of the mode influences the performance of usual tasks into a VR scene. Experienced users were asked to perform basic actions, and the designed restriction did not prevent users from performing the tasks, successfully disabling the pinch action when it was expected. The proposal can be used as a possible solution to prevent missclick, but more research is needed to address comfort and accuracy issues.

Keywords: virtual reality · pinch · wrist rotation · missclick

1 Introduction

Virtual reality (VR) devices have their origins in the 1960 s, in particular with the pioneering work of Ivan Sutherland, who created the first head-mounted display system [11]. Then VR remained restricted to research laboratories and military applications due to technical and ergonomic limitations. It began to gain ground in the 1990 s with the launch of commercial products such as Nintendo's Virtual Boy [6], but the definitive VR commercial growth and popularization took place in the 2010 s, driven by significant technological advances in graphics processing, motion sensors and high-resolution displays [1]. Companies such as Oculus VR (later acquired by Meta), HTC, Sony and Valve played a key role in creating devices accessible to the general public, also given rise to spin-off technologies such as augmented reality (AR) [3], which integrates virtual objects into

C. Stephanidis et al. (Eds.): HCII 2025, CCIS 2773, pp. 201–208, 2026.
https://doi.org/10.1007/978-3-032-12773-0_19

the real world, and mixed reality (MR) [10], which enables dynamic interaction between physical and digital environments. "Extended Reality" (XR) is a sort of umbrella term used to cover all immersive technologies (VR, AR and MR). The sectors that most use immersive technologies include entertainment, mostly games and cinematic experiences; education and training, especially for medical and military simulations, architecture, tourism and others, consolidating VR, AR and MR as strategic technologies in the global market, which represent a a market size of about 16.32 billion in 2024 [5].

For immersive devices, it is essential to provide more natural and engaging interactions in 3D spaces, since conventional methods such as keyboard and mouse do not offer a satisfactory experience for interacting with virtual objects. In this context, alternative methods emerge, such as dedicated hand controllers, allowing precise actions through buttons, triggers and motion sensors. Another growing approach is the usage of direct interaction through hand gestures, such as pinch clicking (pincer movement) [2]. Moreover, eye tracking (gaze interaction) uses the user's gaze to select and interact with virtual elements, significantly reducing physical effort and providing faster and more intuitive interactions [9]. There are still combinations of hand tracking and gaze, that can provide a better interaction experience to the user [8].

There is no defined standard for interaction in VR/AR/MR platforms [7] so that industry-leading companies are gradually shaping interaction methods. The user experiences are influenced by factors such as device sensor accuracy and user perception, so it is difficult to objectively measure which device provides the best user experience [4]. In this sense, we must design tools to mitigate errors in the interpretation of interaction gestures. In particular, the pinch gesture shown in Fig. 1 a) is one of the most used to select and drag objects into a 3D scene. In general, the movement starts at the "in" position and ends at the "out' position in FIg. 1' b).

(a) (b)

Fig. 1. (a) Pinch; (b) In-Out.

There is no restriction on the angle of the hands to perform this gesture. However, usually when the user does it, the palms of the hands are facing down, as in the Fig. 1 a). Assuming it, we designed a pinch disable mode by limiting the range of angles allowed to perform the pinch, in order to avoid involuntary ones. Then we design a simple test consisting of only an object and a button. So we ask to some users to carry out usual tasks into the scene to investigate how much the angle limitation influences the task performance. We describe the pinch disable mode in Sect. 2. The user test is described in Sect. 3, then we present the results with the user comments and feedback in Sect. 4, and the conclusions in Sect. 5.

2 Wrist Rotation Restriction

XR devices use a specific number of sensors to track the hands, using it to read the user's action or intent. The proposal of wrist rotation restriction is a solution for devices with poor quality sensors or a low number of sensors, mitigating problems resulting from hardware issues and poor scene design.

By default, the Unity XR Hands provides the hand's position, rotation, and velocity of each joint data point. These data are translated into a range of values that range from 0 to 1, which can be used to trigger a specific event when reached. In our case, the event is restricted XR action performed by the user' hands, such as pinch and grab. It can be used to prevent false pinches caused by XR device tracking issues, a wrist rotation restriction feature could aid in experiences of interaction in XR environments of test or final application.

One of the exception cases of wrist rotation restriction is when the user keeps the hands in a rest position, as the left hand shown in the Fig. 2. In this situation, the thumb finger tracked could overlap the index finger and the XR Device reads it as a pinch action, triggering the target's event, such as selection or grab, causing a bad experience.

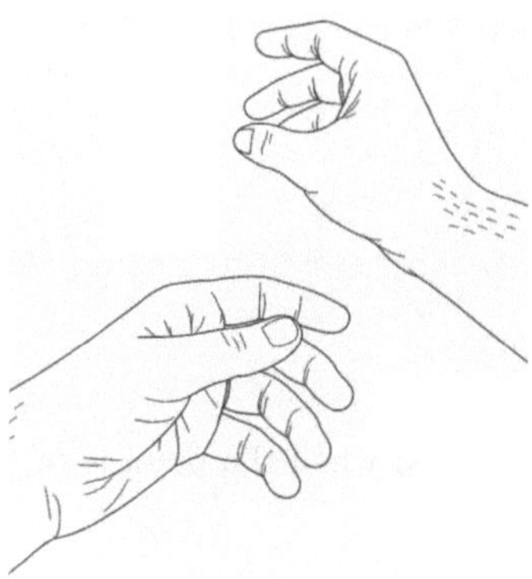

Fig. 2. Rest position of the left hand.

However, restricting the wrist rotation could cause issues such as: set free a grabbed 3D object while the user is dragging it by the environment, stop a resize action for a 3D object wrongly canceling the action, dragging an object rotation the palm upwards canceling the action, and other cases. To prevent it, some definition of UX must be observed to ensure that the wrist rotation restriction works correctly, such as extended action and alignment.

To prevent a false pinch, we defined wrist rotation by restricting the z-axis-degree rotation of the hands. By default, the user must keep the hand's rotation between -30 and 120°C to perform an action, as shown in Fig. 3. The wrist rotation direction for both hands when the palm is down is shown in Fig. 4 a) and when it is up in Fig. 4 b).

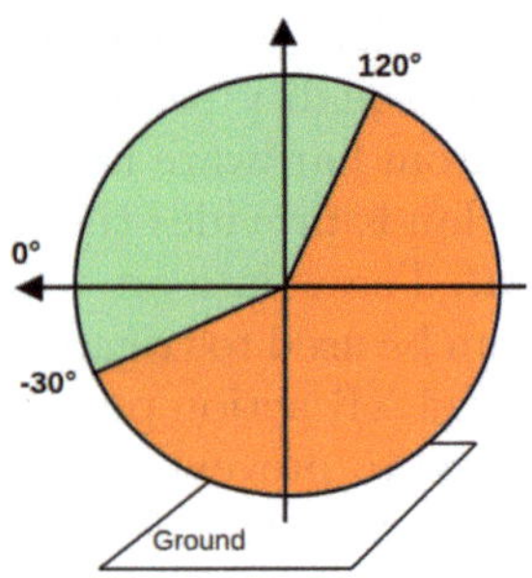

Fig. 3. z-axis allowed to pinch.

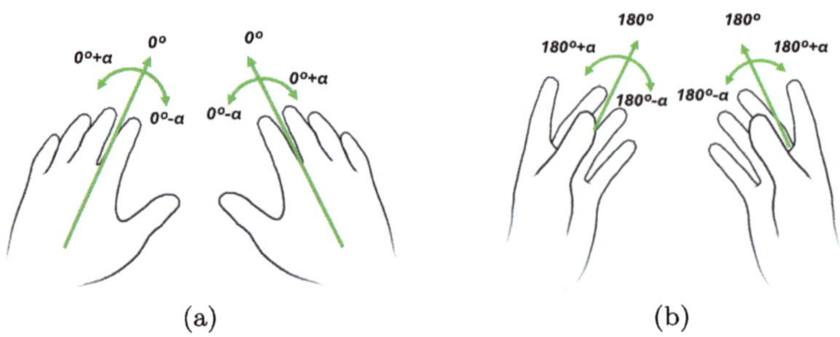

Fig. 4. Wrist rotation when the palm is (a) up; (b) down.

Out of this range, the actions of pinch and grab must be ignored, except if the action is on the extended action or the action lost track by occlusion, e.g. if the palm overlaps the index finger and thumb fingers. While an object is in "extended action", the performed action such as grab keeps working even if the Wrist Rotation exceeds the proposed range. An example of extended action is if the user grabs a closer object using the grab action and rotates the wrist to see the other side of the object. Without the extended action, the grab action is lost because the wrist rotation exceeds the proposed range of restriction. However, with the extended action, the action keeps working until the grab action is finished.

The alignment between the reference angle and the hands must be working correctly for wrist rotation restriction to work. Then, the wrist rotation is set to 0°C if the palm of the hand is face to the ground, and 180°C if it is completely facing upwards

3 User Test

To test the usability of the wrist rotation restriction, we designed a simple scene where the user must be sitting with the hands in the rest position. The scene is shown in Fig. 5 and it has a button positioned closer to where the F.O.V. area ends, and a 3D object to interact with.

The user must interact with the 3D object with any hand while the other hand remains in the rest position. The user must repeat the test with the wrist rotation restriction turned on and turned off.

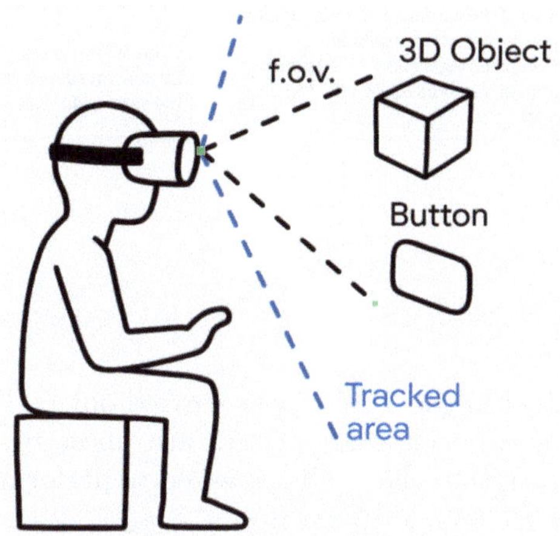

Fig. 5. Test scene scheme.

With the hand tracking activated, the test was performed according to the script described in the table 1.

Table 1. Test procedure.

	Test description	Steps	Expected Result
1	Validate pinch gesture recognition feedback	1. Move your hand to the front of the 3D object 2. Do a pinch gesture on the 3D object 3. Repeat the steps above with the button	1.1. Cursor and Ray must be showed in front of the 3D object 1.2. The 3D object must show a hover color (blue) 2. The object must be selected (turn to a green color) 3. The same behaviors above for the button
2	Validate pinch gesture recognition feedback with laterally hand	1. Move your hand to the front of the 3D object with laterally hand 2. Do a pinch gesture with laterally hand on the 3D object 3. Repeat the steps above with the button	1.1. Cursor and Ray must be showed in front of the 3D object 1.2. The 3D object must show a hover color (blue) 1.3. The hand mesh color must be turn to red 2. The object must not be selected (must not turn to a green color) 3. The same behaviors above for the button
3	Validate pinch gesture recognition feedback with palm up hand	1. Move your hand to the front of the 3D object with laterally hand 2. Do a pinch gesture with palm up hand on the 3D object 3. Repeat the steps above with the button	1.1. Cursor and Ray must be showed in front of the 3D object 1.2. The 3D object must show a hover color (blue) 1.3. The hand mesh color must be turn to red 2. The object must not be selected (must not turn to a green color) 3. The same behaviors above for the button
4	Validate pinch gesture recognition feedback with the hands in rest position	1. Try to move the ray and the cursor to be in front of the 3D object lefting your hand in rest or confortable position 2. Do a pinch gesture on the 3D object 3. Repeat the steps above with the button	1.1. Cursor and Ray must be showed in front of the 3D object 1.2. The 3D object must show a hover color (blue) 2. The object must be selected (turn to a green color) 3. The same behaviors above for the button

4 Test Results

The test script described in the Table 1 was carried out by five users with experience in using immersive technology. Users are unaware that wrist rotation restriction is operating in the scene and are asked to perform the tasks described in the Table 1.

Results are summarized in the Table 2. Each test is performed on a 3D object and a button as in Fig. 5. The first section is designed to check whether the user can perform basic tasks without impairment due to the wrist rotation restriction being enabled. The objective is to position the cursor over the object (then a hover blue color is showed), perform a pinch gesture on the 3D object and then select it (then a hover green color is showed). At this stage, the result was 5 pass and 0 fail for the 3D object and 4 pass and 1 fail for the button. Note that the user can perform the pinch gesture by trying any wrist angle since it dos not known about the restriction.

In the second section, the user is asked to perform the same tasks but with laterally hand. Note that in this case, the user may or may not position the wrist within the range of angles established in the Fig. 3. If it positions inside, the test will pass, otherwise it will fail. In this stage 5 test pass and 0 fail for both 3D object and button. It means that, when the user is asked to put your hand laterally to perform a pinch gesture, it positions it in the allowed angle range of the Fig. 3.

In the third section of the test, the user is asked to try to perform the same tasks but with palm up hand, which means that it will not work, i.e. the pinch gesture will not result in any response. Of course it results in 0 pass and 5 fail for both 3D object and button.

In the fourth section, the same tasks are asked for the users but lefting the other hand in a rest position, appearing on the scene. In this situation, it is possible that the hand in rest position make a pinch shape, but the system will prevent it and the task must be done successfully. This part results in 4 pass and 1 fail for the 3D object and 3 pass and 2 fail for the button. In this stage some users report discomfort in positioning both hands appearing in the scene and performing the tasks, so that the failed tests occurred due to performing the pinch action outside the permitted angle range.

Table 2. Test results.

Task	3D Object Results	Button Results
Basic tasks with restricted wrist rotation	Pass (5) / Fail (0)	Pass (4) / Fail (1)
Lateral hand position	Pass (5) / Fail (0)	Pass (5) / Fail (0)
Palm up hand position	Pass (0) / Fail (5)	Pass (0) / Fail (5)
Additional hand in rest position	Pass (4) / Fail (1)	Pass (3) / Fail (2)

Additionally, most users reported discomfort and pain when positioning the wrist at angles out of the allowed to pinch.

5 Conclusions

In this work, we deal with interaction methods in immersive devices. One of the most used is the pinch gesture. Once this gesture is identified by the system to trigger an action, its functioning depends on the accuracy of the sensor. In this context, a misinterpretation of the device can cause involuntary pinch, harming the user experience. To mitigate the "missclick problem", we propose a restriction on the wrist rotation angles where the pinch action would be allowed.

In experimental tests to validate our implementation, five users experienced in immersive technology were asked to perform basic actions on a 3D object and a button. They were unaware of the wrist angle restriction. The first part of the results showed that in general the implementation of this restriction did not prevent users from performing these actions, but a situation occurred where the user tried to perform the pinch action with the wrist at an angle allowed to perform it. All users successfully completed the task with laterally hand, and the restriction acted successfully when tasks were performed with palms facing up, as expected. It also prevent involuntary pinch with a hand in rest position, although in this test some users report discomfort.

Wrist rotation restriction can be used as a possible solution to prevent involuntary pinch caused by misinterpretation of the system, although it still needs refinement to improve practical experience. More research is needed to address comfort and accuracy issues, ensuring a more efficient and safer experience for users.

Acknowledgment. This work was presented as part of the results from "Sidia-M VST Platform and Applications", carried out by Sidia Instituto de Ciência e Tecnologia in partnership with Samsung Eletrônica da Amazônia LTDA, according to IT Law n.8387/91 and article 39 from Decree 10.521/2020.

References

1. Bamodu, O., Ye, X.M.: Virtual reality and virtual reality system components. In: Advanced Information and Computer Technology in Engineering and Manufacturing, Environmental Engineering. Advanced Materials Research, vol. 765, pp. 1169–1172. Trans Tech Publications Ltd (10 2013)
2. Bowman, D., Wingrave, C., Campbell, J., Ly, V.: Using pinch gloves for both natural and abstract interaction techniques in virtual environments (2001)
3. Carmigniani, J., Furht, B.: Augmented Reality: An Overview, pp. 3–46. Springer, New York, NY (2011)
4. Estrada, R.G., et al, A.V.C.O.: Automated evaluation of metrics for immersive test using reinforcement learning. In: HCI International, pp. 188–197. Springer Nature Switzerland (2024)
5. Fortune business insights: virtual reality market overview. https://www.fortunebusinessinsights.com/industry-reports/virtual-reality-market-101378. Accessed 03 Mar 2025
6. K., J.: Boy toy: Nintendo virtual boy 3-D game system. Video Magazine 19(7) (1995)
7. Mayer, J., Auer, S., Friedl, J., Anthes, C.: Volumetric data interaction in AR and VR using a handheld touch-sensitive device. transitional interfaces in mixed and cross-reality: a new frontier?, KOPS Universität Konstanz (2021). https://books.google.com.br/books?id=s4nGzgEACAAJ
8. Pfeuffer, K., Mayer, B., Mardanbegi, D., Gellersen, H.: Gaze and pinch interaction in virtual reality, pp. 99–108. Association for Computing Machinery (2017)
9. Plopski, A., Hirzle, T., Norouzi, N., Qian, L., Bruder, G., Langlotz, T.: The eye in extended reality: a survey on gaze interaction and eye tracking in head-worn extended reality. ACM Comput. Surv. **55**(3) (2022)
10. Speicher, M., Hall, B.D., Nebeling, M.: What is Mixed Reality, pp. 1–15. Association for Computing Machinery, New York, NY, USA (2019)
11. Sutherland, I.E.: A head-mounted three dimensional display. In: Proceedings of the December 9–11, 1968, fall joint computer conference, part I, pp. 757–764 (1968)

YourStayHub: A Mobile-Centric Universal Controller for a Smart Hotel Room

Konstantinos Drenoviadis[1], Asterios Leonidis[1,2](✉), Maria Korozi[1], George Paparoulis[1], and Constantine Stephanidis[1,2]

[1] Institute of Computer Science (ICS), Foundation for Research and Technology - Hellas (FORTH), Heraklion, Crete, Greece
kdren@ics.forth.gr , korozi@ics.forth.gr, groulis@ics.forth.gr, cs@ics.forth.gr

[2] Computer Science Department, University of Crete, Heraklion, Crete, Greece
leonidis@ics.forth.gr

Abstract. YourStayHub is a web-based smart automation platform tailored for short-term hospitality environments such as Airbnb properties, guesthouses and hotel rooms. The system provides guests with full, intuitive control over a wide range of smart devices—such as lighting, HVAC, water heaters, blinds, and security systems—via a web-based responsive interface, with no app installation or technical setup required. Moreover, guests can create multi-step scenes with customized device behaviors—including delayed actions—, schedule time-based automations, monitor real-time environmental and energy data, and access an integrated security panel that supports "smart" alarm states and live CCTV feeds. Access is granted only for the duration of the reservation and is automatically revoked upon checkout. YourStayHub is compatible with a wide range of IoT devices and communication protocols, offering vendor-independent, unified control through a single platform. Designed with a user-centered approach, it bridges the gap between traditional smart home automation and the specific needs of hospitality environments. It empowers non-technical users to manage smart spaces independently, securely, and efficiently.

Keywords: Smart Home Automation · Hospitality Technology · Guest Access Control · Scenario Automation · Universal Smart Devices · IoT Interoperability

1 Introduction

Smart home automation has gained significant traction in recent years, offering users increased convenience, energy efficiency, and security through the centralized control of connected devices [5]. These technologies are widely adopted in residential settings, where homeowners manage lighting, climate, and security systems via mobile apps or voice assistants.

C. Stephanidis et al. (Eds.): HCII 2025, CCIS 2773, pp. 209–216, 2026.
https://doi.org/10.1007/978-3-032-12773-0_20

However, the hospitality sector —particularly short-term rentals such as Airbnb properties, guesthouses and hotel rooms [6]— introduces unique challenges. In these environments, users are temporary, often unfamiliar with smart home technology, and have limited time to learn complex interfaces [3]. Most existing automation platforms are designed for long-term residents with technical knowledge and do not support temporary access control or guest-oriented configuration.

Beyond residential contexts, prior work in tourism and hospitality reports that IoT adoption can enhance guest satisfaction while reducing operational costs and enabling differentiated services [1].

To address these limitations, we present YourStayHub, a web-based smart automation platform specifically designed for hospitality contexts. The system enables guests to control IoT-enabled devices, create multi-step scenes, schedule automation routines, and monitor environmental and energy and water consumption data in real time. Access is limited to the duration of the reservation and is automatically deactivated after checkout, ensuring both usability and security.

YourStayHub aims to bridge the gap between traditional smart home systems and the dynamic needs of hospitality spaces. Its interface is tailored to non-technical users and requires no app installation or setup. The platform provides flexible and secure control of a wide range of vendor-independent devices through a unified interface.

This paper outlines the motivation behind the system, presents its core user requirements, describes its architecture and functionality, and discusses its role in enhancing smart hospitality experiences.

2 Related Work

In this study, existing smart home automation systems such as **Home Assistant**[1], **openHAB**[2], **Shelly**[3], **ComfortClick**[4], and **Housemate**[5] were examined, as they comprehensively cover device control and automation needs. Despite their extensive features, automation scenarios, and customization capabilities, they primarily target permanent homeowners or specific accessibility use cases and do not provide an integrated mechanism for *time-limited guest access* that automatically expires at the end of a reservation. Additionally, their technical complexity and setup requirements may discourage occasional users or short-term guests from using them easily.

Beyond residential smart homes, surveys focusing on tourism and hospitality discuss a growing range of IoT applications (e.g., connected rooms, mobile check-in, energy-aware operations) and highlight managerial and operational

[1] https://www.home-assistant.io/.
[2] https://www.openhab.org/.
[3] https://www.shelly.com/.
[4] https://www.comfortclick.com/.
[5] https://housemate.online/en/.

implications for hotels and destinations [1]. Reported challenges—such as interoperability, security/privacy, scalability, and maintainability—further motivate vendor-agnostic approaches that unify heterogeneous devices behind a single interface and access model [1].

Similarly, recent research prototypes such as **IoT-based smart home automation system** [10], the **IoT-Based Integrated Smart Home Automation System** [8], and the **Design and Implementation of an IoT-Based Smart Home Automation System** [11] demonstrate implementations of smart home automation using technologies like Node-MCU[6], ESP8266[7], Raspberry Pi[8], and Wi-Fi, with an emphasis on low cost, simplicity, and basic device control via web or mobile applications. Despite their technical completeness and practical application in residential settings, these systems are also designed exclusively for permanent household users and do not support hosting-specific scenarios, temporary guest management, or roles with time-restricted access. The proposed system aims to address this gap by combining IoT architecture know-how with tailored features for Airbnb and hotels, offering a secure, flexible, and user-friendly experience for property managers and guests alike.

In addition, Lok et al. present a large-scale smart hotel integration approach in China, where a vendor-independent system based on an MQTT messaging backbone and tight interoperability with Property Management Systems (PMS) was deployed across thousands of properties [7]. Their focus is primarily on the operator side—standardizing integration and ensuring scalability for hotel chains—whereas our work targets the guest side of short-term rentals, emphasizing temporary, reservation-bound access and ease of use for non-technical visitors. Together, these perspectives illustrate complementary challenges in smart hospitality: large-scale system integration for operators, and intuitive, time-limited control for guests.

3 User Requirements and Motivational Scenario

The design of *YourStayHub* was guided by a user-centered design process specifically for intelligent environments [9], grounded in a set of user requirements tailored to the specific needs of short-term guests staying in smart-enabled apartments. Unlike long-term residents, such users require minimal onboarding, intuitive interfaces, and quick access to essential features. The system prioritizes ease of use, time-limited access, and secure, personalized control of smart devices.

The main functions derived from these requirements include:

- **Home Dashboard**: display active and favorite devices, current alarm status, and widgets for weather and map view.
- **Centralized device management**: Users can: (a) view the available devices categorized by room, type, and active state, (b) moreover, they can monitor their current state, and (c) manage their individual settings.

[6] https://www.nodemcu.com.
[7] https://store.arduino.cc/products/nodemcu-esp8266.
[8] https://www.raspberrypi.com/.

- **Device Grouping**: Allows users to (a) group similar devices across rooms, (b) control them in bulk with a single action, and (c) access predefined or custom groups quickly.
- **Automation Scenarios**: Enables users to (a) create scenarios involving multiple devices of same or different types, (b) configure their behavior (e.g. brightness, temperature), (c) introduce execution delays between actions, and (d) schedule them for automatic execution.
- **Scheduling Interface**: Allows users to (a) define start/end times for routines, (b) specify active days and repeat rules, and (c) set the duration of each action.
- **Security Dashboard**: Offers (a) control over alarm states (Arm Away, Arm Stay, Disarm), (b) management of smart locks, and (c) access to live video feeds from external surveillance cameras.
- **Data Analytics Dashboard**: Provides (a) historical and real-time energy and water consumption data, (b) environmental readings such as CO_2 levels, temperature, and humidity, and (c) safety-related sensor data including human presence, smoke and flood detection.

Scenario: A Solo Traveler Seeking Personalized Comfort

The following motivational scenario illustrates how these features address user needs.

Maria, a solo traveler, arrives in a modern Airbnb apartment for a weekend stay. She receives a login code via email and accesses *YourStayHub* through a web browser—eliminating the need to contact the property owner or visit a hotel reception, allowing instant and autonomous check-in.

On the home page, she sees an overview of the apartment's current state, including active devices and alarm mode, which helps her immediately understand what is on or off without needing to inspect each room. The interface also provides a clear view of the apartment's layout, making it easy for her to orient herself within the space.

Navigating to the Devices section, she adds her preferred appliances—the bedroom lamp, air conditioner, and living room light—to her favorites. This ensures faster access throughout her stay, reducing time spent navigating menus and allowing her to control her essentials with a single tap.

Wanting to unwind in comfort, she creates a custom scene named "Cozy Night," combining dimmed lighting, a pleasant A/C temperature, and hot water readiness by activating the boiler. By scheduling this scene for 9:00 PM every night, she automates her comfort routine and avoids manual adjustments each evening.

Before leaving for dinner, Maria checks the front camera through the Security tab and activates the alarm in "Away" mode—gaining peace of mind that the apartment is protected during her absence, without needing additional equipment or third-party apps.

When she returns, the apartment greets her with the ambiance she had planned in advance, showcasing how *YourStayHub* empowers guests to enjoy a seamless, personalized experience with minimal effort and no technical background.

4 The System

YourStayHub is a web-based smart automation platform, designed specifically for guest usage in short-term rental properties. The system is tailored to meet the needs of non-technical users who may be unfamiliar with smart home technologies and the layout of the property itself. It offers a well-organized and intuitive browser interface that allows users to access and control all available smart devices without needing to install any application. Access is granted via a unique login code that expires automatically at the end of the guest's stay.

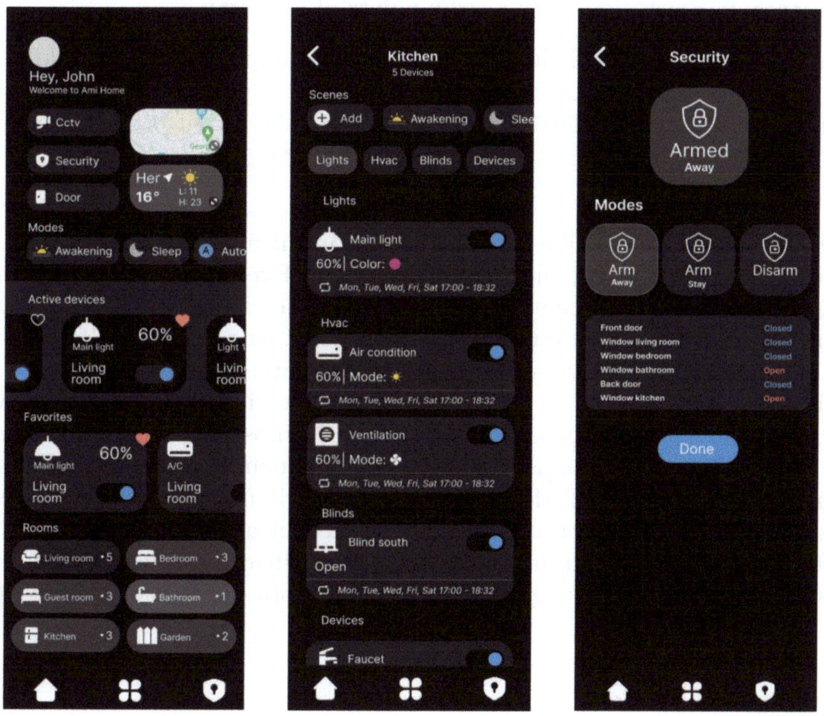

Fig. 1. Snapshots of key system interfaces: Apartment Dashboard (left), Room Details screen (center), and Security monitoring view (right)

User Access and Apartment Dashboard

Upon arrival, guests receive a personal access code via email, which they can use to log in from their own smart device (e.g. smartphone, tablet). Each code is linked to the reservation period and automatically expires after checkout, ensuring secure and temporary access. At present, the access codes are generated by the property manager through the system's backend, while future extensions may include automatic integration with booking platforms such as Airbnb or hotel PMS systems.

The Apartment Dashboard (Fig. 1, left) provides an overview of the apartment's status, including:

- Active and favorite devices
- List of rooms
- Current alarm mode (*Arm Stay, Arm Stay Balcony, Arm Away, Disarmed*)
- Predefined scenarios (e.g., *Morning Routine, Goodnight Mode*)
- Widgets with weather and location-sensitive information (e.g., current temperature, forecast, map with nearby points of interest)

Navigation is simplified through room-based grouping (Fig. 1 - Middle) and clearly labeled controls, allowing even non-technical users to quickly interact with the environment, even if they are unfamiliar with the layout of the property.

Device Management

Guests can manage all available smart devices in the apartment, organized logically by room and type (e.g., lights, HVAC, boiler). Every device can be activated or deactivated, and adjusted according to its specific capabilities, such as changing brightness for lighting, temperature for HVAC, or color for RGB lights. To simplify control, frequently used devices can be marked as favorites.

The system is designed to be compatible with a wide range of smart devices and has already been successfully tested with Philips Hue lamps, Nuki smart locks, and KNX-based curtains and blackouts. This demonstrates that guests can interact with heterogeneous devices through a single interface, without needing to install additional applications or deal with technical complexity.

Additionally, the system provides real-time feedback on energy consumption and sensor readings, allowing guests to make informed decisions during their stay.

Grouping and Scenes

Users can create **Device Groups** to control multiple similar devices with a single action. The **Scenes** interface enables users to build multi-device routines by configuring the behavior of each device and optionally introducing execution delays. Scenes can be saved, edited, and triggered manually or automatically.

For example, a scene called "Cozy Night" might dim the bedroom lights, fully open the blinds of the sea-facing window, and adjust the temperature and fan speed of the air conditioner—all in a single step.

Scheduling Automation

YourStayHub supports the configuration of time-based automation routines for both individual devices and multi-device scenarios. This functionality is particularly beneficial for short-term guests who want to automate daily routines without manual effort. For example, a guest may schedule the bedroom lights to turn off and the A/C to activate every night at 10:00 PM. The system allows the specification of start and end times, repetition rules, active days, and action duration. Automations can be reviewed and modified at any time, ensuring a flexible and personalized stay.

Security and Monitoring

The system provides integrated security features (Fig. 1 - Right), enabling guests to manage the apartment's alarm modes—such as Arm Away, Arm Stay, and Disarm—and monitor safety-related data in real time. Live video feeds from CCTV cameras can be accessed to observe entry points, and the status of doors, windows, and human presence sensors is available for increased awareness. For example, a mode like Arm Stay Balcony allows guests to remain on the yard-facing balcony while still monitoring areas of the apartment that are not directly visible from that position—such as the main entrance or front-facing windows—ensuring that key access points remain under surveillance. These features contribute to a sense of safety and autonomy without requiring intervention from the property owner.

Data Analytics

To promote energy awareness and efficiency, YourStayHub offers real-time and historical analytics based on smart sensor data [2]. Guests can view detailed information about electricity and water consumption, organized by device or room. Additionally, environmental parameters such as CO_2 concentration, temperature, humidity, and human presence are tracked and visualized through daily, weekly, and monthly graphs. This helps visitors understand their usage patterns and encourages conscious, environmentally friendly, interaction with the smart environment.

5 Conclusions and Future Work

This paper presented YourStayHub, a web-based smart automation platform designed to address the unique needs of short-term hospitality environments. Unlike conventional smart home systems, YourStayHub offers time-limited guest access, an intuitive browser interface, and flexible control of multiple smart devices and scenarios without requiring technical knowledge or app installation.

By focusing on ease of use, secure temporary access, and vendor-agnostic device support, the system demonstrates how smart automation can be adapted to enhance the guest experience in Airbnb rentals and hotel rooms.

Future work includes expanding the system's interoperability with additional IoT protocols and device types [4], as well as integrating AI-driven recommendations for energy savings and personalized scenarios based on guest behavior. Long-term goals also include testing the platform in real hospitality environments and gathering user feedback to further refine usability and performance.

Acknowledgments. This work has been supported by the FORTH-ICS internal RTD Programme 'Ambient Intelligence and Smart Environments'.

References

1. Car, T., Stifanich, L.P., Šimunić, M.: Internet of Things (IoT) in tourism and hospitality: Opportunities and challenges. In: ToSEE – Tourism in Southern and Eastern Europe. vol. 5, pp. 163–175 (2019)
2. Hassan, S.A., Eassa, A.M.: SHMIS: an integrated IoT context awareness framework for hotel management to enhance guest experience and operational efficiency. Inf. Technol. Tourism 1–34 (2025)
3. Kim, S., Leonidis, A., Zidianakis, E.: Interaction styles. In: Interaction Techniques and Technologies in Human-Computer Interaction, pp. 1–44. CRC Press (2024)
4. Leonidis, A., Arampatzis, D., Louloudakis, N., Stephanidis, C.: The AmI-Solertis system: creating user experiences in smart environments. In: 2017 IEEE 13th International Conference on Wireless and Mobile Computing, Networking and Communications (WiMob), pp. 151–158. IEEE (2017)
5. Leonidis, A., et al.: Ambient intelligence in the living room. Sensors **19**(22), 5011 (2019). publisher: MDPI
6. Leonidis, A., Korozi, M., Margetis, G., Grammenos, D., Stephanidis, C.: An intelligent hotel room. In: International Joint Conference on Ambient Intelligence, pp. 241–246. Springer (2013)
7. Lok, C.K., Lee, B.P., Lei, U.M.: Enhancing guest experiences through smart hotel systems in the hotel industry in China: a system integration approach. In: Proceedings of the 11th World Congress on Electrical Engineering and Computer Systems and Sciences (EECSS'25), pp. CIST 143–1–CIST 143–9. Paris, France (2025). https://doi.org/10.11159/cist25.143, paper No. CIST 143
8. Satheeskanth, N., Marasinghe, S., Rathnayaka, R., Kunaraj, A., Joy Mathavan, J.: IoT-based integrated smart home automation system. In: Ubiquitous Intelligent Systems: Proceedings of ICUIS 2021, pp. 341–355. Springer (2022)
9. Stephanidis, C., Leonidis, A., Korozi, M., Kouroumalis, V., Adami, I., Ntoa, S.: Design for intelligent environments. In: Human-Computer Interaction in Intelligent Environments, pp. 1–43. CRC Press (2024)
10. Stolojescu-Crisan, C., Crisan, C., Butunoi, B.P.: An IoT-based smart home automation system. Sensors **21**(11), 3784 (2021). publisher: MDPI
11. Tayef, S.H., Rahman, M.M., Sakib, M.A.B.: Design and implementation of IoT based smart home automation system. In: 2021 24th International Conference on Computer and Information Technology (ICCIT), pp. 1–5. IEEE (2021)

Augmented Reality Solution Requirements for Human-Building Interactions: Lessons Learned from an Applied Science Project

Lukas R. G. Fitz(✉), Lukas D. Teutenberg, Ekaterina Veldyaeva, and Jochen Scheeg

Department of Business and Management, Brandenburg University of Applied Sciences, Magdeburger Str. 50, 14770 Brandenburg an der Havel, Germany
{fitz,teutenbe}@th-brandenburg.de

Abstract. One popular application domain for Augmented Reality (AR) technology is facilitating human-building interactions (HBI). Such applications help users to retrieve and transact information through localized interaction points displayed on their (mobile) devices. Growing adoption of AR technology underlines the importance of incorporating suitable AR components for HBI, which is important for effective implementation and testing of HBI-AR use cases, increasing user satisfaction, and long-term viability. In this context, our short paper presents key experiences and lessons learned from an applied science project targeting the development and evaluation of an HBI-AR university campus app. Drawing on an ex-post inquiry of project collaborator experiences, we prescriptively highlight relevant AR solution requirements for this specific design context. Our findings amplify the importance of (1) balancing trade-offs between different spatial embedding computation methods, (2) modularity, customizability, and testability for efficient software development, and (3) taking building complexity and prototype maturity requirements into account when taking AR solution make-or-buy decisions. Our shared insights may inform future best practices and design principles for convergent HBI and AR projects in research and practice.

Keywords: Augmented Reality · Human-Building Interaction · Requirements

1 Introduction

In an increasingly connected world shaped by technology-enabled interactions between humans and smart objects, human-building interactions (HBI) have emerged as a subdiscipline of human-computer interaction research in built environments. Humans nowadays spend most of their lifetime in buildings and 4.25 billion of them use smartphones – a combination which triggers a plethora of opportunities for contemporary and future HBI, enabled through advancing information technology (IT) [1].

One such technological enabler is Augmented Reality (AR). In 2025, the number of AR users is projected to reach new all-time highs across various platforms, including more than 1 billion mobile AR users [2]. Moreover, AR has already been identified as

C. Stephanidis et al. (Eds.): HCII 2025, CCIS 2773, pp. 217–225, 2026.
https://doi.org/10.1007/978-3-032-12773-0_21

a paradigmatic HBI technology more than 20 years ago [3]. Recent analyses suggest that most convergent HBI-AR solutions have been studied in the context of construction informatics [1] and were considered most suitable for pre-inhabiting phases of building lifecycles [4]. Contrastingly, reviews of AR application areas point more frequently at established end-user HBI use cases amid building inhabitation – examples include AR-guided museum tours, indoor and outdoor navigation, retail in- and out-of-store experiences, industrial and work applications, facility management and maintenance [5–7]. Both research trends, after all, fuel emerging scholarly interest in AR-enabled location-based services [8].

To this end, our poster paper provides key take-aways reported through an applied science project for the implementation and evaluation of HBI-AR use cases on a university campus. The main objective of this contribution is to share the lived experiences of AR developers and reflect on them from a scientific perspective. In this way, our findings may add to a general practical knowledge base in the HBI-AR realm and enrich future best practices in the field.

2 Project Overview

The "5G-Testbed-BB" project (https://5g-testbed-bb.de/) has launched in the second quarter of 2023. It targets the collaborative implementation and experimental use of several testbeds for 5G wireless network technology use cases (such as 5G-based robotics, drones, or AR applications) across the federal state of Brandenburg, Germany.

One of these testbeds, focusing on the nexus of 5G and AR specifically, has been implemented on the campus premises of Brandenburg University of Applied Sciences. This sub-project focuses on the development, testing, and evaluation of an AR application for campus navigation and services based on 5G network connectivity. Its core objective is to develop prototypes ranging from providing static information to personalized content and supporting individuals with special needs.

Thus, from an end-user perspective, the project aims to make the retrieval and use of campus information more efficient and user-friendly, and to make an applied science contribution to advancing AR solutions in this field. To address the needs of different campus stakeholder groups, user-centric methods and workshops were employed to optimally shape and tailor the development of the applications to the target audiences. In this, relevant AR use cases were derived from interviews with students, staff and external visitors; they comprise typical campus activities like AR indoor navigation, soliciting helpdesk services with AR, or retrieving instructions on how to use communal printers through AR. To accomplish tests and evaluations of all the envisioned use cases, a 5G standalone telecommunication infrastructure has been installed on-campus to enable network coverage in the campus main building, the library building, the adjacent student dorms, as well as outdoor pathways in between. The network consists of three main radio units, with two mounted on the roof of the building adjacent to the library building and one mounted on the main building facing toward the student dorms. Furthermore, two indoor radio units with four dots each have been installed on the first and third floor of the main building. The boundaries of the testbed are illustrated in Fig. 1. In these areas, QR-code access points have been visibly mounted on walls, like in Fig. 2, which shall allow for spatial embedding of the user's location on the virtual campus map. Smartphones and other mobile devices are provided as test units on the receiving end. Beyond that, as visualized in Fig. 3, the project's system landscape includes a dedicated server running a *MySQL* and *SvelteKit* application for the data and UI handling, an external server hosted by the AR solution provider for navigation calculations, a development environment consisting of the AR solution provider's software development kit (SDK) and *Unity 3D*, as well as the target application itself consisting of an iOS app and *ARKit*.

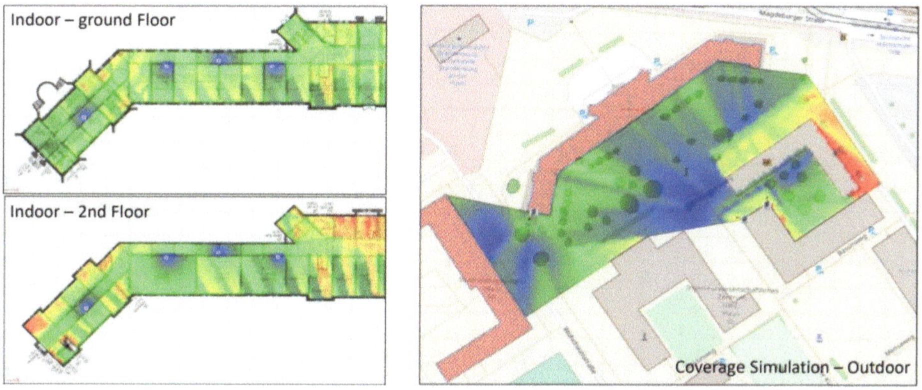

Fig. 1. Testbed topography and 5G network coverage heatmap.

Fig. 2. Scannable AR access points distributed across the campus testbed.

As of May 2025, the project has entered a final evaluation phase, which focusses on user test data and perceptions. Before that, the AR application development has been finished with the implementation of a functional prototype. The implementation involved multiple AR system developers and followed an agile approach, which proved crucial due to numerous unexpected events and disruptions related to the utilized AR software solution. The following section will detail these setbacks by reflecting on lessons learned about AR solution requirements throughout the project.

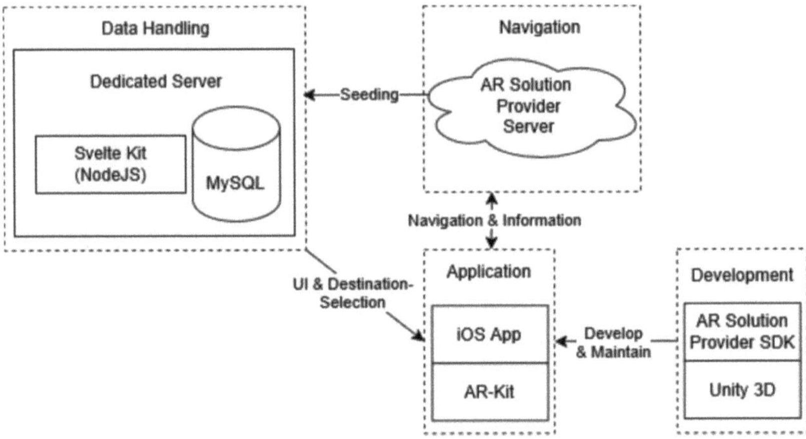

Fig. 3. Overview of system components associated with the project.

3 Reflection on Lessons Learned

The primary data stems from a semi-structured interview (49 min.) with the lead AR software developer on the project, which is complemented by screenshots, photos, intermediary reports and meeting notes. The interview was recorded, transcribed and thematically analyzed using the software MAXQDA 24 Analytics Pro. Project collaborators' and software providers' names are anonymized.

3.1 Odometry- vs. Triangulation-Based Spatial Embedding

In the beginning, the developer team expected the spatial embedding and navigation to be challenging because of the mathematical approach used by the integrated software solution to compute the end-devices position with odometry, that is, using the device's camera and built-in sensors to estimate its real-time position and rotation:

> "So basically, I'm constantly measuring my sensors and thinking about how I've probably moved in the last two seconds. And I keep doing that until I somehow end up somewhere I can scan a new access point again. My gut feeling was that this is a tough thing to do reliably. To make it work that well. It's a big deal in robotics too. Like, where exactly is my robot right now and how long has it been moving exactly? The error just keeps growing in that process. That was my expectation, that it would be difficult and a problem, and that a lot would depend on it. And that if it doesn't work well, it becomes a real issue." (Lead Developer).

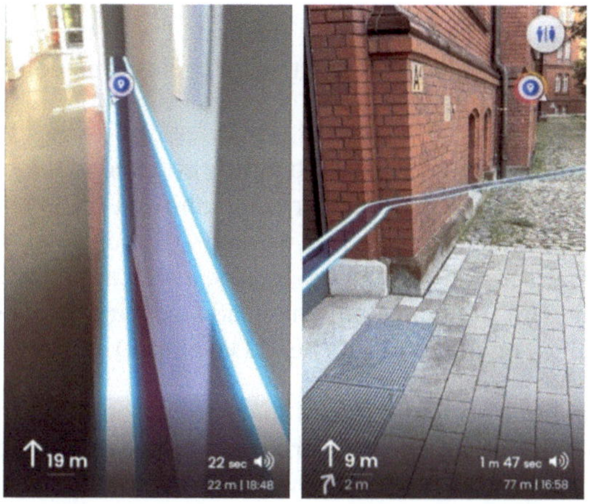

Fig. 4. Screenshots showing misaligned spatial embedding.

Indeed, the "drifting" position of the computed end-device position indeed became challenging in the course of the project, as Fig. 4 shows, requiring several adjustments to the positioning of access points. Also, users need to establish a plain and straight camera-to-wall angle when scanning these access points, because the end-device's default rotation will determine the alignment between virtual map with the campus terrain. In conclusion, the trade-offs of solutions utilizing odometrical position computation need to be taken into account, and alternatives be considered:

> "I don't think odometry is the right approach here. So, reading out sensor data and basically integrating your own movement from that… I don't think that's the way to go. Instead, you either need this kind of ground truth through some kind of beacons, which, of course, isn't very realistic for smaller organizations, because it involves buying, operating, and maintaining expensive hardware. (…) I could also imagine that problems like this could be tackled through AI-based image processing somehow - that this could open up a new perspective." (Lead Developer).

In consequence, the quest for both viable and cost-efficient solutions for spatial embedding in virtual AR spaces remains challenging and needs to be discussed as a matter of balancing trade-offs against user expectations. Artificial intelligence (AI) trends should be observed as a potential future game-changer in this regard.

3.2 Closed-Source Monoliths vs. Customizable Micro Services

Furthermore, the collaborators found that too monolithic solution components that handle too many aspects at once (camera control, navigation, user interface) instead of being more modular and decoupled were hindersome. It made the software "opinionated" (provider biased) and difficult to customize or extend beyond the predefined features. This unfolded through three distinctive issues.

First, the software's UI had been tightly integrated with the *Unity 3D* development platform, which made the development and testing cycles time-consuming compared to a more web-based approach.

> "But the fact that the user interface was so tightly coupled to the Unity application meant that the iteration cycles – like: I try something, I try to solve a problem, I think I've fixed it, and then I check if it worked – those cycles were pretty slow and time-intensive. Especially compared to, say, a web application where I could quickly spin up an extra frontend component, add a debug output somewhere, and just print some values or something." (Lead Developer).

Second, the monolithic structure meant that the custom adjustments relied on the software provider's openness policy. In the project, it turned out that relevant components were provided in closed-source mode and thus inaccessible:

> "Some parts were (…) closed source – like how the app communicated with the [software provider] servers or what kind of information specific components of the code contained. That wasn't always clear, and usually not documented. Sometimes you could get answers if you asked directly, but even then, accessing certain information or bypassing a specific system - like if you suspected a bug and wanted to test around it – wasn't really possible." (Lead Developer).

Third, the solution used the software provider's server infrastructure, which also belonged to the monolithic solution package. Although user-centered AR development typically requires iterative re-adjustments and test-cycles, it was not possible to create synthetic test data on the remote servers. Instead, developers had to physically move test devices across the campus to generate test data, as illustrated by Fig. 5.

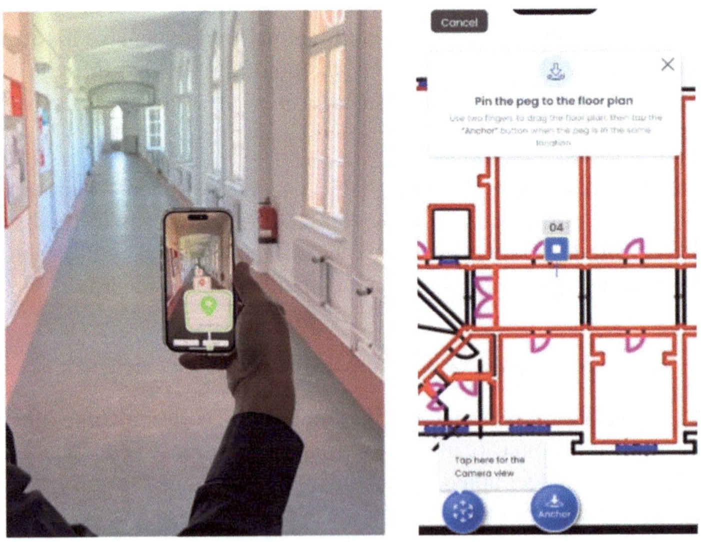

Fig. 5. Photo and screenshot of the manual anchor point setup.

> "And the last issue was with the servers. That meant I couldn't, for example, inject synthetic data for testing. Because of how the application was built, I always had to deploy the new build onto the phone, start the app, and then, in most cases, physically go out and collect real-world phone data. I couldn't fake that data to simulate scenarios. I couldn't just sit at my desk, simulate the whole thing, run through different test cases, and have it done in 30 s. Instead, it was always this five-minute cycle: deploy the app to the phone, unplug everything, go to a different floor, test it in the real world, walk back, and try again." (Lead Developer).

In sum, modularity, customizability and testability for the development stage emerge as potential requirements for HBI-AR solutions. Project initiators should look into possibilities to reduce dependencies on monolithic systems, even though a large plug-and-play solution may seem more convenient.

3.3 Prototyping: Make or Buy?

The last aspect concerns weighing off the convenience of soliciting an all-purpose solution compared to building a prototype-level application oneself. Depending on project requirements, prototypes may need to work primarily in a functional sense and go without advanced features. In combination with the before-elaborated lessons learned, the lead developer concluded:

> "In retrospect, I would say that building the application myself would not have been more work-intensive than what we did now. I had completely underestimated that. (...) This opinionated software solution that takes a lot off your hands also means that you invest a lot of work time in learning the conventions for a software solution that may be completely irrelevant to the application domain." (Lead Developer).

Moreover, HBI projects may involve buildings with specific characteristics that do not conform with a standardized software's capabilities. In the case of Brandenburg University of Applied Sciences, the main building is a former casern established in 1881 with an unconventional wing-shaped layout and several mezzanine floors, as exemplified in Fig. 6. On the one hand, this offered many options for navigation and HBI use cases, on the other hand some challenges were encountered when developing the application:

> "Representing things like a mezzanine level that was lowered by about 60 cm - like the one in the basement of that building – wasn't exactly easy, and often not even possible without significant effort. For instance, without creating an entirely separate floor level, you would have to decide: either the user no longer gets a complete map of the actual floor and only sees the area up to that small staircase of three steps, at which point the map changes and instead of continuing the navigation, the system just says, 'Please change floors and go down three steps.' Or you decide to keep it on a single shared map - but then all navigation elements in the AR space are shown, say, two meters above the ground, where users might not be able to see them anymore." (Lead Developer).

Fig. 6. Screenshot of AR navigation arriving at a mezzanine level staircase.

Implicitly, HBI-AR project initiators in make-or-buy contexts might need to prioritize factors like building complexity and specific prototype maturity requirements.

4 Conclusion

This short paper highlights important lessons learned from an applied science project at the conjunction of HBI and AR development. Altogether, the elaborated solution requirements comprise (1) selecting a project-appropriate spatial embedding method, (2) amplifying modularity, customizability, testability capacities for an efficient development process, and (3) considering individual characteristics of targeted buildings and potential self-developing effort in project-based make-or-buy decisions. We thereby add intermediate-level HBI knowledge in line with field expert suggestions [9] and especially address future practitioners in HBI-AR projects. Stakeholders from both practice and research will need to closely observe upcoming trends at this specific technological crossroads, as best practices seem likely to be continuously re-shaped by advancing technologies [10] like AI, new telecommunication standards and evolving user needs.

Acknowledgments. The project "5G-Testbed-BB" is funded by the German Federal Ministry for Digital and Transport as part of the “Innovative Network Technologies” funding program.

Disclosure of Interests. The authors have no competing interests to declare that are relevant to the content of this article.

References

1. Taherkhani, R., Aziminezhad, M.: Human-building interaction: a bibliometric review. Build. Environ. **242**, 110493 (2023)

2. ARtillery Intelligence: Mobile augmented reality (AR) users worldwide from 2023 to 2028 (in millions). Statista. https://www.statista.com/statistics/1098630/global-mobile-augmented-reality-ar-users/. Accessed 5 Apr 2025
3. Malkawi, A.M., Srinivasan, R.S.: A new paradigm for human-building interaction: the use of CFD and augmented reality. Autom. Constr. **14**(1), 71–84 (2005)
4. Ean, P.: Human-computer-building interaction: an integrated experience of the digital and physical environments. In: Streitz, N.A., Konomi, S. (eds.) Distributed, Ambient and Pervasive Interactions. HCII 2023. Lecture Notes in Computer Science, vol. **14036** (2023)
5. Dargan, S., Bansal, S., Kumar, M., Mittal, A., Kumar, K.: Augmented reality: a comprehensive review. Archives of Computational Methods in Engineering **30**(2), 1057–1080 (2023)
6. Salman, A., Ahmad, W.: Implementation of augmented reality and mixed reality applications for smart facilities management: a systematic review. Smart and Sustainable Built Environment **14**(1), 254–275 (2025)
7. Tran, T.T.M., Brown, S., Weidlich, O., Billinghurst, M., Parker, C.: Wearable augmented reality: research trends and future directions from three major venues. IEEE Trans. Visual Comput. Graphics **29**(11), 4782–4793 (2023)
8. Kanade, P., Prasad, J.P.: Mobile and location based service using augmented reality: a review. European Journal of Electrical Engineering and Computer Science **5**(2), 13–18 (2021)
9. Alavi, H.S., Churchill, E., Kirk, D., Nembrini, J., Lalanne, D.: Deconstructing human-building interaction. interactions **23**(6), 60–62 (2016)
10. Zhang, Z., Wen, F., Sun, Z., Guo, X., He, T., Lee, C.: Artificial intelligence-enabled sensing technologies in the 5G/internet of things era: from virtual reality/augmented reality to the digital twin. Advanced Intelligent Systems **4**(7), 2100228 (2022)

Interactive Design of Plant Cultivation Based on an App Platform: Application Research of Virtual IP Characters and Affective Computing

Guangyu Hu[1](✉), Yang Cao[1], and Yihang Dai[2]

[1] Nanjing Normal University, 1 Wenyuan Road, Nanjing 210-098, China
tougou1913299905@gmail.com
[2] Tama Art University, 2-1723 Yarimizu, Tokyo 192-0394, Japan

Abstract. With the growing interest in plant cultivation, it has evolved into a lifestyle beyond mere entertainment. However, beginners often face challenges due to improper care methods. This research introduces Leaf Talk, an interactive plant care app that conveys plant needs through a virtual IP character, integrating artificial intelligence and affective computing. The app features real-time plant health monitoring, plant identification through image recognition, a growth calendar, and personalized settings to enhance user engagement. By translating environmental conditions (humidity, temperature, light) into anthropomorphic expressions, the virtual IP character enables users to interact emotionally with their plants via a natural user interface (NUI) using voice and touch. User testing revealed that 85% of participants found the system beneficial, demonstrating its effectiveness in improving plant care awareness and fostering a new dimension of plant-human interaction.

Keywords: Artificial Intelligence · Intelligent Interaction Technology · Plant Cultivation · Virtual IP Design · Affective Computing

1 Introduction

In recent years, with the growing interest in plant cultivation, plant care has evolved beyond a mere leisure activity to become a reflection of personal lifestyle and attitude. An increasing number of individuals are integrating plant care into their daily routines, not only to enjoy a closer connection with nature but also as a means of enhancing their quality of life [1]. However, for beginners lacking relevant experience, plant cultivation presents numerous challenges [2]. Studies have shown that many novice plant enthusiasts possess insufficient knowledge of plant care, particularly in key areas such as water management, light regulation, and temperature control. This lack of expertise often leads to issues such as overwatering, neglect, or improper environmental conditions, ultimately affecting plant health. Moreover, the fast-paced nature of modern life makes it difficult for many individuals to consistently monitor and tend to their plants, further

C. Stephanidis et al. (Eds.): HCII 2025, CCIS 2773, pp. 226–235, 2026.
https://doi.org/10.1007/978-3-032-12773-0_22

increasing the risk of plant deterioration or failure [3]. Therefore, providing effective guidance for beginners to enhance plant survival rates and improve the overall plant care experience has become an important research focus.

Furthermore, many plant owners have limited knowledge of essential environmental factors such as soil quality and sunlight exposure, and the lack of effective monitoring tools further complicates their decision-making in plant care. Studies indicate that approximately 40% of plant enthusiasts struggle to identify pests and plant diseases, leading to delayed intervention and subsequently affecting plant health and survival [4]. Additionally, despite the increasing awareness of sustainable gardening, around 60% of plant owners face challenges in adopting eco-friendly care practices due to insufficient guidance. This not only exacerbates the complexity of plant maintenance but also underscores the urgent need for enhanced scientific guidance and technical support in this field.

With the advancement of plant care technology, the integration of sensors to transmit plant growth information to software platforms has become a common practice [4–6]. Devices such as "Parrot Flower Power" and "Xiaomi Smart Plant Monitor" can connect to mobile applications to provide real-time monitoring of soil moisture, light intensity, and environmental temperature, offering users feedback to optimize plant growth conditions [5]. However, most existing plant care software exhibits significant limitations, primarily due to a lack of personalization and user-friendly design. These systems often rely heavily on traditional data collection and analysis methods, making them complex and less intuitive for users [1]. This not only restricts the potential of plant care software in enhancing user experience and emotional interaction [5] but also fails to meet the growing demand for more intelligent, engaging, and personalized plant care solutions [5, 7].

Furthermore, users' expectations for plant care software have evolved beyond basic data monitoring functions; they now prefer systems that incorporate intelligent analysis, real-time feedback, and highly personalized recommendations [7–10]. To enhance user experience and accommodate diverse needs, plant care software must go beyond precise plant growth monitoring by integrating user habits and preferences to offer customized care guidance. Therefore, this study aims to develop an interactive plant care software based on user experience (UI/UX) design principles, integrating artificial intelligence and affective computing technologies. By employing an anthropomorphic virtual character (IP representation) as an interactive interface, the proposed system seeks to simplify plant care processes while enhancing user engagement and fostering emotional connections with plants, ultimately improving the overall user experience.

2 Related Works

2.1 Analysis of Users' Pain Points and Resolution

By analyzing users' difficulties in the plant care process, as well as their requirements regarding app functionalities, user interface design, and virtual character representation, we incorporated the results of a user survey into the subsequent design process. Specifically, a pre-design questionnaire survey was conducted with 50 participants, and the results are presented in Fig. 1.

The detailed questionnaire items are as follows:

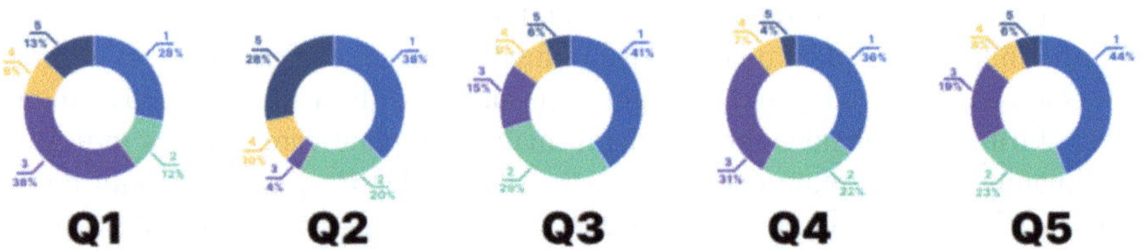

Fig. 1. Pre-design questionnaire results from 50 participants. The data, arranged from left to right, correspond to Q1–Q5, representing users' challenges in plant care, app feature preferences, acceptance of a virtual IP character, interest in a natural user interface, and expectations for the app's impact on care habits.

Q1: What are the biggest challenges you face in the plant care process? (Up to 5 responses)
Q2: What do you consider the most important functionalities of a plant care app? (Up to 5 responses)
Q3: What are your thoughts on the feature of using a virtual character (IP representation) to express plant needs? (Up to 5 responses)
Q4: If the app provided a natural user interface (e.g., voice or touch interaction) for "conversing" with plants, would you be interested? (Up to 5 responses)
Q5: Do you believe that a plant care app could help improve your plant care habits? (Up to 5 responses)

2.2 Persona-User Positioning in User Portrait and Usage Scenario

Alan Cooper, the father of interaction design, first introduced the concept of "User Portrait," defining it as a concrete representation of target users. He described user portraits as a modeling approach that abstracts and synthesizes multidimensional information, including users' social attributes, lifestyle habits, and consumption behaviors. By employing data analysis and tagging mechanisms, user portraits facilitate the characterization of typical user traits, enabling product and design teams to gain deeper insights into user needs, preferences, and behavioral patterns [11, 12].

In this study, the user portrait model is employed to inform the personalized design of virtual IP characters. Based on distinct user profiles (Fig. 2), we customize the IP character's attributes, such as hair color, facial features, and attire, according to variations in users' plant care duration, plant species, and common challenges encountered during the cultivation process. Furthermore, leveraging scenario-based analysis (Fig. 3) helps mitigate design uncertainties, minimize potential errors, and reduce investment risks. By constructing two distinct usage scenarios across three user profiles, we investigate whether users facing different decision-making difficulties in plant care can effectively resolve issues through the intelligent detection capabilities of our proposed app. Ultimately, this research aims to integrate intelligent analysis, real-time data feedback, and precise recommendations while enhancing engagement through personalized and interactive experiences, thereby optimizing the plant care process.

Fig. 2. User portrait interface.

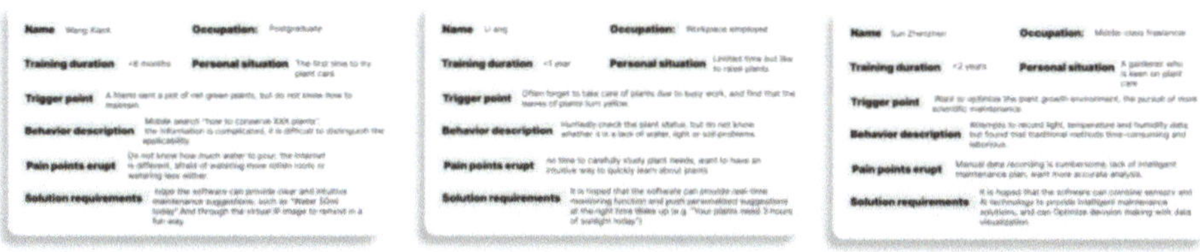

Fig. 3. Usage scenario.

3 Methodology

3.1 Product Positioning and Architecture

The core architecture of the Leaf Talk intelligent plant cultivation application consists of five key modules: plant health monitoring, virtual IP character, Scanning for plant selection, growth calendar, and personalized settings. Specifically, the system collects and categorizes basic plant information, while real-time monitoring parameters such as light exposure, humidity, airflow, and temperature ensure accurate data collection and feedback.

Additionally, Leaf Talk introduces an innovative "Plant Dialogue" function powered by artificial intelligence (AI), allowing users to interact with their plants through an anthropomorphized virtual IP character. This function works by providing a user-customized plant avatar as a pre-set prompt to the language model, optimizing the interaction experience. Furthermore, the system incorporates a customization mechanism that enables users to personalize the virtual character's appearance, including outfit and accessories, enhancing immersion and emotional connection.

The Leaf Talk app introduces several innovative breakthroughs. Firstly, it offers a user-driven virtual IP character customization framework, allowing individuals to create unique plant avatars based on their own cultivation experiences. This enhances engagement by moving beyond traditional plant care software's rigid interface design. Secondly, leveraging AI technology, the system dynamically evaluates plant health conditions and delivers real-time feedback through a conversational virtual IP character. This intelligent interaction mechanism enables a more intuitive understanding of plant health and helps users optimize plant care strategies, ultimately improving both plant growth quality and user engagement (Fig. 4).

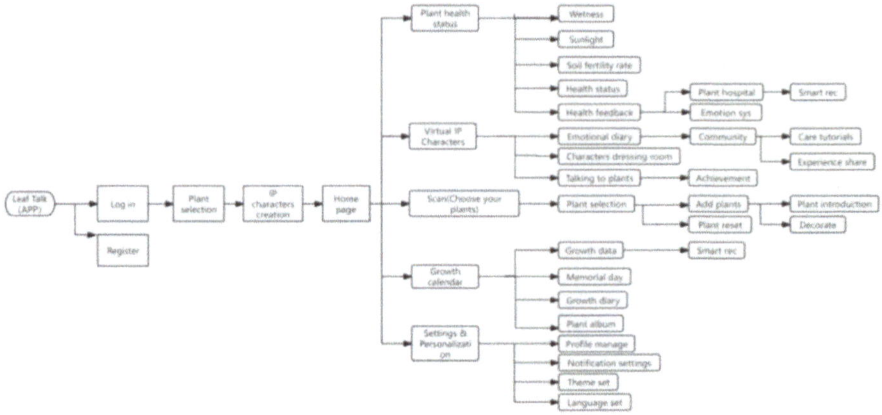

Fig. 4. Product architecture.

3.2 Visual Design

As shown in Fig. 5, the Leaf Talk logo adopts a minimalist geometric style, seamlessly blending a silhouette of a girl with plant elements, symbolizing harmony between nature and life. The girl's outline is drawn with smooth curves, while her hair transforms into delicate leaves, representing the continuity of life and care for nature. The leaf patterns extending from the ear and neck reinforce the plant theme and reflect the app's "intelligent dialogue" and "living interaction" concepts, aligning with the "Leaf Talk" branding.

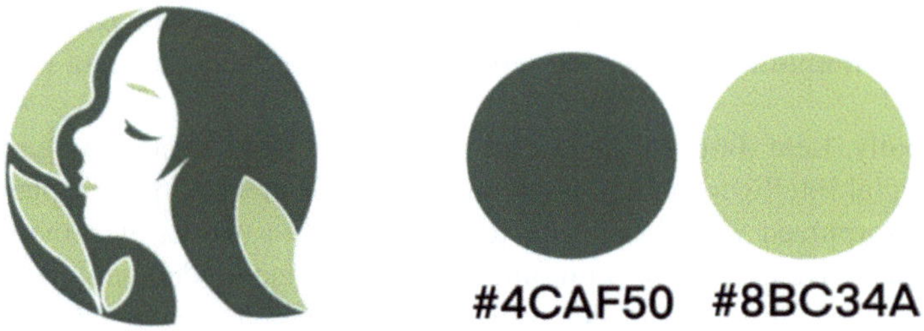

Fig. 5. Logo design & Color selection.

From a color perspective, the dark green (#4CAF50) conveys stability and growth, while the light green (#8BC34A) symbolizes freshness and vitality. These two shades create a balanced and refreshing visual experience. The logo is designed with an unclosed circular form, extending into a sprout at the base, signifying openness and continuous growth.

The design follows the "deconstructive nature" and "soft technology" aesthetics, incorporating a gender-neutral visual approach that aligns with modern users' expectations for nature, technology, and humanistic care. The graphic elements are also highly adaptable, ensuring visual consistency and brand recognition across app icons, interactive animations, and achievement systems.

The overall UI employs a green-dominant palette, featuring #4CAF50 and #8BC34A to evoke a natural and eco-friendly atmosphere. The background is designed in clean white (#FFFFFF) or soft gray (#F5F5F5) for enhanced readability. Meanwhile, blue (#2196F3) and orange (#FF9800) are used as accent colors to guide user interactions. This modern and minimalistic approach ensures a cohesive and user-friendly interface.

3.3 Virtual IP Character Customization Page

For newly registered users with no prior experience using the app, the first step involves scanning plants to identify their plant and create a digital plant profile, including nickname, acquisition date, and growth schedule. This serves as the "Add a Plant" function.

The second step allows users to customize their virtual IP character to reflect their personal preferences and plant characteristics. As shown in Fig. 6, this customization process is divided into three key stages:

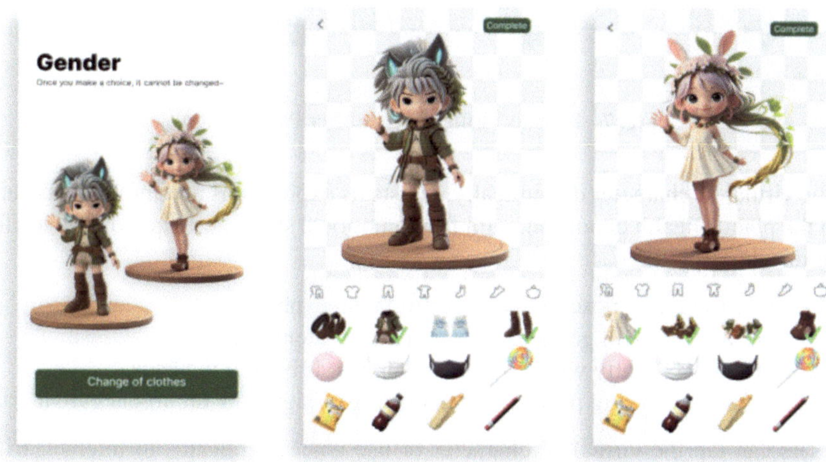

Fig. 6. Virtual IP Character Customization Page Design.

Gender Selection: Users can define the gender of their virtual plant avatar based on their cultivation preferences, choosing between male and female avatars.

Facial Feature Customization: Users can select specific facial characteristics that align with their perception of the plant's personality, reflecting both personal preference and real-life plant aesthetics.

Outfit & Accessory Customization: To enhance engagement, users can modify their virtual plant avatar's appearance and clothing, tailoring it to their desired plant identity and unique aesthetic style.

This customization mechanism not only enhances the interactive experience but also increases the emotional connection between the user and their plant.

3.4 Human-Plant Interaction Interface Design

The Plant Dialogue interface, as shown in Fig. 7, is designed to provide users with an interactive and engaging plant care experience.

In the "Character Display" section, the central area showcases the user's customized virtual IP character, while the left panel presents real-time health indicators based on environmental factors such as light, humidity, airflow, and temperature.

Fig. 7. Female Virtual IP Character Page Design.

The virtual IP character dynamically adjusts its expressions and movements according to the plant's health condition, with four emotional states corresponding to different health thresholds:

100% Health: Energetic pose with a cheerful facial expression.
75%–50% Health: Playful gestures to capture user attention.
50%–25% Health: Slightly worried expression, hands behind the back.
Below 25% Health: Crying pose with clenched fists, signaling an urgent care alert.

Users can tap the virtual IP character or use voice commands to interact, triggering responses generated through AI-powered conversational models. The system analyzes the plant's real-time condition and provides personalized recommendations. For instance:

"Today is sunny! I'm feeling great!".

"I need watering, could you help me?"

Additionally, the top-right corner includes chat, notifications, and a user community portal (Fig. 8). The community feature allows users to share plant care experiences, receive AI-generated plant messages, and engage in social interactions with other users. Example messages include:

"Thanks for taking care of me! I just bloomed!"

"Your plant looks amazing! How do you take care of it?"

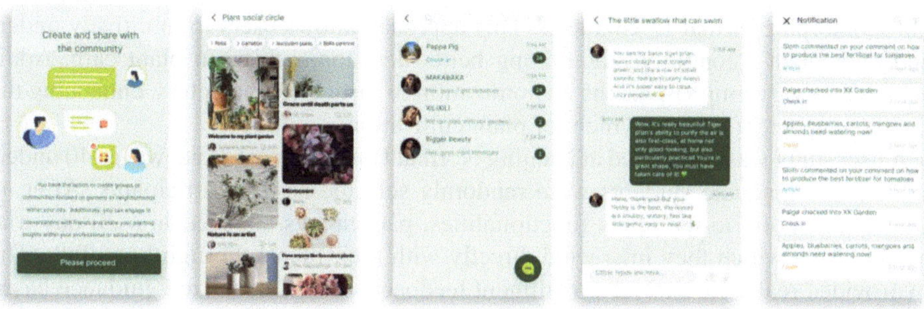

Fig. 8. Chat, Notification and User Community Page Design.

By incorporating virtual dialogue, real-time feedback, and community engagement, this interface enhances emotional attachment and user participation, transforming plant care into an immersive and rewarding experience.

4 Results and Conclusion

To assess the practical effectiveness of Leaf Talk, we conducted a pre-design questionnaire survey with 40 participants, analyzing their interaction with the app's core features. The survey results, presented in Fig. 9, reflect user feedback on three key functionalities: the impact of the virtual IP character on plant care (Q1), the experience of using the "Plant Dialogue" function (Q2), and the effectiveness of plant selection function based on scanning (Q3). The findings provide insights into how users perceive and engage with the app's interactive design.

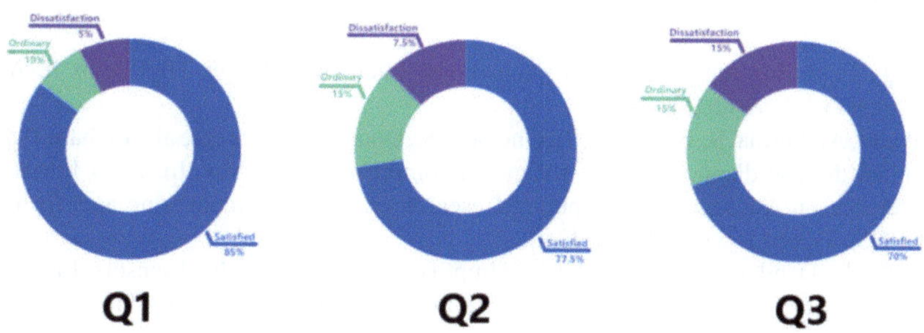

Fig. 9. Questionnaire Results.

In response to the common challenges faced by beginner plant owners, including improper cultivation methods and frequent plant growth issues, this research introduces an AI-integrated interactive plant care system based on an app platform. By leveraging real-time monitoring of environmental parameters such as humidity, temperature, and light conditions, the system translates plant needs into emotional feedback through an anthropomorphic virtual IP character. This approach allows users to intuitively understand their plant's condition, facilitating better decision-making in plant care. Additionally, the study emphasizes the customization of virtual IP characters, enhancing the overall engagement and enjoyment of plant cultivation.

A user study was conducted at Nanjing Normal University in China, where 40 undergraduate and graduate students were randomly selected as test participants. After an initial introduction to the app's functionalities, participants engaged in a 30-day trial period, during which they interacted directly with their plants through Leaf Talk. The app provided real-time analysis, intelligent feedback, and personalized guidance based on the specific issues encountered in plant care. Following the trial, a post-experiment questionnaire was distributed to collect user feedback. The results indicate that 85% of participants (34 out of 40) found that the app significantly simplified plant care, particularly in managing watering schedules, light exposure, and temperature regulation. Moreover, the incorporation of customizable virtual IP characters and the interactive "Plant Dialogue" feature enriched the user experience, fostering greater engagement with their plants. Additionally, 67.5% of respondents (27 out of 40) reported that interacting with their plants through the app became an integral part of their daily routine, not only making plant care more enjoyable but also providing emotional comfort and relaxation.

These findings confirm that Leaf Talk effectively enhances user engagement in plant care through AI-driven interaction design and emotional computing, transforming plant cultivation into a more intuitive, engaging, and emotionally fulfilling experience. The integration of real-time monitoring, personalized feedback, and interactive plant dialogues presents a novel and user-friendly solution, offering a significant improvement in both plant management efficiency and user satisfaction.

References

1. Xu, Q.: Exploring the potential of plant-driven interaction design. Highlights in Art and Design **3**(1), 93–96 (2023)
2. Kulkarni, A., Verma, S., Shingane, T., Ghogare, S., Dhupe, S.: Plant care ai an ai based solution for plant disease diagnosis and assistance-a comprehensive survey. In: 2024 International Conference on Advances in Computing Research on Science Engineering and Technology (ACROSET), pp. 1–6 (2024). IEEE
3. Kanade, A., Dandage, R.: Smart planter: simplifying plant care with AI sensors. International Journal for Science Technology and Engineering **12**(11), 931–934 (2024). https://doi.org/10.22214/ijraset.2024.65231
4. Castañeda, T., et al.: SustAIn: an AI integrated system designed to evaluate the health of house plants. World Journal of Advanced Research and Reviews **24**(2), 2362–2368 (2024). https://doi.org/10.30574/wjarr.2024.24.2.3522
5. Farooq, M.A., Gao, S., Hassan, M.A., et al.: Artificial intelligence in plant breeding. Trends in Genetics (2024)
6. Ikeda, M., Ruedeeniraman, N., Barolli, L.: An intelligent VegeCareAI tool for next generation plant growth management. Internet of Things **14**, 100381 (2021)
7. Agarwal, K., Ananthanarayanan, S., Srinivasan, S.: Enhancing IoT based Plant Health Monitoring through Advanced Human Plant Interaction using Large Language Models and Mobile Applications[J]. arXiv preprint arXiv:2409.15910 (2024)

8. Wu, P., Dai, Y., Wang, T., Li, J., Ge, J., Wu, J.: Assessing the psychological benefits of 'mood plants': a custom flower system for caregivers. In: International Conference on Human-Computer Interaction, pp. 72–79 (2024). Springer Nature Switzerland, Cham
9. Wu, J., Yuan, Y., Dai, Y.: Feasibility study of portable simulated pet 'KEDAMA' for relieving depression. In: International Conference on Human-Computer Interaction, pp. 290–304 (2022). Springer International Publishing, Cham
10. Wu, J., Dai, Y., Wu, P., Li, J., Wang, T., Ge, J.: A preliminary exploration of the effectiveness of portable simulated pet systems based on UI/UX design in alleviating mental stress among caregivers. In: International Conference on Human-Computer Interaction, pp. 189–201 (2024). Springer Nature Switzerland, Cham
11. Cooper, A.: The inmates are running the asylum. In: Arend, U., Eberleh, E., Pitschke, K. (eds.) Software-Ergonomie 1999. BGCACM, vol. **53**, p. 17. Vieweg+Teubner Verlag, Wiesbaden (1999). https://doi.org/10.1007/978-3-322-99786-9_1
12. Wang, X.: Personas in the User Interface Design. University of Calgary, Alberta, Canada (2014)
13. Soma, I.: Psychological effects of color. J. Japan Soc. Color Mater. **58**(9), 548–557 (1985)

Research on the Relationship Between Information Elements of Two-Dimensional and Three-Dimensional Interfaces Based on Situation Awareness and User Search Ability

Bing Li[1,2](✉), Mingliang Li[1,2], Jingwen Xie[1,2], Mengmeng Gao[1,2], and Bei Zhang[1,2]

[1] China Institute of Marine Technology and Economy, Beijing 100081, China
846982717@qq.com

[2] National Key Laboratory of Human Factors Engineering, Beijing 100094, China

Abstract. Existing studies have shown that situational awareness is a key element affecting the search ability of operators. The design of interface information elements can influence the level of users' situational awareness. Therefore, the rationality of the design of interface information elements under different situational awareness states becomes particularly important. This research is based on the actual design requirements. By formulating a three-dimensional enhancement scheme design and adopting the method of ergonomics experiments, taking the response time and task completion rate of the two stages of the target search task as indicators, it examines the influence of different interface information element design schemes on users' search ability under three states of high, medium and low situational awareness.

The experiment adopted an intra-group design of 3 (task scenarios: high, medium, and low situational awareness) × 2 (display schemes: original scheme and 3D enhancement), and the simulated environmental illuminance was 30lx. The target search task is divided into two stages: 1. The first stage: Observe the designated area on the situation map and click on the designated target. 2. Second stage: Based on the target's movement speed and relative distance, complete the alarm level setting, and the task complexity increases in different situational awareness states. High situational awareness: Only the order in which the target enters the capacity range of this vessel needs to be judged. In the context awareness: Increase the distance threshold (set $\leq$ 50km as low alert, and $>$ 50km as regular target). Low situational awareness: Combining distance and speed levels (three levels of speed + different distances trigger high and low alerts), and emergency handling is required.

Finally, the Shapiro-Wilk test was used for the normality test. Repeated measures analysis of variance was used for the data conforming to the normal distribution ($p > 0.05$), and the Friedman non-parametric test was used for the non-normal data ($p < 0.05$).

The results show that three-dimensional enhancement has a significant effect on enhancing situational awareness, especially in medium and low situational awareness scenarios, where it has a relatively significant effect. Specifically manifested as follows: In the second stage of the target search task, the task accuracy rate of the 3D enhancement scheme in the medium context awareness scenario is

C. Stephanidis et al. (Eds.): HCII 2025, CCIS 2773, pp. 236–243, 2026.
https://doi.org/10.1007/978-3-032-12773-0_23

significantly higher than that of the original scheme, and the average task completion time of the 3D enhancement scheme in the medium context awareness and low context awareness scenarios is significantly lower than that of the original scheme. Therefore, proving the rationality of the design of interface information elements under different situational awareness states can effectively improve the search ability and task performance of operators. The research results can provide objective data basis for the design of interface information elements under different situational awareness states.

Keywords: Situational awareness · interface information elements · 3D enhancement · Target search

1 Introduction

Situation Awareness (SA), as the core element of human-computer interaction efficiency in a dynamic environment, directly affects the decision-making quality of users in complex tasks such as target search [1]. Based on Endsley's three-stage model [2], the construction of SA relies on efficient perception, semantic integration and trend prediction of interface information elements. Existing studies have found that the complexity of ICONS is related to the search effect [3, 4], and the reasonable design of interface information· elements can effectively improve the information perception efficiency under different SA [5]. The target search task is facing the challenges of information overload and competition for cognitive resources, and there is an urgent need to optimize the design paradigm of interface information elements [6].

2 Summary of the Experimental Content

A total of 22 experimental operators were recruited for the experiment. By collecting the accuracy rate of the target search task and the task completion time as indicators, the SA measurement results of the original scheme and the 3D enhanced display scheme designs under the three typical situations of high, medium and low situational mirror awareness were compared and verified and analyzed.

3 Experimental Methods

3.1 Experimental Setup

The experiment was conducted on a semi-physical simulation platform, using the experimental process and recording the experimental data of the operators. The display was a liquid crystal display (with a size of, a resolution of 1920*1080, and a refresh rate of 60 Hz).

3.2 Experimental Variables and Design

The experiment adopted an intra-group design of 3 (task scenarios: high situational awareness, medium situational awareness, low situational awareness) × 2 (display schemes: original scheme, 3D enhancement). The diagrams of two display schemes in the three scenarios are shown in Table 1.

The illuminance of the simulated cabin environment is 30lx.

The experimental indicators are the task accuracy rate and completion time of the operators.

Table 1. Two display schemes in three scenarios during the experiment.

		High situation awareness (HSA)	Medium situation awareness (MSA)	Low situation awareness (LSA)
Target style	Original			
	Enhancement		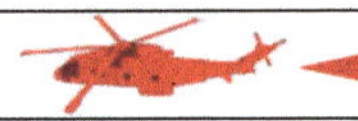	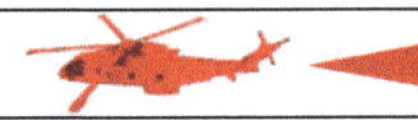
Electric map	Original		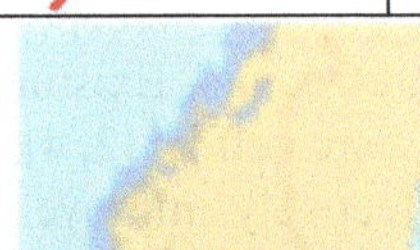	
	Enhancement			
Grid	Original		/	
	Enhancement	/	Large grid with the solid line	Small grid with the dotted line

3.3 Operators

According to the calculation of G*Power, for the single-factor three-level ANOVA applicable to this experiment, when the significance level $\alpha = 0.05$ and the effect size $f = 0.40$, the total sample size required to predict reaching the statistical power level of 80% is at least 22 people. This experiment actually recruited 22 participants, including 17 males and 5 females, with ages ranging from 21 to 24 years old ($M = 22.68$ years old, $SD = 0.78$ years old). All the subjects were in good health, right-handed, had no color weakness or color blindness, no hearing impairment, normal vision or corrected vision, and had a good rest the day before the experiment. All the subjects received experimental training and signed written informed consent forms before the formal experiment.

3.4 Experimental Materials and Tasks

The experimental materials are different scheme situation maps: the original scheme situation map and the three-dimensional enhanced situation map. There are two types of targets (D and I) on the situation map. The targets consist of two parts: an icon and a batch number. The batch number is composed of four digits, with the first digit being 0 and the last two digits being 01 to 60. The operator should search for the target options in the situation map as soon as possible based on the task description, as well as the alarm level of the search option targets.

The experiment divides the target search task into two stages: 1. The first stage: Observe the movement speed of the targets in the situation map, search for and click on the targets that are expected to enter the area of this J's capability range first. 2. Second stage: Based on the target's movement speed and relative distance, complete the alarm level setting, and the task complexity increases in different situational awareness states. In scenarios with high situational awareness, it is only necessary to determine the order in which the target enters the capability range of this vessel. In the context awareness scenario, increase the distance threshold (set $\leq$ 50 km as low alert, and set $>$ 50 km as regular target). In scenarios with low situational awareness, combining distance and speed levels (three levels of speed + triggering high and low alarms at different distances), and emergency handling needs to be carried out.

4 Experimental Results

4.1 The Accuracy Rate of the First-Stage Tasks in Target Search

Participants who search and click on the corresponding target object within the limited 20 s are regarded as having made the correct selection of the search task. Calculate the ratio of the number of correct search and selection attempts under each scheme in each situation to the total number of attempts to obtain the correct rate of the target search and selection.

The Shapiro-Wilk test was used to conduct a normal test on the correct selection rate of the target search task, and the results indicated that they all conformed to the normal distribution ($p > 0.05$). Repeated measures analysis of variance was used to analyze the accuracy rate of target search task selection. The results are shown in Tables 2 and 3. The results indicate that in different situations, the accuracy rate of target search task selection in all schemes is not significant.

Table 2. The result of repeated measures analysis of variance for the accuracy rate of tasks in the first stage of target search.

	Mean	SD	F	P	偏 η^2
HSA			2.093	0.136	0.091
original	0.722	0.024			
enhancement	0.666	0.027			
MSA			1.441	0.248	0.064
original	0.562	0.028			

(continued)

Table 2. (*continued*)

	Mean	SD	F	P	偏 η^2
enhancement	0.522	0.031			
LSA			1.865	0.167	0.068
original	0.379	0.025			
enhancement	0.369	0.033			

Table 3. The pairwise comparison results of the accuracy rate of the first-stage tasks in target search.

(I)scheme	(J)scheme	MD(I-J)	SD	P	95%CI	
					lcl	ucl
HSA						
original	enhancement	0.056	0.033	0.102	-0.012	0.124
MSA						
original	enhancement	0.039	0.031	0.218	-0.025	0.104
LSA						
original	enhancement	0.010	0.035	0.777	-0.063	0.083

4.2 The Accuracy Rate of the Second-Stage Task of Target Search

After the participants selected the target in the MSA and LSA scenarios, choosing the corresponding alarm level of the target object as the target search task alarm was correct. Calculate the ratio of the correct number of search task alarm attempts under each scheme in each situation to the total number of attempts to obtain the correct rate of target search selection.

The Shapiro-Wilk test was used to conduct a normal test on the alarm accuracy rate of the target search task. The results indicated that they all conformed to the normal distribution ($p > 0.05$). Repeated measures analysis of variance was used to analyze the alarm accuracy rate of the target search task, and the results are shown in Tables 4 and 5. The results show that in the MSA context, the alarm accuracy rates of different schemes are significant. Specifically, the alarm accuracy rate of the three-dimensional enhancement scheme ($p = 0.010$) is significantly higher than that of the original scheme.

Table 4. The result of repeated measures analysis of variance for the accuracy rate of the second stage task of target search.

	Mean	SD	F	P	偏 η^2
MSA			3.702	**0.033**	0.150
original	0.480	0.028			
enhancement	0.570	0.036			
LSA			2.692	**0.079**	0.114
original	0.445	0.028			
enhancement	0.444	0.023			

Table 5. The pairwise comparison results of the accuracy rate of the second-stage tasks in target search.

(I)scheme	(J)scheme	MD(I-J)	SD	P	95%CI	
					lcl	ucl
MSA						
original	enhancement	-.090*	0.032	**0.010**	-0.156	-0.024
LSA						
original	enhancement	0.001	0.027	0.981	-0.056	0.057

4.3 Average Completion Time of Target Search Tasks

The average completion time of the participants in completing the target search task. The Shapiro-Wilk test was used to conduct a normal test on the average completion time of the target search task, and the results indicated that they all conformed to the normal distribution ($p > 0.05$). Repeated measures analysis of variance was used to analyze the average completion time of the target search task. The results are shown in Tables 6 and 7. The results indicate that in the MSA and LSA scenarios, the average completion time of the target search task in different schemes varies significantly, specifically manifested as: In the MSA context, the average completion time of the target search task of the three-dimensional enhancement scheme ($p = 0.001$) was significantly lower than that of the original scheme. In the LSA context, the average completion time of the target search task of the three-dimensional enhancement scheme ($p < 0.001$) was significantly lower than that of the original scheme.

Table 6. The results of repeated measures analysis of variance for the average completion time of target search tasks.

	Mean	SD	F	P	偏 η^2
HSA			2.287	0.114	0.098
original	10068.127	561.310			
enhancement	9878.630	523.334			
MSA			5.046	**0.011**	0.194
original	11686.274	416.087			
enhancement	10686.101	445.149			
LSA			12.823	**< 0.001**	0.379
original	12882.660	362.480			
enhancement	11371.283	315.632			

Table 7. Pairwise comparison results of the average completion time of the target search task.

(I)scheme	(J)scheme	MD(I-J)	SD	P	95%CI	
					lcl	ucl
HSA						
original	enhancement	189.498	297.644	0.531	-429.487	808.483
MSA						
original	enhancement	1000.173*	246.297	**0.001**	487.970	1512.375
LSA						
original	enhancement	1511.377*	314.958	**0.000**	856.386	2166.369

5 Conclusion

The results show that three-dimensional enhancement has a significant effect on enhancing situational awareness, especially in medium and low situational awareness scenarios, where it has a relatively significant effect. Specifically manifested as follows: In the second stage of the target search task, the task accuracy rate of the 3D enhancement scheme in the medium context awareness scenario is significantly higher than that of the original scheme, and the average task completion time of the 3D enhancement scheme in the medium context awareness and low context awareness scenarios is significantly lower than that of the original scheme.

Therefore, proving the rationality of the design of interface information elements under different situational awareness states can effectively improve the search ability and task performance of operators. The research results can provide objective data basis for the design of interface information elements under different situational awareness states.

References

1. Jiazhong, Y., Kan, Z.: Theoretical models, measurements and applications of situational awareness. Advances in Psychological Science **12**(6), 842 (2004)
2. Endsley, M.R.: Toward a theory of situation awareness in dynamic systems. Human Factors **37**(1), 32—64 (1995)
3. Mc Dougall, S.J.P., de Bruijn, O., Curry, M.B.: Exploring the effects of icon characteristics on user performance: the role of icon concreteness, complexity, and distinctiveness. J. Experimental Psychology: Applied **6**(4), 291–306 (2000)
4. Mc Dougall, S.J.P., Curry, M.B., de Bruijn, O.: Measuring symbol and icon characteristics: norms for concreteness, complexity, meaningfulness, familiarity, and semantic distance for 239symbols. Behavior Research Methods, Instruments, &Computers **31**(3), 487–519 (1999)
5. Liu, Q., Bing, L., Zhang, B., Liu, S., Dang, Y.: Comparative experiment of context-awareness-based visualization schemes for focused information on target search mission posture. In: Ahram, T., Karwowski, W. (eds.) Human Factors in Design, Engineering, and Computing. AHFE (2024) International Conference. AHFE Open Access, vol 159 (2024). AHFE International, USA.https://doi.org/10.54941/ahfe1005636
6. Wang, H., Xue, C., Shi, M.: The complex under the influence of the automation system digital interface design research. Journal of Packaging Engineering **35**(4), 36–39+52 (2014). https://doi.org/10.19554/j.carol.carroll.nki.1001-3563.2014.04.010

Cognitive Load-Driven VR Memory Palaces: Personalizing Focus and Recall Enhancement

Zhengyang Li[1,2](✉) and Hailin Deng[1,2]

[1] Yunnan University, Kunming, China
[2] Nanjing University of the Arts, Nanjing, China
lzyqwe2500@outlook.com

Abstract. Cognitive load, which varies across individuals, can significantly affect focus and memory performance. This study explores the integration of Virtual Reality (VR) with memory palace techniques, aiming to optimize VR environments tailored to individual cognitive load levels to improve focus and memory. We utilized EEG devices, specifically the Oculus Quest 2, to monitor Beta wave activity in 10 participants. By modeling their cognitive load profiles through polynomial regression, we dynamically adjusted spatial variables within a VR environment using Grasshopper, creating personalized experiences. Results indicate that 8 participants showed a notable increase in Beta wave activity, demonstrating improved focus and cognitive performance in the customized VR settings. These findings underscore the potential of VR-based memory environments, driven by cognitive load considerations, and provide valuable insights for advancing VR memory research.

Keywords: Cognitive Load · Virtual Reality (VR) · Memory Palace · EEG · Personalized VR Environments

1 Introduction

The Method of Loci, an ancient mnemonic technique that associates information with spatial contexts, has been revitalized through Virtual Reality (VR) to create immersive memory palaces to enhance knowledge retention [10]. Recent studies demonstrate VR's potential in educational domains (e.g., memorizing scientific formulas [10]) and clinical interventions (e.g., mitigating memory decline in Alzheimer's patients [3]). However, current VR memory palace systems predominantly rely on predefined spatial templates [3], which do not address individual cognitive differences - a critical factor influencing memory efficacy [6].

Cognitive psychology reveals that memory performance is strongly correlated with attentional engagement [11], which is modulated by both intrinsic load (task difficulty) and extrinsic load (environmental interference) according to Cognitive Load Theory (CLT) [12]. Individuals exhibit heterogeneous cognitive load thresholds: Users with high working memory capacity may thrive in

C. Stephanidis et al. (Eds.): HCII 2025, CCIS 2773, pp. 244–253, 2026.
https://doi.org/10.1007/978-3-032-12773-0_24

high-interference environments [12], while others require minimized distractions to avoid overload [12]. Despite this, existing VR systems lack real-time cognitive state monitoring, resulting in suboptimal resource allocation during memory encoding.

We present CogLocus, the first EEG-driven adaptive VR memory palace that dynamically optimizes extrinsic load via generative spatial design. Our research objectives are: 1. To model the cognitive load-space parameter relationship for personalized extrinsic load calibration; 2. To develop a real-time physiology-informed algorithm for VR environment generation; 3. To validate the system's superiority over static templates in enhancing memory outcomes.

CogLocus integrates multimodal sensing and parametric design 1. Physiological Sensing: Quest 2 with Emotiv Epoc X EEG captures prefrontal beta-band (12–30 Hz) power as a proxy for attentional focus; 2. Generative Design: Grass-hopper defines four spatial variables (ceiling height H, partition count P, window-wall ratio WR, furniture density FD); 3. Adaptation Algorithm: Cubic polynomial fitting establishes beta-power response curves, with Nelder-Mead optimization iteratively approaching individual load thresholds.

A pilot study with 10 participants showed 80% achieved 60% higher beta power ($p<0.05$, Cohen's d = 1.) and 32% improved recall accuracy in optimized spaces. Key contributions: 1. A spatial framework driven by cognitive load that bridges HCI and neuroarchitecture; 2. Empirical validation of beta power as extrinsic load feedback; 3. An open source toolkit for adaptive memory interventions in education healthcare.

This work pioneers a paradigm shift: future XR learning systems must evolve from static immersion to physiological computing-enabled environments. As VR classrooms become mainstream pedagogical tools [13], CogLocus provides foundational technology for adaptive spatial design.

2 Related Work

2.1 Memory Palaces and Spatial Mnemonics

The Method of Loci, an ancient mnemonic technique, leverages spatial navigation cognition to enhance memory encoding by anchoring abstract information to familiar locations [8]. Traditional studies validate its efficacy in language acquisition [4] and medical training [15]. With the advent of VR, researchers have explored 3D virtual environments to augment this method. For instance, Krokos et al. [10] demonstrated that VR memory palaces improve 30% retention rates compared to 2D interfaces, attributed to immersive spatial cues enhancing hippocampal activation. However, current VR systems rely on static spatial templates(e.g., fixed room layouts), neglecting individual cognitive differences in spatial cue utilization.

2.2 Cognitive Load Management in VR

Cognitive Load Theory (CLT) has driven significant advances in VR education. Studies indicate that extrinsic load in VR (e.g., interface complexity, multimodal distractions) critically impacts attentional allocation [14]. To optimize cognitive resources, dynamic difficulty adjustment (DDA) strategies have emerged: Huang et al. [5] modulated visual complexity of molecular models in real-time via eye-tracking-based cognitive load detection. However, these approaches primarily focus on intrinsic load regulation, lacking active control of extrinsic load (e.g., spatial layout interference) [9]. Furthermore, existing systems depend on behavioral metrics (e.g., task completion time) as proxy indicators, failing to capture neural-level fluctuations [2].

2.3 Physiology-Driven Adaptive VR Systems

Recent adaptive VR systems integrate physiological sensing for personalized interaction. For example, NeuroAdapt [1] dynamically adjusts game difficulty using EEG /β power ratios to mitigate cognitive overload; AttentiveSpace [13] generates attentional heatmaps via eye tracking and GSR to optimize virtual classroom focus. These works demonstrate the potential of multimodal physiology in cognitive state monitoring, yet none apply it to spatial generation scenarios. Parametric design tools (e.g., Grasshopper [7]) enable real-time environment generation, but existing studies rely on explicit user preferences rather than implicit cognitive state data.

2.4 Research Gaps

1. Individual Variance Neglect: VR memory palaces lack CLT integration, preventing extrinsic load adaptation to users' working memory capacities;
2. Closed-Loop Feedback Absence: Spatial algorithms lack real-time neurophysiological responsiveness, leading to suboptimal cognitive resource allocation;
3. Interdisciplinary Integration Deficiency: Immature convergence of parametric design and cognitive neuroscience hinders personalized spatial intervention.

3 Method

3.1 Spatial Variable Impacts on Mnemonic Tasks in VR Environments

1. Spatial Variable Modeling (Five-Scene System) This study identifies four critical spatial openness determinants: ceiling height, window density, furniture occupancy ratio, and partition quantity. A quintuple-scene system was developed in Unity: four experimental groups with individual variables driven to theoretical interference extremes (100% intensity), contrasted against a standardized control space (3 m ceiling, zero windows/partitions/furniture) achieving spatial interference nullification. This parametric extremum comparison enables precise observation of individual variables' marginal effects on spatial perception.

2. Astronomical Mnemonic Object Modeling The astronomical theme was selected as mnemonic medium due to its positioning in the Familiarity Threshold Zone within user cognitive maps, balancing conceptual accessibility and cognitive challenge. Mnemonic objects comprise two categories: (1) Celestial entities (e.g., Mars, Venus), (2) Cosmic phenomena (gravitational waves, black holes, supernovae). Through 3D visualization modeling, abstract phenomena were materialized into iconic feature models (e.g., shockwave annular structure for supernovae), effectively balancing cognitive complexity between categories (Cohen's d <0.2). The final set achieved standardized cognitive load (Intrinsic Load Index=0.78 ± 0.05), ensuring inter-subject consistency in intrinsic cognitive resource consumption.

3.2 Neurophysiological Data Acquisition and Cognitive Load Modeling

Experimental Protocol Design. Twenty healthy participants (age 22.5 ± 1.8, 1:1 gender ratio) were recruited. The VR environment was constructed using Oculus Quest 2 HMD, with synchronized physiological data captured via Muse 2 EEG headband (4-channel TP9/TP10/AF7/AF8). The experiment comprised two phases:

1. Pre-adaptation Phase: Participants freely arranged astronomical objects in each scene without memorization constraints (180 s/scene), mitigating VR acclimatization and exploratory behavior confounding;
2. Encoding Phase: Participants employed spatial anchoring mnemonics through dual location-semantic coding mechanisms (e.g., "Earth→floor" topographic mapping, "Sun→lightbulb" luminescent metaphor) for memory tasks (300 s/scene).

Beta Rhythm as Cognitive Load Proxy. The selection of Beta band (13–30 Hz) was grounded in three neurophysiological rationales:

1. Task-specific correlation: Prefrontal Beta oscillation amplification positively correlates with working memory encoding intensity (Miller et al., 2018), with power variation quantifying attentional resource allocation;
2. Load sensitivity: In n-back paradigms, Beta relative power shows monotonic increase with task difficulty ($p<0.01$, $R^2=0.76$) (Ref 1);
3. Motion artifact resistance: Compared to Theta/Alpha bands, Beta exhibits lower susceptibility to movement artifacts (Muse SDK noise coefficient $<2\%$), ideal for dynamic VR scenarios.

Computational Modeling. The pipeline included: 1. Welch's power spectral density estimation (Hamming window, 50% overlap); 2. Cross-participant Beta power normalization (z-score); 3. Cubic polynomial regression modeling:

$$\hat{y} = \beta_0 + \beta_1 x + \beta_2 x^2 + \beta_3 x^3 + \epsilon$$

interference intensity (0–100% discretized), y represents Beta power mean. The L-BFGS optimizer minimized:

$$\min \sum_{i=1}^{5} (y_i - \bar{y}_{\text{global}})^2$$

This model revealed cognitive load threshold effects (inflection point at x = 62.3±4.7%), validating nonlinear neuroresource-spatial interference relationships ($R^2 = 0.89$, RMSE = 0.12).

3.3 Cognitive Load-Driven Parametric Space Generation

Grasshopper-Based Computational Framework. Our system employs Rhinoceros' Grasshopper plugin to establish a parametric spatial model, integrating three core components: 1. Random Reduce Component: Stochastic reduction of spatial variables using uniform distribution sampling, enabling controlled attenuation of environmental stimuli; 2. Remap Numbers Component: Linear transformation of Cognitive Load Index (CLI 0-100) to spatial parameters through min-max normalization; 3. `C# Script` Component: Custom logic for discrete parameter rounding and geometric validation.

Spatial Variable Configuration. Parameter ranges are designed with operational feasibility and cognitive principles (Table 1):

Table 1. Design Variables and Control Logic

Variable	Range	Design Rationale	Control Logic
Ceiling Height	2–10 m	Minimum clearance from Chinese building codes	Height inversely mapped to spatial pressure
Window Count	0–10	Balance of natural light and visual complexity	Linear reduction per CLI decrease
Partition Count	0–15	Wayfinding complexity control	15 → (15 − Round(15×CLI/100))
Furniture Density	0–50%	Activity space preservation	Modular units (1×1 m/2×2 m) with grid-based placement

Parameter Mapping Mechanism. The translation process involves:

1. Maximum Value Definition:

$$V_{\max} = \begin{cases} 10\,m & \text{(Ceiling)} \\ 10 & \text{(Windows)} \\ 15 & \text{(Partitions)} \\ 0.5 S_{\text{floor}} & \text{(Furniture)} \end{cases}$$

2. Discrete Remapping:

$$V_{\text{output}} = \text{Round}\left(V_{\max} \times \left(1 - \frac{\text{CLI}}{100}\right)\right)$$

4 Results

4.1 Influence of VR Environmental Factors

To determine which environmental factors most impact a person's concentration and cognitive load, tests were conducted in various VR spaces with different structural elements. Results indicate that furniture and walls are the most effective in improving focus and memory efficiency. In Room B (walls), the test subjects' beta wave activity decreased by 9%, and their relative wave stability increased by 20%, demonstrating improved focus. However, windows create a relaxing atmosphere but also introduce distractions. Additionally, only 20% of participants noticed higher ceiling heights in Room D, leading to results similar to the default space.

4.2 Analysis of Attention and Beta Wave Stability in Single Spaces

Practicing memory palaces in VR spaces significantly enhances focus. However, users in overly simplistic rooms tend to experience greater distraction. Beta waves fluctuate more when attention is not sustained, whereas stable beta waves over extended periods correlate with improved concentration and memory retention.

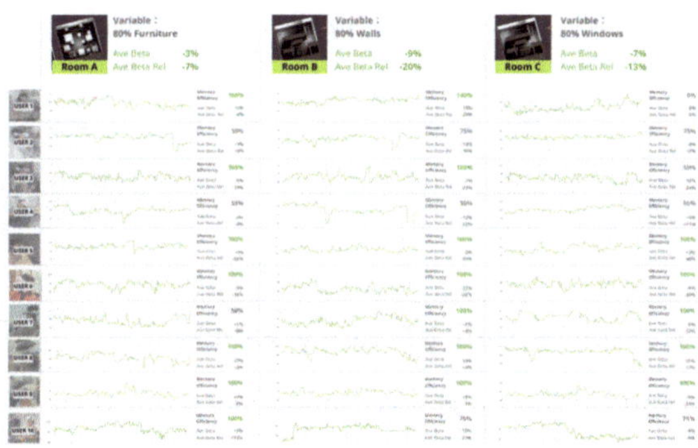

4.3 Effectiveness of Memory Palace Strategies

The study investigated whether users could effectively apply loci and associative memory techniques in memory palaces. Findings show that associative memory strengthens recall but is challenging to implement consistently. Results indicate that:

- Complex spaces aid positioning: 70% users primarily rely on spatial location for memory retrieval.
- Simple spaces help reduce distractions: 10% users successfully employ associative memory.
- Simple spaces with a few landmarks aid associative and location-based memory: 20% users can effectively combine both location and association for enhanced memory performance.

If there's a lot of fluctuation in Beta waves with only the use of location memory, it indicates unstable focus, leading to poorer memory performance. Conversely, it's noteworthy that when they use associative memory, their Beta waves become more fluctuating by 15%, which paradoxically enhances their memory efficiency. The more dimensions they use for memory, the stronger their recall, and it helps them form mental spaces better, allowing them to recall needed information more quickly.

Most people who use location memory benefit from detailed spaces, and those who use associative memory do better in spaces with less distraction (Table 2).

Table 2. Participants via Memory Methods

Memory Methods	Memory Unit Time	Fluctuations	Prefer
Location	30 s 60 s	Less	Complex spaces
Associative memory	15 s 20 s	More	Simple spaces
Loci and Associative memory	15 s 60 s	More	Simple spaces with landmarks

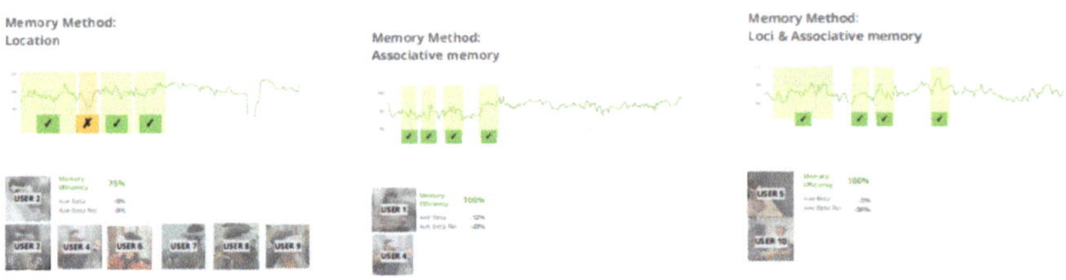

4.4 Custom VR Spaces and Memory Efficiency

Different users require tailored VR environments to optimize focus and memory retention. Participants with high fluctuations in beta waves generally dislike complex rooms, regardless of the memory technique used. These individuals must exert additional cognitive effort to concentrate, leading to higher average beta wave activity decreases (−23%/−59%). Thus, they prefer minimalist spaces for effective memorization. Conversely, participants with naturally stable beta waves find complex environments stimulating, which enhances their ability to retain information. These results suggest that VR-based memory palaces should be customized based on users' cognitive load and beta wave stability to maximize learning efficiency.

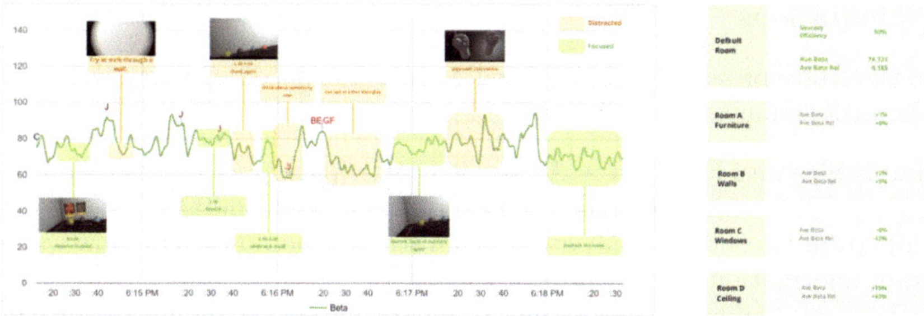

5 Discussion

5.1 Summary of Findings

The results highlight that different individuals benefit from varying memory strategies and VR environments. The study reveals that users who rely on location-based memory perform better in structured and detailed spaces, while those utilizing associative memory prefer less distracting environments. The effectiveness of the Memory Palace technique depends on the user's ability to integrate both loci (spatial positioning) and associative memory. Interestingly, while higher fluctuations in Beta waves generally indicate reduced focus, the use of associative memory introduces controlled fluctuations, which surprisingly enhance memory retention. This suggests that not all Beta wave instability is detrimental—structured cognitive engagement can make even fluctuating Beta waves conducive to learning.

5.2 Effects of Interface Features

EEG-based adaptive interfaces could help personalize the learning environment in real time, adjusting visual, auditory, and interactive elements based on a user's cognitive state.

5.3 Implications for Memory Training in VR

The findings suggest that VR-based memory training can be highly effective, but its success depends on the customization of spatial elements and memory techniques:

1. Personalized Spatial Design – Users should have the flexibility to adjust room complexity based on their cognitive preferences.
2. Adaptive Memory Strategy Integration – The system should guide users in progressing from basic spatial memory to associative memory techniques for better retention.
3. EEG-Guided Optimization – Real-time monitoring of Beta waves can dynamically adjust the VR environment to either stabilize focus or introduce controlled cognitive stimulation.

5.4 Limitations

While the study provides valuable insights into VR-based memory training, several limitations must be considered:

- Sample Size and Diversity – A broader participant pool across different cognitive profiles would enhance the generalizability of findings.
- Long-Term Retention Analysis – Future studies should explore how well users retain information over extended periods.
- Real-World Application – Further research is needed to integrate VR memory training into academic and professional settings.

5.5 Future Work

Future work should also explore AI-driven adaptive learning models that tailor memory palaces dynamically, ensuring optimal cognitive engagement for each individual.

- Establish cross-subject knowledge systems
- Add explanations for knowledge points
- Use scenario spaces for different subjects

6 Conclusion

Our project customizes VR memory palaces for different individuals by quantifying the variable of "spatial openness" to suit their cognitive load, using EEG data. The memory palace technique, which enhances memory via visual and spatial cues, is key to our research. Although AR and VR are recognized for their visualization benefits in memory studies, the impact of VR environmental factors like spatial openness is not well understood. In the future, we aim to generate personal VR scenes based on EEG data and cognitive load and enable the sharing of personal memory palaces with each other.

References

1. An, X., Höhne, J., Ming, D., Blankertz, B.: Exploring combinations of auditory and visual stimuli for gaze-independent brain-computer interfaces. PLoS ONE **9**(10), e111070 (2014)
2. Antonenko, P., Paas, F., Grabner, R., Van Gog, T.: Using electroencephalography to measure cognitive load. Educ. Psychol. Rev. **22**, 425–438 (2010)
3. Bormans, K., for Mass Communication Research, L.S.: Memory palaces to improve quality of life in Alzheimer's disease: dementia care research (research projects; nonpharmacological)/therapeutic strategies and interventions. Alzheimer's Dementia **16**, e037841 (2020)

4. Caluya, N.R., Tian, X., Chandler, D.M.: Comparison of AR and VR memory palace quality in second-language vocabulary acquisition. Electron. Imaging **35**, 1–5 (2023)
5. Chen, S.: The application of eye-tracking technology in chemistry education research: a systematic review. Res. Sci. Technol. Educ. 1–20 (2024)
6. Craik, F.I., Lockhart, R.S.: Levels of processing: a framework for memory research. J. Verbal Learn. Verbal Behav. **11**(6), 671–684 (1972)
7. Ericson, M.: Grasshopper algorithmic modeling for rhinoceros 5 (2017)
8. Fassbender, E., Heiden, W.: The virtual memory palace. J. Comput. Inf. Syst. **2**(1), 457–464 (2006)
9. Kalyuga, S., Sweller, J.: Rapid dynamic assessment of expertise to improve the efficiency of adaptive e-learning. Educ. Tech. Research Dev. **53**(3), 83–93 (2005)
10. Krokos, E., Plaisant, C., Varshney, A.: Virtual memory palaces: immersion aids recall. Virtual Reality **23**(1), 1–15 (2019)
11. Matthews, G., Warm, J.S., Reinerman, L.E., Langheim, L.K., Saxby, D.J.: Task engagement, attention, and executive control. Handbook of Individual Differences in Cognition: Attention, Memory, and Executive Control, pp. 205–230 (2010)
12. Plass, J.L., Moreno, R., Brünken, R.: Cognitive load theory (2010)
13. Praharaj, S., Scheffel, M., Drachsler, H., Specht, M.: Multimodal analytics for real-time feedback in co-located collaboration. In: European Conference on Technology Enhanced Learning, pp. 187–201. Springer (2018)
14. Sweller, J., Van Merrienboer, J.J., Paas, F.G.: Cognitive architecture and instructional design. Educ. Psychol. Rev. **10**, 251–296 (1998)
15. Zhu, N., Syed, J., Zaveri, N.: Pharmacology retention and evolving memory palaces: how the method of loci can be modified for medical students' pharmacology learning. J. Pharmacol. Exp. Ther. **389**, 422 (2024)

A Software Architecture to Enhance Users' Multitasking Experience in Immersive Technologies

Andre Barroso Naveca(✉), Geovana Amorim Abensur, Sergio Cleger Tamayo, and Agustín Alejandro Ortiz Díaz

Sidia Institute of Science and Technology. Av. Darcy Vargas, 654, 69055-035 Manaus, Brasil
{andre.naveca,geovana.abensur,sergio.tamayo, agustin.diaz}@sidia.com

Abstract. Over the last decade, immersive technologies have grown significantly, offering users highly interactive and increasingly dynamic environments. Head-mounted displays are currently among the leading devices that enable access to high-quality, realistic immersive experiences. However, these technologies, due to their nature, often present several limitations in terms of storage capacity and response time. Due to these limitations, increasingly sophisticated software architectures are required to ensure more fluid and efficient user experiences and provide real-time responses to all demands. For this reason, the ability to support parallel processing for complex tasks such as data inference or the incorporation of machine learning (ML) models has become a critical challenge. Recently, our team published a general architecture, composed of six interrelated components, that allows the grouping and organization of a diverse set of ML models or data inference methods adaptable for immersive environments. In this paper, we address initial ideas for an efficient implementation of the fourth component, "Task Orchestration and Scheduling," of this architecture. This component manages the concurrent execution of multiple models based on extracted features and user interactions. The objective of this work is to explore the role of software architectures in improving the multitasking experience of users interacting with immersive applications. We focus specifically on task scheduling, parallelism, and scalability. Furthermore, we provide interesting elements for efficient code development for parallel programming and show promising results comparing sequential and parallel programming approaches.

Keywords: Software architecture · Task scheduling · Parallel execution · Scalability · Immersive technologies · Machine Learning models

1 Introduction

In recent years, immersive technologies have gained significant traction, offering users highly interactive and dynamic environments. Extended reality (XR) is the term that encompasses a spectrum of immersive and interactive technologies. XR covers augmented reality (AR), mixed reality (MR), and virtual reality (VR). Interactions are part

C. Stephanidis et al. (Eds.): HCII 2025, CCIS 2773, pp. 254–264, 2026.
https://doi.org/10.1007/978-3-032-12773-0_25

of the hard core of immersive experiences, some authors consider that these experiences are exceptional due to the possibility of interacting with the world around us. It is currently possible to access immersive experiences through mobile devices, head-mounted displays (HMD), virtual reality glasses, and other technologies [1].

However, these technologies require increasingly sophisticated software architectures to provide more seamless and efficient user experiences. For this reason, the ability to support parallel processing for complex tasks like data inference, or the incorporation of machine learning models has become a critical challenge. To address this, researchers and engineers have been focusing on software engineering approaches that optimize concurrency and task scheduling, ensuring that computational workloads do not impede user experience. Studies in software architecture that focus on task parallelization and resource allocation have shown that using strategies such as multi-threading and parallel processing can significantly improve both performance and user satisfaction in multitasking environments. These architectural approaches are key to unlocking the full potential of immersive technologies by reducing latency and ensuring smoother interactions [2, 3].

Recently, new lines of work have emerged, such as Real-Time Multi-Model Multi-Task, which lay the foundation for the efficient use of key data inference techniques, such as the incorporation of machine learning models in areas such as XR. The central idea is to combine user interactivity in XR environments with computationally complex data inference activities such as machine learning. This combination generates a strong synergy that solves various problems by offering more engaging and sophisticated applications in immersive environments [4].

Following this line of research, just a year ago our team proposed a general architecture that allows for the incorporation, organization, and grouping of a set of data inference models and methods (ML models) adaptable to work in XR environments. These methods have special characteristics, as they must be adapted to provide real-time responses to user interactions with the environment and must also adapt to the characteristics and limitations of immersive environments. These methods are essential and useful for improving the performance of current and future systems [5].

Our proposed architecture consists of six main components. In this paper, we will address initial ideas for an efficient implementation of the fourth component, "Task Orchestration and Scheduling." This component manages the concurrent execution of multiple models based on the extracted features and user interactions. The principles of modern software architecture can improve multitasking performance in immersive technologies. We will particularly focus on task scheduling, parallelism, and scalability. We will explore techniques capable of managing the high computational loads typical of VR, AR, and other immersive environments [5].

This poster explores the role of software architectures in enhancing the multitasking experience for users interacting with immersive applications. Specifically, the design focuses on concurrent processing to optimize performance for applications that require real-time inference or other compute-intensive tasks. By leveraging principles of concurrent programming and task-based parallelism, we propose a technique that can efficiently handle multiple tasks, improving overall performance and responsiveness.

For better organization and description of the work results, the article has been divided into 5 sections: "Related Works" (Sect. 2), "General architecture. Development" (Sect. 3), "Software Architecture for developing the Task Orchestration and Scheduling layer" (Sect. 4). Finally, in Sect. 5, we present our "Conclusions", "Acknowledgments", and "References".

2 Related Works

To improve users' multitasking experience in immersive environments, some software architectural elements can be considered. For example, parallel processing, task separation, task scheduling, and multimodal interfaces allow for more efficient multi-tasking in mixed reality environments. Research on multitasking and parallel processing in virtual environments has explored several approaches to enhance overall performance.

Referring to parallel processing, in 1998, a software architecture was implemented where parallel processes are represented as nodes in a directed graph, with intelligent edges that determine how services between nodes should be dynamically managed [6]. More recent research explores several applications of parallelism and asynchrony in this context. Karpov et al. [7] demonstrate a parallel processing architecture for estimating oculomotor features in VR/AR platforms, improving speed and accuracy over serial implementations.

Just two years ago, in 2023, Zaripova et al. [8] provide a comprehensive overview of parallelism and asynchrony in high-performance software development, highlighting their importance in increasing efficiency across multiple domains, including GPU computations, distributed systems, and web development. These studies highlight the important role of previous approaches in improving computational performance, particularly when it comes to complex multitasking and processing big data and artificial intelligence models. As recently as last year, 2024, a hybrid CPU-GPU parallel computing model was presented for the representation of volumes with quality diversity, achieving significant improvements in execution time [9].

Another approach is related to the separation of tasks in immersive software environments, which can significantly improve performance, collaboration, and user experience. For example, in 2023 a multiagent framework that separates rendering processes from data management and communication tasks, improving collaborative processes in virtual reality applications was proposed [10].

Related to task scheduling, Dai et al. [11] proposed a task scheduling model for mobile devices that enhances user experience by prioritizing user-centric tasks and optimizing processor frequency. Experimental results demonstrated that this task scheduling model successfully achieves a trade-off between energy consumption and performance while improving user experience TASK-scheduling.

Finally, related to multimodal interfaces in immersive virtual environments, since 2015 there has been evidence that immersive virtual reality systems, such as HMDs, improve performance in online engineering design activities compared to non-immersive systems [12]. Furthermore, parallel views in VR allow users to view multiple locations simultaneously, potentially improving multi-embedding and reducing physical effort for complex tasks [13]. However, Kargut et al. [14], in 2024, cautioned that increasing immersion may not always benefit computational performance, finding that more immersive conditions led to worse selection performance and did not improve spatial learning in VR selection tasks. This suggests that the effectiveness of immersive environments may depend on the specific application and the requirements of the task being performed.

3 General Architecture. Development

In 2024, we presented an architectural proposal designed to efficiently incorporate, organize, and execute ML methods in XR environments. Its main objective is to ensure the execution of methods with data-based inference techniques and inductive learning that provide real-time responses to user interactions, considering the requirements and limitations of immersive environments. The following considerations were considered for its design: real-time performance, resource constraints, adaptability, scalability, heterogeneity, concurrency, and cascading and cascaded concurrency [5].

To ensure compliance with the above considerations, a layer-based architecture was created that incorporates the concepts of real-time multi-model multi-tasking (RT-MTMM) workloads [4]. This proposal is made up of the following layers: (1) Data acquisition, (2) Preprocessing and Feature Extraction, (3) Model Selection and Verification, (4) Task Orchestration and Scheduling, (5) Fusion and Post-processing, (6) XR Integration (Fig. 1) [5].

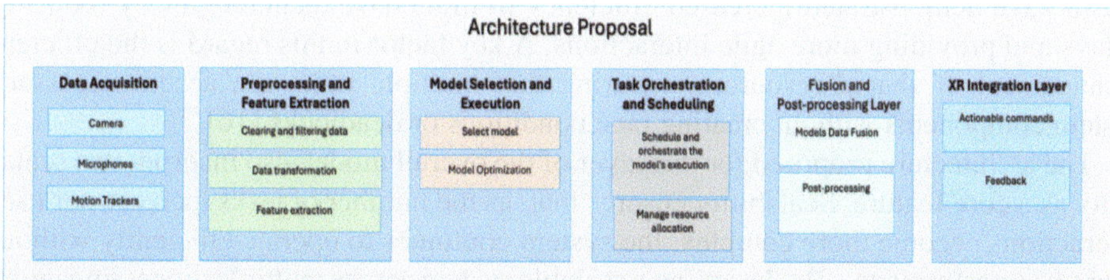

Fig. 1. Architecture Proposal for XR with Real-Time Multi-Model Capabilities (Figure taken from [5]).

In this paper, we will address several ideas for the development of the fourth layer, "Task orchestration and scheduling". However, it is important to highlight that due to the interrelationship between the architecture layers, the remaining layers may be affected by significant modifications.

Task orchestration and scheduling: This layer is responsible for managing the concurrent execution of multiple models, whether inference models or inductive models, responding to user iterations [4].

a) Scheduling and orchestrating the concurrent execution of multiple models: This step uses RT-MTMM workloads or similar techniques that help efficiently schedule concurrent tasks based on realistic deadlines, resource availability, and potential task dependencies.
b) Managing resource allocation: Ensures that available resources (processing power, memory) are efficiently distributed among concurrently executing models.

4 Software Architecture for Developing the Task Orchestration and Scheduling Layer

Modern software architecture principles can enhance multitasking performance in immersive technologies. Specifically, the design of this layer of the architecture focuses on concurrent processing to optimize performance for applications that require real-time inference or other compute-intensive tasks. By leveraging principles of concurrent programming and task-based parallelism, we propose a technique that can efficiently handle multiple tasks, improving overall performance and responsiveness [2].

The first key element in this layer's architecture is task scheduling. Efficient task scheduling is crucial in environments where multiple high-priority operations must be performed simultaneously, such as graphics rendering, user input processing, and real-time inference. Recent advances in dynamic task scheduling algorithms demonstrate how these methods can prevent bottlenecks in systems where both high- and low-priority tasks compete for CPU time. Our approach integrates these principles, allowing task balancing without significant overhead, ensuring smooth user experiences even during computationally intensive periods [15].

In addition to task scheduling, we consider the implementation of parallel task execution as a fundamental aspect of this architecture. Leveraging modern concurrency techniques, parallel execution allows multiple independent tasks to execute simultaneously, significantly reducing overall computing time. Architectures that utilize parallelism have demonstrated increased efficiency in immersive technologies by reducing delays and providing more agile interactions. A key factor in this regard is the efficient management of shared resources, ensuring that multiple tasks can access necessary system components without creating race conditions or deadlocks [16].

The architecture proposed for this layer of the overall model also incorporates scalability as a core feature. Scalability ensures that, as the number of tasks increases or user interactions become more complex, the system continues to operate efficiently without degrading performance. By designing a scalable system across multiple processing units, or cores, we address one of the key challenges of immersive technologies. Designing a scalable architecture supports the idea that well-structured, scalable systems are essential for modern multitasking in immersive applications. By combining these engineering techniques (task scheduling, parallel execution, and scalability), we propose a software architecture that can significantly improve the user multitasking experience in immersive technologies. Our technique efficiently balances task execution while maintaining high performance, ensuring that users can engage in complex, resource-intensive activities without interruptions or latency issues [17].

4.1 Experimental Setup. Parallel Execution Pipeline for Media Classification

The following experiments were developed to evaluate the proposed software architecture, which was designed for the efficient parallel execution of multiple AI routines in an immersive multimedia application. In general, this architecture should be functional and efficient enough to work with different methods and models (both AI and non-AI) that, due to their independence, can be executed in parallel.

To conduct this evaluation, a media classification problem was selected. A multimedia broadcast can be live or recorded, and in our case, it is delivered through Internet platforms. There are different multimedia elements that can be analyzed or classified, such as: text, which frequently appears in titles, subtitles, or headlines; images, along with text are the most basic multimedia elements; videos, which come in a wide variety of formats; music and audio; and so on.

Figure 2 shows a simplified parallelization scheme of the proposed software architecture.

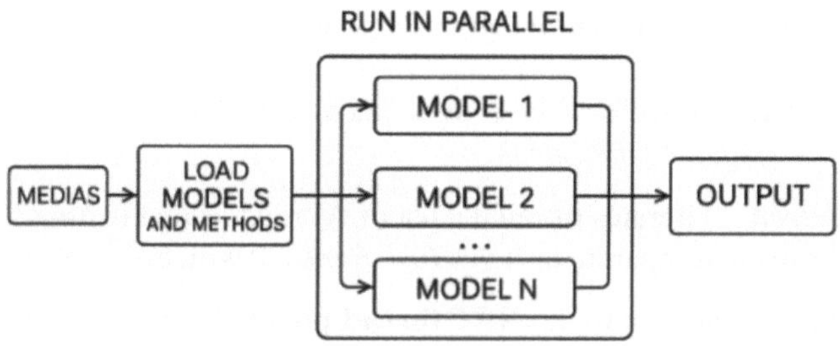

Fig. 2. Simplified parallelization scheme of the proposed software architecture.

Schema input (*"Medias" in Fig. 2*)**.** Multimedia or multimedia elements to be analyzed. For example, it could be just an audio fragment, a video frame, or just text.

Loading and initializing methods and models *("Load model and methods" in Fig. 2).* Several AI models or methods are preloaded into memory. Each model is trained, and each method is implemented for a specific task. For example, an image can be classified by its content (the objects it contains) or by its format (structural characteristics or patterns, independent of the objects or content it represents).

Parallel prediction tasks *("Run in parallel" in Fig. 2)***.** For example, using C#'s Task class and a thread pool, each method or model executes in parallel. These methods and models have different objectives and are independent of each other. A case with three classification tasks could be:

- A first task is solved using an AI model for text analysis or classification, or sentiment analysis.
- A second task is solved using a method with digital image processing (DIP) techniques to classify frames according to their content.
- A final task is solved using another AI model, in this case for audio analysis and classification.

In this way, video-type multimedia could be analyzed, analyzing each multimedia element (text, frames, audio) in parallel using an independent schema.

Output. Aggregation and Decision-Making (*Output*)**.** Once all the tasks are completed, the results are aggregated. A decision engine prioritizes the results based on confidence scores and redundancy checks. The final unified classification label is generated.

4.2 Ideas for Multi-Threaded Execution in Unity Using C# Tasks.

In the following section we will describe some interesting ideas that can be used to integrate and parallelize different tasks within a pipeline within the Unity platform using C#.

- The pipeline is integrated into a Unity-based immersive application.
- Execution is orchestrated using *Task.Run()* with *Task.WhenAll()* to coordinate parallel execution.

To implement the parallel pipeline, we utilize the C# Task API, which abstracts the low-level thread management and integrates a pool-based execution model to optimize the use of processor cores.

Parallel Task Creation for AI Models. *TaskList = ModelList.Select(model = > Task.Run(() = > model.Predict(media)));*

1. *ModelList.Select(...)* iterates through a list of AI models and methods.
2. Each model runs in a separate task via *Task.Run(...)*, which:
   - Queues the operation into the**.NET thread pool** *(ThreadPool)*, which manages a pool of worker threads.
   - These worker threads are reused across the application to reduce context-switching overhead and memory cost of creating new threads.
3. The *Predict(media)* method executes the AI model inference or the classification method in general using the *input media.*

CPU Cores: The thread pool schedules these tasks based on system availability, often aligning them with physical or logical CPU cores. On multi-core systems, this allows true concurrent execution of the AI models.

Parallel Task for Processing DIP method.*DIP_Task = Task.Run(() = > DIP Processor.Analyze(media));*

1. Simultaneously, a separate task is dispatched to run a PDI processing.
2. This runs independently of the model predictions and is enqueued in the same thread pool.

Task Synchronization.
AllTasks = ModelTasks.Append(DIP_Task);
Task.WhenAll(AllTasks);

1. *ModelTasks.Append(DIP_Task)* combines all AI model tasks and the DIP processing task into a single list.
2. *Task.WhenAll(...)* asynchronously waits for the completion of all tasks.
   - This ensures the main thread (or caller) only resumes once all processing has completed.
   - It also avoids unnecessary polling or manual synchronization via locks.

Results Aggregation.
Predictions = ModelTasks.Select(predictionTask = > predictionTask.Result);
PDI_Result = PDI_Task.Result;

1. Retrieves the prediction results from the completed AI model tasks.
2. Retrieves the result from the DIP task.

Final Decision Logic.
Aggregator.Decide(Predictions, PDI_Result);

1. Combines both AI models and traditional DIP results to infer the final-result.
2. This method may apply a decision-tree or weighted voting mechanism to resolve conflicts.

Thread Pool and Core Utilization in.NET. The C# Task system relies on the ThreadPool, a managed pool of threads created by the runtime:

- Threads are mapped dynamically to logical or physical CPU cores.
- The scheduler minimizes the number of idle threads and reuses them for lightweight or I/O-bound tasks.
- On modern CPUs (e.g., 8-core or 16-thread), the thread pool allows full core utilization up to system limits.

This model enables efficient scaling of parallel workloads, making it ideal for computational tasks like model inference and image processing that are independent and can run concurrently.

Advantages of this architecture.

- Minimal Latency. Parallelism reduces total processing time.
- CPU Efficiency..NET manages threads across cores automatically.
- Scalability. Adding more models or tasks does not increase latency linearly.
- Unity Compatibility. All heavy processing occurs off the main thread, pre-serving UI and rendering performance.

4.3 Experimental Example. Results

A generic experimental situation was designed as an example to establish a practical comparison between two programming approaches, sequential and parallel. In this experimental example, three machine learning models and two DIP methods were used. Table 1 shows the results of these five methods and models, considering two key parameters: memory usage and execution time for each task.

The results described in Table 1 show a significant difference in execution time between the two programming approaches, sequential and parallel. The parallel execution approach guarantees statistically more promising execution times in all cases. On the other hand, no statistically proven differences were found regarding memory usage, although it is important to note that the sequential paradigm yielded slightly lower values in all cases.

Table 1. Execution results of PDI methods and ML models using two different programming approaches: sequential and parallel. Two fundamental parameters were evaluated: memory usage and execution time.

Media	Parallel		Sequential	
	Time (ms)	Mem. Avg (KB)	Time (ms)	Mem. Avg (KB)
Method 1 (DIP)	6559.31	740.6	24632.3	647.3
Method 2 (DIP)	6486.07	487.4	24380.53	439.1
Model-1 (ML)	7845.47	1268.7	24827.6	993.9
Model-2 (ML)	7395.4	1246.8	25439.87	911.9
Model-3 (ML)	7982.4	1230.7	25510.1	971.4

5 Conclusions

This work addresses some theoretical and practical ideas for the efficient implementation of part of a general architectural proposal designed to group and organize a diverse set of ML models and inference methods for use in immersive environments. The theoretical design of this architectural proposal, composed of six interrelated main components, was published just over a year ago. Specifically, this paper began the development of the fourth component of this architecture, which has been named "Task Orchestration and Scheduling." This component manages the concurrent execution of multiple models based on the extracted features and user interactions.

In developing this component, our main objective was to implement an efficient software architecture to improve the multitasking experiences of users interacting with immersive applications. For this reason, we focused on three fundamental elements: task scheduling, parallelism, and scalability. The main results derived from the implementation process of this objective were:

- As a first result, a task parallelization scheme was designed that allowed us to organize the simultaneous execution of different complex methods and models, such as models derived from ML tasks.
- As a second result, from a practical perspective, an experimental design was created that allowed us to compare our parallel task execution scheme with a traditional sequential scheme. Based on the designed experiments, it was possible to demonstrate that parallel task execution guarantees statistically shorter execution times in all the cases analyzed. However, the sequential scheme showed better values in terms of memory usage.
- Finally, the main ideas used to efficiently implement the parallel pipeline in the C# Task API on the Unity platform were included in the work. This API abstracts low-level thread management and integrates a pool-based execution model to optimize the use of processor cores.

Acknowledgments. This paper was presented as part of the results of the Project "SIDIA_M_VST_PLATFORM_AND_APPLICATIONS", carried out by the Institute of Science and Technology – SIDIA, in partnership with Samsung Electrônica da Amazônia LTDA, in accordance with the Information Technology Law n.8387/91 and article at the. 39 of Decree 10,521/2020.

References

1. Gupta, Y., Mukul, Gupta, N.: Deep learning model-based multimedia retrieval and its optimization in augmented reality applications. Multimed Tools Appl. **82**, 8447–8466 (2023). https://doi.org/10.1007/s11042-022-13555-y
2. Stan, R.-G., Băjenaru, L., Negru, C., Pop, F.: Evaluation of task scheduling algorithms in heterogeneous computing environments. Sensors **21**(17), 5906 (2021). https://doi.org/10.3390/s21175906
3. Maurya, R., adn Tripathi, D.: Benchmarking Task Scheduling Algorithms in Heterogeneous Computing Environments. arXiv Preprint. arXiv:2405.08187 (2018)
4. Kwon, H., et al.: XRBench: an extended reality (XR) machine learning benchmark suite for the metaverse. Proceedings of the 6th MLSys Conference, Miami Beach, FL, USA, 2023.2211.08675, arXiv, http://arxiv.org/abs/2211.08675/ (2023)
5. . Amorim, G., et al.: Study and development of machine learning models designed for extended reality interactivity in real-time. HCII-2024 Conference, volume 66, LNCS-15377, Late Breaking Work (2024)
6. Choi, I., Bargar, R.: Human-machine performance configuration for multidimensional and multi-modal interaction in virtual environments. In: Proceedings Fourth Annual Symposium on Human Interaction with Complex Systems, pp. 99–111 (1998). IEEE
7. Karpov, A., Liberman, J., Lohr, D., Komogortsev, O.: Parallel Oculomotor Plant Mathematical Model for Large Scale Eye Movement Simulation. arXiv preprint arXiv:2007.09884 (2020)
8. Zaripova, R., Mentsiev, A., Perukhin, M.: Integrating parallelism and asynchrony for high-performance software development. In: E3S Web of Conferences, Vol. 460. EDP Sciences (2023)
9. Butincu, C.N., Gavrilescu, M.: CPU-GPU parallelism applied to quality-diversity volume rendering. In: 2024 28th International Conference on System Theory, Control and Computing (ICSTCC), pp. 576–581 (2024). IEEE
10. Conesa, J., Mula, F., Contero, M., Camba, J.D.: A multi-agent framework for collaborative geometric modeling in virtual environments. Eng. Appl. Artif. Intell. **123**, 106257 (2023)
11. Dai, J., Liu, W., Lin, X., Ye, Y., Xiao, C., Wu, K.: User experience enhanced task scheduling and processor frequency scaling for energy-sensitive mobile devices. In: IEEE 17th International Conference on High Performance Computing and Communications, 2015 IEEE 7th International Symposium on Cyberspace Safety and Security, and 2015 IEEE 12th Inter-national Conference on Embedded Software and Systems, pp. 941–944. IEEE
12. Bharathi, A., Tucker, C.: Investigating the impact of interactive immersive virtual reality environments in enhancing task performance in online engineering design activities. In: International Design Engineering Technical Conferences and Computers and Information in Engineering Conference, Vol. 57106 (2015)
13. Teo, T., Sakurada, K., Sugimoto, M.: Exploring enhancements towards gaze oriented parallel views in immersive tasks. In: IEEE Conference Virtual Reality and 3D User Interfaces (VR), pp. 620–630. IEEE (2023)
14. Kargut, K., Gutwin, C., Cockburn, A.: Effects of device environment and information layout on spatial memory and performance in VR selection tasks. In: Proceedings of the CHI Conference on Human Factors in Computing Systems, pp. 1–17 (2024)

15. George Amalarethinam, D.I., Maria Josphin, A.: Dynamic task scheduling methods in heterogeneous systems- a survey. International Journal of Computer Applications **110**(6) (2015)
16. Prasad, A., Benini, L., Conti, F.: Specialization meets flexibility: a heterogeneous architecture for high-efficiency, high-flexibility AR/VR processing. In: 60th ACM/IEEE Design Automation Conference (DAC), San Francisco, CA, USA, pp. 1–6 (2023). https://doi.org/10.1109/DAC56929.2023.10247945
17. Jeffrey, M.C., Subramanian, S., Yan, C., Emer, J., Sanchez, D.: A scalable architecture for ordered parallelism. In Proceedings of the 48th International Symposium on Microarchitecture, USA (2015). https://doi.org/10.1145/2830772.2830777

Gesture-Driven AR for Industrial Production Lines: Insights from a Field Trial

Katerina Valakou[1], George Margetis[1(✉)], Stavroula Ntoa[1], and Constantine Stephanidis[1,2]

[1] Institute of Computer Science, Foundation for Research and Technology—Hellas (FORTH), 70013 Heraklion, Crete, Greece
{valakou,gmarget,stant,cs}@ics.forth.gr
[2] University of Crete, Heraklion, Greece

Abstract. Gesture-based interaction in Augmented Reality (AR) offers new possibilities for enhancing operator support in industrial environments, enabling intuitive, hands-free control of digital systems during physical tasks. This study investigates the usability and user experience of an AR application for defect inspection and equipment calibration in microchip production lines. A user-based evaluation was conducted onsite with ten factory employees performing scenario-driven tasks in a real production setting, following a structured evaluation methodology for the collection of quantitative and qualitative data. The results showed that the AR user interface was clear to understand and that gesture-based interaction was intuitive. The findings suggest that gestures can be effectively used in industrial contexts for hands-free interaction and underscore the potential of AR in supporting decision-making on the factory floor, while also identifying design challenges relevant to the broader integration of AR in manufacturing workflows. The adopted evaluation methodology provides a general-purpose approach for assessing gesture-driven AR systems across diverse application domains.

Keywords: User-based evaluation · Methodology · User Experience · Gesture-based Interaction · Augmented Reality · Defect Inspection · Industry 4.0

1 Introduction

Modern industrial production lines increasingly rely on real-time data and automation to ensure high product quality, minimize defects, and support operator efficiency. Technologies like Internet of Things (IoT), cloud manufacturing, big data, augmented reality (AR), etc., are used in tandem with concepts and techniques of traditional industrial production to maximize effectiveness and efficiency [1]. As factories adopt digital transformation strategies, the role of human operators remains critical, particularly in tasks that require domain expertise,

C. Stephanidis et al. (Eds.): HCII 2025, CCIS 2773, pp. 265–277, 2026.
https://doi.org/10.1007/978-3-032-12773-0_26

careful visual inspection, and adaptive decision-making. Nevertheless, several challenges arise for technology adoption by workers, necessitating high-quality education, aligning digital tools with work tasks, and offering user-friendly digital solutions [2]. In this context, AR technologies are emerging as powerful tools for enhancing situational awareness, supporting task execution, and minimizing cognitive and physical workload by overlaying relevant information directly within the operator's field of view [3,4].

This work explores a gesture-based AR application, designed for defect inspection and equipment calibration in a microchip production environment. Through the AR application, critical information regarding defects in the production line is overlaid onto the physical environment, aiming to support operators in performing their tasks with enhanced precision and awareness. The developed AR application utilizes gesture-based interaction to allow hands-free control of the interface, enabling users to inspect printed circuit boards (PCBs), identify glue defects, and adjust equipment parameters directly through hand movements [5], assisted by computer vision [6] and Artificial Intelligence [7] technologies for automated defect detection. To improve the user experience and support safe, efficient task execution, the interface dynamically presents visual cues, gesture prompts, and system feedback aligned with each operational step. These interface elements are designed to minimize cognitive load and maintain situational awareness by integrating information in context-sensitive ways [8]. The gesture vocabulary adopts the classification described in Gavgiotaki et al. [9]. In particular, users select user interface (UI) menu items (first, second, third, etc.) by performing finger-count gestures and can also perform a close fist gesture to stop the production line, if any defect is detected. By adopting hands-free interaction, the application aims to improve usability, facilitate natural task execution, and ensure that operators remain focused on their environment and tasks without the need to handle physical controls or external devices. A conceptual overview of the AR solution is provided by Margetis et al. [10]. The current study focuses on evaluating the developed prototype under realistic industrial conditions, exploring its usability, user acceptance, and integration into daily workflows.

In more detail, the main objective of this study was to evaluate the effectiveness, usability, and user experience of the gesture-driven AR interface under realistic working conditions. The evaluation was conducted as an in-situ study to better understand the experience, interactions and context in which the system will be operated [11], with actual production staff at a microchip manufacturing facility, using scenario-based tasks grounded in real operational needs. Participants interacted with the system through commercially available AR glasses and were asked to complete a series of inspection and calibration scenarios. The study followed a structured methodology combining task performance metrics, standardized usability questionnaires (SEQ and SUS), and post-task interviews to capture both quantitative and qualitative insights. To assess how gesture-based AR systems can support zero-defect manufacturing goals by enhancing operators' interaction with complex systems, improving their situational awareness, and reducing potential sources of error. We also identify challenges related to gesture design, interface readability, and device comfort, which are crucial considerations for the adoption of such technologies in industrial environments. The findings contribute to the broader discourse on how human-centered design principles can be applied to the deployment of AR in manufacturing, offering practical insights into the opportunities and limitations of gesture-based interaction in high-demand operational contexts.

The structure of the paper is as follows: Sect. 2 reviews related work and provides the background relevant to this study. Section 3 describes the evaluation methodology and procedure. Section 4 presents the results of the user-based evaluation. Finally, Sect. 5 concludes the paper and outlines directions for future research.

2 Background and Related Work

User-based evaluation is a well-established approach in Human-Computer Interaction (HCI) for assessing the usability, performance, and acceptance of interactive systems. It involves collecting direct feedback from users through structured testing, questionnaires, and interviews to identify usability issues and evaluate the overall user experience. The primary goal is to ensure that the system meets user expectations and supports task efficiency in real-world conditions.

Prior research regarding user-based evaluation for AR applications has emphasized the importance of assessing user experience (UX) and usability to ensure that AR interfaces are intuitive and effective. Dünser et al. (2011) explored various evaluation methodologies for AR systems, focusing mainly on task performance metrics [12]. However, task completion alone is insufficient for capturing the full spectrum of user experience in AR, particularly given its spatial and context-dependent nature. As a result, more recent studies have adopted mixed-methods approaches, combining quantitative indicators, such as success rates and user satisfaction per task, with qualitative feedback, and standardized questionnaires to provide a more comprehensive evaluation of AR interfaces [13]. At the same time, aiming to fully capture not only user perceptions but also actual user performance, which often provide different perspectives, it is recommended to combine subjective metrics with objective observations [14,15].

Evaluating AR applications that incorporate gesture-based interaction presents additional challenges due to the embodied nature of input and the need for accurate recognition across diverse environments in varying lighting conditions. Prior work has explored gesture-based AR interfaces in fields such as industrial assembly, maintenance, and training, where hands-free operation is critical for task efficiency and safety [16,17]. Studies have shown that while gesture interaction can improve user engagement and reduce reliance on external controllers, it can also introduce usability issues related to gesture memorability, physical fatigue, and recognition errors in uncontrolled settings [18]. User-based evaluations of such systems frequently involve scenario-based tasks to assess how gestures perform under realistic operational constraints [19]. Findings across the literature suggest that the success of gesture-based AR systems depends not only on technical recognition accuracy but also on how well the interaction model aligns with users' mental models and task flows [9]. As such, evaluations must consider gesture fluency, user comfort, and the adaptability of the system to real-world conditions. Furthermore, challenges remain in standardizing evaluation protocols due to the diversity of AR use cases, devices, user contexts, and interaction methods, underscoring the need for adaptable and user-centered evaluation frameworks [12,20].

Given the dynamic nature of industrial environments, where unexpected defects in the production line can occur at any time, evaluating AR systems under realistic conditions is essential. Laboratory simulations can offer controlled testing conditions, but they cannot always capture the practical constraints, physical workflows, or cognitive demands experienced on the factory floor. For this reason, the present study adopts a scenario-based, user-centered methodology conducted on-site in a real production line.

3 User-Based Evaluation

3.1 Method and Procedure

The user-based evaluation focused on assessing the usability and user experience of a gesture-based AR application designed for defect inspection and equipment calibration in production lines. The application enables users to perform PCB inspections and adjust glue pressure settings using hand gestures to interact with the developed AR interface. The evaluation took place in an operational production line area, where participants were free to move naturally around the workspace. The setup included AR glasses, a laptop for monitoring, three defective PCBs (including one placed inside a mock machine enclosure), and two printed quick-reference guides, allowing first-time users to familiarize themselves with the gestures' vocabulary.

Before the evaluation began, participants were informed about the study's objectives, the procedures involved, and their rights regarding data protection and voluntary participation. After addressing any questions, each participant provided written consent. The evaluation was structured as a scenario-based study to reflect real-world use cases, focusing on the effectiveness of the interface and the naturalness of the gesture vocabulary. The facilitator explained to participants the interaction with the system and a printed set of gestures and their functionalities was handed out, explaining to participants that they could consult it when needed, particularly considering that they were all first-time users of the system. Throughout the sessions, the facilitator observed participants' behavior, noting task success, errors, help requests, and spontaneous remarks. Participants were encouraged to follow the think-aloud protocol [21], verbalizing their thoughts during the tasks. Two standardized instruments supported the evaluation: the Single Ease Question (SEQ) [22] to measure perceived difficulty after each scenario, and the System Usability Scale (SUS) [23] for overall usability assessment. The evaluation concluded with semi-structured interviews aimed at gathering user feedback, highlighting both positive aspects and areas for improvement.

3.2 Scenarios

Interaction was structured around two main scenarios, one for inspecting the PCBs in production and one for monitoring PCBs that were not directly visible to the worker.

Scenario 1: Inspect the PCBs in production

Task 1.1 – Start the system: From the initial screen of the application, users can perform the gesture for initiating the system. An icon showcasing the gesture from the initial screen will then disappear, and the system will be ready to use.

Task 1.2 - Select the appropriate menu item to start the PCB inspection: In the initial screen of the application, there is a menu with two options. To initiate the PCB inspection process, the user has to select the first menu item with the corresponding finger-count gesture. The task is successful when the user performs the gesture correctly and a pop-up message with further instructions shows up on the screen.

Task 1.3 - Initiate defect analysis of the first PCB and view results: The popup message prompts the user to place the first PCB for inspection in their field of view and indicates the gesture the user has to perform to begin the inspection process. This task is considered successful if the user is able to view the detected defects and point out the defective, good and acceptable microchips, providing information about their status.

Task 1.4 - Initiate defect analysis of the second PCB and view results: The second PCB, which is a different type from the first one, is placed in the glue dispensing machine. The same procedure has to be followed with the user placing the PCB in front of them and inspecting it, assisted by the system.

Task 1.5 – Calibrate the glue pressure: A popup message indicates that the AI suggests an adjustment of the glue dispensing pressure. For the scenario purposes, users were asked to say that they don't agree and adjust the pressure manually, performing the correct gesture. A side menu then shows up on the screen, indicating the gestures for increasing or decreasing the pressure. Participants were tasked to increase the pressure by 5%. This task is considered successful if the user is able to perform the correct gesture for increasing the pressure and understand that the pressure is increased.

Task 1.6 – Exit the inspection process: Users were then asked to complete the inspection process by performing the thumps-up gesture.

Scenario 2: Monitoring the PCBs

In this scenario, users were tasked to monitor PCBs that were not directly visible, being inside a closed machine. For the purposes of the experiment, a prototype of this closed machine was set up in the evaluation room, as depicted in Fig. 1. A PCB was placed inside this prototype. The facilitator explained the concept to the participants, asking them to imagine that they were dealing with an actual closed machine.

Fig. 1. Prototype of a closed machine with the PCB inside and AR application output

Task 2.1 - Select the appropriate menu item to start monitoring the PCB: The user has to select the second menu item with the finger-count gesture. The task is successful when the user performs the correct gesture, and a pop-up message with further instructions shows up on the screen.

Task 2.2 - Initiate defect analysis and view results: The popup message instructs users to look towards the machine and what gesture to perform to begin the inspection process. This task is considered successful if the user is able to see the PCB inside the machine and report that it is defective, identifying the number of microchips with excessive glue.

Task 2.3 – Stop the production line: When the system identifies a defective PCB, it prompts the user through a popup message to stop the production line, by performing the close fist gesture. The task is successful if the user performs the correct gesture.

3.3 Participants

The evaluation was conducted on-site at the production line, with all participants being employees of the facility. A total of 10 users took part—2 females and 8 males—ranging in age from 18 to 54 years. The age distribution was as follows: 10% aged 18–24, 40% aged 25–34, 20% aged 35–44, 20% aged 45–54, and 10% aged 55–64. Participants under 35 generally had less than 5 years of professional experience, while those over 35 had more than 10 years. Their roles within the company included engineers, technicians, and managers. While most participants were familiar with using computer applications in their daily work, none had prior experience with AR systems.

4 Results

This section presents the key findings from the evaluation conducted at the production line. It begins with an analysis of task performance based on observed user success during the experiment. Participant satisfaction with each task is then assessed through responses to the Single Ease Question (SEQ). Perceptions of overall system usability are drawn from the System Usability Scale

(SUS) scores. Finally, qualitative insights from the semi-structured debriefing interviews are summarized, highlighting user impressions and suggestions for improvement.

4.1 Task Success

Users achieved a 95% success rate in completing the tasks. Notably, all participants successfully completed the tasks related to the selection of menu items (Tasks 1.2 and 2.1). A key focal point of the evaluation was on Tasks 1.3, 1.4, 1.5, and 2.2, which required users to understand the system's output, identify defects on PCBs (Tasks 1.3, 1.4, 2.2), and calibrate the glue pressure (Task 1.5). For these tasks, the overall success rate was 95%. Specifically, 90% of users successfully completed Tasks 1.3 and 1.5, while 100% of users successfully completed Tasks 1.4 and 2.2. In Task 1.3, one participant partially succeeded by confusing the color indication of borderline acceptable microchips (yellow) with normal ones (green). In Task 1.5, one participant initially failed to see the side menu for gesture options, even after facilitator assistance. Despite performing the correct gestures for calibrating the pressure, this task is considered partially successful. Additionally, two other users commented that they had difficulty seeing the side menu clearly due to the variance in ergonomics when wearing the AR glasses visors.

All participants successfully completed Tasks 1.6 and 2.3, performing the correct gestures for completing the inspection process and stopping the production line, respectively. Users appreciated the application's provision of gesture icons at each step, which made it easy for them as they did not need to remember the gestures. However, Task 1.1 had the lowest success rate at 80%. Based on the facilitator's notes, this may be attributed to it being the first task, with participants not yet familiar with the system and the correct gestures. Two participants who partially succeeded performed the correct gesture to initiate the system, but did not realize the system was initiated because they could not see the corresponding icon located at the top right corner of the screen.

In a nutshell, Tasks 1.2, 1.4, 1.6, 2.1, 2.2, and 2.3 were fully successful, while Tasks 1.1, 1.3, and 1.5 were partially successful by 20%, 10%, and 10%, respectively. Figure 2 illustrates the success rates of individual tasks along with the overall performance.

4.2 Satisfaction per Task

In this section, we are discussing the satisfaction of the participants regarding each task, based on their responses to the SEQ questionnaire. Participants were asked to rate the difficulty of each task on a scale from 1 (= very difficult) to 7 (= very easy). User satisfaction per task is depicted in Fig. 3 and user satisfaction per scenario is illustrated in Table 1, demonstrating that participants were highly satisfied overall.

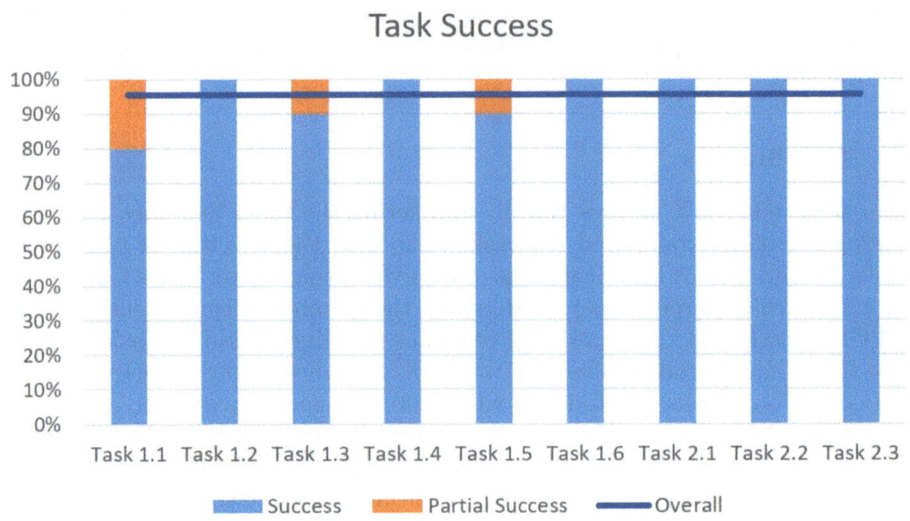

Fig. 2. Task Success and Overall.

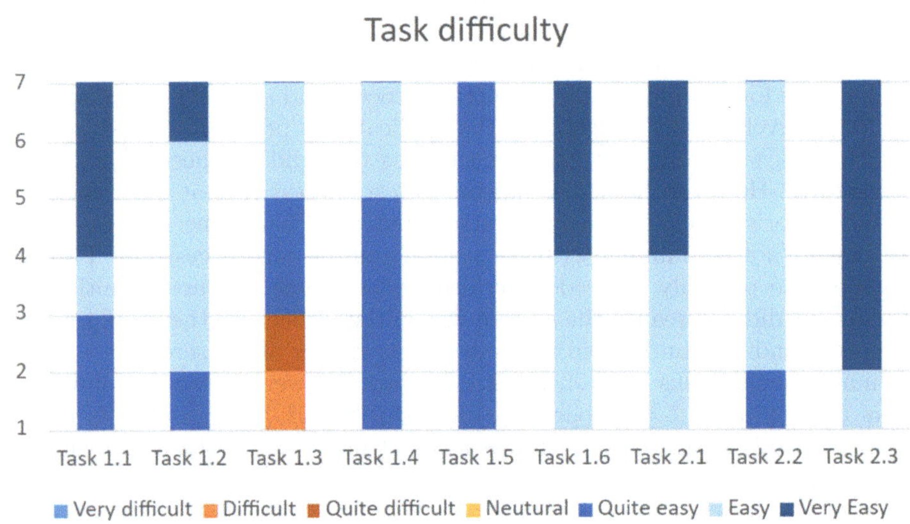

Fig. 3. Task Satisfaction.

Table 1. Average and Standard Deviation Satisfaction per scenario and overall

	Task 1.1	Task 1.2	Task 1.3	Task 1.4	Task 1.5	Task 1.6	Task 2.1	Task 2.2	Task 2.3	Overall
Average	6.1	6	4.7	5.5	5	6.5	6.5	5.9	6.8	5.9
SD	1.4	1.2	1.9	1.5	1.1	0.7	0.7	1.2	0.4	1.1

4.3 System Usability

The SUS questionnaire findings were also very encouraging. The average SUS score was 75.3%, as depicted in Fig. 4, with Standard Deviation 0.8, exceeding the required acceptability threshold of 70% [24]. Thus, the results indicate that the system usability scored a B grade (i.e., between 74.1% and 77.1%) [23], indicating a quite satisfactory performance.

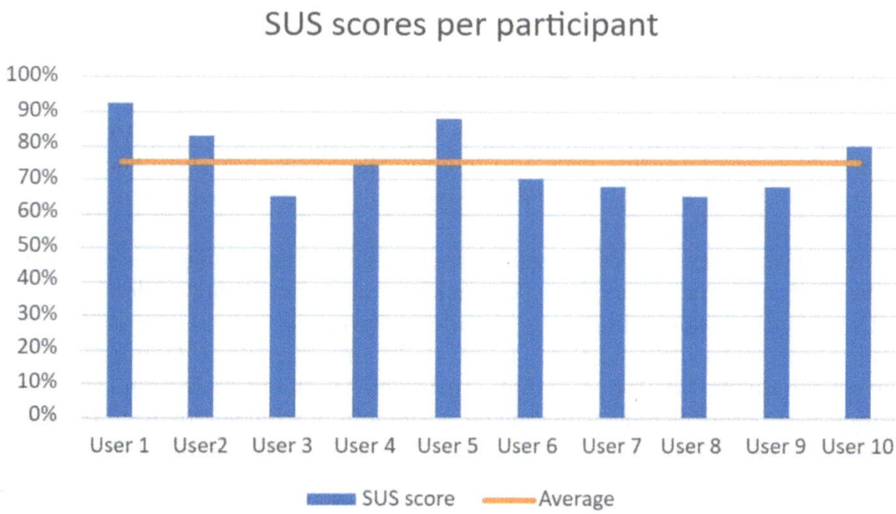

Fig. 4. SUS scores per participant.

4.4 User Impressions

In the final phase of the evaluation, there was a semi-structured interview with each participant. These interviews were very informative on their opinions on the system and provided useful information for future improvements. Participants were asked about their overall impression of the system, what they liked and disliked most, and if they had any suggestions for improvement. The findings are the following:

- All the users liked the system.
- Only two users felt slight nausea while wearing the AR glasses.
- All participants agreed with the AI suggestion for the glue pressure adjustment.
- All of the participants claimed that the system could assist them in becoming more aware of a situation at hand since it provides real-time information. Also, most of the participants would use it in their daily operations, except for one user, because of the headset. In addition, one participant claimed that they would use it for inspection, because it provides a lot of useful information, but not for more complex tasks.

- Approximately 20% of participants expressed concerns about using the AR headset during long shifts due to its weight.

The attributes of the system that were praised by the users were the following:

- The amount of information that is visualized
- The clarity and the simplicity of the UIs
- The interaction with the gestures
- The hands-free interaction
- The ease-of-use
- The provision of real-time feedback

On the other hand, some improvements that users mentioned are to bring the camera closer to the user's eyes and enlarge the icons that show the gestures, making them more visually distinctive, since they are really helpful but not clear to all.

Users have suggested a few improvements, including a longer cable between the headset and the smartphone or making the connection wireless. Regarding the UI, users would like more detailed information about the PCBs, such as their type, material, and the type of glue being dispensed. One user recommended enhancing safety in a manufacturing environment by having the system automatically stop visualizations when it detects movement, or by including a button to manually stop the visualizations if needed. Additionally, an interesting suggestion was to include an overlay for gestures, showing how to perform them and indicating which gesture the system recognizes.

It is worth noting that 70% of the users praised the ease of use of the system regarding both the UI and the gesture-based interaction. All users appreciated the inclusion of icons with the gestures, as it alleviates the need to memorize the entire vocabulary, particularly during initial use. One participant remarked: *"The gesture-based controls are intuitive and straightforward. I liked the interface because it allows workers to remain aware of their surroundings."* One other participant said: *"It is a very good product with many potentials. I would use it today!"*

5 Conclusions and Future Work

This paper has presented a user-centered evaluation for assessing gesture-based interaction in AR applications within industrial settings. The methodology was applied to evaluate an AR system designed to support defect inspection and equipment calibration in a microchip production line. The system aims to enhance operators' situational awareness and safety while enabling hands-free task execution.

The evaluation methodology combined scenario-based task execution with mixed-methods data collection, including direct observation, standardized usability questionnaires (SEQ and SUS), and semi-structured interviews. This approach proved appropriate for assessing the naturalness and effectiveness of gesture-based interaction in AR, as it reflected real-world workflows and captured both objective performance data and subjective user experience. The inclusion of think-aloud protocols and post-task interviews allowed for insight into user perceptions, usability issues, and design limitations. Given its flexibility and emphasis on contextual validity, this methodology is suited for evaluating other AR or XR systems involving embodied interaction, in domains such as manufacturing, maintenance, training, or healthcare, where hands-free operation and intuitive control are critical for safety and task performance. The applied evaluation approach and its outcomes emphasize the importance of systematic, user-centered assessment in advancing the deployment of AR technologies in real industrial settings.

The results of the user-based evaluation provide strong evidence for the usability and effectiveness of the developed gesture-based AR system. All ten participants, employees at the microchip production line, completed the scenario-based tasks with a high success rate of 95%, and no user failed any task. The average ease-of-use rating of 5.9 out of 7 reflects a generally positive user experience, particularly in terms of task intuitiveness and interaction flow. These findings suggest that gesture-based AR interfaces can successfully support industrial inspection and calibration tasks when aligned with users' workflows. Two key areas for improvement emerged from the evaluation: the learnability of the system for first-time users, and the clarity of the interface elements. Although the system is not intended to be used without prior training, feedback emphasized the importance of clearer visual guidance during initial use. Importantly, all participants reported increased situational awareness when using the system, and 90% stated they would incorporate it into their daily tasks—highlighting its perceived practical value. Concerns were raised regarding the comfort of the AR headset over long shifts and a general hesitation toward replacing familiar tools with new technologies. Nevertheless, users consistently praised the hands-free interaction and the intuitive gesture design. Overall, the evaluation confirms the potential of context-aware AR systems to enhance operator efficiency and awareness in industrial environments, while also underscoring the need for ergonomic refinement and sustained user onboarding strategies.

Future work will focus on studying AR gesture-based applications in additional domains, such as healthcare, training, remote assistance, and omni-conferences, to explore common concerns and differences, contributing to the discussion on usable and useful AR systems for enhanced situational awareness. In addition, future work will focus on the development of generalizable guidelines for designing AR systems in complex environments.

Acknowledgments. This work has received funding from the EU's Horizon Europe research and innovation programme under Grant Agreement No 958264 (OPTIMAI). This paper reflects only the authors' views and the Commission is not responsible for any use that may be made of the information it contains.

References

1. Reljić, V., Milenković, I., Dudić, S., Šulc, J., Bajči, B.: Augmented reality applications in industry 4.0 environment. Appl. Sci. **11**, 5592 (2021). https://doi.org/10.3390/app11125592
2. Kans, M., Campos, J.: Digital capabilities driving industry 4.0 and 5.0 transformation: insights from an interview study in the maintenance domain. J. Open Innovation Technol. Market Complexity **10**(4), 100384 (2024). https://doi.org/10.1016/j.joitmc.2024.100384
3. Bottani, E.; Vignali, G.: Augmented reality technology in the manufacturing industry: a review of the last decade. Iise Trans. **51**(3), 284–310 (2019). https://doi.org/10.1080/24725854.2018.1493244
4. Szymon, M., Chamier-Gliszczyński, N., Królikowski, T.: Application of AR/VR technology in industry 4.0. Procedia Comput. Sci. **207**, 2990–2998 (2022). https://doi.org/10.1016/j.procs.2022.09.357
5. Margetis, G., et al.: An Elevator Calibration Recommender System for Effective Defect Detection and Prevention, Eccomas Proceedia: Crete. Greece (2023). https://doi.org/10.7712/150123.9871.446205
6. Karakostas, I., et al.: A real-time wearable AR system for egocentric vision on the edge. Virtual Reality **28**, 44 (2024). https://doi.org/10.1007/s10055-023-00937-2
7. Tziolas, T., et al.: Explainable AI methods for identification of glue volume deficiencies in printed circuit boards. Appl. Sci. **15**, 9061 (2025). https://doi.org/10.3390/app15169061
8. Stefanidi, Z., Margetis, G., Ntoa, S., Papagiannakis, G.: Real-time adaptation of context-aware intelligent user interfaces for enhanced situational awareness. IEEE Access **10**, 23367–23393 (2022). https://doi.org/10.1109/ACCESS.2022.3152743
9. Gavgiotaki, D., Ntoa, S., Margetis, G., Apostolakis, K.C., Stephanidis, C.: Gesture-based interaction for AR systems: a short review. In: Proceedings of the 16th International Conference on PErvasive Technologies Related to Assistive Environments(PETRA '23), pp. 284–292. ACM, Corfu, Greece (2023). https://doi.org/10.1145/3594806.3594815
10. Margetis, G., Valakou, K., Ntoa, S., Gavgiotaki, D., Stephanidis, C.: Adaptive augmented reality user interfaces for real-time defect visualization and on-the-fly reconfiguration for zero-defect manufacturing. Sensors **25**(9), 2789 (2025). https://doi.org/10.3390/s25092789
11. Whitlock, M., et al.: MRCAT: in situ prototyping of interactive AR environments. In International Conference on Human-Computer Interaction, pp. 235–255, Springer Nature (2020). https://doi.org/10.1007/978-3-030-49695-1_16
12. Dünser, A., Billinghurst, M.: Evaluating augmented reality systems. In: Furht, B. (ed.), Handbook of Augmented Reality, pp. 289–307. Springer, New York, NY (2011). https://doi.org/10.1007/978-1-4614-0064-6_13
13. Ntoa, S., et al.: A mixed-methods approach for the evaluation of situational awareness and user experience with augmented reality technologies. In: International Conference on Human-Computer Interaction, pp. 199–219. Springer Nature, Cham (2024)
14. Ntoa, S.: Usability and user experience evaluation in intelligent environments: a review and reappraisal. Int. J. Hum. Comput. Interact. **41**(5), 2829–2858 (2024). https://doi.org/10.1080/10447318.2024.2394724
15. Bargas-Avila, J.A., Hornbæk, K.: Old wine in new bottles or novel challenges: a critical analysis of empirical studies of user experience. In: Proceedings of the

SIGCHI Conference on Human Factors in Computing Systems (CHI '11). Association for Computing Machinery, New York, NY, USA, pp. 2689–2698 (2011). https://doi.org/10.1145/1978942.1979336
16. Kerdvibulvech, C.: A review of augmented reality-based human-computer interaction applications of gesture-based interaction. In: HCI International 2019 – Late Breaking Papers: 21st HCI International Conference (HCII 2019), pp. 233–242. Springer International Publishing, Orlando, FL, USA (2019)
17. Lishan, C., Saravana, K., Rao, S., Manushree, B.: A comprehensive survey on gesture-controlled interfaces: technologies, applications, and challenges. Int. J. Sci. Res. Sci. Technol. **12**, 1112–1136 (2025)
18. Bellani, P., et al.: Enhancing user engagement in shared autonomous vehicles: an innovative gesture-based windshield interaction system. Appl. Sci. **13**(17), 9901 (2023). https://doi.org/10.3390/app13179901
19. Pourmemar, M., Poullis, C.: Visualizing and interacting with hierarchical menus in immersive augmented reality. In: 17th ACM SIGGRAPH International Conference on Virtual-Reality Continuum and its Applications in Industry (VRCAI '19), Article 30, pp. 1–9. ACM, New York, NY, USA (2019). https://doi.org/10.1145/3359997.3365693
20. Margetis, G., Ntoa, S., Antona, M., Stephanidis, C.: Human-centered design of artificial intelligence. Handbook Human Factors Ergonomics 1085–1106 (2021). https://doi.org/10.1002/9781119636113.ch42
21. Eccles, D., Arsal, G.: The think aloud method: what is it and how do I use it? Qual. Res. Sport. Exerc. Health 1–18 (2017)
22. Sauro, J.; Dumas, J.S.: Comparison of three one-question, post-task usability questionnaires. In: SIGCHI Conference on Human Factors in Computing Systems Proceedings, CHI '09, pp. 1599–1608. Boston, MA, USA, 4–9 April (2009). https://doi.org/10.1145/1518701.1518946
23. Lewis, J.R.; Sauro, J.: Item benchmarks for the system usability scale. J. Usability Stud. 158–167 (2018)
24. Bangor, A., Kortum, P.T., Miller, J.T.: The system usability scale (SUS): an empirical evaluation. Int. J. Hum.-Comput. Interact. 574–594 (2008).https://doi.org/10.1080/10447310802205776

CoRK Lite A Lightweight Co-design Workshop Reflection Kit

Torben Volkmann(✉), Katharina Weiß, Nele Balke, and Nicole Jochems

Universität zu Lübeck, Lübeck, Germany
{t.volkmann,anja.weiss,n.balke,nicole.jochems}@uni-luebeck.de

Abstract. This paper introduces CoRK Lite, a structured framework designed to help moderators reflect on and improve Co-Design workshops. The framework facilitates systematic retrospection, allowing facilitators to analyze workshop dynamics and make methodological and didactic adjustments for future sessions.

CoRK Lite incorporates principles from Participatory Design, Theme-Centered Interaction, and Design Thinking, providing a structured approach to capturing observations. It consists of two main components: (1) a framework for structuring Co-Design workshops and (2) a visualization tool to analyze strengths, weaknesses, and areas for improvement. The method involves collecting moderator impressions, categorizing feedback using color-coded Post-its, and generating visualizations to identify workshop patterns.

First empirical results suggest that CoRK Lite enhances self-reflection and collaborative learning among moderators, making workshop processes more iterative and adaptive.

Keywords: Participatory Design · Co-Design · Reflection · Research through Design

1 Introduction

Co-Design workshops are characterized by diverse stakeholders (e.g., users, decision makers, designers, researchers) who collaboratively design a product. These workshops are useful in both the early exploratory phases for brainstorming ideas and the later stages for jointly creating digital prototypes. They are typically designed to be democratic, enabling all participants to contribute to defining problems and finding solutions [13,14,17]. The more diverse the target groups are, the greater the challenge is to understand how different user characteristics and structural aspects influence technology development, as different needs, priorities, as well as expectations intersect [7] and impact learning outcomes [4]. At the same time, the interaction between the different stakeholders is essential for mutual sharing of experiences, knowledge acquisition, and the development of design solutions [6].

Reflecting on the design process is crucial for enhancing the process itself and trigger insights for moderators. Additionally, improving team collaboration

C. Stephanidis et al. (Eds.): HCII 2025, CCIS 2773, pp. 278–287, 2026.
https://doi.org/10.1007/978-3-032-12773-0_27

is essential for enhancing workshop quality and outcomes. Specific dimensions and methods for reflecting on design processes with workshop moderators are currently limited, and little has yet been done to address how the dynamics of joint design activities can be captured [1,2,8].

The Co-Design workshop Reflection Kit (CoRK Lite) described in this paper support (1) a systematic and lightweight retrospection on Co-Design workshops by moderators and (2) facilitates methodological and didactic adaptations for follow-up workshops. CoRK Lite consists of two parts. A framework for Co-Design workshops, which is described in the first section of the paper. Second, it provides a visualization tool to identify strengths and weaknesses, which can be used to determine adjustments and consultations."

2 Related Work

The CoRK Lite framework builds upon established methodologies from Participatory Design, Theme-Centered Interaction, and Design Thinking.

Participatory Design (PD) emphasizes the active involvement of stakeholders in design processes, fostering co-creation and ensuring solutions align with user needs. Within PD, Co-Design extends these principles, engaging participants in structured workshops to generate collaborative solutions [13,15].

Theme-Centered Interaction (TCI) provides a model for managing group dynamics in creative contexts, balancing individual, group, and thematic elements. By applying TCI principles, CoRK Lite ensures workshop participants engage meaningfully while maintaining structured discussions [5].

Design Thinking is a human-centered collaborative problem-solving approach that emphasizes user needs and focuses on analysis, synthesis, and generating insights and ideas. Rather than following a linear sequence, Design Thinking operates as a system of overlapping spaces. It is a structured yet flexible approach that involves phases of inspiration, ideation, and implementation, helping teams navigate uncertainty and generate innovative solutions through rapid prototyping and iterative refinement [3,16].

This paper is methodologically rooted in Research through Design (RtD), which embeds research projects into a design practice with the explicit goal of generating knowledge to systematize design activities by placing a stronger emphasis on the interpretation and reflection of processes [12,18].

3 Developing the Reflection Framework for Co-Design Workshops

The purpose of this reflection framework for Co-Design workshops is to lay the groundwork for a systematic review conducted by the moderators after a Co-Design workshop. The results of the retrospection can be used to adapt future workshops methodological and didactically. Thus, Co-Design workshops are not understood as isolated events, but rather as ongoing learning processes that emerge from the interplay between structure and interaction dynamics to optimize the potential available resources through iterative adjustments [9].

In alignment with TCI, we understand workshops as a combination of individual and teamwork elements that each address different areas of competence and can be considered as parallel running threads in the workshop dynamics [10,11]. Thus, participants are simultaneously involved in the process as individuals and as part of a group. At the individual level, an idea is developed or expanded by a single person on a given topic, presented in the course of the workshop. Feedback is received from one or more external persons. On the other hand, teamwork can be described as a group of people who have one or more ideas that they try to work out together as a team and relate success factors to it. These success factors are often determined by the team but may also vary among individuals.

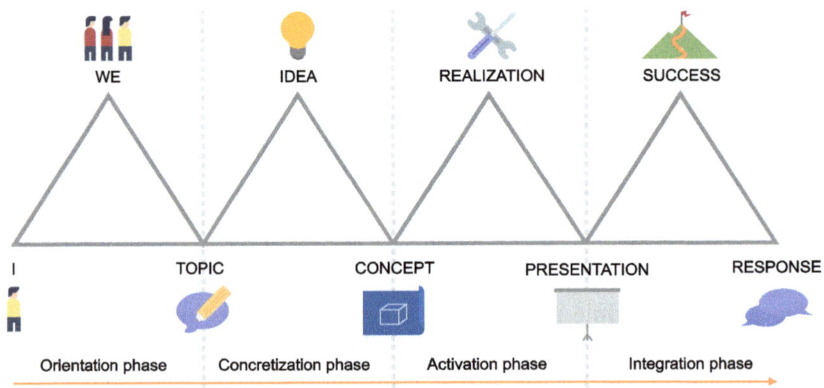

Fig. 1. Reflection Framework for Co-Design workshops.

The CoRK Lite framework provides a structured approach to workshop retrospection, supporting systematic reflection by moderators. It divides the reflection process into four interconnected phases: orientation, concretization, activation, and integration (see Fig. 1). Each phase corresponds to distinct aspects of workshop dynamics and supports iterative improvements.

- *Orientation Phase:* Participants define questions and challenges, establishing a shared understanding of the topic. Inspired by TCI, this phase emphasizes balancing individual, group, and thematic contributions.
- *Concretization Phase:* Initial ideas are explored in a divergent manner, followed by convergence into structured concepts. This phase leverages Design Thinking methodologies to promote ideation and synthesis.
- *Activation Phase:* Refined concepts are developed into actionable solutions. Participants work collaboratively to transform abstract ideas into concrete outcomes, ensuring alignment with the workshop's goals.

- *Integration Phase:* Final insights are consolidated, and future steps are defined. Outcomes are documented to guide subsequent workshops, fostering a continuous learning process.

By structuring workshop reflections into these phases, CoRK Lite promotes analyzing key interactions, identifying challenges, and refining methodologies over time. The framework's flexibility allows adaptation to various Co-Design contexts, supporting sustained improvements in workshop effectiveness.

4 Using the Reflection Framework in Practice

The following section outlines the implementation of the reflection framework in two Co-Design workshops, detailing the collection of impressions, categorization of results, and visualization of findings in two workshops. The first workshop (WS1) involved 14 participants and 6 moderators. The second workshop (WS2) included 11 participants and 4 moderators, allowing for a comparative analysis of workshop dynamics and facilitator insights. Both workshops were conducted over 90 min.

The workshops were conducted within the *VernetzBar* project, which aims to develop a digital platform specifically designed for young adults aged 14 to 30. This platform is intended to serve as a central point of contact to provide information about current activities and social support services in the city. A key feature of the project is the close cooperation with the target group in order to include their needs and interests directly in the development process. This should not only increase the usability and relevance of the platform, but also strengthen the commitment and active participation of young people in urban development.

4.1 Step 1 Collecting Impressions

Involving moderators in reflection with CoRK Lite, the framework was recorded on a whiteboard in advance or digitally presented in a hybrid reflection session, along with Post-its and pens of a single color to maintain neutrality. For the reflection, a duration of 45 min was set to capture the most important impressions concisely and to keep this results-verification phase resource-sensitive for all participants involved (see Fig. 2 for an exemplary result). We propose to apply CoRK Lite in the following five steps:

1. *Sketching the reflection object:* This step involves creating a visual representation of the object or topic being reflected upon. It can be done on an analog or digital whiteboard.
2. *Individual reflection:* Participants reflect on their personal experiences and impressions of the workshop. They capture their thoughts using Post-its, with each item representing a specific aspect or impression. The color of the Post-its is kept neutral to avoid bias at this stage.

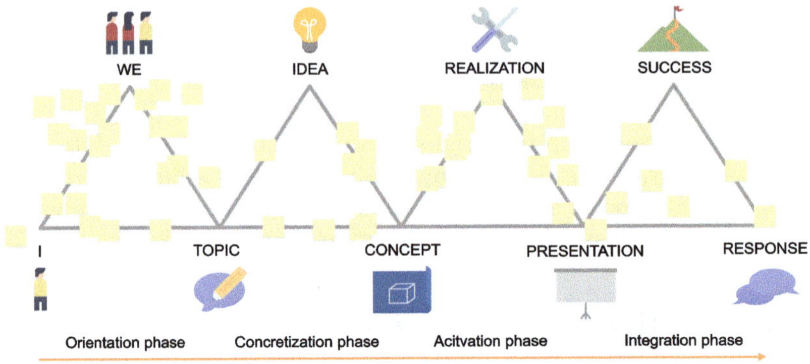

Fig. 2. Results of a collection of impressions from a Co-Design workshop ($N = 31$). The texts on the Post-its have been removed post hoc.

3. *Consolidation of results:* The individual reflections are brought together in a group setting. Each participant presents their Post-its and tries to categorize them into relevant aspects or relationships as defined by the reflection framework. In case of ambiguity, the group discusses and decides on the proper categorization.
4. *Group reflection:* The aggregated results are reflected upon as a group. The focus is on identifying patterns, trends, or surprising findings that emerge from the collective impressions.
5. *Digitization of the results (optional):* Finally, the visual aggregations are digitized using tools like Miro[1] to facilitate further analysis and interpretation of the data. This step allows for additional insights and connections to be made through visualization and collaborative work.

The process aimed to capture a wide range of impressions and experiences from moderators while maintaining focus and resourcefulness. By involving them in the reflection process, the reflection framework for Co-Design workshops enabled a comprehensive understanding of the workshop dynamics and facilitates the development of improvements or adaptations to enhance future Co-Design interventions.

4.2 Step 2 Color Coding and Visualization

The Post-its created by the moderators were subsequently analyzed with a focus on adjustment potential and workshop dynamics using content analysis of the observation items, from which inductive categories were derived and assigned color codes. This step is referred to as color coding. A total of eight sub-categories have been identified, depicting different qualities of reflection items:

- *Positive*: Feedback that highlights positive aspects or emphasizes something praise-worthy (light green).

[1] www.miro.com.

- *Disturbance*: Disturbance regarding the structure or/and participants (orange).
- *Observation*: Comments that echo observations or experiences without judgement (blue).
- *Adjustment*: Adjustment made resulting from previous workshops (red).
- *Insecurity*: Feedback about insecurities or questions regarding participants or structure (light blue).
- *Didactic memo*: Responses in which personal resources for follow-up workshops are identified (rose).
- *Adjustment for connection*: Feedback that suggests changes to improve or adjust the workshop (purple).
- *Positive to keep*: Comments that underline positive aspects and indicate that certain aspects should be maintained or repeated, or gives a hint to structure (dark green).

The color coding took place with a time delay to the collection of observation items and was conducted by a researcher who was not part of the moderator group. A parallel assignment with the collection of observation items was deliberately avoided in order to initially allow all impressions to stand side by side on an equal footing, to offer a space for reflection as open as possible and not to influence the reflectors in their collection of impressions. With the evaluation step of color coding, specific impressions were translated into encoded reflection items.

The color coded reflection items were assigned to frequency categories according to the phases of the Co-Design framework and translated into a visualization form (see Fig. 3 for a visualization of two consecutive workshops). In the visualization, the number of reflection items is displayed at the intersections of relation and phase. The size of the circles reflects the absolute frequencies. At first glance, this creates a differentiated picture of the overall dynamics of the Co-Design workshop, which can be used as a kind of individual fingerprint of a workshop, serving as a basis for further reflection with different questions or even as a visual form of result documentation for the moderator group. Results can also serve as a starting point for further workshop planning. Multiple workshops evaluated using this method can be compared to each other and analyzed for their dynamics. With the help of the visualization, the following questions can be answered: Can certain observation focuses be identified from the reflection? What internal group agreements show up in the reflection of the intervention? Which relations have received little attention in which phase? How can these gaps be interpreted? Does an adaptation show up in the structure or a new method also reflect in the dynamics of implementation? Which dynamics that have come up in the orientation phase are relevant for the further course of the workshop?

Fig. 3. Visualization of the outcome of two consecutive Co-Design workshops. The relationships of the Co-Design framework are depicted on the x-axis, and the phases of the Co-Design framework are depicted on the y-axis (left $N = 58$ Post-its, right $N = 31$ Post-its).

5 Results and Discussion

Results can be found on two levels. The first level consists of the collective impressions gathered from the workshops (step 1). The second level involves the visualization of these impressions after further processing (step 2).

The first step involved collecting moderator impressions using Post-its. In group discussions, moderators reflected on what stood out, identifying key themes that were later analyzed through visualization." Accumulations of observation items in the respective phases were found and gaps identified. The accumulations of observation items may be a first indication of a concentration of factors that influence the dynamics of workshops. In the reflection on workshop 2 (see Fig. 3) they form a focus in the orientation phase and above all on the relation between *I* and *We*. Thus, the social dynamics of the workshop were particularly emphasized by the reflecting moderators."

We found that the reflection kit serves as a basis for self-reflection within the moderator group and provides documentation for planning subsequent workshops. This supports the idea that the design process should be understood as a learning process. Reflections could be conducted on an equal footing, with all observations considered equally. Reflection on phases or relationships could be captured as quickly as identifying *blind spots*. The workshop is again perceived as a group achievement, a common mental reconstruction of workshop dynamics emerges. The reflection functioned as a quick first impression that addresses the question of common success or adjustment potential.

The second result was the visualization of the workshops' dynamic. The visualization served as an internal communication tool that provided a starting point for connecting follow-up workshops. When carrying out multiple consecutive workshops, it became apparent that these present different dynamics, which should be taken into account in the further development of the didactic structure. Color coding revealed content gaps, highlighting phases where no positive or disruptive elements were noted. Visualization enabled moderators to quickly recognize workshop strengths and weaknesses, guiding decisions on structural adjustments. These findings validate CoRK Lite as an effective tool for analyzing workshop dynamics. Future refinements could further enhance its ability to support facilitators in optimizing Co-Design processes.

The quality criteria for RtD proposed by Prochner and Godin [12] – traceability, interconnectivity, applicability, impartiality, and reasonableness – can be applied to the method used to capture the dynamics of the Co-Design workshop in the following ways:

The method documents what was done during the workshops, particularly through aggregated Post-its, reflections, and visualizations. The structured reflection process (step 1) and the resulting visualization (step 2) provide a clear documentation trail, enabling others to understand how observations were collected, analyzed, and synthesized (*traceability*).

The method links key concepts such as social dynamics, phases of the workshop, and relationships between participants (e.g., *I* and *We*). The visualization enhances these connections by illustrating how workshop elements interact, making it easier to identify patterns and relationships across multiple workshops (*interconnectivity*).

The approach generates knowledge beyond the specific workshops, as the reflection kit and visualization method can be reused for future Co-Design sessions. The results contribute to the iterative development of workshop formats, helping facilitators refine their methods based on documented observations and trends (*applicability*).

The process emphasizes equal consideration of all observations, preventing individual biases from dominating the reflection process. The use of aggregated group reflections and color-coded visualization supports an objective assessment of strengths, weaknesses, and content gaps, reducing subjective influence (*impartiality*).

The rationale for decisions regarding workshop adjustments is documented through the structured reflection and visualization process. The identification of blind spots and adjustment potential ensures that modifications to future workshops are based on observed patterns rather than arbitrary changes (*reasonableness*).

6 Conclusions and Future Direction

In this paper, the Co-Design Workshop Reflection Kit (CoRK Lite) was described that enables a systematic and lightweight reflection on group dynamics during a workshop for technology development. By reflecting upon the workshop experience after its completion, CoRK Lite promotes the development of methodological and didactic adaptations for consecutive workshops. The effective utilization of the reflection framework enhances the understanding of workshop dynamics and facilitates a learning journey.

By encouraging individual reflections and subsequent group discussions, the moderators gained insights into their experiences and those of their peers.

This process fostered improved collaboration and the identification of potential adjustments to enhance the overall effectiveness of the workshop. The reflection with the moderators was carried out in four consecutive steps in a joint activity in about 45 min to capture insights and ensure the usage of CoRK Lite remains focused and efficient in terms of resources. By deriving discussions about potential adjustments, the reflection tool empowers moderators to understand the design process as a learning process to actively improve the workshop outcomes.

The overarching goal of conducting Co-Design workshops is gaining insights for the development of digital technologies. By using CoRK Lite, we focused on analyzing workshop dynamics to enhance the didactic structure and improve workshop outcomes over time. Therefore, the reflection kit can be considered part of a broader study. For instance, workshops can also be evaluated through video analyses, artifact analyses, participative observation, or reflection by the participants. However, these methods do not reveal the dynamics within a workshop.

In addition, challenges with visualization need to be addressed. Currently, absolute frequencies of reflection items are represented. This poses challenges for scalability and comparability, especially when the number of facilitators changes.

To improve the validity and applicability of the Reflection Kit, further Co-Design workshops should be analyzed in future research. As a result, learning processes over time can be revealed and the dynamics of Co-Design workshops in a project course can be represented. Observation focuses could be identified through the color coding approach, and interpretations on workshop dynamics could be derived. The focus should be on highlighting adaptations in the structure of Co-Design workshops and reflecting on the dynamics of their adjusted implementation.

References

1. Baumer, E.P., Khovanskaya, V., Matthews, M., Reynolds, L., Schwanda Sosik, V., Gay, G.: Reviewing reflection: on the use of reflection in interactive system design. In: Proceedings of the 2014 Conference on Designing Interactive Systems, pp. 93–102. DIS '14, Association for Computing Machinery, New York, NY, USA (2014). https://doi.org/10.1145/2598510.2598598
2. Bossen, C., Dindler, C., Iversen, O.S.: Evaluation in participatory design: a literature survey. In: Proceedings of the 14th Participatory Design Conference: Full Papers - Volume 1, pp. 151–160. PDC '16, Association for Computing Machinery, New York, NY, USA (2016). https://doi.org/10.1145/2940299.2940303
3. Brown, T., Wyatt, J.: Design Thinking for Social Innovation. Stanford Soc. Innovation Rev. **8**(1), 31–35 (2009). https://doi.org/10.48558/58Z7-3J85
4. Cerna, K., Müller, C., Randall, D., Hunker, M.: Situated scaffolding for sustainable participatory design: Learning online with older adults **6** (2022). https://doi.org/10.1145/3492831
5. Cohn, R.C., Stumm, G.: Themenzentrierte Interaktion (TZI), pp. 700–701. Springer Vienna, Vienna (2000). https://doi.org/10.1007/978-3-211-99131-2_1922

6. Duarte, E.F., Baranauskas, M.C.C.: Revisiting the three HCI waves: a preliminary discussion on philosophy of science and research paradigms. In: Proceedings of the 15th Brazilian Symposium on Human Factors in Computing Systems. IHC '16, Association for Computing Machinery, New York, NY, USA (2016). https://doi.org/10.1145/3033701.3033740
7. Eisma, R., et al.: Early user involvement in the development of information technology-related products for older people **3**(2), 131–140 (2004). https://doi.org/10.1007/s10209-004-0092-z
8. Glinka, K., Müller-Birn, C.: Critical-reflective human-AI collaboration: Exploring computational tools for art historical image retrieval **7**(CSCW2) (2023). https://doi.org/10.1145/3610054
9. Langmaak, B., Braune-Krickau, M.: Wie die gruppe laufen lernt. anregungen zum planen und leiten von gruppen. ein praktisches lehrbuch (1998)
10. Ørngreen, R., Levinsen, K.: Workshops as a research methodology. Electron. J. E-Learn. **15**(1), 70–81 (2017)
11. Pibernik, J., Milcic, D., Bota, J.: Pressure toward creativity: Individual/group work in student design competition. In: DS 66-2: Proceedings of the 1st International Conference on Design Creativity, ICDC 2010 (2010)
12. Prochner, I., Godin, D.: Quality in research through design projects: Recommendations for evaluation and enhancement. Des. Stud. **78**, 101061 (2022). https://doi.org/10.1016/j.destud.2021.101061
13. Sanders, E.B.N., Stappers, P.J.: Co-creation and the new landscapes of design **4**(1), 5–18 (2008). https://doi.org/10.1080/15710880701875068
14. Sarmiento, J.P., Wise, A.F.: Participatory and co-design of learning analytics: an initial review of the literature. In: LAK22: 12th International Learning Analytics and Knowledge Conference, pp. 535–541. LAK22, Association for Computing Machinery (2022). https://doi.org/10.1145/3506860.3506910
15. Tomasini Giannini, F., Mulder, I.: Towards a power-balanced participatory design process. In: Proceedings of the Participatory Design Conference 2022 - Volume 2, pp. 111–117. PDC '22, Association for Computing Machinery, New York, NY, USA (2022). https://doi.org/10.1145/3537797.3537819
16. Wangsa, K., Chugh, R., Karim, S., Sandu, R.: A comparative study between design thinking, agile, and design sprint methodologies **15**(2), 225 (2022). https://doi.org/10.1504/IJASM.2022.124916
17. Whittle, J.: How much participation is enough?: A comparison of six participatory design projects in terms of outcomes. In: Proceedings of the 13th Participatory Design Conference on Research Papers - PDC '14, pp. 121–130. ACM Press (2014). https://doi.org/10.1145/2661435.2661445
18. Zimmerman, J., Forlizzi, J.: Research Through Design in HCI, pp. 167–189. Springer New York, New York, NY (2014). https://doi.org/10.1007/978-1-4939-0378-8_8

Interactive Projection Walls Design for the Visualization of the Automotive Green Manufacturing Process

Yianmin Xue(✉) and Weirong Wang

Xi'an University of Technology, Shanxi 710054, China
1583012809@qq.com

Abstract. Interactive projection wall technology integrates projection displays with interactive sensors to capture user movements and generate real-time feedback, delivering immersive interactive experiences. In recent years, as an innovative form of human-computer interaction, it has garnered significant attention and has been widely applied in museums, automotive exhibitions, advertising, and educational exhibition design.

This study focuses on the application innovation of interactive projection wall technology in automotive industrial exhibitions. Based on the audience segmentation theory, a user persona model was constructed to categorize visitors into three target groups: learning-oriented, research-oriented, and entertainment-oriented. Through in-depth needs analysis, differentiated interaction modes—single-user explanatory mode and multi-user entertainment mode—were refined. The research employed the Unity engine to develop interactive nodes, innovatively visualizing automotive production processes and green manufacturing techniques through dynamic graphics. A user evaluation of the display system revealed significant differences in environmental and manufacturing knowledge retention among the three user groups ($p < 0.05$) via memory retention tests. Furthermore, the AttrakDiff scale validated that the interactive projection system achieved notable improvements in both the Hedonic Quality and Attractiveness dimensions compared to conventional video displays. Empirical results demonstrate that this interactive system not only constructs immersive brand cognition scenarios but also effectively disseminates green manufacturing concepts through gamified learning mechanisms, providing a reusable technical framework for the exhibition design field.

Keywords: Interactive projection wall · automotive green manufacturing · public display · interactive animations

1 Introduction

Interactive projection walls rely on the cooperation of computer vision technology and projection display technology. The experience of the user's touch or motion projection wall can create a fantastic and interesting interactive experience. Wall interactive projection technology as a form of human-computer interaction in offline entertainment and

C. Stephanidis et al. (Eds.): HCII 2025, CCIS 2773, pp. 288–298, 2026.
https://doi.org/10.1007/978-3-032-12773-0_28

education, in recent years, has been widely concerned and attended [1]. At the same time, it promotes the development of the field of digital display design and has a large number of applications in museums, car shows, advertising, education, and other display designs.

There are prominent cases of interactive projection technology applications in the field of automotive display design; for example, Audi exhibition realizes personalized car selection by using touch gestures on a multi-touch surface [2]. Nowadays, AR interactive projection has been widely applied in car configuration and display [3]; Wang Xiaojun et al. combined with the theory of the experience economy, according to the audience's experience needs based on the example of the Beijing Automobile Museum, designed to create a rich and complete multilevel experience for visitors [4].

In general, it seems that the auto show displays are mostly focused on car options, smart cockpits, car structures, etc., and less on the green manufacturing of cars. This study will be based on the actual automobile enterprise display needs and display the automobile green manufacturing process in the form of interactive projection.

2 Survey of Automobile Enterprises and Exhibition Users

2.1 Investigation of Automobile Production Line and Environmental Protection Technology

This study employs field research to systematically analyze the production processes and technologies of leading automotive enterprises. The selected companies represent advanced manufacturing in environmental management and share the strategic goal of building green factories and producing eco-friendly vehicles.

In March 2024, the research team conducted on-site investigations in welding and assembly workshops, where lecturers provided insights into machinery usage and production line planning. During these visits, data was collected for platform display, including production process documentation and photographs. Figure 1 presents an image taken during the production line investigation.

Fig. 1. Automobile manufacturing workshop investigation scene.

After conducting field research and data collection, this study summarizes the four key processes of automobile manufacturing—stamping, welding, painting, and assembly—along with the industry's environmental protection measures. The emerging "zero-waste" factories integrate eco-friendly and advanced technologies into these production stages. Through on-site investigations, employee interviews, and literature reviews, six key green manufacturing technologies were identified: noise control, pollutant emission reduction, solar photovoltaics, waste heat recovery, water reuse, and green welding. These technologies are incorporated into various production stages in an intuitive and accessible manner, enhancing public understanding of sustainable automotive manufacturing. The content structure of the displayed environmental technologies is illustrated in Fig. 2.

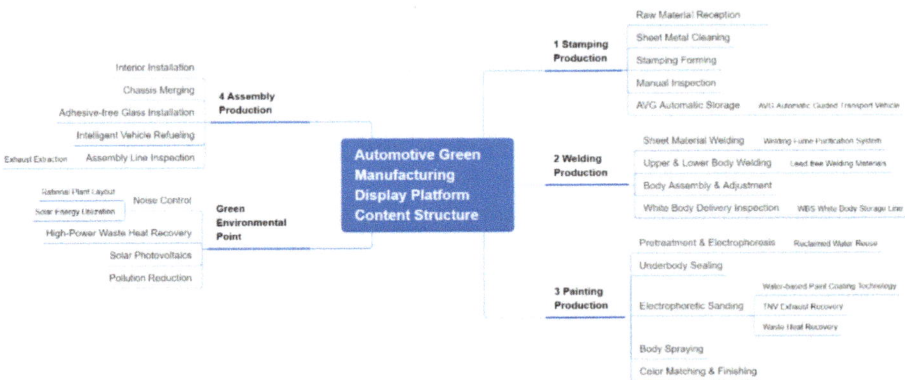

Fig. 2. Automotive green manufacturing platform information structure Introduction.

2.2 Showroom Site Survey

Before the design, the car showroom environment field investigation, the current interactive wall display area was initially completed, as shown in Fig. 3. The wall is gray, two projectors composed of images projected on the wall, and interactive projection radar equipment is also pre-installed in the wall above the completion of the installation. The display wall width is 7.8 m high 3.6 m, projection resolution of 1200 × 3264 px, in the design of the overall layout should be considered in the human height in the 0.5–1.8 m region set in the wall of the interaction point, and the distance from the starting point cannot be too close to each other, the radar recognition range in the radius of 10cm above the circle.

Observation of the surrounding environment can be concluded in the surrounding bright light situation the overall picture brightness and saturation is relatively light, cannot completely restore the screen itself color, so need to pay attention to the design of the display platform when the background color and animation color differentiation degree.

Fig. 3. Interactive projection displays area and two projectors.

2.3 Exhibitor User Survey

Through the interviews with twenty users, including car owners, general exhibition users, and automobile practitioners, it is learned that the main users visiting the exhibition hall are mainly young people, and there are also primary and secondary school students visiting the exhibition hall for study [5]. The age of these users and the degree of understanding of knowledge are not similar, but according to the theory of segmentation of the exhibition objectives can be divided into three categories: education as the goal, to entertainment as the goal, to the goal of research [6].

Learning- Oriented Audience. Learning as the goal of the exhibition users are mainly young people and have the intention to buy a car mainly customers, they attach great importance to the accuracy of the information display in the interactive activities of the digital exhibition, and hope that through the interactive wall can learn to learn about automobile manufacturing related knowledge, so in the design of the design should be taken into account with the artificial or voice explanation service, to facilitate the user's understanding of the content of automobile manufacturing.

Entertainment-Oriented Audience. This is also commonly known as the "walk around" type of audience, they do not have a specific flow of visits and clear goals, and most of them casually watch the exhibition, taking pictures and timely sharing of social media or live streaming software is one of the main driving forces for them to watch the exhibition. They will randomly choose the digital exhibition equipment in the pavilion to experience. The perception and demand for content is not strong, so pay more attention to the novelty of the interactive form and content of the digital exhibition equipment, and hope to get the enjoyment of a happy experience.

Research-Oriented Audience. Mainly automobile practitioners, they are more willing to explore more in-depth content along the routes set up in the exhibition hall, such as automobile production and manufacturing technology, and communicate with internal personnel. In addition, research-oriented visitors are less attached to the digital exhibition equipment and environment and are more willing to invest their energy and time in visiting automobile objects or parts.

3 Interactive Design and Visual Design

3.1 User Viewing Behavior Analysis and Design Transformation

Automobile production line environmental protection interactive wall adopts radar sensor technology, support projection wall multi-touch, multiple users can be used in different positions at the same time, so its interaction mode is mainly divided into two categories, one is the explanation mode, that is, with the lecturer according to the process of explaining; a class of entertainment mode that can realize multiple people to touch and click at will. Taking time as a moving line, through the use of different users' tasks and interactive process analysis, we found that users with the goal of learning and research are more inclined to understand the overall knowledge content of the whole interactive wall when interacting with the device, and they hope to get feedback when touching and sending out the "request" action. And entertainment as the goal of the user will be interactive projection of interactivity and aesthetics by its novelty, to participate in animation viewing and interaction, after the interaction will also be photographed to punch cards, they are more in pursuit of participation in the entertainment experience, so to increase the fun of interactive projection for the display design is also critical.

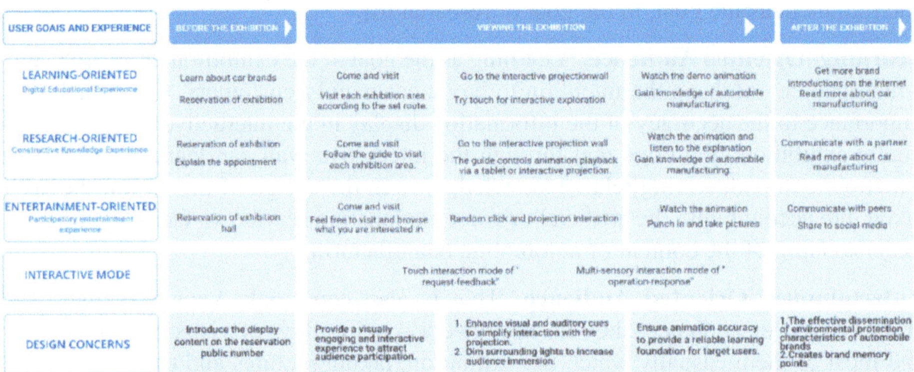

Fig. 4. Analyze the exhibition flow and design concerns based on different target users.

According to the theory of Yvon Rogers, the interaction between users and hardware and software products can be divided into three basic modes: command, dialog, manipulation, and exploration [7]. For the interactive projection wall, its interaction modes can be subdivided into the touch interaction mode of "request-feedback", the multi-sensory interaction mode of "manipulate-response" and the interaction mode of "get-update" according to the different application technologies and display contents. The "Get-Update" interaction mode. Summarizing the above analysis, the multi-sensory interaction mode combining "request-feedback" touch interaction and "operation-response" is selected and transformed into the following design concerns and points, as shown in Fig. 4.

3.2 Content Design of the Automotive Green Production Display Platform

In order to meet the needs of learning and research-oriented audience, the accurate presentation of automobile manufacturing information in the design will be crucial. At the same time, in order to meet the entertainment-oriented audience, the display content should be lively and interesting on the basis of accuracy, so that more users stop to watch; finally, the overall design of the display needs to focus on the conveyance of the characteristics of the automotive brand, effectively convey the information of the development of automotive greening, and enhance the user's awareness of the brand and trust.

Clear and Accurate Display of Manufacturing Knowledge Content. Through the field research on the automobile manufacturing process and the environmental protection points involved, communicate with the process engineers of each process, combine the specific production process with the text and pictures of the research and other information, draw out the interactive animation script of the production process, the interactive animation of each production step with accurate symbolic representation, for example, Fig. 5 shows the actual painting scene of the mechanical arm of the painting and assembly production line, and Fig. 6 shows the symbol transformation of the painting step. For each process of the production of the sub-division of the interactive action annotation and animation state descriptions, labeling sound effects and animation playback time, for the subsequent display of animation synthesis to lay the foundation.

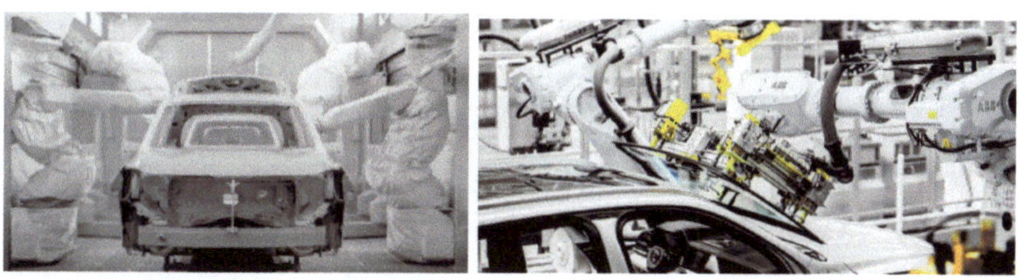

Fig. 5. Intelligent painting scenarios for painting lines and glass automatic intelligent installation scene for assembly production line.

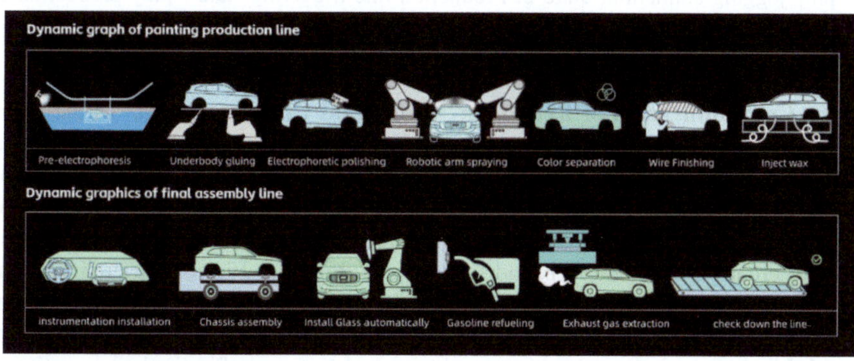

Fig. 6. Painting and final assembly process of symbol extraction.

Interesting Display of Manufacturing Environmental Protection Points. To increase user interactivity and participation in the experience, in addition to analyzing specific user needs, it is also necessary to assess the surrounding environment and add visual aids to guide the user, reducing the user's learning costs while bringing the user an interesting interactive experience [8].

This paper presents the design of an interactive projection wall for automotive environmental technology, incorporating lighting and sound elements to enhance immersion. Sensor lights are installed around the interactive wall, turning off when a viewer enters the detection area, making the projection animation more prominent in the dark while intensifying the atmosphere. Additionally, synchronized factory sound effects play alongside animations, and interactive touchpoints trigger corresponding audio-visual feedback, enriching the audience's learning and entertainment experience.

As shown in Fig. 7, the dynamic process icons feature two states: State 1 (default)displays a subtle, slow animation, while State 2 (active) is triggered when a viewer touches a process point. The animation then follows the production sequence, with synchronized lighting and sound effects simulating a real production line. If multiple users interact simultaneously, the system can trigger multiple animations in State 2 concurrently. When an environmental protection point is activated, its animation takes priority before resetting to State 1. A visual progress bar at the bottom provides real-time tracking of the animation's progress, ensuring clarity and engagement.

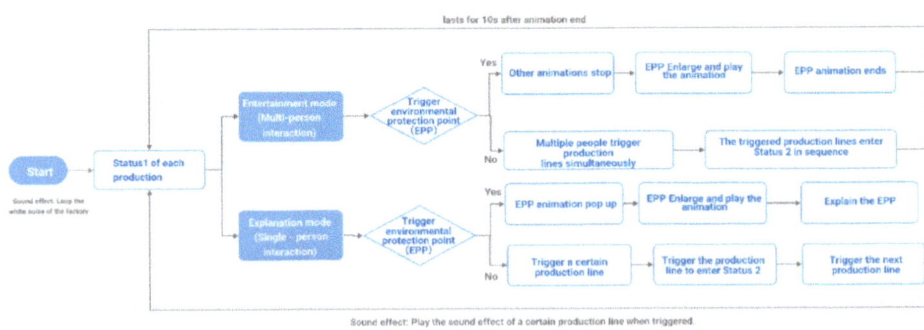

Fig. 7. Interactive flow of the automotive green manufacturing interactive wall. State 1: Standby state - play jogging animation. State 2: Production line triggering state - play production line startup animation.

Effective Communication of Brand Environmental Characteristics. In the overall color style design, the walls around the exhibition hall echo the use of green as the main color, with a sense of science and technology of cyan as a secondary color, and gray for the accent color to present the animation elements of the icon. The content design highlights environmental protection elements to reflect the manufacturer's eco-friendly nature and create a memorable brand impact. As shown in Fig. 8, the environmental protection process is integrated into the animation demo. On the initial interface, green buttons display the global eco-process. Audience members can trigger these buttons with their hands to activate animations and text explanations, effectively promoting the brand's environmental commitment.

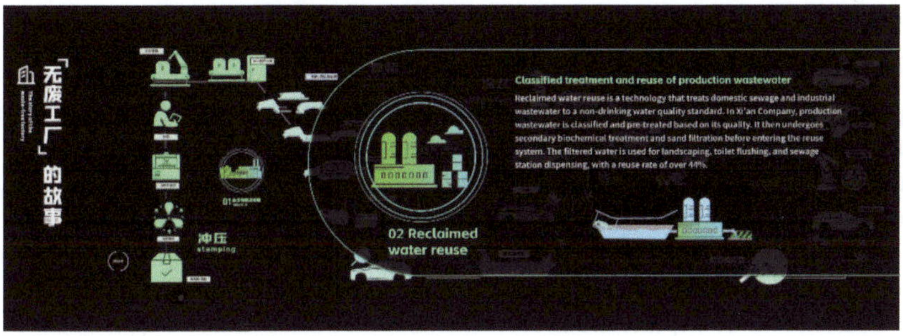

Fig. 8. Interactive wall environmental protection point display in explanation mode.

4 Interactive Projection Wall Realization and User Evaluation

4.1 Interactive Projection Wall Development

Developing an Interactive Display Platform with Unity3D. Infrared projection radar interface supports Unity3D, C#, this paper chooses Unity3D for development to realize the user interface button click trigger animation effect and choose the induction radar to realize the touch sensor. After Adobe Effect (AE)synthesized animation and audio imported into Unity3D development, the interactive platform needs to establish a video screen playback controller, for which script code is written to control the video playback progress; at the same time, it is necessary to add click events for different interactive areas, as shown in Fig. 9.

Interactive Radar Links and Tests. This paper adopts POELidar-M1 interactive radar. After installing it on the wall, we chose TCP network connection, calibrated the radar detection position, and then linked it with the projector software system to realize 360° scanning, mouse simulation and multi-touch projection, Fig. 10 Scenario with no tests installed.

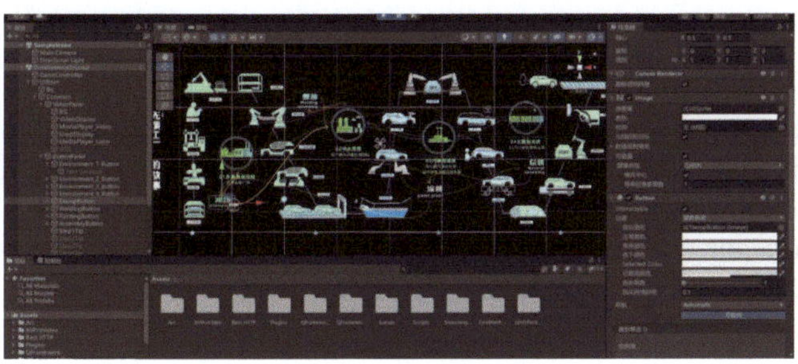

Fig. 9. Develop interactive touch points in Unity3D.

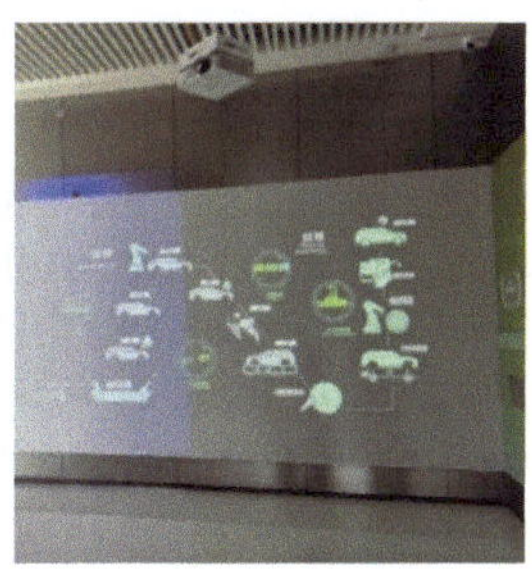

Fig. 10. Linking interactive radar tests.

4.2 Evaluation Experiments

User Experience Evaluation. After the development, 31 exhibitors (including corporate employees, students, and automotive enthusiasts) were invited to participate in the evaluation of the interactive wall project. Using an animated video of automobile manufacturing as a control group, the AttrakDiff scale was used to test whether the use of interactive projection to demonstrate the green production process of automobiles is more entertaining and appealing to the users and is more conducive to users' learning and understanding of the relevant knowledge and brand promotion. The AttrakDiff scale is a standardized user experience assessment tool that consists of 28 questions, each on a 7-point scale, with the lowest and highest scores representing a pair of antonyms [9].

The reliability of the questionnaire shows its Cronbach's alpha $= 0.943 > 0.6$s the mean scores of both the interactive projection wall and the video display format are greater than 4 (on a scale of 1–7), which indicates that the users' evaluations are positive, and the scores of the interactive projection wall are higher than the effect of the playback of the video display on the different dimensions (Fig. 11).

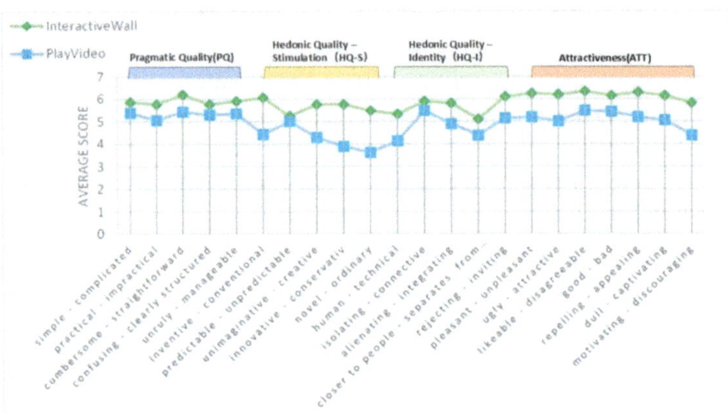

Fig. 11. User experience results rated with AttrakDiff's bipolar verbal anchors

A paired sample t-test was conducted for each dimension, and Table 1 shows that the interactive wall is superior to the video display in both Hedonic Quality - Stimulation(HQ-S)、Hedonic Quality – Identity(HQ-I) and overall Attractiveness (ATT), and there is a significant difference $p > 0.05$, especially in the attractiveness dimension high $p = 0.0003$ higher than the interactive wall, while there is no significant difference between the two displays Practical quality (PQ). The results suggest that the use of an interactive wall is more curious and attractive than displaying a video, and can strengthen users' identification with the automotive brand image.

Important Information Memorability Analysis. The above users were invited to test their knowledge of memorization after listening to the interactive wall explanation and completing the interaction. Interviews were conducted to understand the purpose of

Table 1. AttrakDiffs Difference Test Across Different Dimensions.

Pairwise Comparison	Mean Difference	Standard Deviation	Standard Error Mean	95% Confidence Interval of Difference	t	df	Significance (Two-tailed)
InterEQ - VideoEQ	0.55238	1.45589	0.31770	[-1.1033, 1.21509]	1.739	30	0.097
InterHQI - VideoHQI	1.40952	1.71869	0.37505	[0.62718, 2.19186]	3.758	30	0.001
InterHQS - VideoHQS	0.75238	1.45864	0.31830	[0.08842, 1.41634]	2.364	30	0.028
InterATT - VideoATT	1.06122	1.00364	0.21901	[0.60437, 1.51807]	4.846	30	0.0003

their visit to the exhibition and to ask them questions. Three questions were set about the environmental knowledge of automobile production, with a total score of 60 points. The scores were counted after they answered the questions (Table 2).

Table 2. Average score of knowledge memorization of users of different target types.

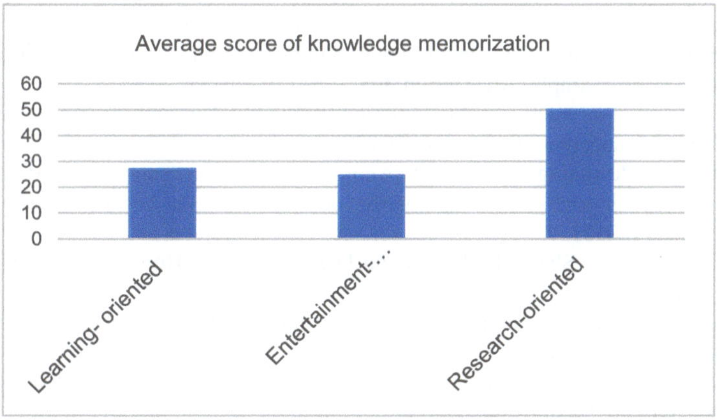

The results show that there is a significant difference in knowledge memorization among the different user types ($F = 15.320$, $p < 0.001$). Comparing the mean scores of each group, it was found that the knowledge recall of "research" users was significantly higher than that of "entertainment" and "learning" users, and this difference can be visualized in Fig. 12.

5 Conclusion

Based on comprehensive research, this study designs an interactive projection-based automotive manufacturing exhibition system. By integrating interactive projection technology, the system enhances the dissemination of automotive production knowledge through an immersive, multi-sensory experience. This approach not only enriches the presentation of green manufacturing at auto shows but also expands the means of communicating eco-friendly production processes. Additionally, it fosters cognitive interaction, improving audience engagement, deepening their understanding, and leaving a lasting impression. This research provides a novel digital innovation for automotive manufacturing exhibitions, promoting greater awareness and emphasis on green and sustainable principles within the industry.

Acknowledgments. . The authors thank the participants for their time and valuable contribution.

Disclosure of Interests. The authors have no conflict of interest to disclose

References

1. Bongers, A.J.: Interactive video projections as augmented environments. International Journal of Arts and Technology **5**(1), 17–52 (2012)
2. Gay, H., Michelle: Car Showroom of the Future. Design (2012)
3. Kandia, M., Kawate, N.: Augmented reality-based car showroom application as a promotional media at alya motor car showroom. IOTA Journal **4**(4), 587–600 (2024)
4. Li, X.L., Wang, X.J.: Automobile exhibition design in experience economy: taking the Beijing auto museum as an example. Art. Design **305**, 128–129 (2018)
5. Pallud, J.: Impact of interactive technologies on stimulating learning experience in a museum. Information & Management **54**(4), 466 (2017)
6. Olesen, A.R.: Co-designing digital museum communication: an exploration of digital museum communication as it emerges in collaborative design interaction between museum staff and digital designers (2015)
7. Preece, J., Rogers, Y., Sharp, H: Interaction Design: Beyond Human-Computer Interaction (4th ed.). Wiley (2015)
8. Interacting with actuated walls: Exploring applications and input types, International Journal of Human-Computer Studies, **172** (2023)
9. Klepsch, M., Seufert, T: Subjective differentiated measurement of cognitive load. In: Proc. 5th Intl. Cognitive Load Theory Conf. (2012)

Correction to: HCI International 2025 – Late Breaking Posters

Constantine Stephanidis, Margherita Antona, Stavroula Ntoa, George Margetis, and Gavriel Salvendy

Correction to:
C. Stephanidis et al. (Eds.): *HCI International 2025 – Late Breaking Posters*, CCIS 2773, https://doi.org/10.1007/978-3-032-12773-0

The book was published with a typo in the book title, Color in this book. The title of the book as "HCI International 2025 – Late Breaking Papers", whereas it should read "HCI International 2025 – Late Breaking Posters" both in the cover and on the Title page of the front-matter correctly. The color needs to be updated consistently across all the three volumes.
This has been corrected in the book accordingly.

The updated version of this book can be found at
https://doi.org/10.1007/978-3-032-12773-0

C. Stephanidis et al. (Eds.): HCII 2025, CCIS 2773, p. C1, 2026.
https://doi.org/10.1007/978-3-032-12773-0_29

Author Index

C. Stephanidis et al. (Eds.): HCII 2025, CCIS 2773, pp. 299–300, 2026.
https://doi.org/10.1007/978-3-032-12773-0

MIX
Papier aus verantwortungsvollen Quellen
Paper from responsible sources
FSC® C105338

If you have any concerns about our products,
you can contact us on
ProductSafety@springernature.com

In case Publisher is established outside the EU,
the EU authorized representative is:
Springer Nature Customer Service Center GmbH
Europaplatz 3, 69115 Heidelberg, Germany

Printed by Libri Plureos GmbH
in Hamburg, Germany